Australian urban land use planning

Principles, systems and practice

Second edition

Nicole Gurran

SYDNEY UNIVERSITY PRESS

Published 2011 by Sydney University Press
SYDNEY UNIVERSITY PRESS
University of Sydney Library
sydney.edu.au/sup

First published by Sydney University Press 2008
Second edition published by Sydney University Press 2011

National Library of Australia Cataloguing-in-Publication entry

Author: Gurran, Nicole.
Title: Australian urban land use planning : principles, systems and practice
            / Nicole Gurran.
Edition: 2nd ed.
ISBN: 9781920899776 (pbk.)
Notes: Includes bibliographical references and index.
Subjects: Land use, Urban--Australia--Planning.
            City planning and redevelopment law--Australia.
            Land use--Australia--Planning.
Dewey Number:
            333.77130994

Cover design by Miguel Yamin, the University Publishing Service

Contents

Acknowledgements

I completed this manuscript while on a University of Sydney Brown Fellowship, and I want to thank the University for the award, and for its commitment to supporting women and those of us with caring responsibilities to maintain research activity.

I also need to acknowledge a number of people who have helped me bring this book to fruition.

John Lea painstakingly reviewed each chapter and, as always, provided substantial content and editorial advice. I am indebted to Mary-Lynne Taylor for examining the chapters on New South Wales.

I am grateful to Stephen Hamnett, Robin King-Cullen, Michael Lockwood, Carey Curtis, and Rebecca Leshinsky for generously reviewing passages on the planning systems in their respective jurisdictions. David Wright helped me understand the fascinating arrangements in the Australian Capital Territory.

Of course, all mistakes and omissions are my own.

Agata Mrva-Montoya gave excellent design and production support and my thanks go to her and to Susan Murray-Smith from Sydney University Press.

Peter Phibbs, who egged me on to finish this book and Vivienne Milligan, Barbara Norman, Elisabeth Hamin, Bill Randolph, and Kristian Ruming will find many references to our joint work. My collaborations with you all continue to shape my thinking.

Adrienne Keane, who stepped in to teach for me on many occasions, and in the most wonderful way, deserves particular thanks.

On the home front, thanks to Kathleen Gurran for making things possible, Raju for putting up with me, and Ravi, Neeva, Saru and Anoushka, for creating wonderful distractions.

Introduction

Why is planning important?

This book has evolved during a national renaissance of interest in urban and regional affairs. Aside from brief flirtations with urban and regional policy over the past century (particularly during the nation building eras of Federation and the postwar years), planning has been largely absent from Australia's national policy agenda. However, by the turn of the new millennium, pressing urban, regional and environmental problems – such as housing affordability; inadequate infrastructure and transportation systems; biodiversity loss, natural disasters human-induced climate change – had begun to capture the national attention. The spectrum of interests engaged in the process of managing urban and regional change – from local residents and their elected representatives, to developers, industry sectors and Indigenous groups – ensure that debates about planning are lively and well reported in the media.

Some claim that land use planning unnecessarily restricts development, discouraging investment and threatening the 'great Australian dream' of home ownership. 'Planning restrictions in particular, are choking our cities and increasingly pushing up the prices in what were once the most affordable places to purchase a home' (Ron Silberberg, in Moran 2006, pii). On the other side of the debate, global concerns about the environmental impacts of urbanisation and associated patterns of consumerism, from biodiversity loss through to climate change, strengthen calls for stronger and more effective urban and environmental planning: 'The 21st century agenda of climate change, understood as a dramatic manifestation of the sustainability crisis, is a "call to arms" demanding changes to the focus of planning purpose and action' (Steele & Gleeson 2010, p109).

In general terms, the land use planning system helps to establish the conditions needed to protect and create attractive and efficient urban environments. By establishing a legal process to manage land use change and development, urban planning can ensure the provision and maintenance of public goods that might otherwise be underprovided by the free market, such as open space or community infrastructure. Planning can also contribute to the pursuit of greater social equity in urban development, by securing opportunities for the diverse housing forms needed to promote mixed communities within new and changing areas.

Importantly, the planning system also provides a process for public participation and an opportunity for groups and individuals to express their views about particular developments, including proposals that may have a direct or unjust impact on them. Organised planning processes can also coordinate different but potentially complementary objectives associated with urban land development, such as the need to provide for new housing and infrastructure, and the need to protect the environment (Barker 2006, p26).

Positive or 'reactive' planning?

The postwar era in particular was a period of strong government intervention in urban and regional development across Britain, Europe, North America and Australia. This intervention was often undertaken directly, through large-scale infrastructure programs such as Australia's Snowy Mountains Scheme or public housing developments, for lower- and middle-income families. Using capital funding provided under the Commonwealth State Housing Agreement, (CSHA) whole new suburbs on the metropolitan fringes of Australia's capitals were developed by state governments during the 1970s. At the same time, disadvantaged inner city areas underwent massive programs of 'urban renewal', including the construction of large public housing tower developments.

This direct government involvement in urban and regional development is often described as a form of positive planning in contrast to the more passive role associated with regulating development initiated by the private sector. However, as the majority of urban change and growth occurs beyond the public sector, regulating and managing this process to achieve positive community outcomes should involve far more than a 'reactive' form of development control.

Rather than tinkering around the edges of private development, the regulatory land use planning system should be about setting and implementing decision-making frameworks that establish the goals, criteria and standards for future development actions by the public or private sector. For this to occur, statutory land use planning should operate within a context of strong government policy, informing all scales of the planning process – ideally from a strong national level of policy setting and implementation through to the local and site based plan and assessment of proposals. Thus, rather than conceiving land use planning as a narrow form of regulation that 'reacts' in a passive way to proposals put forward by the private sector, it is argued in this book that statutory planning processes can and should underpin the proactive governance of urban and regional change.

Implementing strategic urban and environmental policy through land use planning

The main purpose of this book is to provide an accessible introduction to the principles, policy objectives, systems and levers that can be used to achieve such a strategic and proactive form of urban governance. The focus is on the statutory land use planning systems in the Australian states and territories and the mechanisms and tools employed by planners in practice. To use a traditional distinction, the book concentrates predominantly on the procedural aspects of planning – that is, how planning systems are organised and how planning decisions are made. However, the intention is to show how these processes and the system itself can be used to achieve the substantive objectives of planning, for instance, contributing to ecological sustainability, responding to climate change, or achieving more equitable access to jobs, housing and recreation areas across an urban region.

Thus the early chapters of the book set out what might now be understood to be the 'normative' policy objectives or principles of urban and environmental planning, within the paradigm of ecological sustainability. Within this paradigm, the field of urban planning has expanded to encompass a broad spectrum of disciplinary and public policy. This book focuses on just two broad policy areas – environmental sustainability in an era of climate change, and housing supply, affordability and choice – but it would be possible to address many more, and to conceive of the policy remit of contemporary urban or environmental planning in almost infinite ways. Some of the other policy areas that may now be addressed in part through land use planning include economic growth and revitalisation, transportation, urban design, disaster preparedness, cultural heritage protection, community development and engagement, public health, cultural development and the arts.

In illustrating the way in which planning processes and mechanisms can be used to achieve environmental sustainability and housing policy objectives, the book addresses two issues that will already be familiar to most readers, whether or not they have a background in urban planning or policy. It is through their own homes that many people first encounter the planning system. For instance, those seeking to build a house or to renovate will often need planning approval. Those seeking to find a home to rent or buy in the right place at a price they can afford, may also be interested in the urban development policies and processes that help shape the type, amount, and cost of housing that is available within a particular locality.

Similarly, issues relating to environmental sustainability and climate change engage people from the household scale right up to the global level. Is it possible to store and re-use water on a residential site, or to return energy to the electricity grid? What measures are in place to enable residents of new urban areas to walk or cycle to school, the shops, or the train station? How does the land use planning framework ensure that our internationally iconic koala populations will not be further threatened by new housing development within their core habitats? Are potential climate change impacts factored into planning controls for the location and design of new developments?

This book examines how local and state planning authorities in Australia are beginning to address these issues within the broader national and international policy context in which they sit. It shows how standard planning mechanisms can be used to prevent undesirable outcomes from occurring – for instance, avoiding a proliferation of homogenous new housing developments that do not meet community needs; or prohibiting development that would destroy important wildlife habitat. But it also shows how the planning system can be used creatively to encourage desirable outcomes – for example, encouraging denser, vibrant mixed use centres with affordable housing for key workers; securing additional conservation areas and environmental remediation when new development lands are released; or ensuring that neighbourhoods and centres promote walking and cycling. These approaches, while presented in relation to housing or environmental policy objectives, can equally be transferred to other policy areas.

The statutory context in which planning takes place

In showing how the planning system is used, and can be used, to achieve urban and environmental policies, it is sometimes necessary to undertake a detailed discussion of legislation, but this book is not intended to substitute for an environmental law handbook or text. Many practising planners operate within a 'statutory' context, achieving strategic urban and environmental planning objectives through the legal control of land use change and development. In showing how this process operates in Australia the aim is to demonstrate how this system can aid policy implementation through day-to-day planning decisions and through the more comprehensive forward planning process. To illustrate the operation of the system in more detail, two chapters deal specifically with the NSW planning system, one on the policy and legal framework surrounding the plan-making process, the other on development and environmental assessment. The book is therefore a resource for policy-makers, practitioners, students and members of the community who are interested in how planning systems can be used to achieve strategic policy goals.

Information sources

In addition to the primary analysis of urban and environmental planning legislation and policy all of which have been updated from the 2007 edition, several research projects on comparative land use planning systems and approaches to strategic environmental and housing policy, undertaken by the author between 2000–2009, form the primary information sources for much of this book. The majority of examples used refer to state and local planning jurisdictions within Australia, but international examples and comparisons are drawn where helpful to contextualise Australian approaches or to demonstrate creative ideas that might be transferable.

As the status of legislation and planning instruments changes rapidly, the book seeks to introduce the basic elements of key legislation, land use planning instruments and assessment processes across the Australian jurisdictions. The jurisdiction of NSW is often provided as a particular example. Knowledge of these basic elements of a planning system should enable readers to identify and interpret the latest legislation available online through databases of state and national law (www.legislation.nsw.gov.au and www.austlii.edu.au).

Additional resources and readings are suggested in relation to the range of specific issues addressed in each chapter.

Structure of the book

The book is divided into three sections. The first section introduces the key principles – policy goals and system or operational criteria – underpinning statutory land use planning both in Australia and internationally. Chapter 1 introduces the basis for government intervention in private development through a legal land use plan and establishes contemporary principles or objectives for spatial and land use planning. Chapter 2 outlines the essential features of planning systems and the key stages in the land use planning, development and environmental assessment process. Chapter 3 sets out the major land use planning techniques for strategic development control.

The second section of the book introduces the Australian land use planning system. It aims to provide readers with an operational understanding of Australian urban governance, including the major laws, institutional arrangements and systems for strategic land allocation as well as development and environmental assessment. Chapter 4 explains Commonwealth government responsibilities, policies, and legislation relevant to urban land use planning in Australia. Chapter 5 compares the state and territorial land use planning systems, highlighting key policy and legislation. The chapter also outlines approaches to strategic regional and metropolitan planning, and development contributions for local infrastructure.

The remaining chapters in section 2 illustrate in more detail the operation of Australian planning systems. Chapter 6 reviews and compares the key plan-making, development assessment and dispute resolution provisions across the states and territories. Chapters 7 and 8 focus specifically on strategic planning and development control processes in the nation's most populous state of NSW. Chapter 7 focuses on strategic planning, including state planning policy, legislation and plan-making in NSW. Chapter 8 outlines development assessment processes, including environmental impact assessment in NSW. It also explains the development contribution system for local and regional infrastructure provision.

The third section of the book highlights emerging local practice in addressing key policy areas. Chapter 9 updates and extends the chapter contained in the first edition of this book on local planning practice for environmental sustainability – including planning approaches for biodiversity conservation and environmental performance at domestic, neighbourhood, city and regional scales. Chapter 10 builds on this theme with specific reference to planning for climate change – drawing on new practice in land use planning for reduced greenhouse gas emissions ('mitigation planning', and adaptation to impacts of climate change already underway ('adaptation planning'). Chapter 11, on planning for housing supply, affordability and choice, updates and expands the original first edition chapter on this theme.

The final chapter considers the strengths, weaknesses and priorities for reform across Australian planning systems and practice within the broader set of normative planning principles established in section 1 of the book, for environmental integrity, social equity, and community prosperity in urban and regional Australia.

Section 1

Principles: urban and environmental planning and policy

What is planning and why do we plan? In this section of the book the planning system is introduced as a framework for reconciling the range of public objectives and private interests associated with the urban development process, to achieve key overarching principles such as environmental protection, social equity and community prosperity. Chapter 1 begins with the rationale for land use planning as a form of government intervention in private development, to achieve a range of strategic objectives. There are several basic building blocks and sequential processes common to all land use planning systems and these are introduced in chapter 2, with reference to planning systems in the UK and the US. In constructing land use plans there are a number of key tools or mechanisms that form the basis for development control, and these are outlined in chapter 3.

Chapter 1

The objectives of land use planning

This chapter begins by establishing a definition of spatial land use planning and the key rationales or policy arguments for planned intervention in the development process. The second part of the chapter outlines the historical progression of modern town planning from its origins in sanitation and urban reform through to the current, far broader, sustainability agenda. There are many excellent volumes on planning history so the objective here is not to provide a detailed history but to show how the policy goals underpinning urban planning have evolved over time. The final section of the chapter draws together the discussion about the meanings of planning and the evolution of its normative goals. Referring to the concept of planning as a form of urban or environmental governance (Gleeson & Low 2000), a set of expectations or principles for the 'procedural' aspects of planning (how the planning system operates), and the 'substantive' outcomes of this process (what the planning system delivers) are proposed.

Defining planning

Before understanding why we undertake a process such as land use planning and the objectives of this process, it is important to clarify what we mean by 'planning'. The term 'planning' has different meanings in different contexts. In the context of urban policy, the expressions 'town and country planning', 'urban planning', 'land use planning', 'environmental planning' and, increasingly, 'spatial planning' are used to refer to a formal process regulating the use of land and the development of the built environment, in order to achieve strategic policy objectives. In this strict sense, planning is a 'particular form of public policy intervention in the arena of private decisions with regard to the use of land, governed by particular legislation' (Bramley et al. 1995, p38).

The International Society of City and Regional Planners (ISOCARP) describe the activity of land use planning as anticipating, preparing for, 'regulating and promoting changes in the use of land and buildings' (ISOCARP 2001, pxi). Consistent with this definition, planning can be understood as a methodology for identifying appropriate future actions to occur within a defined environment, including the use of various aspects or 'resources' contained within it. More broadly, and in relation to the Australian context, Brendan Gleeson and Nicholas Low argue for an understanding of spatial planning as a form of urban governance justified by the 'ideal of social justice' and directed to the 'challenge of ecological sustainability' (Gleeson & Low 2000, p2). We return to these concepts below.

Rationale for planning intervention

A primary justification for public intervention through the land use planning system relates to the potential negative impacts, or 'externalities' of an individual's activities in the private use of land upon neighbouring landholders and the broader community (Bramley et al. 1995). In other words, 'one householder's environmental gain from a new or improved dwelling may well signify a loss of amenity for their neighbours' (Blake & Collins 2004, p124).

To use a common example, a new addition to a house next door that achieves an additional storey and better views can also result in a loss of sunlight, privacy and outlook for the neighbours, and, depending on the design, may also detract from the visual appearance of the streetscape. Inappropriate development adjoining a nature conservation area could reduce experiential values for visitors and result in the spread of exotic plants and weeds, threatening the delicate ecological systems within the adjoining reserve. Over time, the cumulative effect of many such developments can make a significant impact on the qualities of our shared urban and regional landscapes.

Therefore, a clear land use plan, developed with public input, and setting out the rules governing future changes and the parameters for assessing particular development proposals, gives members of the community a degree of certainty and involvement about future changes. In other words:

> [The] certainty provided by a publicly accountable land use plan, supported by consistently applied development controls, may be seen as a social freedom outweighing the traditional right of the individual to develop land anywhere and in any manner (Blake & Collins 2004, p124).

In her review of the land use planning system in Britain, Kate Barker concluded that the planning system plays an important role in managing urban growth and particularly in addressing areas that are not effectively dealt with by the private market (Barker 2006). For instance, if it were solely up to the private market there would likely be an insufficient provision of important community infrastructure or protection of open space, or only those areas able to incorporate these amenities within private developments, such as premium master planned estates, would enjoy access to them, exacerbating social inequalities. The planning system can also directly contribute to socially fair outcomes in urban development, for instance, by structuring strategies to encourage the regeneration of areas suffering economic decline, or the promotion of socially mixed communities within new and changing areas.

Planning is intended to provide a key mechanism for public participation and representation to protect all sectors of the community from developments that may have an unjust impact on them. It provides a process for generating and disseminating necessary knowledge needed to inform urban development strategies. Planning also provides a defined methodology and policy framework for coordinating and resolving the different components of urban development – housing, employment opportunities, public space, transportation, water, biodiversity protection, and so on. Often these matters seem to relate to rival objectives – for instance, the need to provide new housing and infrastructure, and the need to protect the environment. Planning provides a process and forum for resolving these competing issues.

Finally, the planning system helps overcome blockages to essential development of land that could arise if landowners choose to act in a monopolistic manner (by refusing to sell sites needed for essential urban developments). Planning interventions including the compulsory acquisition of land can help to address this problem (Barker 2006, p26).

Early town planning

It is difficult to know where to begin a historical account of urban planning. Many histories start with the emergence of a professional movement in the early 20th century, which, as discussed further below, was in many ways a response to the urban problems associated with industrialisation. Others begin the history much earlier, with Lewis Mumford's epic history of the city starting at the genesis of human society itself (Mumford 1961). Mumford traces human congregation from the cave, to the hunting camps where people learned to domesticate animals and farm, through to villages and fortified hamlets and finally the Greek and Roman cities. His urban history documents the changing physical form of settlement but also emphasises the social and economic forces that led to the development of urban areas. He describes an 'urban implosion', with the evolution from village to urban city a sequential concentration of functions. Cities themselves represented a new form of social and economic organisation. More than just big villages, cities were fundamentally different, integrating a variety of discrete activities and administered by increasingly complex bureaucracies.

Ultimately these bureaucracies turned explicitly towards the management of urban growth itself. One of the earliest (unsuccessful) attempts to regulate land uses was recorded in New Amsterdam in 1648, as a complaint about the potential negative impacts of a proposed tannery between two houses (Beyer 1965). Later the introduction of 'land use zoning', or separating land uses based on potential conflict, was successfully defended in New York, appealing to precisely this argument.

By the mid 19th century, the poor housing of the working classes in the industrial cities of America, Britain and Australia became a focus for urban reformers. In the late 1830s, an epidemic of cholera in English industrial cities prompted an inquiry into the sanitary conditions of labourers, led by Edwin Chadwick. Reflecting a new awareness of the connections between living conditions and the spread of disease, the Public Health Act was introduced in 1848, which mandated new standards for drainage, ventilation and lighting in new dwellings. Subsequently, the Health Act (passed in 1875) established requirements for rear gardens and minimum road widths between dwellings.

At the same time, rapidly growing urban populations in New York City, Boston, Philadelphia, Chicago and other cities in the US contributed to the development of substandard tenement housing (Beyer 1965). New York City introduced the first Tenement Act in 1867 which required basic health and fire safety standards in tenement construction. This legislation was followed by a series of laws seeking to improve the housing conditions of the poor until the enactment of the comprehensive Tenement Housing Act 1901, which formed the basis for much of the later housing legislation in New York City.

By the early 20th century, despite the existence of laws to organise the process of land subdivision and basic building controls, there was very little in terms of comprehensive spatial planning or control. As well as concern about the urban slums, many were alarmed about the fate of rural areas, which were depressed and depopulating. It was in this context that new and ambitious planning visions to improve the housing conditions of the working class, while protecting rural landscapes from the negative effects of industrial development, were proposed.

The 'Garden City' model put forward by Ebenezer Howard in England involved the planned dispersal of urban populations into new towns serviced by public transport. These new towns were to be relatively self-contained populations of about 32,000 on 1000 acres, surrounded by a permanent green belt and linked to other garden cities and London by a modern mass transit system (Hall 1996). The model was underpinned by strong communitarian ideals, including the objective of providing affordable housing to accommodate the workers who would be attracted by the jobs and services to be provided in the new community.

There were many early experiments of the Garden City model although few were faithful to the comprehensive spectrum of policy goals implicit in their original design. The ideals of self-containment, a balance between employment and homes, and green belts, were variously eroded even in the earliest models – such as Letchworth and Hampstead Garden Suburb in the UK. In New York City the Forest Hills Garden suburb was sympathetic to Howard's ideas and intended to demonstrate that good design, based on the neighbourhood unit, could revive community. In Australia the suburb of Daceyville in Sydney's east was inspired by the Garden City model and some of the housing in the area remains in the public rental sector for low-income households today (Garnaut 2000).

Similarly in Scotland, Patrick Geddes advocated what are now considered to be the first social housing schemes, including models for state-sponsored and voluntary housing cooperatives and self-help housing schemes in Edinburgh for students and artists. Geddes, a biologist by training, was interested in the concept of the natural region – a geographical territory that combines settlements and hinterlands, uniquely shaped by the ongoing relationships between humans and their environment.

At the same time a new interest in the city as monument emerged in the US. The 'City Beautiful' movement emphasised grand civic architecture and a monumental scale of design, inspired by the boulevards of the European capitals. Georges Eugène Haussmann's reconstruction of Paris was the epitome of this model. In Australia at this time similar ideas were beginning to penetrate. Throughout the period the architect planner John Sulman promoted ideas of civic beautification, arguing that aesthetic qualities of place influence society: 'the beauty, or otherwise, of town or city must have an effect on its inhabitants' (Sulman 1921). Australia's new national capital Canberra was conceived as an ideal opportunity to demonstrate the benefits of town planning. In 1912, an American, Sir Walter Burley Griffin won a national design competition for Canberra, with a plan that reflected elements of City Beautiful and wider influences from the UK and Europe, although the full plan itself was never properly realised (Hamnett & Freestone 2000).

In the 1920s the Regional Planning Association of America was established and began to advocate at the regional scale, initially focusing on natural regions with their flagship experiment a comprehensive river basin planning scheme for the Tennessee Valley (Hall 1996). By 1929 the concept of spatial planning across a metropolitan region underpinned the first New York Regional Plan, prepared by Thomas Adams.

In contrast to this broader, more strategic approach to spatial planning and regulation, there was also a growing emphasis in US cities on the control of land uses at the level of individual site through rules and codes, particularly land use zoning. Debates regarding the potential benefits of land use controls and zoning focused on whether the mechanisms would constrain or enhance their land values. By setting limits on what a landowner could do on their own land, was the value of that land diminished? On the other hand, were land values enhanced by the certainty of knowing what could and could not occur on adjacent properties? Land use zoning was seen as a way to protect private amenity and property values, and create a better shared urban environment, but it was also used as a tool to keep out certain social groups (the poor, certain races and religious groups) from exclusive residential areas (Sandercock 1998). In Australia, local authorities were empowered by state legislation in the first quarter of the 20th century to enact minimum subdivision and set standards and building controls, which were also used to exclude lower income earners from new suburbs: for instance, as brick was a more expensive building material than timber during the interwar years, lower income earners could be 'kept out' of suburbs with mandatory requirements for brick housing construction (Frost & Dingle 1995, p31).

Although many jurisdictions in both Australia and the US have tried to remove such barriers to lower cost housing, in 2005 the US Department of Housing and Urban Development found that 'exclusionary' zoning and tight development controls continued to prevent many low-income people and others with particular housing needs from finding homes to rent or buy in many US cities and suburbs (HUD 2005). This issue is discussed further in chapter 11.

Twentieth-century planning

The first half of the 20th century saw the emergence of a defined planning profession, inspired by the exchange of ideas about cities and planning through international conferences and meetings. Leonie Sandercock (1990) describes this as a shift from 'an "ideas" phase" to a "legislative" phase in the evolution of city planning', noting that in Australia there was vigorous opposition to planning. This derived from a number of sectors, including:

> the real estate lobby, who saw planning regulations ... as threatening their business interests; from surveyors and engineers and some architects, who saw planning as a rival and unnecessary new profession; and from politicians in state parliaments representing the interests of both the rural property owners to do what they liked with their property (Sandercock 1990, p7).

In Sandercock's analysis, the struggle to establish a legislative basis for planning resulted in a contraction of its scope:

> the search for cross-class political support for planning measures and the need to appease urban commercial, industrial, and finance capital produced planning agencies and planners

who were more concerned with facilitating commercial and industrial growth and the activities of the subdividers and construction industry than with the problems of urban social reform (Sandercock 1990, p8).

By 1945 all of the Australian states with the exception of South Australia had enacted legislation for local governments to prepare statutory land use plans (Howe 2000). In 1948 Sydney's first planning scheme, the 'Cumberland County Council Plan for Sydney' was completed. The late 1940s also saw the establishment of Australia's first planning school. In 1949 Denis Winston, a former student of the British planner Patrick Abercrombie, was appointed as the first Professor of Town and Country Planning at the University of Sydney.

After World War Two there was a new, international urgency to city building and postwar reconstruction, particularly in Britain and Europe. In Australia and North America the postwar period precipitated significant economic and population growth so in these countries too there was an urgent need for the rapid provision of new urban areas, new roads, schools and public infrastructure. The role of the state in providing housing and managing the land market was largely uncontested during this time and planning itself conceived as far more than the regulation of land uses. Government planning meant direct urban intervention and development, including the provision of infrastructure, transport and housing. Regulating private development through planning control was seen as a balance between support for enterprise on the one hand (by coordinating the provision of infrastructure and encouraging investment in new urban growth) and control of the market on the other (through the provision of welfare and by controlling the shape and design of urban areas) (Hall 1996).

By the late 1950s the concept of a land use plan had shifted from that of a static document setting out the shape of future development in perpetuity to something that would accommodate and facilitate the complex processes of incremental change that characterise urban growth. Amongst the new academy, 'planning' was seen as a technical and scientific practice of making 'rational choices' amongst scientifically determined alternatives (Hall 1996; Taylor 1998). The 1960s was a period of great social and political change and planning itself was soon regarded by many to be the antithesis of rational science. Many perceived, and continue to regard, planning as a political activity, with planners consciously or not, acting as advocates for a particular side: 'Plans are policies and policies, in a democracy at any rate, spell politics. The question is not whether planning will reflect politics but whose politics it will reflect.' (Norton Long 1959, quoted in Taylor 1998, p168).

There was a distrust of the type of planning that emerged from bureaucracies in an autocratic, top-down manner, without opportunities for public participation. If planning is a political decision-making process, some hold the power in this process (such as the bureaucracy, or wealthy developers), and others – certain members of the 'community' – do not. Some scholars argued that it was up to the professional planner to advocate on behalf of those disadvantaged in this political arena, and to develop approaches to remain effective in this context (Forrester 1989).

Figure 1.1: Developing the Australian suburbs in the postwar years

The low density, detached housing on a single block encapsulates the model of suburban development facilitated by government housing schemes in the postwar years. While the housing and environmental amenity in the new suburbs was of high quality by international standards, problems of social isolation soon emerged, particularly for those without access to a private car. Source: the Author 2003.

Australia's major cities entered a period of significant suburban development between the postwar years and the 1970s. This process was facilitated by government home ownership policies, including the War Services Homes Scheme, which provided finance for the construction of houses on single lots. By the 1960s the larger metropolitan regions were under significant strain in terms of urban land supply and infrastructure provision to support new population growth and increased consumption (Morison 2000). Increasing car ownership rates and the decentralisation of industries to suburban areas reinforced the pattern of dispersed, low-density development across Australia's primate metropolitan areas. A degree of spatial differentiation emerged over this time – for instance, workers and their employers tended to settle in distinct sub-regions and there was an uneven spread of environmental amenities and services, particularly on the urban fringe (Gleeson 2006). However, the social divisions and racial segregation that characterised cities in the US over this period did not eventuate to the same degree in Australia. Also in contrast to the US, inner suburbs in Australian cities remained settled by successive waves of new immigrants, and later 'gentrifiers' (Gleeson 2006). Brendan Gleeson comments that the development of Australia's cities until the mid 1970s reflected strong government intervention including, but not limited to, relatively strong urban planning regulation:

> From Federation until the end of the Long Boom, Australian governments used a range of powers and initiatives to ensure the creation of cities that embodied the ideals of the Australian Settlement. The goals were simple: the expansion of collective welfare through orderly and inclusive suburbanisation and the protection of the most vulnerable through a modest public housing sector (Gleeson 2006, p22).

However, a desire to facilitate 'free market' economic development processes has never been far from the surface, despite the range of other social and environmental goals associated with planning. In relation to the history of European settlement in Australia, Margo Huxley (1994) highlights the tensions associated with establishing a system of land allocation and later the regulation of land use through bureaucratic planning that purports to promote the 'public good', by encouraging the accumulation of private wealth through individual property rights. Similarly, Leonie Sandercock commented that the private sector soon found ways to benefit from the planning system:

> the private sector proved remarkably adept at influencing the decisions of planning agencies, either before plans were released or, when necessary, by pressing for changes to published plans if those plans threatened their material interests. In other words, those groups who had opposed the introduction of planning in the interwar period discovered that they could use the planning process for their own ends. (Sandercock 1990, p10)

During the neoliberal era of the 1980s, the role of the government in regulating economic markets, including private development and land markets, came under persistent challenge. This meant that much existing planning legislation was bypassed to facilitate 'growth' (Lennon 2000). Often higher levels of government used their powers to create exceptions to the regulations established by local planning controls, using vehicles such as enterprise zones, where laissez-faire regimes replaced standard requirements. Beyond conservation areas, planning controls were standardised or wound back so as not to impede development. Such approaches are still being implemented throughout Australia. For instance, in 2005 the NSW state government approved legislation to enable the minister for planning unprecedented freedom to bypass planning controls, standards, and matters for consideration when assessing projects he declares to be of 'major' significance. The reforms, contained in the Environmental Assessment Amendment (Infrastructure and other Planning Reform) Bill 2005, were justified to the NSW Legislative Assembly on the basis that the question should not be 'whether' major infrastructure should proceed, but 'how':

> The government has moved decisively with its planning reform agenda to cut red tape and provide the regulatory conditions to support a strong economy, jobs growth and both public and private sector investment. The competitiveness of New South Wales to attract sustainable infrastructure and investment opportunities depends on having an efficient and clear development approval

system underpinned by an up-to-date planning regime ... I thank those in the various industry groups who have participated in the formulation of this legislation ... that will underpin the State's economy for generations to come (Craig Knowles, Second Reading Speech to NSW Legislative Assembly, 27 May 2005).

These reforms and their ongoing legacy in NSW are discussed at greater length in chapter 7. In early 2010 the positive role of the planning system was placed explicitly under the microscope of Australia's competition policy (National Competition Council 2011). In February of that year, the Council of Australian Governments' (COAG) Business Regulation and Competition Working Group (BRCWG) announced a Productivity Commission review of states and territories' planning, zoning, and development assessment systems. The terms of reference focused specifically on 'planning and zoning laws and practices which unjustifiably restrict competition and best practice approaches that support competition' (Sherry 2010).

Figure 1.2: Sydney Harbour

Sydney's attractive harbour, beaches, and architectural icons have reinforced its status as Australasia's financial capital and a beacon for the 'creative class.' Source: the Author 2011.

The rise of neoliberal policies within Australian government has coincided with a broader set of related international trends often described in relation to the umbrella term 'postmodernism'. Literally 'after modernism' (Gleeson & Low 2000), 'postmoderism' refers to the transitional period from Fordist modes of industry and production, and strong government intervention in social and economic policy, to new economies based on less tangible commodities relating to information and financial services, fashion and the arts, leisure and tourism.

This shift paralleled the emergence of distinct global (rather than regional or national) centres of capital accumulation and power. The 'world city' hypothesis, initially proposed by John Friedmann (1986) posited the emergence of a new, global hierarchy distinguished by a handful of international cities – London, Paris, New York, Tokyo; that were concentrated centres of capitalist accumulation. In a world increasingly characterised by competition for footloose, borderless capital, these so-called world or global cities attract the international headquarters of multinational firms and act as magnets for the establishment of higher order financial services and related forms of growth. Combined with perceived lifestyle amenity, as well as high social and cultural capital, Australia's largest cities – Sydney and Melbourne – also attract the highest concentrations of the so-called creative class – scientists, designers, educators, writers and musicians – as well as a wider circle of creative professionals in business, law, health care and finance (Florida 2003).

Despite Melbourne's prominence as the largest and wealthiest Australian city at the time of Federation, less than a century later Sydney had emerged as the financial capital of Australasia (Daly & Pritchard 2000). Sydney's status as a global city (the only Australian city to be ranked amongst the world's second order or Beta cities, including San Francisco, Toronto, and Zurich [Hall 2003]) can be attributed to a number of factors. Sydney overtook Melbourne as the focus of business activity during the postwar commodities boom, housing the Reserve Bank and many of Australia's other largest financial institutions (Daly & Pritchard 2000). The Sydney Olympics in 2000 confirmed Sydney's status as a city firmly in the global spotlight. Today Sydney has Australia's only Futures Exchange and the greatest concentration of the funds management industry and related specialist financial services. Maurice Daly and Bill Pritchard (2000) observe that once Sydney became the hub of financial activity in Australia, a number of other features combined to reinforce its status:

> Sydney was seen as an attractive city. Its climate, its harbour and beaches, its lifestyle benefits, its growing cosmopolitanism: the expatriates who came there to work prized these features. Sydney also had the principal international airport, so business people from overseas naturally passed through the city. This process of 'cumulative causation' acted to reinforce the dominance of Sydney in the financial sector and to encourage the location of corporations linked strategically to finance. (Daly & Pritchard 2003, p173)

Sydney's emergence as financial centre had its spatial expression in the appearance of a 'global arc' of financial and business services extending across the Central Business District to North Sydney, Chatswood, and business parks in Ryde and the North West. These spatial shifts coincided with the downturn in manufacturing industries, affecting Sydney's western suburbs, and large areas of the former industrial cities of Wollongong and Newcastle. Thus a distinct landscape of socio-economic polarisation has emerged with stark differences in property prices and rents between the highest and lowest value markets.

Such spatial polarisation is not unique to Sydney and apparent to varying degrees in each of the state capitals, although to date Sydney's status has arguably contributed to greater socio-spatial differentiation than those of other Australian cities. This socio-economic disparity has been described as the negative side of the broader socio-cultural diversity that is another characteristic of 'postmodernism' (Gleeson & Low 2000).

Figure 1.3: Liên Hoa Temple, Livingstone Rd, Marrickville

Ethnic diversity is increasingly a feature of Australia's urban areas. This temple in Marrickville completes a cluster of places of religious worship, from St Brigid's Catholic Church a few hundred metres away on Marrickville Rd, to the Greek Orthodox Church opposite. Source: the Author 2006

Since the 1970s, Australia's cities have also become far more ethnically and culturally diverse (Thompson 2000). Expressions of this diversity include the vibrant ethnic eating and shopping precincts of the state and territorial capital cities, and the revitalisation of suburbs such as Sydney's Chinatown, Canberra's Dickson, or Carlton in Melbourne. But despite the visible commercial and economic changes associated with cultural diversity, the use and design of our public spaces, business districts and residential areas and forms has not necessarily changed much (Watson & McGillivray 1995). Indeed, local resistance to the development of religious facilities, in particular Islamic schools and mosques in suburban and peri-urban areas, reveal fractures in planning and development assessment processes which have proved ill-equipped to resolve underlying racial tensions and concerns about cultural difference (Dunn 2005).

By the close of the first decade of the new millennium, a century after Federation, Australia's capital cities were again the focus of national policy concern, relating particularly to economic growth, the provision and condition of infrastructure, and housing affordability. Growing awareness of the potential implications of global climate change and the need for radically different approaches to urban form and infrastructure provision in the future has placed urban and regional planning firmly on the agenda. More than a century after modern urban planning emerged from the public health reforms of the late 1880s, the new health crises – obesity, respiratory disease and mental illness have all been linked in part to the built environment (Garden & Jalaludin 2009; Wells et al. 2010).

In sum, the past three decades have represented a number of distinct new challenges for land use planning in Australia. Firstly, there is a series of changes in approach to urban development and policy associated with the shift towards neoliberal policies. These include a retreat from direct government involvement in the development of cities and regions through capital investment in infrastructure or services, and pressure to reduce forms of regulation on private sector development through land use planning. Broad economic changes, including the shift away from the Fordist economy towards hyper-mobile service- or knowledge-oriented industries, have seen the emergence of a hierarchy of world cities competing for global capital, resulting in significant socio-economic differentiation, within such cities themselves and between other, less advantaged areas of the region or nation overall. In addition to economic cleavages, Australia is also characterised by increasing social diversity, of ethnicity, of household structure, of religious or cultural beliefs. Such challenges may not be as stark beyond Australia's primary metropolitan regions of greater Sydney and Melbourne. But the implications of economic restructure and globalisation for urban governance and policy extend across Australia and the Pacific islands region:

> Set within a contemporary framework of structural adjustment, deregulation and cost recovery, with the downsizing … of bureaucracies, governments have become both less willing and less able to assume planning responsibilities, whilst urban residents are no better informed or organised, in what is often an information vacuum. Sustainable development may be as distant now as it has ever been (Connell & Lea 2002, p210).

The question is how cities and urban regions can improve their environmental performance and liveability while engaging in 'hyper-competition' for global capital investment (Douglass 2002, p55). Further, how should we address the emerging social inequalities associated with globalisation, let alone the historical legacies of postcolonialism?

Town planning and Indigenous interests and connections to land

While there are significant differences in the colonial histories of North America, New Zealand, Australia, and parts of the Pacific islands, the impacts of colonisation on Indigenous society and culture in all nations have been universally catastrophic. These include the ongoing social, cultural and economic impacts of dispossession from territorial lands and loss of sovereignty, as well as environmental and cultural heritage degradation and disruption of traditional knowledge and management systems (Gurran & Phibbs 2004, p4). In Australia, even in major urban areas like Sydney, Melbourne and Brisbane, many iconic landmarks, parks and beaches – Bondi, Sydney Harbour, New Farm Park and King's Square in Brisbane, Melbourne's Yarra River, signify very different meanings and layers of history for their traditional Indigenous owners (Read 2000). As Nick Blomley writes in relation to Vancouver, 'colonial dispossessions and displacements cast long shadows … that are still with us', yet are easily overlooked in the day-to-day decisions about the future uses of this land (Blomley 2004, p106). In relation to the US, Leonie Sandercock notes that planning and urban histories have ignored the relationship between urbanisation and Indigenous displacement:

> There could be no more glaring absence from the pages of the planning history of the United States than that of its original inhabitants, Native Americans, who were forcibly removed from their lands in order for most American cities to be built and farms to be established (Sandercock 2004, p53).

John Connell and John Lea write about the close relationship between spatial planning and control of Indigenous populations across the Pacific islands:

> Different measures were devised by the colonial authorities to ensure the continuity of 'urban apartheid', a division that emphasised the European city in opposition to the Indigenous village … Land was firmly alienated where necessary. Colonial towns in the Pacific, whilst simultaneously offering some forms of economic and social development, established and regularised an ordered and largely intransigent inequality (Connell & Lea 2002, p44).

There are several aspects of the new 'sustainability' paradigm that are relevant to considering the particular interests and concerns of Indigenous communities in relation to land use planning decisions. In relation to the principle of social equity and justice within and between generations, it is crucial to acknowledge the social, cultural and environmental legacies of colonisation and land dispossession, as well as their localised impacts when planning with a particular community in a particular place. We also need to understand and attend to aspects of contemporary planning practice that may reinforce patterns of inequality between Indigenous and non-Indigenous people.

There are now clear policy and legal obligations to recognise Indigenous land interests and incorporate Indigenous participation in land use planning processes both in Australia and in other postcolonial nations, although admittedly these obligations are often very weak indeed. New Zealand's Resource Management Act 1991 recognises Indigenous Maori rights in managing natural and physical resources, and requires that local plans promote Maori interests and participation (Berke et al. 2002, Gurran & Phibbs 2004). In Australia, federal legislation (the *Native Title Act 1993*), discussed in chapter 4, establishes a framework to recognise the continued existence of native title in certain circumstances, and to manage this cooperatively with non-Indigenous uses. But there is still a very long way to go.

Figure 1.4: Flats in Cabramatta

Despite housing a distinctly multicultural community, predominant urban forms in south-western Sydney are distinctly homogenous, as shown in this image of apartments in the suburb of Cabramatta within the Fairfield Local Government Area. The image also shows increasing concerns for personal security and the sharp differentiation between the 'winners' and 'losers' in the postmodern city increasingly characterised by pockets of wealth and poverty. Source: the Author 2002.

The sustainable city?

Whether properly realised or not, underpinning many of the early urban planning experiments were broad goals that continue to influence urban planning practice – the need for an organised and coordinated process to provide the land and infrastructure to support economic development, environmental protection, and social equity, as it was then conceived. Today the goal of environmental protection is expressed in the terms of sustainable urban development: 'development that meets the needs of the present without compromising the ability of future generations to meet their own needs' (WCED 1987), and environmental sustainability more broadly. This adds to the traditional objectives of urban planning (which included the conservation of natural and rural landscapes, protection of waterbodies, and minimisation of pollution), more rigorous expectations regarding the need to protect biodiversity, wildlife habitat, and contain urban expansion, while introducing technologies to reduce dependency on non-renewable sources of energy.

Sustainable development

In the most general sense, 'sustainability', means ensuring that human activities do not compromise the essential natural and social systems on which life depends, now or in the future (Beatley 1995; Beatley & Manning 1997; Dixon & Fallon 1989). The concept gained prominence during the late 1970s and 1980s as a reaction to environmental degradation and atmospheric pollution on a global scale. Central to notions of sustainability are changing perceptions of the environment itself. Traditional meanings of environment amongst western cultures reflect deep Judeo-Christian beliefs about 'man's' place in relation to his surroundings, or the 'natural' world. Definitions of the 'environment', including legal definitions, reflect this human-centred or 'anthropocentric' focus (Farrier & Stein 2006). So the environment is often defined in relation to human 'surroundings', or by reference to the resources contained within it (as in 'natural resources'). Another distinction refers to the level of modification by humans, with 'natural' areas being environments with limited or no evidence of human modification (Cronon 1996). Contemporary definitions of the environment tend to recognise all elements of the living and non-living world, from the natural and built landscape, to waterbodies, atmosphere, and the social and biophysical processes of interaction between these elements (Gilpin 1990; Conacher & Conacher 2000).

In Australia, the phrase 'ecologically sustainable development' prevails in most official policy documents and environmental legislation, most frequently defined as 'using, conserving and enhancing the community's resources so that ecological processes, on which life depends, are maintained and the total quality of life, now and in the future, can be increased' (Commonwealth of Australia 1992). While this interpretation of sustainability still implies a continuation of economic growth, it also emphasises the connections between social and ecological wellbeing and quality of life in its entirety (Berkes & Folke 1998). As such, the definition straddles what have become known as the radical 'deep' forms of environmentalism, which advocate fundamental change in approaches to urban governance, management and consumption; and the more conservative 'shallow' forms of environmentalism, which emphasise the potential for the market and technology to solve environmental problems, without the need for significant government-sponsored intervention. It is often argued that government policies reflecting 'shallow' environmentalism focus primarily on issues of resource depletion and pollution to secure the health and affluence of the so-called developed nations (e.g. Naess 1983, 1989). For instance, stricter environmental regulations in affluent nations have meant that many global companies simply shift their practices to developing nations where standards are not so strict. Similarly, there has been a recent proliferation of market-based schemes such as carbon trading which allow corporations or individuals to purchase 'credits' (often in the form of conservation works carried out on their behalf). The implication of these market-based schemes is that, by 'pricing' pollution appropriately, market signals will trigger technological innovation, leading to less polluting technologies over time. While such schemes are intended to discourage pollution and 'offset' environmental impacts, they do little to challenge the systemic patterns of behaviour or consumption that lead to resource depletion and pollution.

This approach is often described as 'environmental modernisation':

> The core argument of ecological modernisation is that although democracy, the state and the market have gone astray, they can be restructured in a way that will make them sustainable ... Ecological modernisation argues that economic growth can be decoupled from raw material throughput, energy use and waste generation by applying new technology and redesigning institutions ... well designed interventions by government are assumed not to hinder economic growth but instead to stimulate new and more efficient industries. (Byrne et al. 2009, p138)

Australian environmental policy has arguably favoured 'environmental modernisation', rather than more active intervention through strategic and coordinated spatial strategies for infrastructure, transportation, and urban and regional change (Byrne et al. 2009).

Limits to growth

These radically differing perspectives regarding the meanings of 'sustainability' make it difficult for decision-makers, especially land use planners, to be confident that they are acting to implement sustainable development in practice. It is often suggested that, like other aspirational terms such as 'freedom' or 'justice', concepts of sustainability may remain ambiguous but that the value of the notion is in the extent to which it can inspire beneficial change (e.g. Beatley 1995; Lafferty 1998; Harding 1998).

Even if the precise meaning of sustainability remains unclear, there are several important principles for urban policy and land use plan-making. The notion of fundamental physical and ecological limits to growth establishes a basis for land use planning strategies to contain settlements and activities representing an unacceptable risk to the environment.

If considered in relation to 'natural' systems, like forests, soils or ocean fisheries, 'sustainability' means using and managing these resources in a way that preserves their capacity for renewal. Applied to social systems, 'sustainability' means pursuing individual and community wellbeing in a way that promotes equity. This involves both environmental and social fairness. For instance, it is not consistent with the principles of sustainability to prohibit the operation of polluting industries or activities within a particular area (such as a local government area, or even a nation), but to support the continuation of such activities elsewhere (without attempting to influence their environmental impact) through patterns of investment or consumption.

Similarly, principles of social sustainability and equity are not promoted when specific groups are deliberately or effectively excluded from particular communities. This can occur because of physical designs or rules which mean lower-income people, singles, or people with a disability cannot find suitable housing options or access the public realm. The principles of equity also apply over time – that is, policies should not exploit environmental and other resources at the expense of future generations. In summary, rather than emphasising the economic growth model as a method for satisfying human needs and aspirations, sustainability principles emphasise the renewal and *enrichment* of natural and social forms of capital rather than their *exploitation* in the pursuit of private wealth (Beatley & Manning 1997; Gleeson & Low 2000; Gurran 2001, p15).

Over the past two decades there have been a number of attempts to synthesise the key themes of sustainability as a set of principles relevant to environmental governance, including spatial land use planning. Consistent with the traditional distinction introduced above between 'procedural' planning (the planning system and planning decision-making processes) and 'substantive' planning (the matters addressed by planning) (Taylor 1998), sustainability principles reflect expectations regarding the urban decision-making process as well as the outcomes of this process.

Integration of the 'Three Es' – Environment, Equity, Economy

With regard to the decision-making process, a key principle is that decision-making systems must be able to integrate a variety of potentially competing social, cultural, economic and environmental considerations. Such integration must operate across the traditional sectoral boundaries (industry, transportation, housing, the environment and so on) and administrative boundaries (local, regional, state or nationally managed jurisdictions), as well as space and time (Beder 1993, pp4–5; Harding 1998). This principle reflects ecosystem concepts of holism and interdependence – that is, that individual species are dependent on an ecosystem and the processes it supports in their entirety.

As discussed above, the creation of safe, healthy, and functional living environments, and minimisation of negative social, economic, or environmental impacts of private development, has always been the rationale for the town and country planning movement. But the sustainability agenda extends traditional expectations of social and environmental responsibility in urban development. It also challenges conventional models of land use planning which focus on the fragmentation of landscapes into isolated management units, such as land use zones, in favour of a more ecologically informed perspective (Beately & Manning 1997; Conacher & Conacher 2000; Gurran 2001, p15). It has been argued that advancing scientific understandings about ecosystem functions actually challenge western philosophical and technocratic assumptions that the world can be divided into discrete components for analysis, utility and management (Aplin 1998). Arguably such notions underpin approaches to spatial land use planning that are primarily driven by zoning, or the categorisation and separation of land use functions. Recent scientific advances also challenge the notion of the environment as subject to predictable, controllable processes of change. Just as it is difficult to predict the full social implications of planning (e.g. Rittel & Webber 1973), the notion of 'ecosystem surprise', where unexpected and unpredictable environmental events occur, underpin the need for a precautionary approach to the environmental risks of development (Berkes & Folke 1998; Harding 1998).

In Australia, the principles of ecologically sustainable development, including the 'precautionary principle' are now enshrined in Commonwealth environmental legislation:

3A Principles of ecologically sustainable development

The following principles are *principles of ecologically sustainable development*:

(a) decisionmaking processes should effectively integrate both long-term and short-term economic, environmental, social and equitable considerations;

(b) if there are threats of serious or irreversible environmental damage, lack of full scientific certainty should not be used as a reason for postponing measures to prevent environmental degradation;

(c)   the principle of intergenerational equity – that the present generation should ensure that the health, diversity and productivity of the environment is maintained or enhanced for the benefit of future generations;

(d)   the conservation of biological diversity and ecological integrity should be a fundamental consideration in decisionmaking;

(e)   improved valuation, pricing and incentive mechanisms should be promoted. (*Commonwealth Environment Protection and Biodiversity Conservation Act 1999*).

Enshrining these principles in law means that decision-makers are bound to take them into account when considering specific proposals. However, as discussed throughout this book, the interpretation of these principles in relation to individual cases and alongside the other considerations associated with a particular development or plan mean that their actual implementation in practice is far from clear cut.

Sustainable and resilient communities

Recognising the broader social and economic objectives associated with the land use planning process, contemporary discourse emphasises the concept of 'sustainable communities', which are places rich in both social and ecological forms of wealth (Beatley 1995; Beatley & Manning 1997). Good practice would dictate that each community should collectively define their own measures of social and ecological wellbeing. These measures should be interpreted in relation to particular local and regional environments, subject to the broad principle that natural and social assets should be protected and enhanced, rather than undermined by exploitative or destructive patterns of settlement and production. One appealing vision of sustainable communities focuses on 'sense of place' as the basis for generating 'social sustainability' and a high quality of life:

A sustainable community nurtures built environment and settlement patterns that are uplifting, inspirational, memorable, and that engender a special feeling of attachment and belonging. A sustainable community also nurtures a sense of place by understanding and respecting its bioregional context – its topography and natural setting, its creeks, rivers, hilltops, open lands, native flora and fauna, and the many other unique elements of its natural context (Beatley 1995, p387).

Spatial planning strategies can help to encourage and preserve strong social networks, places where people have room to meet and encounter each other, 'where people are committed, invested, and involved … know and care about one another' (Beatley 1995, p390). Such communities will be distinguished by a strong sense of involvement, extending to local stewardship responsibility for the condition and health of the environment.

In policy terms, the United Kingdom has defined sustainable communities as:

Sustainable communities are places where people want to live and work, now and in the future. They meet the diverse needs of existing and future residents, are sensitive to their environment, and contribute to a high quality of life. They are safe and inclusive, well planned, built and run, and offer equality of opportunity and good services for all.

Sustainable communities should be:

- ACTIVE, INCLUSIVE AND SAFE – fair, tolerant and cohesive with a strong local culture and other shared community activities
- WELL RUN – with effective and inclusive participation, representation and leadership
- ENVIRONMENTALLY SENSITIVE – providing places for people to live that are considerate of the environment
- WELL DESIGNED AND BUILT – featuring a quality built and natural environment
- WELL CONNECTED – with good transport services and communication linking people to jobs, schools, health and other services
- THRIVING – with a flourishing and diverse local economy
- WELL SERVED – with public, private, community and voluntary services that are appropriate to people's needs and accessible to all
- FAIR FOR EVERYONE – including those in other communities, now and in the future. (HM Government 2005, p121).

Many aspirations of sustainability have emerged in relation to specific communities of place in Australia. For instance, the 'Melbourne Principles for Sustainable Cities' were articulated at a meeting jointly organised by the United Nations Environment Program and the Environmental Protection Authority of Victoria held in April 2002 (Low et al. 2005). These principles provided a reference point for the development of more place specific approaches, proceeding from the following vision: 'To create environmentally healthy, vibrant and sustainable cities where people respect one another and nature, to the benefit of all' (Low et al. 2005, p209). Specific principles relate to intergenerational, social, economic, and political equity and the individuality of cities, long-term economic and social security, the protection and restoration of biodiversity, the minimisation of ecological footprints, empowering citizens and fostering participation, supporting sustainable production and consumption; continual improvement and good governance (UNEP 2003).

There is growing awareness of the impending impacts of human induced climate change, and the contribution of the built environment to reducing the harmful greenhouse gas emissions that contribute to global warming. In this context, more recent conceptions of sustainable communities often refer to the concept of 'resilience'. 'Resilience' implies the ability for both human and natural systems to accommodate and adapt to increased climatic volatility.

In theory, all of these objectives are potentially complementary and mutually reinforcing. However, in practice, helping 'communities of place' to resolve the range of private and public interests associated with the protection and enhancement of their shared spaces is a key challenge and rationale for planning (Healey 1997):

Spatial planning efforts should thereafter be judged by the qualities of process – whether they built up relations between stakeholders in urban region states and whether the relations enable trust and understanding to flow among the stakeholders and generate sufficient support for policies and strategies to enable these to be relevant to the material opportunities available and the cultural values of those involved, and have the capacity to endure over time (Healey 1997, p72).

These procedural criteria recall the notion of planning as a form of urban or environmental governance.

Figure 1.5: Community Farm, Eugene, Oregon

This community farm is a focal point for the town of Eugene, Oregon. Situated along a rehabilitated river bank, and accessible by cycle and footpath, it provides a focus for sustainability education, fosters social networks, and offers a place for recreation and nature contemplation. Source: the Author 2003.

Planning as urban or environmental governance

Governance itself is a term that requires some explanation. Gleeson and Low (2000) describe governance as a formal system of authority articulated through legislation and administered by bureaucratic departments at national, state and local levels. Implied in the notion of governance is an expectation of leadership, consistent with democratically defined strategic policies.

The United Nations Centre for Human Settlements (UNCHS) regards 'good urban governance' as a system of decision-making that promotes 'sustainability, decentralisation, equity, efficiency, transparency and accountability, civic engagement and citizenship' (UNCHS 2000, p5). This recognises that governance may extend to processes or relationships beyond the realm of government itself, such as community (voluntary) and private sectors (Hyden 1998). Thus governance may also be described as the relations between government, the private sector and civil society (Carley & Smith 2001). This reflects the understanding that governments cannot act in isolation to effectively address problems associated with urban development and environmental degradation but depend on collaboration between these three sectors (IIED 2001). This broader understanding is consistent with a view of planning as a form of urban spatial governance (Gleeson & Low 2000), regulating the physical evolution of cities and regions according to democratically defined policies designed to promote social equity, economic vitality and ecological integrity, and mediating across the public and private sectors and civil society.

Expectations associated with these processes for urban policy and spatial planning, relate to transparency and openness in decision-making, including the sources of knowledge and information on which decisions are made, and the factors taken into account. Genuine public involvement in such decision-making processes is critical, including contributions to the way in which decisions are framed, and provisions for diverse forms of communication and expression.

What is the role of the 21st-century planner within this wider conceptualisation of urban and environmental governance; where the planner might be situated within or across the public, private or non-profit sector? Wendy Steele conceptualises a hybrid stance whereby planners, particularly those working for private consultancy, may be simultaneously engaged by government to prepare planning studies or strategies, and by developers to prepare application and assessment material in support of particular proposals (Steele 2009). While these competing roles raise complex questions about professional integrity, influence and ethics, similar issues have always characterised planners in practice.

The planning profession operates within a challenging context where stakes are particularly high. Members of professional planning associations subscribe to ethical charters by which they undertake to promote and uphold principles such as fairness, impartiality, public participation, addressing the needs of the disadvantaged, protecting the natural environment, as well as professional standards relating to independence, due diligence, avoiding conflicts of interest, confidentiality and disclosure (Barrett 2001).

Ethics in planning practice includes three distinct concepts and obligations. The first, relates to a professional charter or code, which usually includes a wide charter for planning professionals to uphold throughout their working life. The second, relates to the obligations and requirements of particular organisations – which tend to focus more narrowly on issues such as conflicts of interest, confidentiality and the use of information. The third set of ethical requirements for professional planners is established by law, but it is a mistake to think that so long as a practice is strictly legal, that it is also ethical. Many planning theorists draw on the various traditions of moral and environmental philosophy – not only to underpin and explain planning ethics – but also to support planning itself, as a practice organised by and oriented towards particular societal and environmental values or principles (Hendler 1995).

Summary and conclusions

This chapter began by defining planning as a form of urban governance, directed towards the goals of social justice and environmental sustainability. An important rationale for planning intervention in development is the need to address matters not effectively managed by the private market (such as the provision of infrastructure or the protection of community resources), and the capacity to mitigate the negative externalities that can arise from private development. Planning can promote socially fair outcomes in the urban development process and provide an opportunity for broad public participation in decisions regarding the use of shared environments. Essentially planning provides a policy framework and a methodology for informing, coordinating and resolving the different components of urban development.

The historical evolution of planning ideas, techniques and the profession itself shows that while planning interventions have focused predominantly on the physical environment, the objectives and scope of planning have always extended to the social or economic spheres (Keeble 1959). If there has been a tension between seeking broad objectives for environmental sustainability and community wellbeing through the protection of private property rights (and, in postcolonial societies, in the original vesting of those rights); the sustainability paradigm provides a normative policy framework within which some of these tensions may be addressed. The ways in which the spatial planning system can contribute to this agenda are outlined in the following chapters.

Chapter 2

The land use planning process

Urban land use planning systems have emerged in different forms across the world. But there are some basic elements and procedures that are common to all countries with an organised system for regulating land use and development through legal statute. This chapter introduces the key elements common to land use planning systems within Australia and internationally. It then compares the different roles undertaken by levels of government in different international planning jurisdictions. Finally, the chapter outlines the basic procedural steps associated with the planning process.

Elements of a planning system

The International Society of City and Regional Planners (ISOCARP) has identified five basic elements of a planning system:

- Source(s) of power (for planning intervention), articulated through national, state, regional, local or equivalent levels of government and legislation;
- A balance of strategic policies underpinned by incentives to encourage preferred development, and controls to constrain undesirable impacts;
- Regulation: the need for consent to carry out change;
- Legal rights for public consultation, including rights to object to a plan or decision; and,
- Financial arrangements for public infrastructure and for planning administration (ISOCARP 2001).

These elements are discussed in turn.

A source of power

All planning systems need a legal source of power to legitimise their bureaucratic and development control functions. This source of power will typically be articulated within a major or principal piece of legislation, or, in some cases, may be drawn from several legislative sources. This legislation is often described in Australia as 'enabling legislation' because it provides the basis for the establishment of a bureaucracy to administer the planning process, to prepare particular plans or other forms of land use control, and to actually regulate development proposals.

This source of power may operate at a national level or at a lower level of jurisdiction. For instance, New Zealand has national planning legislation, with primary responsibility for detailed land use planning activities, delegated to local governments. In carrying out their planning activities – making plans and assessing development, local governments remain bound by the procedural objectives and requirements enshrined in New Zealand's Resource Management Act 1991. Similarly, in Britain the planning system is based on the original Town and Country Planning Act 1947 which provided for local planning authorities to have responsibility for plan-making and development assessment within the context of national planning policies. In the US and Australia, there is limited national involvement in urban policy or planning and the states are responsible for enacting their own enabling legislation to establish land use planning systems. Again the detailed responsibilities for preparing plans and assessing developments are delegated to local government.

A balance of constraints and incentives

The statutory land use planning system can only address prospective or future activities. In general, the statutory planning system has no power to stop or modify existing activities or developments that were previously legitimately approved and carried out in a way that is consistent with this approval. Nor can it require that a particular development or series of developments take place. Thus planning controls must be designed to effectively encourage preferred developments consistent with community objectives, while constraining forms of development that would undermine these objectives.

This is often more difficult than it sounds. For instance, a local government may be concerned about the unsightly impact of tourist cabins within an aging caravan park on an area of beach foreshore earmarked for enhancement. The planning authority has no real power to compel the caravan park owner to enhance their property. New design controls would ensure that future developments would be consistent with the new image of the beach foreshore, and meet stricter environmental criteria, but if they are too stringent, they are likely to deter the caravan park owner from any form of upgrading at all. On the other hand, if the new controls contain some incentives, such as provision for additional tourist cabins on the site or for some other form of appropriate additional use, like a café, the potential value associated with upgrading may outweigh the costs associated with complying with the new requirements. In this case, the incentive encourages the private developer to undertake development, or to sell to a new owner who will, helping achieve the broader community objectives.

Regulation

The requirement for consent to carry out change in the use or development of land or buildings activates the regulatory planning system. The degree of regulation inherent in each planning jurisdiction depends on the triggers for this consent, defined in planning legislation.

Legal rights for public consultation

All planning systems include some provisions for public involvement in plan-making or in assessing developments. At a minimum these rights usually provide for some ability to comment on, or object to, a planning regulation that affects an individual's own property, or a development proposal that adjoins property boundaries. However, the thresholds for these opportunities vary from planning jurisdiction to jurisdiction.

Opportunities for public consultation, or, more broadly, involvement in the planning system, may also include the right to comment on proposed new plans or planning policies and larger developments that are thought to have wider significance to the community. Many planning systems also include provisions for legal appeal against planning decisions (with differing opportunities for individuals to initiate this action), and for public inquiries into significant planning issues or decisions.

Figure 2.1: Foreshore parks, Cottesloe, Western Australia

Provisions exist within most planning systems to secure basic contributions, (financial or in kind) from developers to provide for the shared infrastructure that supports urban development, such as the reservation of water foreshores or the construction of playgrounds. Source: the Author 2004.

Financial arrangements

All planning systems include arrangements to ensure adequate provision of the public or shared infrastructure needed for private development, such as roads, electricity, water services, and often public space and community facilities. It is common for planning authorities to require, as a condition of planning approval, contributions from developers towards this shared infrastructure, and sometimes, to offset other impacts of the development. In other cases developers will provide this infrastructure directly. Obviously, requiring such contributions from private developers is not uncontentious and there is a vase spectrum of requirements and justifications among the Australian planning jurisdictions and internationally. There are also important policy considerations associated with establishing fee requirements. These are discussed at greater length in the following chapter. Arrangements for developer contributions in the Australian states are compared in chapter 5 and the NSW system as an example is described in greater detail in chapter 8.

Funding is also needed to cover the costs associated with administering the planning system. One way in which these funds are acquired is through development application fees paid to planning authorities by the proponents of developments. Generally the principal planning legislation (including any more detailed guidance or regulations supporting it) will establish the parameters for compulsory fees and charges within the planning system and the ways in which they must be managed and dispersed.

Administration of planning systems

Local government authorities typically have the main responsibility for land use planning, operating within a policy and legal framework established by a higher level or levels of government (regional, state or national).

The Town and Country Planning System in the United Kingdom

The national framework for planning in the United Kingdom (UK) is established by the Town and Country Planning Act 1990 (TCPA 1990) (as substantially amended by the Planning and Compulsory Purchase Act 2004 [PCPA 2004]). The TCPA 1990 establishes the processes and mandatory considerations for plan-making and development assessment. It was derived from the original Town and Country Planning Act 1947 which represented a radical juncture in British planning from a zoning system to a system of nationalised development rights (that is, development entitlements vested in the planning authority to be allocated through planning permissions, rather than a land use zoning designation).

The system provides for a tiered process of planning:

- National level policies issued by central government ('Planning Policy Guidance'), which establish national planning policy including matters of 'material consideration' that must be taken into account by local authorities in plan-making or development assessment; and 'Circulars' which contain more detailed guidance to assist in the interpretation of national planning policy;
- Local Development Frameworks; and,
- Site level assessment of specific proposals (Barker 2006; Department of Communities and Local Government 2011b).

The system is described as a 'plan-led' process, whereby regulations contained in land use plans prevail unless a 'material consideration' (defined in central government policy) indicates otherwise (Barker 2006, p28). In reality this means that each development is subject to a highly discretionary process of local deliberation. While this discretionary process enables each proposal to be considered on merit, these deliberations occur within the context of the tiered system of national and local policy and plans. A strong planning appeals system, conducted centrally by trained planning inspectors adds weight to the implementation of these policies.

Local planning authorities are responsible for the preparation of local development plan frameworks which include a 'core strategy' as well as other development plan documents which may contain more detailed provisions to implement the core strategy (Department of Communities and Local Government 2011b). 'Area Action Plans' are prepared in areas where 'significant change or conservation are needed' (Department of Communities and Local Government 2011, p27b). An 'adopted proposals map' identifies 'areas of protection, such as nationally protected landscape and internationally, nationally and locally designated areas and sites, and Green Belt land; show areas at risk of flooding; and allocate sites for particular land use and development proposals included in any adopted development plan document and set out the areas to which specific policies apply' (Department of Communities and Local Government 2011, p32b). While plans identify sites suitable for particular types of development, this does not signify an 'as right' entitlement. Other sites not identified in plans may also be proposed by developers for housing or other land uses (Monk & Whitehead 1999) but these proposals will be determined against adopted plans and policies.

Local planning authorities are responsible for managing and determining most applications for planning permission (consisting of an outline application, often involving negotiation with professional planning staff, followed by a more detailed application considered by an elected local planning committee) (Monk & Whitehead 1999). Every development proposal must secure planning permission through this discretionary planning process. In addition to the provisions of the relevant development plan, local planning authorities are required to have regard to any other material consideration established by national policy guidance. Following planning permission, building work itself usually requires permission under separate building regulations.

Section 106 of the TCPA has enabled local planning authorities to enter into an agreement relating to the use of land, including provisions for financial or other types of contributions made by the developer to the planning authority. These contributions have in the past included the provision of local or regional infrastructure like parks, highway alterations and, particularly, affordable housing. Agreements under s106 have been negotiated (Crook & Whitehead 2004), but the introduction of a Community Infrastructure Levy allows local authorities to impose a set tariff based approach for funding new local infrastructure. It is intended that the new levy system will have wider application across all developments, and provide greater certainty than the negotiated system (Department of Communities and Local Government 2011b). In setting charges, authorities need to demonstrate economic viability, that is that the charge is not so high that it will make development unviable. Development specific planning obligations under s106 of the TCPA may still apply, for instance, for affordable housing provision.

Urban planning in the US

The American planning system has many similarities to that of Australia. The federal government has limited responsibilities for urban planning, although it can influence matters indirectly through federal legislation (for instance, environmental impact laws). The federal government can also influence planning approaches at the local level through stipulations attached to grant funding. The states are responsible for managing the land use planning system. They establish the enabling legislation and policy within which local planning can occur. While these policies and legislation establish the parameters for local planning, the extent to which each state can directly intervene in local decisions varies from jurisdiction to jurisdiction. Some US states require local authorities to prepare a comprehensive plan consistent with either a state or regional plan, or both, and to draft regulatory controls to implement the goals and principles of the comprehensive instrument (Witten 2003, p510). These regulations include zoning or subdivision ordinances, and may also include other local policies, guidelines, strategies or agreements (Cullingworth & Caves 2009).

Where states mandate the adoption of a comprehensive plan, land use zoning should be consistent with that plan (Witten 2003). To prepare a comprehensive plan, state legislation requires 'elements' to be included in the plan. 'Land use' and 'transportation' elements are always required, although other elements, such as a 'housing element' in comprehensive plans are not always mandatory.

States without comprehensive planning requirements allow local jurisdictions far more freedom in establishing development controls, although these controls must still conform to relevant state or federal legislation. Even in these states, local development controls – and particularly land use zoning – are very much the responsibility of local government units. Across the 50 states, there were around 19,000 municipalities at the time of the 2002 US Census of Governments, and a similar number of counties and townships (which also have the status of local government unit) (Cullingworth & Caves 2009 p80). Accordingly there are vast differences in land use planning legislation and policy approaches across the US, and even greater diversity at the local authority level.

Land use zoning is a very important component of planning regulation in the US. In 1924 a Standard State Zoning Enabling Act was published providing a model for land use zoning ordinances across the country. The concept of zoning spread rapidly across the nation – within two years 43 states had passed laws to enable land use zoning; and over 400 local governments representing major population areas had adopted zoning ordinances (Cullingworth & Caves 2009 p72). Rather than establishing a strategic policy framework, these zoning ordinances were intended to facilitate orderly development while protecting property rights and providing certainty for investment:

> Zoning was seen as the instrument for providing the necessary security against both unwanted development and legal challenge. In particular it provided protection to home owners from uncongenial neighbouring uses which would affect both amenity and market value (Cullingworth and Caves 2009 p71).

The emphasis on zoning and legally defined development entitlements has meant that the courts play a significant role in the US planning process. Both federal and state constitutions include provisions which relate to land law through their protection of property rights. In the US, the Fifth Amendment to the Federal Constitution states that private property cannot be 'taken for public use without just compensation' (Cullingworth and Caves 2009 p84) . This has presented two specific problems for land use regulators: firstly, the need to ensure that zoning regulations are not so onerous that they constitute a 'taking' and, secondly, that if they do constitute such a 'taking' they also conform to what is termed the 'public use doctrine' – that is, they meet an appropriate public purpose.

Figure 2.2: Comprehensive planning and urban renewal in Portland, US

The state of Oregon in the US requires comprehensive plans to be prepared. In the city of Portland, the comprehensive planning process included integrated land use, transportation and housing elements resulting in reduced urban sprawl, renewal of inner city areas including the downtown (above), affordable housing and free public transport around the CBD. Source: the Author 2003.

A more fundamental issue associated with the heavy reliance on land use zoning in the US has been the challenges zoning presents for achieving mixed uses and urban intensification around centres and public transit (Hirt 2007), illustrating the ways in which particular types of planning regulation can have profound impacts on urban structure and form.

The planning process

The urban planning process itself is characterised by two key stages (Figure 2.3):

- Forward planning – defining strategic objectives and policies to achieve them, which are usually expressed through legally enforceable guidelines or controls on land use and on the dimensions of development contained with a planning instrument or instruments;
- Development control – assessing development proposals, by private or public developers, against these planning controls, and issuing a decision to approve (usually with conditions), refuse, or negotiate to further modify the proposal.

Strategic land use planning is intended to establish a framework for achieving the desired future of a particular place, by articulating a shared vision or objectives, and by establishing a legally enforceable basis for guiding future decisions and actions consistent with these objectives. In this way, strategic land use planning underpins effective development assessment, because if the rules and decision-making criteria are clear and robust, assessing particular developments against these rules becomes much more straightforward. Of course, a strong strategic planning process will incorporate more than the legal framework for managing future development, but will encompass wider strategies for infrastructure and transport investment, environmental management and conservation, affordable housing and social inclusion. In practice, however, this holistic framework is rarely achieved, because it depends on a high degree of coordination and control, particularly in relation to policy and funding decisions for transport and infrastructure. This raises a perennial problem for the urban planning process, particularly for nations such as Australia, where urban and environmental governance functions are distributed across discrete Commonwealth and state agencies for transport, infrastructure, housing, environment and natural resource management. Rather than representing a proactive policy arm, with overarching control or influence over policies for transport, infrastructure, or natural resource management, these parallel bureaucracies can undermine the effectiveness of plan-making and implementation.

Therefore, while in theory strategic planning and development assessment should be complementary parts of an integral whole, in practice there is often a greater emphasis on development control. Often the resources of a planning authority are limited, especially during a period of high development activity, when it is necessary to consider large volumes of applications very quickly. Frequently the environmental or social data needed to fully inform strategic planning processes are costly or difficult to obtain, so this research is deferred to the development assessment stage. Often plans include a requirement that the developer fund the necessary environmental or social impact studies needed to support their proposal. Yet by requiring costly studies to be paid for by private developers, the stakes are raised and it becomes harder to refuse a proposal that already represents a significant investment of funds by the proponent. Further, it might be expected that, when studies are commissioned and funded by the proponent they are most likely to be directed towards demonstrating how the proposal could be achieved rather than whether it should proceed at all.

Thus it is clearly preferable for the objectives, standards and expectations regarding developments to be clearly established in a legally enforceable plan. Ideally, sufficient information will be available during the strategic planning stage, to provide a clear, if not definitive signal, as to the type of development that will be approved within a particular area. Without this type of certainty, it is likely that the assessment process will be lengthier, subject to more disputes, and often result in suboptimum outcomes from the perspective of the developer or the local community, or both.

Figure 2.3: The planning process

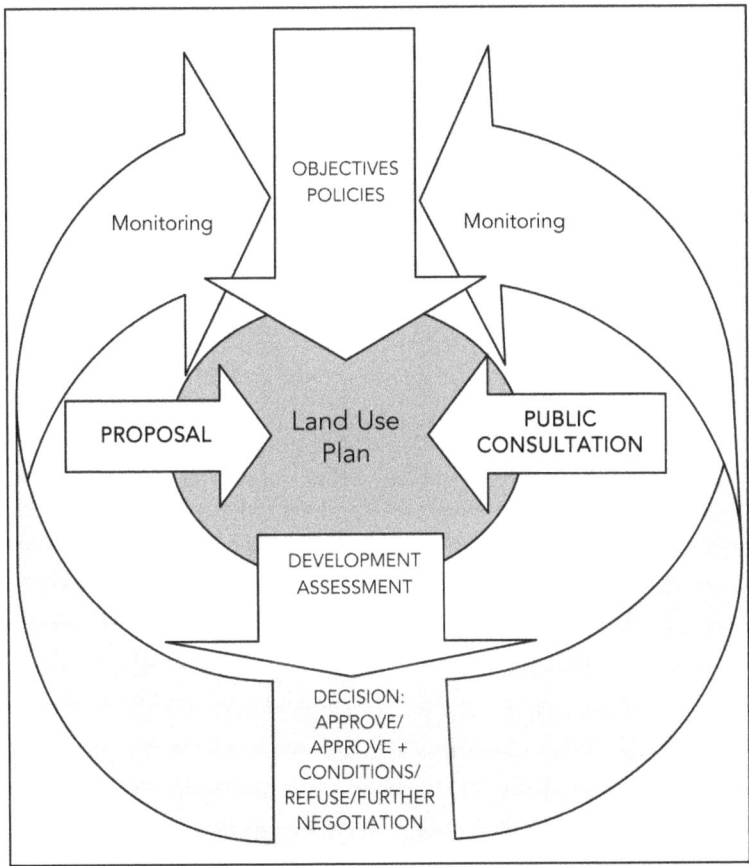

Source: the Author 2007

The need for as much certainty as possible notwithstanding, there is a tension between specifying all of the rules or parameters to govern developments in advance and providing for the flexibility to assess particular developments on their own merits; as highlighted by the brief comparison of the approach to planning in the US and the UK. We return to this issue in the following chapter.

Operation of the planning process

The operation of these basic processes is illustrated in relation to a more detailed sequence, involving a range of key stakeholders:

- Research and consultation
- Establishment of objectives
- Land allocation
- Articulation of development standards or criteria
- Formal public consultation and finalisation of land use plan
- Development assessment (including consultation on specific proposals)
- Decision (including potential appeal)
- Monitoring.

The first five of these activities (research and consultation, establishing objectives, allocating land and articulating specific development standards) relate to forward, or strategic, planning. The next two activities, including consultation on specific development proposals, are part of the development control process, while 'monitoring' focuses on the results of the development control stage but ultimately informs the next strategic planning phase.

Research and consultation

The research phase seeks to identify existing and likely future needs in relation to demographic factors (population growth and change), economic factors (income, labour market trends) and existing land supply (for commercial, residential, industrial or related development). Research is also needed to determine or review the environmental, cultural heritage, social, or economic values and attributes of the area that need to be enhanced or protected. In undertaking research on land capacity, values and opportunities for future growth it is also necessary to consider the governance or implementation capacity of the local planning authority. In other words, what is the availability of and condition of the 'delivery systems' that will enable the planning and development process itself to take place? Do staff have the requisite training and capacity to assess complex proposals in line with the expectations and criteria outlined in national, state, or local policy and legislation, or likely to be defined during the strategic planning process? Are there sufficient numbers of staff in the critical areas? What provisions for data capture, monitoring and reviewing the achievement of plan objectives need to be set in place?

The research and consultation stage should engage key community groups, residents, developers and other public agencies. Different terminology is used to refer to the involvement of people in the urban and environmental planning processes. The broad term 'public involvement' can include both formal consultation processes as well as actual public involvement in decision-making itself:

> Public involvement is the *process* for involving the public in the decision-making procedures of a municipality or corporation. This can be brought about through a series of approaches or

techniques that range from consultation to participation, the key difference being the degree to which those involved in the process are able to influence, share, or control decision-making (Marshall & Roberts 1997, p8).

'Consultation' tends to involve information sharing – in land use planning this is often achieved by the exhibition of a plan or proposal and an invitation for members of the public to comment. Often this is a formal legal requirement or an established procedural policy, as discussed below. But this form of public involvement is relatively limited.

Public 'participation' includes more direct forms of involvement beyond the relatively static activities of receiving, sharing, or responding to information provided by a planning authority. Public participation could include involvement in an advisory committee, or attendance at a focus group, conference or forum designed to understand the different perspectives, interests and aspirations of community members in relation to future urban growth and change.

Public involvement is important at all stages of the planning process, and different techniques are likely to be appropriate at different stages. For instance, community representatives and even local businesses may provide important sources of information to assist in identifying future needs for infrastructure, residential, commercial, or industrial land, while the support of local resident groups may be needed to implement specific components of the plan, such as changes to provisions governing the height or density of buildings.

The term 'stakeholder' is commonly used to refer to members of the public, business, government, or community sectors who have an interest or 'stake' in particular planning decisions. However, the term may imply that some people have a more legitimate interest than others in certain decisions, or that it is not necessary to pursue broadly based public involvement. A summary of people and groups likely to have an interest in or be affected by land use planning decisions is contained in Box 2.1.

Ensuring that all these individuals and groups are able to participate meaningfully in strategic urban planning processes or have an opportunity to comment on specific development proposals can be extremely difficult. It is much easier to build on ongoing participatory structures if these have been established or are already supported by a local planning authority – for instance, resident or precinct committees, Indigenous advisory or liaison groups, local heritage committees or environmental associations. However, it should not be assumed that such structures encompass all who may wish to have a voice on a particular issue. When considering a specific public involvement strategy it is a good idea to develop structures that can continue or regroup when needed, beyond the life of the specific issue being considered. It is also beneficial to ensure that there are as many diverse opportunities for interested people to participate as possible, particularly during comprehensive, strategic planning processes, while providing more focused opportunities at other stages of the decision-making cycle.

Aside from the formal opportunity to comment on a draft plan or proposal, public meetings are perhaps the most common opportunity for public involvement or consultation in land use planning processes. However, there are many limitations to public meetings – they are an inherently adversarial structure; only the most assertive voices will be heard;

and they provide little scope for members of the community to actively deliberate on particular issues. Special strategies are likely to be needed to engage particular groups, such as Indigenous people or their representatives. It is good practice to consult with local Indigenous groups to determine the best and most appropriate approach (Baker et al. 2001).

Box 2.1 Groups and individuals with an interest in land use planning

Those likely to be interested in, or affected by, land use planning processes include:

- Local residents (including the full spectrum of people who live in a community and have particular interests, values, and needs, such as seniors, children and youth, people with a disability, single people, families, extended families, gays and lesbians, people with particular religious needs, the unemployed, renters and homeowners, and so on)
- Traditional landowners or those Indigenous people and groups with traditional or ongoing links to the area
- People who work in the area but might not live there
- Landowners ('rate payers'), who are not necessarily resident in the area
- Frequent/seasonal visitors
- Government agencies that have significant land holdings
- Adjoining local council authorities and constituents
- Government agencies responsible for human service provision
- Local community organisations and service providers
- Heritage societies, sporting and recreational clubs, environmental groups, tourism associations (at local, state, and sometimes national levels)
- Development industry representatives including real estate agents, developers, builders, major land holders
- Chambers of commerce
- Representatives of particular industries

For further discussion on public participation, particularly in relation to the Australian planning context, see Zehner and Marshall 2007.

Table 2.1 lists approaches to public involvement at different stages in urban or environmental planning processes. It is not always necessary to undertake formal consultation at each of these stages, although regular consultation helps build support for implementation. Some stages, such as the land allocation stage, need to be managed carefully so as to not raise expectations regarding potential land use decisions that could encourage land speculation or monopolistic behaviour.

Table 2.1: Public involvement in the land use planning process

Planning Stage	Possible public involvement/consultation approach
Research/initial consultation	Establishment of an overall steering/advisory committee
	Community survey
	'Future search' conference (involving representatives of all stakeholder groups, to identify key issues and goals)
	Workshop/focus groups, targeting key groups (e.g. community sector, developers, residents, tenants, youth, the aged, etc.)
	Social media/twitter
	Targeted meetings with key stakeholder representative groups and individuals (within local authority and external stakeholders)
Establishing objectives	Focus groups/workshops, public meetings
	Shopfront/information display/Q&A sessions
	Printed information/newsletter/website
	Social media/twitter
	Presentation/discussion at open planning authority meeting
Land Allocation	Meetings with major landholders likely to be affected, key developers, industry groups, relevant stakeholders – Indigenous, environmental, community, recreation, heritage groups etc.
	Meetings with expert advisors/steering committee, if available
	Guided field trips, focus groups/workshops
Articulating development standards	Meetings with expert advisors/steering committee, key developers
	Design charettes (intense, facilitated workshops to collaboratively define options or preferred designs for specific localities – such as a neighbourhood or commercial centre, or a new residential subdivision or release area)
Formal consultation on draft plans	Public exhibition of draft plan – planning authority offices, libraries, shopping centres, schools, community centres, internet
	Provision for feedback (submissions/verbal feedback)
	Shopfront/information displays/Q&A sessions
	Printed information/newsletter/website
	Social media/twitter
	Presentation/discussion at open planning authority meeting

Planning Stage	Possible public involvement/consultation approach
Development assessment	Public exhibition of draft plan – planning authority offices, libraries, shopping centres, schools, community centres, internet
	Provision for feedback (submissions/verbal feedback)
	Independent forum/hearing to negotiate issues between neighbours/ residents and developers
	Presentation/discussion at open planning authority meeting
	For developments associated with significant environmental or social impact, shopfront/information display/Q&A sessions
	Printed information/newsletter/website
Monitoring	Regular publishing of indicator data (e.g. through an annual report or community feedback report)
	Forum for regular community/stakeholder feedback about plan outcomes – local newsletter/website/annual or bi-annual events
	Ongoing meetings with advisory committee (if available)

Source: Adapted from Marshall 2003

Establishment of objectives

It is important to establish a clear set of objectives or aims, to guide the overall direction of the plan. Sometimes these are described as a community 'vision' of their community and environment in the future. Sometimes these aims are expressed as or supplemented by guiding principles for how the specific provisions of the plan should be interpreted by decision-makers. Information acquired during the research and consultation stages will contribute to the articulation of these overall objectives or aims.

Land allocation

The allocation of land involves identifying appropriate development opportunities to meet forecast needs, subject to environmental capacity, landscape characteristics, existing and preferred settlement patterns and so on. This stage involves identifying or reassessing existing and potential sites for industry or housing within existing urban areas (infill and brownfield development) and on previously undeveloped land (greenfield sites). This is a highly contentious process that involves making decisions to include some land for certain types of development and excluding other land from development for urban purposes. Some landowners will gain hypothetical increases in land value as a result of these decisions, while others will not.

Depending on the specific regulations within each planning jurisdiction, it is unlikely that strategic processes of land allocation would seek to avoid designating lower or more limited land uses than the current classification or zoning permits. In the case that land is to be designated for future public purposes (for instance, infrastructure, a road, or a nature reserve) there will usually be a provision allowing the landholder to require the acquisition of the land.

Other jurisdictions have different regulations to ensure that potential land use classifications or zones cannot be arbitrarily downgraded to a lower use, irrespective of whether there are sound environmental or social reasons to do so, without the consent of the owner or provision for financial compensation. This ensures that land values are somewhat protected from sudden changes in land use planning decisions. Therefore once the land has been designated for urban purposes, it is very difficult to change this designation, even in response to environmental change in the future (such as rising sea levels), or if new information about environmental values becomes available. The difficulty of 'down zoning' or reversing a zoning decision means that it is very important to tie decisions about land supply to rigorous data on existing and projected demand, recognising that some over-supply may be necessary to achieve adequate quantities of new development, given that not all landholders will opt to sell or develop their land.

Figure 2.4: Greenfield development, South-East Queensland

Source: the Author 2002

Even when land has not been already zoned for an urban purpose, land holders, particularly on the fringes of urban areas, often enjoy higher land values based on the speculative expectation that future planning changes will permit the land to be used for urban growth. In these cases it can be very difficult to ensure that comprehensive strategic planning processes focus on identifying the most appropriate locations for new development in relation to the needs of the broader community.

It is important to make a final comment about the allocation of land to particular uses. Most, if not all, strategic planning processes relate to existing communities or places that are already occupied or used in some way – from existing settlements, towns or city suburbs through to farming lands or forests. When establishing the land uses to be allocated through a strategic planning process and recorded within the statutory land use plan, the existing uses of the land are unaffected by the new planning designation. The only way in which new land use planning law will result in a changed land use is through the process of lodging a development application with the relevant planning authority. Most planning jurisdictions have specific provisions to recognise and permit the continuation of activities even when they no longer conform to the current land use specified by the plan. These are known as 'existing use rights' or 'non-conforming uses'. There are different procedures in each planning jurisdiction to regulate these 'non-conforming uses', including provisions to encourage the establishment of a conforming use when the current activity ceases or changes.

Figure 2.5: Dispersed development, Western Sydney

When there are no mechanisms to control the sequencing of urban development, the result is a degraded landscape no longer suitable for agricultural uses but unattractive and poorly serviced for residential development. Source: the Author 2004

Articulation of development standards

Once the land has been identified or assigned to particular classes of land use, mechanisms for regulating the way in which this land becomes available for urban development and the standards for the construction and appearance of this development are needed. This occurs by establishing development standards or controls in land use plans. One of the most basic controls is land use zoning, which is an operational mechanism for implementing the land allocation decisions described above. A land use zone defines the uses or activities that the land within the zone may legally be used for. In addition to land use zones or their equivalent, specific standards and controls to govern the configuration, appearance and design of particular development types are also defined at this stage in the planning process.

Traditionally, these standards were expressed in a highly prescriptive way, often with reference to specific numerical standards or detailed requirements. However, in Australia some jurisdictions now use 'performance-based' standards or criteria. These are intended to be more flexible by allowing proposals to demonstrate compliance with the underlying objectives of the control rather than a rigid numerical standard. Queensland's *Sustainable Planning Act 2009* allows developers to choose between a 'code assessable' track, whereby preset controls must be met, and a potentially more flexible 'impact assessable' option, whereby compliance with more interpretive criteria must be demonstrated. As already noted, in the UK, policy criteria are used to assess particular proposals in a highly discretionary planning system, while in the US more prescriptive zones and standards apply. Overall, in Australia, there is a trend towards greater standardisation and codification of routine development types, and greater flexibility for more significant proposals – although this dichotomy can be problematic. These issues are discussed at greater length in following chapters, with reference to the Australian state and territorial planning systems.

Formal public consultation about the content of draft plans

Once a draft plan has been prepared, most jurisdictions have a formal requirement for the plan to be publicly exhibited for a specified period of time. This is often called 'advertising' or 'public notification', as notices about the plan's exhibition are usually placed in newspapers with wide circulation. During the exhibition period there are usually opportunities for members of the public to make submissions about the plan's content, and an expectation that these submissions will be formally considered by the authority responsible for making the plan. If plans change substantially following public consultation, there are often legal requirements for the plan to be exhibited again. Table 2.1 outlines additional forms of public participation to supplement the formal exhibition of draft plans.

Development assessment

Following the finalisation of the land use plan, it may be many years before specific proposals for development are submitted to the planning authority in relation to particular sites. Upon receipt of the proposal, or development 'application', the authority will assess it against the criteria or rules contained in the land use plan and any other relevant legislation or policy. Depending on the nature of the proposal, there will often be a public exhibition of the application, again with the opportunity for members of the public to make comments in relation to it. The assessment process often entails extensive negotiation between the planning authority and the developer, sometimes extending to neighbouring landholders, public agencies, or other community stakeholders.

More complex proposals undergo a formal environmental impact assessment process, discussed in the following section.

Decision

Once the development or environmental assessment process is completed, the authority will usually issue a decision to approve, or refuse the application, or negotiate a changed outcome. If approved, this is generally subject to conditions set by the planning authority. In cases of dispute between the planning authority, the person making the planning application, and sometimes a third party, there are often alternative courses of action available to seek a resolution through mediation or through proceedings in a court of law. Access to legal review of planning decisions by the applicant as well as by affected individuals or concerned members of the public is an important safeguard of the system, although the emphasis should be on good consultation arrangements up front when the planning instrument itself is being prepared (Low et al. 2005).

Monitoring

Most academic descriptions of the planning process advocate the need to monitor the implementation of planning goals, against specified indicators of progress. Ultimately, there should be a system to evaluate the extent to which the planning framework has delivered expected outcomes and to review and amend it in relation to changed circumstances, new information, or because aspects of the plan had unanticipated consequences.

In practice it has proved difficult to monitor the implementation of a statutory land use plan where the achievement of broad goals depends on the voluntary actions of private developers to initiate a development process. However it should not be impossible to monitor the extent to which environmental or social objectives are achieved in relation to specific developments or within particular areas covered by a plan. There is a trend towards the development of broader, non-statutory policy and action planning frameworks setting out the general objectives for a community and identifying benchmarks or indicators to enable progress to be measured against these objectives. Local Agenda 21 plans and the State of the Environment reporting framework (discussed in chapter 9) provide an example of this strategic planning and monitoring approach. When a statutory land use plan is prepared within this broader framework, the process for monitoring the implementation of land use planning objectives is more straightforward, but explicit provisions to do this are still required.

Some state jurisdictions in Australia have requirements that local planning instruments be reviewed within a specified time frame (usually between three and five years). Regular reviews of local planning instruments provide a process for ensuring that planning provisions remain in line with local development needs while discouraging the type of incremental revision on a site by site basis that can undermine the whole rationale of a comprehensive land use planning instrument. Increasingly Australian jurisdictions maintain data relating to the development assessment process. For instance, in NSW there are now requirements for local councils to report on the types of development applications they process, the extent of public notifications and referrals to other agencies, the financial value of development applications, decisions reached, and legal action (DOP 2006b). Many local councils themselves maintain such data even in the absence of state government requirements. This provides useful information for monitoring types of new development within specific areas, relative to local trends and forecast need – for example, types of housing or commercial approvals relative to forecast demographic or business trends and anticipated needs.

Environmental impact assessment (EIA)

The term 'environmental assessment' or 'environmental impact assessment' (EIA) is used to describe the process of assessing developments likely to present significant environmental or social impact. EIA arose during the late 1970s in the context of significant public concern about the impact of pollution on public health and the natural environment (Thomas & Elliott 2005). It provides a basis for identifying risks to the environment that might arise from particular actions, and ensuring this information is available to decision-makers. EIA is intended to protect the environment from damage by ensuring that decision-makers take relevant information into account, facilitating coordinated decision processes between agencies. Despite community expectations, EIA processes rarely result in outright project refusals, but rather influence and modify project design, siting, and environmental management (Weaver et al. 2008). Ideally the process will actively improve a project design so that, where possible it will result in positive environmental impacts. A parallel form of impact assessment focuses specifically on social impacts (known as 'social impact assessment' or SIA). Many of the processes applying to EIA are also followed for social impact assessments, and it is common for a specific SIA to form part of a wider environmental assessment process.

Procedures for public exhibition and consultation through the environmental assessment process are intended to support public scrutiny and contestability of the scientific information used to assess proposals (O'Faircheallaigh 2010). Consultation during the EIA process should also reveal how a proposal might be modified to reduce negative impacts during its construction or long-term life.

Although the specific procedural requirements differ from jurisdiction to jurisdiction, environmental impact assessment processes follow a relatively standard methodology. Firstly, a scoping phase identifies the full range of environmental features or processes likely to be affected by proposal ('before state'), and ongoing trends – that is, what would happen if the project (and a range of alternative scenarios) did not go ahead. Secondly, the assessment process seeks to predict the magnitude of impact on these features, drawing on a variety of scientific and other forms of data. Both spatial impacts – the local and 'downstream' effects of the proposal – and impacts over time – must be considered, as well as their probability. Thirdly, the relative importance of these impacts and the potential of mitigation approaches to reduce them are considered. Finally, the overall impact of the proposal is assessed, vis-a-vis other potential options (including a 'do nothing scenario') to identify a preferred option (see Thomas & Elliott 2005). The document supporting this assessment process is called an Environmental Impact Statement (EIS).

It is controversial that the EIS is usually prepared by the proponents of the activity, rather than an independent agency. For these reasons, scrutiny of the EIS through open public consultation processes, and contestability via the rights of those not directly party to the decision to challenge an approval in court, are particularly important safeguards. An alternative model, designed to ensure the independence of the EIS, would be for proponents to fund, but not to directly commission, the EIA process.

Addressing concerns that the EIA process focuses too narrowly on specific proposals in isolation, rather than the wider strategic context, or the cumulative impacts of many similar projects, there are two more strategic variations of EIA (Gunn & Noble 2009). 'Strategic environmental assessment' (SEA) provides for an upfront assessment of a specific plan or series of proposals, ahead of preparing a statutory planning instrument. The subsequent statutory plan is then able to include specific provisions to manage identified developments with significant environmental impacts, avoiding detailed project-based assessment later. The second variation, 'Cumulative environmental impact assessment' provides a methodology for considering the cumulative impacts of similar proposals or a single proposal over time, and for considering regional impacts.

Planning at different scales

As noted, spatial planning can occur at different geographical or administrative scales. Some countries have a national level at which broad development goals, settlement, conservation and infrastructure programs (particularly transportation infrastructure) are articulated. In nations where there is a national framework for land use planning, such as the UK, it is common for national planning goals and principles to be established. Other nations, like Australia and the US have limited federal government involvement in urban spatial policy, although there are certainly programs to fund spending on the environment and national infrastructure that can have significant implications for spatial strategy.

State/territorial planning

In nations where state or territorial jurisdictions exist, spatial planning functions at this broad geographical level are usually limited to the articulation of legislation and policies that are then interpreted in relation to smaller units through the making of land use plans or when developments are assessed.

Regional and metropolitan planning

Regional planning provides an important basis for addressing interests that extend across the boundaries of a single local government unit. In densely populated areas regional planning is often synonymous with metropolitan planning. Regional plans may provide a comprehensive spatial strategy for managing urban and regional change or focus on specific matters such as water quality or biodiversity, social issues, like housing needs, or matters relating to economic development and infrastructure. Regional plans may have a statutory basis or have the status of guiding strategy or policy.

Local planning

Local planning is the level at which most detailed land use planning activity takes place. Local government units have many different names across the world ('local authorities', 'shires', 'counties', 'cities', 'municipalities'), but in Australia are usually referred to as local government areas, or by reference to their elected representative 'councils'.

Neighbourhood/precinct planning

Within the local planning framework there may be provisions for, or requirements for, a more detailed planning approach focusing on particular neighbourhoods or precincts. This type of planning may recognise a specific need, such as the need to protect heritage, or to provide for revitalisation. Often the release of new land for urban development (greenfield land), or the remediation and re-use of land that was formerly used for other urban purposes (brownfield land) is accompanied by a 'master planning' process, which is another way to describe the identification of detailed planning objectives and controls for development within a specific area. 'Masterplanned' communities are usually large, predominantly residential or mixed residential, retail, and employment estates, typically with the defining characteristic of being controlled by a 'master-developer' (Minnery & Bajracharya 1999, p34).

Site planning

When a new development proposal is conceived, a process of site planning will be undertaken. This may be as simple as the preparation of plans for a new home, or extensions to an existing building, or as complex as the preparation of a detailed plan for the subdivision of a large residential area and subsequent development of hundreds or thousands of new homes. The site plan will be formally lodged when the application for development approval is made, and the planning authority will consider this plan against the requirements set out in all of the relevant other instruments applying to the site, beginning with the local planning scheme.

Principles for strategic environmental planning

The Development Assessment Forum (DAF) is a coalition of Australian government and industry representatives which has come together to 'lead, reform, and harmonise' development systems and processes by undertaking research and best practice initiatives. In 2001, the DAF completed a project to establish 'best practice' in development assessment and planning. The project emphasised the close connections between effective strategic planning and development control, and articulated the following principles for 'strategic environmental planning' in Australia.

The DAF advises that "strategic environmental planning" should focus on a defined local or regional spatial area, rather than broader forms of strategic policy that have no specific geographic application and so are more difficult to interpret in relation to a specific plan or development. A 'holistic, long-term vision' is needed, rather than an incremental approach to reactive plan amendment in response to individual development proposals. Strategic environmental planning must 'integrate economic, environmental, social, cultural and equity factors' and be based on sound 'social and environmental research and analysis'. Strategic planning processes should 'respect' the capacity of the environment, 'involve the community and recognise its diversity'. The 'principle of subsidiarity' should be applied, whereby higher levels of government should not undertake functions that can reasonably be performed by lower levels of government. Finally, 'suitable benchmarks and performance indicators for monitoring and evaluation' should be identified (DAF 2001). These principles are consistent with the broader set of expectations for urban planning and governance proposed in chapter 1 and provide a more applied basis for evaluating the performance of particular planning systems in practice.

Summary and conclusions

Knowing the basic elements or components in a planning system provides a basis for understanding the way in which specific planning systems work within particular juris-dictions. As discussed in this chapter, planning systems at national, state and local levels have evolved in many ways that often seem very different and difficult to understand and compare. But all planning systems emanate from a source of legislative power, and all seek to combine constraints to prevent negative impacts of development, with incentives to encourage positive outcomes consistent with the objectives of a land use plan. The trigger for the regulatory planning process is the need for permission to undertake a development. In comparison to other forms of public policy-making, urban land use planning systems enshrine formal opportunities for public participation, although such rights vary between jurisdictions. Lastly, to a greater or lesser degree, planning systems can organise funds to coordinate and provide the public infrastructure on which private development depends, as well as the other financial arrangements for the operation of the planning system itself.

This chapter also outlined the need for effective strategic planning to inform development assessment or control, and the basic steps or approaches involved in these two distinct components of planning. It concluded with the specific principles for good practice in strategic environmental planning identified by a national coalition of policy-makers and development industry representatives in Australia (The Development Assessment Forum 2001). The following chapter turns to the more detailed considerations associated with selecting which tools or planning mechanisms to use in articulating the standards for development control.

Chapter 3

The development control tool kit

Sometimes, the broader, strategic activity of spatial land use planning is confused with the more specific subset of activities described here as 'development control'. Development control is, however, a very important means by which the spatial planning system can achieve strategic directions for urban growth and environmental enhancement. Development control includes establishing specific parameters, rules, or decision-making criteria to guide the location, type, configuration and design of development within a particular area, and assessing actual proposals against this control framework.

There are a number of key tools or mechanisms for strategic development control and for land use regulation that are used to greater or lesser degree across local planning jurisdictions in many parts of the world. This chapter provides an overview of these approaches to development control and highlights the main policy considerations in deciding upon which particular controls to apply when preparing a statutory land use plan. There is a necessary bias towards development control approaches used across the Australian states and territories.

What is development?

In order to impose legal controls or restrictions on the way that land and buildings are developed or used, it is necessary to first define which activities constitute development. Each planning jurisdiction will establish its own definition of 'development'. Usually, definitions of development are broad, because they need to include all activities that the planning system seeks to regulate through the development control process, such as:

- activities on land (it is often necessary to regulate changes in land uses even when these do not involve the erection of any buildings or works, such as the introduction of grazing animals, the establishment of a weekend community market, or a change in the operational hours of commercial premises)
- subdivision of a parcel of land
- the erection of buildings or the carrying out of other works on land (for instance, an excavation)
- the demolition of buildings or works
- the establishment of advertisements and signboards
- the establishment of temporary structures (for example, the erection of a circus tent or a fairground).

Depending on the operational scope of planning legislation within particular jurisdictions, other activities, such as conservation works, or even the provision of affordable housing, may fall within the definition of development.

Development controls

Many of the mechanisms used to control development through land use planning instruments have been introduced in the previous chapters. It is useful to recapitulate here in relation to the full spectrum of development control approaches before turning to decisions regarding their use within a particular plan.

Land use categorisation (zoning)

As discussed in chapters 1 and 2, a system of land use categorisation (often called zoning) assigns permissible uses to parcels of land depending on the characteristics and the capacity of the land. The approach is often intended to separate uses that are thought to be incompatible. For instance, a 'residential zone' would permit residential dwellings to be built, while an 'agricultural zone' would permit agricultural development but prohibit most residential dwellings unless associated with rural activities. In some nations, such as Germany, mixed uses are a feature of zoning categories (Hirt 2007). In other nations, there is a trend towards encouraging as many mixed compatible uses as possible to reduce distances between homes, work and services, however, this can be difficult to achieve retrospectively in established areas.

Development controls/standards

Specific development controls or standards can regulate the configuration, appearance, density (concentration of development relative to the overall site), heights, building materials, landscaping requirements, provisions for parking and so on. In Australia, standards governing the density of particular types of development (such as housing) are usually enforced through a numerical requirement regarding the amount of site coverage to total building area ('floor space ratio') or by specifying minimum lot sizes for residential subdivision, or for the erection of housing. Building heights, the number of storeys or floors in a building, minimum building front, rear and side setbacks and other such criteria can also control the density of development. Other development controls regarding design issues such as height, building materials or landscaping are intended to achieve objectives relating to urban design, heritage conservation, privacy or environmental conservation. Basic construction standards for health and safety are contained in building codes, but these differ from development controls in planning instruments as they are usually associated with particular types of building rather than tied to a specific place.

Coordination of activities and services

The strategic planning process of allocating land is underpinned by the objective of coordinating the amount and location of different types of development (such as housing, industry, services, retail). In general a guiding principle is to ensure reasonable 'self containment in local labour markets, shopping and services' (Bramley et al. 1995, p40). This coordination can be promoted through the process of land use categorisation, although ultimately this cannot guarantee that the envisaged mix of activities and services will result within a particular time frame. In some jurisdictions a 'master planning' or comprehensive approach is used to designate actual activities (as opposed to general classes of activities) on specific sites. It is possible to promote greater coordination of activities and services by including triggers within the land use planning instrument to manage the release of new areas for development in a way that maximises the efficient provision of infrastructure (for instance, by requiring the endorsement of infrastructure providers before new subdivisions or housing developments can be approved). As discussed in following chapters, there is a trend towards such coordination at metropolitan levels in Australia whereby metropolitan strategic plans are accompanied by infrastructure or transport strategies.

Figure 3.1: Rural land

Maintaining a clear separation between urban and rural land uses protects agricultural, scenic and landscape qualities. Once agricultural land is zoned to allow more intense forms of development, its value is likely to increase. Even without an immediate change of land use, the increase in potential land value makes it more difficult for the land to remain in the agricultural sector in the long term. Source: the Author 2005

Urban boundaries

An important principle of urban planning has been to maintain a distinction between settled and rural or natural areas. This separation is needed to ensure the efficient and affordable provision of infrastructure and services. It is more expensive to establish road networks, water and electricity utilities, let alone other public facilities like parks, schools, health centres and so on if development is dispersed. Further, without a critical mass to ensure patronage, public transport services cannot be effectively provided. There are other economic and social reasons for concentrating settlements, including the protection of agricultural activities. Rural lands of a certain size are needed to maintain viable rural industries, so if this land were to be sold for more concentrated development activities (a 'higher' economic use), it would appear uneconomic for individual farmers to continue their rural activities and they would be unable to afford the costs of land for expansion. Local shops and businesses need a certain catchment in order to operate, so scattered, low density housing developments can rarely support basic services and conveniences, meaning residents are fully dependent on the private car to get to shops, schools, places of work and recreation.

The allocation of land uses through mechanisms such as zoning result in a separation between urban and rural land uses (provided that these functions are themselves separated uses). But many local or urban areas wish to establish more formal urban boundaries to contain the expansion of settlement. Such boundaries may simply arise from the land use category (with agricultural land forming a default periphery) or they may represent a more formal barrier to expansion, such as the 'green belt' system used in the UK and parts of Australia, and the designated 'urban growth boundary' approach applied in parts of the US.

As well as the boundaries created by land use categorisation and zoning, it is important to acknowledge the administrative boundaries established by local government area jurisdictions. In Australia, the population and size of local government areas can vary greatly, at the national level and between the states and territories. For instance, as discussed further in chapters 4 and 5, capital city metropolitan regions may be comprised of a core local government area – such as the City of Brisbane, or multiple units – such as the Sydney Greater Metropolitan Region which comprises more than 40 local councils. At the interface between urban and rural areas, the issue of local government boundaries may arise, particularly if the criteria and policies for growth management and development differ. Further, in some instances tensions can arise between the differing functions and amenities contained in adjacent urban and semi-rural localities, with rural residents able to utilise locally provided urban infrastructure and services without contributing towards them through rates or development contributions.

Provision of local and regional infrastructure

An important component of the development control toolkit is the capacity to require contributions towards the shared infrastructure on which urban development depends. These contributions may be required on a compulsory or negotiated basis depending on the legislative provisions within each planning jurisdiction. These provisions also determine the range of facilities that such contributions may fund – ranging from car parking to open space to community centres or subsidised housing for low-income people. The contributions may be levied through a defined formula or plan, or negotiated through the development process. Many jurisdictions specify the way in which certain contributions must be provided – either as a monetary contribution or as land, buildings, or another 'work in kind'. Obviously the imposition of such requirements is contentious and developer contributions are often viewed as a 'tax' on development.

Accordingly, there is a substantial literature on the rationale for development contributions (Been 2005; Crook et al. 2002; Evans-Cowley & Lawhon 2003; Fensham & Gleeson 2003). A clear justification for the collection of such contributions has become very important. It is obviously important in policy terms, because if there is too much opposition from developers or the community, elected governments will not support the mechanism. A clear rationale for the establishment of specific contribution requirements is also necessary when levying individual fees on particular developments because most jurisdictions enable developers to contest these requirements in a court of law.

Impact fees

There are two basic approaches to the justification of development contributions. The first focuses on the impact that the new development has on the need for public services, and seeks to recover a contribution towards offsetting this impact. Contributions levied on the basis of this approach, are often called 'impact' or 'linkage' fees in the US. When compelling developers to contribute towards the costs of essential infrastructure or services on the basis of the impact their development will make on the need for such services, the amount of the fee must be clearly linked to the impact of the development (Gurran et al. 2009). This link or connection is described as a 'nexus'. Typically planning legislation requires that there must also be a nexus between the development and the use to which the impact fee is put.

Windfall gains and taxing planning 'betterment'

The second approach seeks to capture some of the financial benefits that accrue to private individuals following a beneficial planning decision. By substantially changing the way in which a parcel of land may be used (for instance, by rezoning it to enable more concentrated or profitable forms of development) its potential value in the land market is substantially increased. This type of positive change to land value associated with a planning decision is often described as 'betterment' (the converse, when a parcel of land is assigned a more restrictive use due to heritage or other reasons is often described as 'down-zoning', and compensation or acquisition may be required).

The benefits accruing to individuals through planning betterment are frequently referred to as a 'windfall gain' because unlike cases in which land value increases due to direct 'improvements' to the land (erecting a building, for example), the increase in land value occurs at the stroke of a bureaucratic pen. Many argue that a proportion of this 'windfall gain' should be recaptured for public benefit, but in practice there are many difficulties associated with doing this in a formal way.

A short-lived experiment in NSW in the early 1970s highlights the political difficulties associated with introducing a betterment tax. The *Land and Development Contributions*

Act 1970, introduced by a conservative government, required landowners to pay a levy of 30 per cent of the 'increased price or value of re-zoned land … on the sale of the land or on the issue of a development consent' (Roseth 2003, p96). Funds were collected by the State Planning Authority and held in a dedicated Land Development Contribution Fund to pay for physical infrastructure. However, not surprisingly, the levy was unpopular with landowners and the Labor opposition party promised to remove it – a promise that was matched by the re-elected Liberal government who repealed the levy in February 1973. The substantial $16 million that had been collected was distributed to outer Sydney councils (Roseth 2003).

There have also been several attempts to introduce a betterment tax in the UK. In practice, contributions for development in the UK have been justified on the basis of betterment or planning gain. In the UK there is a clearer sequential connection between favourable planning decisions and betterment because all proposals are considered 'on their merits' and development approvals are negotiated in relation to specific proposals and sites. However, it has proved difficult to measure the theoretical increase in land value associated with a particular planning decision, let alone to develop an accurate tool to tax this (Oxley 2006). Even with both of these approaches in place, the contribution requirement is triggered by a specific development proposal and the timing of this proposal may not always coincide with a beneficial change in planning controls. The question has been resolved through the introduction of a flat levy to apply to all development (Department of Communities and Local Government 2011b).

In the Australian Capital Territory (ACT) a type of betterment tax has been applied in the form of a change of use charge when development is approved. However, this is peculiar to the ACT system of leasehold land tenure, discussed further in chapter 6.

In sum, the practical difficulties associated with implementing a formal betterment tax mechanism in most jurisdictions, let alone opposition from landholders and developers, have meant that the approach has not been used widely. But the concept of 'windfall gain' can be used as an additional policy argument to justify developer contributions, without needing a formal measure for calculating or hypothecating this gain in precise terms. There are limits to this approach, however. In general, it is difficult to rely on the concept of 'windfall gain' and high development contributions to finance major regional infrastructure items. Irrespective of the hypothecated windfall, development contributions alone are unlikely to provide a sufficiently reliable source of upfront funding to ensure that important facilities precede, rather than follow, significant urban growth. It is also important to recognise that while development contributions may provide an efficient source of funding towards the infrastructure and services required by local residents and businesses, the mechanism is largely inadequate in contexts with significant short term or seasonal fluctuations in population, such as resort or mining towns. In these situations, other resources are often needed to fund services to meet 'peakload' requirements.

Conditions of development approval

Developments are usually approved under certain conditions established by the planning authority. These conditions might relate to the retention of trees on the site or landscaping requirements for gardens to be planted with endogenous (locally occurring) species.

They might relate to special treatment of windows or balconies to ensure the privacy of neighbours, or to the hours of operation of a commercial establishment. Development conditions are usually a combination of standard requirements (for instance, that all buildings comply with certain construction or safety codes), as well as matters that are determined in relation to the particular proposal. Conditions can provide an opportunity to implement arrangements or agreements between the developer and the planning authority that have been negotiated through the assessment process, for instance, an agreement regarding the provision of an infrastructure contribution.

The tension between certainty and flexibility

In establishing the rules to govern future development within a particular area, there is a considerable tension between providing certainty about what may and may not occur on a parcel of land, and enabling sufficient flexibility to accommodate unanticipated proposals that may still represent good design or a positive contribution to the community. Another way of considering this issue relates to the difficult task of protecting the public from the negative externalities associated with private development, while still providing individual landholders with sufficient freedom to achieve the style of building they aspire to on their own property.

Both developers and members of the community want the certainty of being able to anticipate the likely future development within a particular locality, or at least what is likely and not likely to be permitted by the planning authority on a specific site. This is important for members of the community who want assurances that a valued forest or park is not threatened by unsympathetic development on its periphery, or that a significant heritage precinct will be protected from development that is out of character to the prevailing building forms. It is also important for developers to have a degree of certainty about what types of development will and will not be permitted on a particular site because major investment decisions – for instance, to acquire the site itself – are made on assumptions about the permissibility of various potential land activities.

However, it is rarely possible to anticipate all of the potential future activities and proposals that may relate to a particular site or locality. Many different sorts of proposals may represent good development outcomes, depending on the specific circumstances of the project. It is particularly difficult to predict the range of conditions that will factor into decisions about specific development proposals many years before such proposals may be actually lodged with a planning authority. At the same time, a reasonable medium- to long-term planning horizon is needed to ensure that land use planning instruments are not undermined by constant incremental change.

One approach maximises certainty for potential developers (but not for community residents) by applying minimal restrictions to the range of activities that are likely to be permitted on a parcel of land. This approach represents the 'lowest common denominator' control on the basis that a more restrictive set of regulations would unacceptably impede development options. If the planning jurisdiction allows, some of the problematic issues that may arise from this rather laissez-faire approach could be addressed when development conditions are specified for particular proposals.

The other side of this coin maximises certainty for community residents by establishing very strong parameters around the type of development that can and cannot occur within a particular area. This highly prescriptive approach may be best in established urban areas or in areas of significant natural or cultural heritage. However, if the objective is to encourage new development, particularly over a medium- to long-term period of time, highly prescriptive controls are problematic. Even within areas designated by the community for relatively homogenous land uses, such as low-density residential development, developers often object to a control framework that is extremely rigid. The community can also be at a disadvantage in this scenario because the planning instrument might act to deter development that would otherwise be welcomed. Inflexible planning frameworks can also discourage or prevent creative forms of design or unforeseen projects that might be beneficial to the area.

Prescriptive or 'performance based' development controls

In establishing development control frameworks there are different ways to approach this dilemma. In the US the approach is largely to codify development rights and requirements as much as possible with little room for merit-based evaluation by local land use planners (but often much room for legal disputes about the interpretation of statutory entitlements and restrictions). In the UK all developments must be assessed 'on their merits' with statutory land use plans providing a strong guide to the types of development and land uses that are likely to be supported. Across the Australian states and territories there has been a progressive move towards a hybrid of both approaches, although each jurisdiction retains their own distinctive approach (summarised in chapter 5).

This hybrid approach attempts to codify simpler forms of development (like garages or single storey houses) to enable their assessment against predetermined standards. If the site is not situated within an environmentally sensitive area or subject to some other specific constraint, and the proposal meets all of the specified standards, it must be permitted. Other forms of development are subject to more qualitative merit-based deliberation, although if a proposal complies with all of the controls specified in the relevant statutory land use plan it would be unlikely for the proposal to be refused. For major developments there is a tendency in some Australian jurisdictions to liberate proposals from planning controls altogether, subject only to an environmental assessment process informed by a site-specific study of impact rather than a framework of statutory requirements and prohibitions. We discuss this trend further in the following section of the book.

An additional approach to managing the tensions between certainty and flexibility focuses on the way in which controls themselves are expressed. It is argued that controls are established to fulfil a particular outcome or set of objectives. If these objectives are articulated then any given proposal able to demonstrate that these objectives are met should be approved. Thus the emphasis moves to a 'performance-based' assessment of proposals, rather than a more technical assessment of compliance with set standards and requirements. Performance-based plans often permit a dual approach, with developers able to follow predetermined criteria and be sure of securing certain approval, or propose an alternative solution that demonstrably meets the established performance criteria. The latter course permits flexibility but the onus is on the proponent to demonstrate to the planning authority that the performance criteria have been met.

Are there likely to be any unintended consequences of the development control?

While the objectives associated with land use planning promote social welfare, the land use planning system itself is not inherently benign, as noted in chapter 2: 'The formal activity of urban planning can reinforce and perpetuate injustice, environmental degradation and vested interests as easily as it can reform, mitigate or even improve environmental quality' (McManus 2005, p25). Thus in selecting particular approaches to development control it is important to consider the range of outcomes likely to arise and the potential for unintended consequences to result from the control. For instance, will the control deter development that would otherwise be desirable? Could the control lead to outcomes that may conflict with other community objectives for the plan? Does the control impose unnecessary or unfair burdens that have wider social or economic impacts? In the following sections we consider some of the unintended or negative consequences that may arise from particular development controls. In some cases, controls will still be justified on the basis of other important planning reasons and so it becomes necessary to consider strategies that offset or mitigate these unavoidable impacts.

Do we need planning at all?

Some claim that the planning system per se unnecessarily restricts development and has caused the problem of rising house prices in Australia (Moran 2006). These arguments are based on the reasoning that land use planning controls restrict the amount of land that is available for development and the way it can be used, therefore creating an artificial shortage of developable land and increasing prices:

> Where planning restricts land access it creates scarcity, thereby artificially bringing higher cost homes … If Australia were applying the liberal systems to development that prevail in Texas for example, a house/land package price would at least halve. Australia's ration-induced high prices for new developments on the periphery lift prices throughout the city (Moran 2006, pp3–4).

These claims represent a fundamental misunderstanding about the objectives of the land use planning system. Rather than seeking to create an undersupply of land relative to the need (or demand) for such land, a normative planning principle is to establish the optimal balance between the release of land in the right location and at the right time, in order to create the most favourable conditions for development to occur, while still meeting community objectives, including the protection of areas where development should always be prevented.

Within the constraints established by environmental characteristics and land capacity, any shortage of land zoned for residential development relative to the need for such land, reflects a systemic deficiency in the operation of the planning system. Such shortages might relate to a failure on behalf of the planning authority to undertake long-term strategic planning or to adequately predict the scale of likely future demand. Monitoring the take-up of existing developable land and identifying potential future opportunities is an important strategic planning task that should continue throughout the implementation of the plan itself to avoid a sudden land scarcity that could inflate prices. Other systemic deficiencies that might be associated with an artificial shortage of developable land include delays in the land use plan approval process, or in assessing applications for land subdivisions.

As increased land prices are associated with a scarcity of land in the market relative to demand, supply blockages may arise because of monopolistic or semi-monopolistic behaviour of landholders. In fact, too much land zoned for urban development can depress land values such that landholders will choose not to sell until conditions become more favourable for them (Bramley & Leishman 2005). To understand the relationship between land use planning decisions and the value of land in the private market it is necessary to turn briefly to some basic principles of land economics.

Planning and land values

As any real estate agent will attest, the value of a parcel of land is closely associated with its location. Demonstrating the significance of location, a hypothetical model of land value posits falling values or 'rents' as distance increases from the city centre (where commercial activities are concentrated), until the value is below that of land used in agricultural production (Alonso 1964; Golland & Gillen 2004). The political economist David Ricardo (1817) explained land values in relation to the unique attributes of land (including its location) and its limited supply or scarcity value. Ricardo distinguished between what are described as 'transfer earnings' – or the value associated with land at its current use (and needed to be paid to secure its transfer from one owner to another); and 'economic rent', which is the amount above this transfer value that is associated with the potential to apply this land to another land use (Oxley & Dunmore 2004). Using this terminology, the value of land under an existing planning control or zone may be understood as its 'transfer value', while the 'economic rent' is the difference between this point and the new value that might be associated with a favourable change in planning controls that enable a 'higher' or more commercially profitable land use.

So, in theory, land values are established by the activity or form of development associated with the highest potential earnings, minus the costs associated with realising these benefits. This means that although land may be more freely available at the urban periphery within this idealised scenario without planning constraints, this very availability reduces its value until it ultimately falls below its potential value for other uses such as agriculture. This is why land on the urban periphery is not necessarily taken up by developers even when a scarcity of developable land exists within more accessible areas:

> So even in this theoretically ideal world without planning, land that is useful for housing and other urban purposes, by virtue of its location, is semi permanently scarce and commands a corresponding rent (Bramley et al. 1995, quoted in Gurran et al. 2007, p18).

Even if the potential market price of land that could be developed is higher than that of its current use, landholder expectations regarding future land prices may lead them to hold out until pent-up demand increases prices even further. This often occurs if land is held in monopoly by a single owner, or if a group of landowners act in cooperation to release land slowly.

Further, as discussed above, an oversupply of vacant land zoned for urban purposes leads to piecemeal growth across a region. As well as diminishing scenic, biodiversity or agricultural values of such land, these developments are expensive and difficult to service and are situated far from transport, employment and infrastructure. Residents are at increased risk of social isolation and related disadvantages. In other words, without planning, the negative externalities arising from unregulated development and uncoordinated or inadequate provision of infrastructure are likely to create disincentives to investment in new development:

> If there was no planning system the pervasive externalities associated with urban development would have a severe effect on the market and on supply. In general, because of the lack of certainty about future developments on adjacent land in this unplanned situation, individual investors could be less sure about the future value of their own particular housing investments. This could be a general deterrent [to development] … Much of the land in theory available for development would not be developable in practice because of the lack of services … the supply of infrastructure itself would be a risky investment because of uncertainty about the extent and nature of development to be served in particular areas, and so urban services would be under provided (Bramley et al. 1995, quoted in Gurran et al. 2007, p19).

Thus we return to the difficult task of ensuring that the right amount of land in the right locations is allocated for urban development. At the same time there is a need to avoid creating an oversupply that might degrade landscape values and entrench social disadvantages associated with isolation, make infrastructure provision uneconomic, or encourage the monopolistic behaviour of landholders.

Urban containment policies and a shortage of housing supply

Restricting urban expansion to protect land and biodiversity and to reduce the costs associated with dispersed development and the inefficient provision of infrastructure is an important urban planning goal, as discussed above. However, it is often argued that when restrictions on the release of new land for residential development greatly limit opportunities for new housing during a period of high demand, housing prices will increase (Monk & Whitehead 1999). A number of studies in the US have sought to examine the affordability impact of planning approaches (frequently described as 'growth management' techniques) designed to restrict the expansion of urban land (Anthony 2003; Nelson et al. 2002, Quigley & Rosenthal 2005).

These studies have been unable to identify a clear link between the price impacts of growth management or urban containment strategies on the affordability of housing (Gurran et al. 2009). While prices often increase following the introduction of growth management policies, these increases may reflect other reasons such as rapid population growth, or increases in house size and quality (Anthony 2003). It is important to note that these pressures often precipitate the introduction of a growth management strategy, making the determination of cause and effect even more complex. Further, the increased certainty and protection of environmental quality resulting from the establishment of urban containment measures might explain any subsequent increases in land values (Anthony 2006). Finally, given that new housing construction accounts for a very small proportion of total housing stock (for instance one per cent of total supply in the UK represents annual additions to the housing stock), any deflationary price impacts associated with the release of new residential land relate to market perception rather than a significant shift in supply (Barker 2004, p4).

Figure 3.2 Abandoned residential land (small town America)

If there is too much land available for residential development, relative to demand, values will drop and the land becomes unnecessarily degraded. Source: the Author 2003

It may be possible to actively counteract negative impacts of planning strategies such as growth management or urban containment controls on housing affordability by ensuring that housing goals are implicit in their design (Nelson et al. 2002; Russell 2003). For instance, housing 'scarcity' effects of growth boundaries could be offset by providing an ample supply of land zoned for higher residential densities, and increasing the supply of dedicated affordable housing (Anthony 2006; Gurran et al. 2008b). These approaches are discussed further in chapter 11.

Restrictive development controls and standards

Development controls impact on the cost of development largely by contributing to the creation and protection of an attractive and well-functioning living environment. None-theless, if controls are extremely restrictive or expensive to comply with, many forms of development may be prevented. In particular, when the cost of complying with planning controls becomes so expensive that it represents a barrier for lower-income groups to enter the housing market, planning controls can be regarded as 'exclusionary' (Liberty 2003; Pendall 2000).

Figure 3.3: Affordable housing in Portland, Oregon

When introducing an urban growth boundary for the city of Portland, Oregon, the city was concerned to offset any potential impacts on housing affordability, by increasing densities within inner areas and including provisions for dedicated affordable housing for low-income residents to rent. This had the effect of stimulating urban renewal as abandoned factories and warehouses were converted for residential uses and the inner Central Business District enjoyed a commercial revitalisation. Source: the Author 2003

In the US, the Federal Department of Housing and Urban Development has established a national program to identify, eradicate or offset development controls that deliberately or inadvertently make housing more expensive. Examples of controls that unnecessarily increase housing costs include requirements for excessively large lot sizes in urban areas, tight restrictions on housing types, or design standards that require the use of expensive materials. Even a small increase in required building setbacks within an area may inflate house prices by between six and seven per cent (HUD 2005). Other development controls that make the cost of housing production more expensive include limited provisions for housing diversity, such as medium-density housing, group homes for people in need of residential support, manufactured housing, accessory dwellings (often called 'granny flats' in Australia), requirements for wide streets and excessive parking spaces (APA 1991, 1997, 2001; HUD 2005; Pendall 2000; Gurran et al. 2008b).

Development controls, architecture and design

Planning control is, as discussed above, intended to protect and enhance attributes of our shared environment. This includes protecting against negative impacts on things like views, solar access or the appearance of the street. In general, the preference is for relative consistency in building heights, setbacks and building styles, especially within heritage areas. In these contexts, controls are designed to achieve development that is compatible with the surrounding built environment and character in terms of its bulk, scale and appearance. Some planning jurisdictions focus not on the aesthetics of development, but on its impact – in terms of building size or nature. Those in favour of specific building controls for aesthetic purposes often argue that the rules are not designed to inhibit good or innovative design, but to preserve the public interest and promote uniqueness and place identity (George & Campbell 2000). Others argue that good aesthetic design cannot be achieved through regulation, and that in fact, such regulations often do little more than preserve socio-economic exclusivity. Elizabeth Farrelly, architecture and planning commentator for the *Sydney Morning Herald* writes that:

> We want to believe that we can reduce beauty to rules, in order to make it replicable. But the fact is, we're deceiving ourselves. Partly because, when it comes to rules, the big question is always: who is applying them, and to whom? … Already an east-west style gradient is palpable in Sydney, with a number of developers strategically offering smart-and-white in Sydney, trimmed with real timber and steel but dumbed-down polychrome out west. (Farrelly 2006, p138).

These comments recall our earlier discussion regarding the introduction of building controls in Australian cities, which were also used as a basis for spatial elitism (Frost & Dingle 1995). But the point should still be made that planning controls must neither act as a surrogate for exclusion, nor stifle the potential for innovative design and architectural expression.

Development costs and charges

Ascertaining the costs and charges to development that arise through the planning process is difficult. There are likely to be direct costs such as compulsory requirements for infrastructure provision and fees for processing development applications, as well as indirect costs associated with seeking planning approval, such as the time taken for a proposal to be assessed, or to appeal an unfavourable decision within an increasingly complex regulatory environment (Gurran et al. 2009). Research suggests that expectations of delays or difficulties in securing consent for development proposals within a particular jurisdiction will lead developers to look for opportunities elsewhere, ultimately reducing the amount of development activity in an area (HUD 2005; Monk & Whitehead 1999).

In relation to residential development, the Housing Industry Association of Australia (HIA) has claimed that between 25 and 35 per cent of the purchase price of new houses comprises 'indirect taxes', including infrastructure charges or levies, securing development approval and other state government taxes relating to the development process (HIA 2003).

The impact of mandatory developer contributions for infrastructure on housing affordability is a major concern, both in Australia and in the US. Several studies in the US have sought to determine the extent to which contributions for public infrastructure impact on the cost of housing production and ultimately, the affordability of housing. Based on the available evidence to date, it appears that while compulsory infrastructure contributions increase the cost of producing housing, as do other planning requirements, the extent of this impact on housing affordability depends largely on characteristics of the market (Evans-Crowley & Lawhon 2003; Gurran et al. 2009).

It appears that in situations where there is high demand for housing, developers are able to pass on compulsory costs to home buyers, thus suggesting that home buyers are subjected to higher costs than would be the case without the compulsory contributions. However, there is also a strong likelihood that developers will set the prices that the market will bear, irrespective of costs associated with production (Been 2005). On the other hand, in a flatter housing market, the developer or landseller is more likely to bear the costs of compulsory infrastructure provision. If these compulsory contributions are set at a very high level, this may discourage housing development in all but the most buoyant of market scenarios. Another variation on this scenario is a reduction in new housing development until demand is sufficient to increase prices again. Finally, developers may simply produce more 'up-market' housing with a greater margin for profit as a way of recouping costs associated with compulsory infrastructure contributions (Gurran et al. 2009, p26). Again, this may undermine affordability objectives.

If the likely level of contribution is known prior to the purchase of land or the submission of a development application, in theory the financial burden can be passed back to the landowner. As discussed above, it should be possible to pass on this burden because the value of the land is determined by its potential use minus the constraints or obligations associated with realising this use. The potential for land values to adjust to infrastructure payment requirements underpins the relatively large contribution expectations often associated with new urban release areas, discussed further in chapters 5 and 7. To be effective, this approach should coincide with a significant planning change that results in higher theoretical land values (such as a rezoning from non-urban to urban uses). Thus landholders share some of the increased value to their own land that arises from a bureaucratic decision to allow the land to be used for more intensive development. At the same time, it can also be argued that the infrastructure contribution is needed to ensure this land can be used for urban development, so is a necessary precondition for achieving higher land values. However, a strategy that requires a substantial new and unforeseen infrastructure contribution from private landholders (at the point of sale) or developers (through the process of development application) can be risky. This is again because the owner may choose to hold onto their land until supply shortages or other interventions will increase land prices sufficiently to offset the new requirement.

Finally, as noted previously, if the costs associated with compulsory development contributions are passed onto the homebuyer, this is not necessarily an unfair burden, as they may benefit from enhanced infrastructure and services and the value of their own property will increase accordingly (Been 2005). Furthermore, as also noted, when development contributions fund essential infrastructure that would not otherwise be able to be provided, they facilitate a supply of developable land that might not otherwise be available.

Offsetting negative impacts of development controls

As noted, sometimes the negative impacts of specific development controls on broader planning objectives may be unforeseen. It is therefore important to regularly review the objectives underlying development controls and the extent to which these are being realised, as well as to consider other potential impacts, positive or negative, that may be occurring. In cases where there is a negative outcome arising from a particular development control but the control itself is justified by other important planning goals, it is important to consider ways in which these impacts might be offset. For instance, if the locality is characterised by significant amounts of land that should not be developed because of environmental sensitivity or potential exposure to natural hazards, it is desirable to increase development potential in other areas in order to avoid a scarcity of land supply that could make development overly expensive.

If strict design controls regarding the height, external appearance and so on of buildings within a conservation area are needed to protect the cultural heritage values of the precinct, these controls may act as a disincentive to even necessary developments like ongoing home renovations or maintenance work. They may also discourage the conversion or adaptation of housing stock in relation to changing housing needs (such as the trend to smaller households or the need for seniors' accommodation). Strict heritage controls can also be difficult or expensive for businesses to comply with and so can discourage private enterprise within a community. To counteract these unintended consequences of important development controls, it is possible to offset the financial impact of compliance by offering incentives or development bonuses for activities that will not undermine the objective of the control. For instance, many land use plans contain heritage 'incentives' that enable heritage items (buildings or sites that are listed in a statutory planning instrument as requiring special protection) to be used for other purposes that might not otherwise be permissible within the plan.

Table 3.1 summarises strategies proposed by the US Department of Housing and Urban Development to evaluate the extent to which development controls, planning requirements or processes unnecessarily increase housing production costs. It establishes criteria that can be used to ensure that development controls and planning processes are more likely to encourage more diverse and affordable homes.

As shown in the table with respect to affordable housing, one way to counteract unintended impacts of compulsory infrastructure contributions on development that is actively desired is to waive or reduce the imposition of such fees for projects meeting defined criteria. Such strategies may be used more broadly, not just in relation to housing. For instance, if a local community wished to encourage new tourism development within the area it may choose to waive or reduce required infrastructure contributions within a set timeframe (to encourage take-up of the scheme). A locality could demonstrate its support for community-based ventures (and perhaps contribute to stronger social capital) by offering infrastructure contribution or development application discounts to development proposals by non-profit organisations. Another possibility would be to permit the deferred or staged payment of contributions over time rather than up-front while overall development costs are high.

Table 3.1: Removing excessive development controls or planning requirements that make housing more expensive

Constraint/Regulation	Criteria
Zoning/development controls	Sufficient supply of zoned residential land for five years
	Minimum of 1/3 residential zone for attached dwellings
	Capacity for second unit development
	Growth constraints based on defined environmental or infrastructure limitation
	Growth constraint to expire if environmental/infrastructure constraint resolved
	Growth constraints offset by requirements that industrial/commercial development that is likely to increase affordable housing need/ contribute to meeting that need
	Growth constraints offset by affordable housing provisions
	Permit mixed use development
	Relax development standards for affordability
	Permit manufactured homes, single-room occupancy and group homes.
Administration/consent requirements	More residential developments approved than refused
	At least 2/3 of proposed number of housing units approved in majority of applications
	Fewer than six months for development approval (without rezoning)
	Clear permit processing requirements
	Minimum off-street parking requirements and road reservations
	Cost-effective local infrastructure design
	Waive/reduce compulsory infrastructure fees for dedicated affordable housing.

Source: (Gurran et al. 2007; Gurran et al. 2009 p48)

These examples of ways to identify and counteract unintended or negative impacts of development controls are by no means exhaustive. The intention is to illustrate the need for planners to consider the potential for these inadvertent outcomes when drafting development controls and reviewing these controls as plans are implemented, and to weigh up the need for the particular control against other goals underpinning the overall plan. Where the need for the control is established, it is then important to consider whether any negative outcomes can be avoided or offset by drafting the control in a different way, introducing other measures to mitigate its impact, or waiving it if the circumstances so require.

Summary and conclusions

This chapter has introduced the basic suite of tools, mechanisms or procedures used by land use planners to manage development – land use categorisation, standards and specific controls, coordination of urban activities and identification of urban boundaries, arrangements for infrastructure provision, and conditions of development approval. In deciding which mechanisms to implement, a tension arises between establishing a regime of land use control that maximises certainty regarding what will and will not be permitted in the future, versus a system that can accommodate unforeseen proposals that represent good design and achieve overall planning goals. The potential to allow a performance-based system of development controls was described as well as the emerging dual approach where developers can ensure approval by complying with prescribed requirements, or seek approval by demonstrating how they meet alternative performance criteria.

The final section of the chapter highlighted the range of factors to consider when selecting and using specific development controls, or imposing particular charges such as compulsory developer contributions. In some cases planning controls, such as environmental protections, are necessary but may have a negative impact on the achievement of other planning goals. In these cases the comprehensive planning framework provides a basis for including particular measures or provisions to offset this impact. In selecting from the range of tools canvassed here – and indeed the many other strategies for planning and managing urban change, the policy and legal framework governing each jurisdiction may be a constraint. However, in most cases there are ways to adapt existing mechanisms to suit a specific set of goals. Above all, it is important to use such development control terms mindfully – alert to their potential impact in relation to overall community objectives.

In summary, this first section of the book has shown that the planning system impacts on our shared environment through its functions of allocating land for business, services and residential development, requiring compliance with development controls and standards, by imposing fees and charges associated with the provision of infrastructure and public facilities, and more broadly, by creating or preserving attractive places in which to live. Thus planning interventions are central to efficient urban structure, but they also serve to protect the favourable environment needed to maintain investment in industry and residential development.

Accepting the need for the planning system and the important role it plays in contributing to social equity, economic vitality and environmental protection, it is nevertheless important to address any potentially negative impacts that may arise through the planning process. In the second section of the book we turn to the specific policy frameworks and legal arrangements characterising the land use planning system in Australia.

Box 3.1: Additional readings and resources

There are many potential additional readings and resources relating to the range of matters covered in section one of this book. The following is a limited selection of additional introductory material.

Planning history

Lewis Mumford's epic tome *The city in history* (1961) is a classic text.

Sir Peter Hall's *Cities of tomorrow: an intellectual history of urban planning and design in the twentieth century* (1996) is an accessible and lively account of the modern urban planning project.

For a straightforward account of the progression of planning ideas see Nigel Taylor's *Urban planning theory since 1945* (1998).

Urban planning in a changing world: the twentieth century experience (2000), edited by Robert Freestone, contains a stimulating collection of reflective articles on the past century.

For an overview of metropolitan planning history in Australia see *The Australian metropolis*, edited by Robert Freestone and Stephen Hamnett (2000).

Also by Robert Freestone, *Urban nation: Australia's planning heritage* (2010) is a comprehensive account of the historical legacy of urban planning and design across Australia, from early European settlement to the new millennium.

In relation to Sydney's planning history, *Sydney planning or politics: town planning for Sydney region since 1945* (2003), edited by John Toon and Jonathon Falk, offers a detailed insider's analysis, including original commentary by many of the state's leading practitioners.

Leonie Sandercock's original Cities for sale and subsequent updated Property, politics and urban planning: a history of Australian city planning 1890–1990 provides a critical historical analysis of the 'failure' of city planning in Australia (Sandercock 1990).

Urban planning and governance in Australia

Planning Australia: an overview of urban and regional planning (2007) edited by Susan Thompson, is an essential reference, drawing together a comprehensive set of articles on Australian planning history, concerns and practices.

Brendan Gleeson and Nicholas Low's book *Australian urban planning: new challenges, new agendas* (2000) is still a classic text for scholars of urban policy and governance in Australia.

Clive Forster's analysis of Australian cities: *Australian cities, continuity and change* (2004) now in its third edition, is an important reference for Australian urbanists.

Sustainability and planning

The ecology of place by Timothy Beatley and Kristy Manning (1997) provides one of the first accounts of how land use planning processes and techniques can contribute to the sustainable community.

The green city; sustainable homes, sustainable suburbs (2005) by Nicholas Low, Brendan Gleeson, Ray Green, Darko Radovic (2005), offers an inspiring articulation of sustainability in cities, drawing on practical examples from Australia, Europe and North America.

Planning sustainable cities: global report on human settlements 2009 is a benchmark publication by the United Nations Human Settlements Program. It provides a comprehensive report on global trends and indicators relating to social and environmental aspects of urbanisation (Earthscan, London, 2009).

Healthy spaces and places

For comprehensive information about planning and design for sustainability and healthy living, see the website: www.healthyplaces.org.au , a joint initiative of the Australian Local Government Association, the National Hart Foundation of Australia, the Planning Institute of Australia and the Commonwealth Government.

Planning systems and processes

The Green Book as it is called in the US contains a collection of useful introductory essays on the planning system and critical elements of local policy development: Hoch J, Dalton C and So F (2000) *The practice of local government planning* (2000) (3rd edn).

Again focusing on planning systems in the US, but covering a range of policy issues and planning techniques or mechanisms more broadly, *Planning in the USA*, by Barry Cullingworth and Roger Caves (2009), is a useful resource.

Introducing Planning, Clara Greed (2000) provides another contemporary introduction to the planning system and processes, albeit with a focus on the UK.

The United States Department of Housing and Urban Development (USHUD) maintains a comprehensive collation of research, data, and practice advice on matters relating to urban planning and development regulation (www.hud.gov).

Professional planning organisations also contain useful resources for policymakers and planning scholars. The American Planning Association website contains extensive resources and publications relating to planning research, legislation, and policy development (www.planning.org), as does the UK's Town and Country Planning Association (www.tcpa.org.uk) and the Royal Town and Country Planning Institute, (www.rtpi.org.uk/index.html).

The Planning Institute of Australia (www.planning.org.au) contains links to all of the state planning divisions which generally offer sources of information about legal and policy changes and issues within each Australian planning jurisdiction, as well as links to other government and industry organisations relevant to urban policy and planning in Australia.

Section 2

Systems: urban land use planning in Australia

This section of the book introduces Australia's urban land use planning system, or, more properly, systems. Land use law was not in the minds of the legislators at the time of Australia's Federation, so responsibility for the environment devolved to the Australian states and territories by default. Over the years the Commonwealth government has undertaken different levels of policy intervention in relation to urban and regional planning and in chapter 4 current Commonwealth responsibilities, policies and legislation relevant to urban and environmental planning are reviewed. State planning arrangements, including legislation, policy, and regional approaches are introduced in chapter 5. Chapter 6 compares plan-making, development assessment and dispute resolution arrangements in each of the states and territories. Chapters 7 and 8 examine Australian urban land use planning systems in more detail, focusing on the example of New South Wales which is Australia's most populous state. The NSW planning system – including environmental planning legislation, institutions and processes for planmaking, and public participation, is set out in chapter 7. Chapter 8 outlines processes for development assessment and approval in NSW, including arrangements for requiring contributions for local infrastructure and planning appeals.

Chapter 4

Intergovernmental responsibilities for the environment and land use planning in Australia

Australia became a federation in 1901 when six formerly independent British colonies agreed to combine as a new nation comprising of states: (New South Wales (NSW), Queensland (Qld), South Australia (SA), Tasmania (Tas.), Victoria (Vic.), and Western Australia (WA). It was agreed that the remaining areas would have the status of territory (including the Australian Capital Territory [ACT] and the Northern Territory [NT], which are self governing). This federation provides for a national level parliament and government with lawmaking powers in areas defined by the *Commonwealth Constitution Act 1900* ('the Constitution'). In addition to this two-tier (national and state or territorial) system of government, the different states and territories have enacted their own legislation to establish a devolved tier of local jurisdiction.

This chapter provides an overview of these intergovernmental responsibilities relating to the environment and land use planning in Australia. It outlines the different roles played by the Commonwealth, states, territories and local government in relation to the environment, urban policy and planning. It also discusses key national policies and collaborative intergovernmental processes. While the Commonwealth government does not traditionally have a strong role in relation to the environment or urban planning, there are several key Commonwealth laws that have implications for planning, environmental protection and land management at national, state and local government levels. The final part of the chapter introduces this legislation, particularly the *Commonwealth Environment Protection and Biodiversity Conservation Act 1999*. The information contained in this chapter was current at the time of writing.

Commonwealth involvement in urban and regional affairs

Despite limited Commonwealth involvement in matters relating to the environment or planning, Australia's earliest comprehensive town planning schemes were actually prompted by the Commonwealth government using its powers of tied grants. The first Commonwealth State Housing Agreement (CSHA) in 1945 provided loans from central government to the states for the construction of dwellings to house low-income families. The loans were made contingent upon each state developing legislation to control matters such as town and country planning and slum clearance (Gleeson & Low 2000, p31).

Brendan Gleeson and Nicholas Low note that despite limited direct federal government involvement in urban and regional policy till this time, Australian state and federal governments sought to promote social democratic ideals in city building and in urban development:

> The goals were simple – the expansion of collective welfare through rational suburbanisation, and the protection of the most vulnerable through a modest public housing sector – but they were seriously pursued. Although the actual redistributive capacities of the state town and country planning systems that emerged after World War II were modest, the commitment to welfare was sincerely registered in spatial policies that sought to regulate, if not command, urban land markets for the common good (Gleeson & Low 2000, p33).

The immediate period post-World War Two under the Curtin Labor government included an intense, if brief, focus on regional planning. This activity included an emphasis on decentralisation, motivated in part by concern over the fate of declining country towns. However, a change of federal government soon meant that regional decentralisation policies were left to the states (Self 1995, p248). The states pursued regional development goals in different ways, but the focus tended to be on attracting investment to regional areas, often by subsidising loans or making development sites available. While these initiatives may have slowed the process of urban concentration in the major cities, the 'scattergun' approach reflected political pressures to offer 'something to everyone'. By spreading available assistance unselectively over wide geographical areas, rather than a planned strategic approach to promoting growth in selected areas with distinct locational advantages, these approaches failed to gain any serious momentum.

In 1972 the election of the Whitlam Labor government meant another serious attempt at regional development via decentralisation. Concerned with regional disadvantage and disparity both within and beyond the growing metropolitan areas, the Whitlam government established the Department of Urban and Regional Development (DURD). Amongst the initiatives of the DURD was the attempt to establish several 'growth centres'. The growth centres included Campbelltown in NSW, which was to be a 'new town' on Sydney's southern outskirts, with a central business area, local industrial employment opportunities and affordable housing and recreation. Other growth centres in NSW were Gosford–Wyong, and Bathurst–Orange. The Albury–Wodonga growth centre is regarded the most successful, perhaps because of its equidistance location between Sydney and Melbourne on the main inland transportation route. Development in Albury–Wodonga was facilitated by a dedicated development corporation which managed to attract firms to establish in the urban centre. Government policies to decentralise state agencies were also intended to support the process.

Perhaps because of the short term in which the DURD had to implement and support the growth centres projects, and some ambivalence from the states, few of the projects have been judged successful. Commonwealth involvement in the growth centres was largely abandoned following the return to Liberal government in 1975.

One of the legacies of the Whitlam era was the establishment of voluntary Regional Organisations of Councils ('ROCs'), which have provided a bottom-up focus for regional policy-making and coordination (Howe 1995). Subject to varying levels of commitment, activity and funding security, there is little formal recognition of the ROCs and both state and federal governments define their own regions based on administrative convenience, with little reference to the self-organising regions of local government authorities (Howe 1995). However, many ROCs remain influential today, particularly in metropolitan regions.

Figure 4.1: Public housing, Melbourne

Public housing in Melbourne, funded under the Commonwealth State Housing Agreement. Source: the Author 2003.

In the early 1990s the federal (Labor) government again demonstrated an interest in urban and regional development, through research and policy initiatives sponsored by the short-lived Department of Housing and Regional Development. These included a series of initiatives and demonstration projects funded under the 'Building Better Cities' program which sought to demonstrate best practice in urban renewal and development in the last years of the Keating Labor government.

A new era of Commonwealth interest in urban and regional affairs began with the election of the Australian Labor Party (ALP) in September 2007. One of the first initiatives was to establish a Major Cities Unit within a new infrastructure portfolio. Key outcomes have been the release of a national urban policy (Department of Infrastructure and Transport 2011) and a national population strategy (Department of Sustainability 2011).

In releasing the national urban policy, the Commonwealth Government asserted a commitment to 'planning for and delivering, an urban Australia that is more productive, sustainable and liveable' (Department of Infrastructure and Transport 2011 p123). This commitment was supported by a range of funding measures in the 2011/12 Federal Budget for urban infrastructure and renewal and for regional planning and development (Burke 2011; Swan 2011). Announcing the Government's new emphasis on urban and regional affairs during the second reading budget speech to parliament, the Federal Treasurer Wayne Swan declared:

> We want prosperity and opportunity to reach all corners of the nation, especially our outer suburbs and regional towns. This is crucial to managing population growth and promoting sustainability right around the country. Among the most important things we can do to help deal with population pressures is to make regions more attractive places to work and raise a family. This Budget delivers for regional Australia like no Budget before it (Swan 2011).

Roles and responsibilities of Australian governments for the environment and land use planning

When the Constitution was drafted, concepts of environmental protection, management, or land use control were not in the minds of the legislators (Bates 2006; Harding 1998). The range of matters (or 'heads of power') that the Commonwealth is directly authorised to legislate on are set out in section 51 of the Constitution and no mention is made of the environment. By default this has meant that the main responsibility for environmental and land use planning legislation has traditionally fallen to the states and territories, who have in turn delegated certain powers to local government (Harding 1998). The Commonwealth is, however, able to use any of its existing powers to pursue environmental objectives, and so has established a variety of indirect approaches to influence environmental outcomes. Its powers relating to corporations, overseas trade and taxation have all been used to guide environmental policy at a national level. The system of tied grants (section 96 of the Constitution) also enables the Commonwealth government to direct the operation of environmental programs administered by the states (Harding 1998). Moreover, the Commonwealth has direct and exclusive jurisdiction over Commonwealth-owned land, Australian external territories and much of the marine environment (Bates 2006, p51). Legislation relating to Commonwealth-owned and managed areas is discussed further below, as is the Commonwealth's increasing role in shaping urban and regional policy at the national level. The Commonwealth government is also referred to as the 'Australian government'.

The states and territories

The Australian states and territories have primary responsibility for the legal framework governing urban policy and land use planning in Australia. These state and territorial legislative frameworks (often described as 'enabling frameworks') establish the parameters for strategic urban and regional planning, including the range of matters that can be addressed by statutory land use plans, the processes by which these plans must be prepared and the matters that must be considered when developments are assessed. The states and territories also define the powers and operating arrangements of local government in Australia.

Much of the responsibility for detailed strategic planning and development assessment is delegated by the states and territories to local government. Local government, overseen by elected representatives who form a local 'council', relates to a specific jurisdiction or local government area (LGA). As noted above, the policy, administrative, procedural and financial responsibilities of local government in Australia, are wholly regulated by state legislation. Thus, the degree of responsibility delegated to local government in relation to urban planning functions differs in each state and territory.

The role of local governments in Australia is generally much narrower than that of local authorities in comparable nations including the US and the UK. For instance, in the US, local authorities are responsible for the provision of education and policing services while in the UK, local authorities have been responsible for developing and managing significant social housing programs. By contrast, local governments in Australia have traditionally been perceived in terms of a narrow 'roads, rates and rubbish' remit – referring to their responsibilities for the provisions of local infrastructure and related services (primarily relating to local roads, recreation areas, community facilities and waste management). In recent years this has expanded to include more strategic expectations in relation to urban planning and environmental conservation and management. The different intergovernmental roles in relation to the environment and urban planning in Australia are summarised in Figure 4.2.

In 2008 the Australian government established the Australian Council of Local Government (ACLG) to provide a basis for direct Commonwealth/local government engagement. The ACLG comprises elected local government leaders (mayors and shire presidents) and its representative body, the Australian Local Government Association (ALGA). Members of state and territorial government also attend ACLG meetings which focus on issues of national interest affecting local government and communities, as well as the provision of information and data to support local government development (Australian Council of Local Government 2010).

Planning authorities

The term 'planning authority' or 'consent' authority is often used to refer to the organisation responsible for setting the statutory development controls and assessing proposals in relation to a particular place or development. Planning or consent authorities may operate at Commonwealth, state or local levels. While in most situations, local councils are the relevant planning authority for development within their local government area boundary, state governments are also increasingly intervening in the preparation of strategic plans for significant new urban areas and in the assessment of major projects. In the two territories, plan-making and development assessment powers are retained by the territorial governments.

Figure 4.2: Intergovernmental roles for the environment and urban planning in Australia

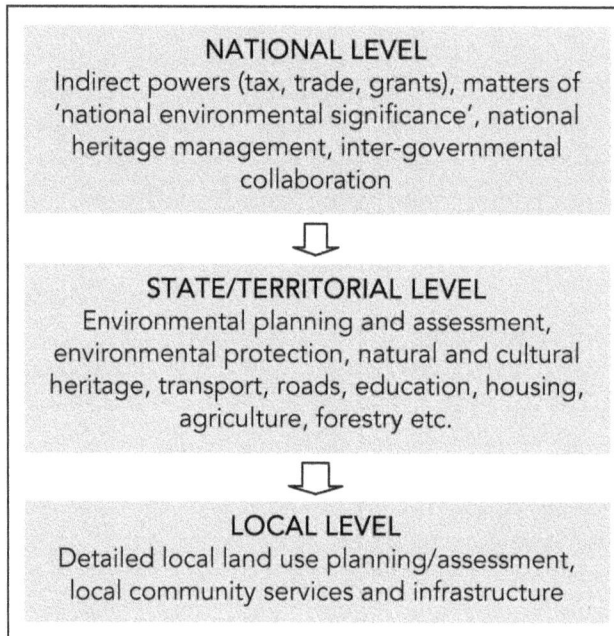

NATIONAL LEVEL
Indirect powers (tax, trade, grants), matters of 'national environmental significance', national heritage management, inter-governmental collaboration

⬇

STATE/TERRITORIAL LEVEL
Environmental planning and assessment, environmental protection, natural and cultural heritage, transport, roads, education, housing, agriculture, forestry etc.

⬇

LOCAL LEVEL
Detailed local land use planning/assessment, local community services and infrastructure

Source: the Author 2007

Intergovernmental processes and committees

The Council of Australian Governments (COAG) provides the basis for intergovernmental cooperation, policy development and reform in Australia. Formed in 1992, COAG comprises the prime minister, the premiers and chief ministers of the states and territories, and the president of the Australian Local Government Association.

Intergovernmental cooperation on matters relating to the environment is bound by the 'Intergovernmental Agreement on the Environment', made in May 1992. The agreement defines the roles of the respective governments in relation to the environment, and is intended to reduce the number of disputes between the Commonwealth and the states and territories on matters relating to the environment, and result in better environmental protection (Box 4.1). Subsequent meetings of COAG have refined elements of this original agreement, as national environmental policy has progressed. In particular, the 'Heads of agreement on Commonwealth and state roles and responsibilities for the environment' (COAG 1997) established a basis for identifying matters of national environmental significance and other Commonwealth responsibilities. Much of this subsequent agreement has been implemented through the *Commonwealth Environmental Protection and Biodiversity Conservation Act 1999*, discussed further below.

In late 2009 the COAG Reform Council, which is a special committee of COAG, agreed to reforms in a number of government portfolios, including urban planning and housing. Planning commitments related to the establishment of new criteria to improve the strategic planning frameworks for capital cities and the relationships between capital cities and regional areas. The overall goal of these commitments as stated by the COAG Reform Council is 'to ensure Australian cities are globally competitive, productive, sustainable, liveable and socially inclusive and are well placed to meet future challenges and growth' (COAG Reform Council 2009). The COAG criteria for capital city planning include integration across land use and transport, economic and infrastructure development, and environment assessment. Plans should span near- and long-term land use and infrastructure plans, provision of nationally significant economic infrastructure (transport corridors, international gateways, major communications and utilities, and reservation of appropriate lands for future expansion). Plans should also address nationally significant policy issues such as population growth and change, climate change, productivity and global competitiveness, social inclusion, housing affordability and matters of national environmental significance (COAG Reform Council 2009). It is intended that future Commonwealth funding for infrastructure will be linked to the ways in which states and territories demonstrate adherence to these criteria.

Box 4.1 Environmental roles of Australian governments

SECTION 2 – ROLES OF THE PARTIES – RESPONSIBILITIES AND INTERESTS

2.1 RESPONSIBILITIES AND INTERESTS OF ALL PARTIES

2.1.1 The following will guide the parties in defining the roles, responsibilities and interests of all levels of Government in relation to the environment and in particular in determining the content of Schedules to this Agreement.

2.2 RESPONSIBILITIES AND INTERESTS OF THE COMMONWEALTH

2.2.1 The responsibilities and interests of the Commonwealth in safeguarding and accommodating national environmental matters include:

- matters of foreign policy relating to the environment and, in particular, negotiating and entering into international agreements relating to the environment and ensuring that international obligations relating to the environment are met by Australia;

- ensuring that the policies or practices of a state do not result in significant adverse external effects in relation to the environment of another state or the lands or territories of the Commonwealth or maritime areas within Australia's jurisdiction (subject to any existing Commonwealth legislative arrangements in relation to maritime areas).

- facilitating the cooperative development of national environmental standards and guidelines as agreed in Schedules to this Agreement.

2.2.2 When considering its responsibilities and interests under paragraph 2.2.1(ii), the Commonwealth will have regard to the role of the States in dealing with significant adverse external effects as determined in 2.5.5 of this Agreement, and any action taken pursuant to 2.5.5.

2.2.3 The Commonwealth has responsibility for the management (including operational policy) of living and non-living resources on land which the Commonwealth owns or which it occupies for its own use.

2.3 RESPONSIBILITIES AND INTERESTS OF THE STATES

2.3.1 Each state will continue to have responsibility for the development and implementation of policy in relation to environmental matters which have no significant effects on matters which are the responsibility of the Commonwealth or any other state.

2.3.2 Each state has responsibility for the policy, legislative and administrative framework within which living and non living resources are managed within the state.

2.3.3 The States have an interest in the development of Australia's position in relation to any proposed international agreements (either bilateral or multilateral) of environmental significance which may impact on the discharge of their responsibilities.

2.3.4 The States have an interest and responsibility to participate in the development of national environmental policies and standards.

2.4 RESPONSIBILITIES AND INTERESTS OF LOCAL GOVERNMENT

2.4.1 Local Government has a responsibility for the development and implementation of locally relevant and applicable environmental policies within its jurisdiction in cooperation with other levels of Government and the local community.

2.4.2 Local Government units have an interest in the environment of their localities and in the environments to which they are linked.

2.4.3 Local Government also has an interest in the development and implementation of regional, Statewide and national policies, programs and mechanisms which affect more than one Local Government unit.

Intergovernmental Agreement on the Environment (DSEWPC 1992)

Additionally, there are numerous other intergovernmental processes and committees to coordinate matters relating to environmental policy across jurisdictional boundaries. Key national level intergovernmental committees relevant to environmental or urban policy are summarised in Table 4.1.

As shown, the Environmental Protection and Heritage Council (EPHC) comprises ministers from the Commonwealth, the states and territories, and New Zealand. It is a statutory body with the power to make laws and issue National Environmental Protection Measures, against which each jurisdiction must report on an annual basis. National Environmental Protection Measures address air and water quality, amenity in relation to noise, site contamination, hazardous waste, re-use and recycling (EPHC 2010).

Table 4.1 National ministerial councils, intergovernmental committees or other structures relevant to environmental or urban planning policy in Australia

Structure	Description	Date
Council of Australian Governments	Described as the 'peak intergovernmental forum in Australia'; intended to develop and monitor the implementation policy reform of significance to Australian governments and which require intergovernmental cooperation (COAG 2010b). Issues addressed to date include water reform and reform of environmental regulation. Comprises the prime minister, state premiers, territory chief ministers and the president of the Australian Local Government Association.	1992
National Environment Protection Council (NEPC)	Comprises the Australian state, territory and Commonwealth governments; has lawmaking powers to enact National Environmental Protection Measures (Council functions subsumed within the EPHC; lawmaking functions preserved as separate entity).	1992
Development Assessment Forum (DAF)	Representatives of Commonwealth, state/territorial and local governments, and professional industry associations. Aims to promote national consistency and improvement in development assessment processes.	1998
Environmental Protection and Heritage Council (EPHC)	Council of environmental ministers of Australia and New Zealand. Addresses environmental protection, conservation and heritage matters.	2001
Ministerial Council on Energy (MCE)	Established by COAG, sets national policy and governance arrangements for the Australian energy market.	2001
Natural Resource Management Ministerial Council (NRMMC)	Comprises the Australian state, territory and Commonwealth governments focuses on sustainable natural resource management.	2001
Local Government and Planning Ministers' Council (LGPMC)	Established by COAG, focuses on strategic, national level policy matters for local government and planning in Australia and New Zealand. Supported by senior officer level committees (the Local Government Joint Officers' Group) and the Planning Officials' Group (POG).	2001
National Housing Supply Council	Monitors national housing supply, demand, and affordability trends.	2008
National Building Industry Innovation Council	Advises Australian government on priorities and opportunities for building industry innovation to meet challenges like climate change, sustainability, competitiveness, as well as issues such as regulatory reform, workforce capability, and skills needs.	2008

Source: the Author (January 2011)

The Local Government and Planning Ministers' Council within the COAG is an important structure for pursuing national urban policy and planning matters in a coordinated way. The National Housing Supply Council provides independent expertise and information on Australian housing supply, demand and affordability trends.

Several other national level advisory committees and councils (many of which involve scientists, industry, and or community representatives) address specific issues relating to the environment and resource management.

The Murray Darling Basin Authority aims to manage the river basin's water resources in the national interest, and reports to the Commonwealth government. The six-member authority is supported by over 300 staff, responsible for the preparation, implementation and enforcement of the Murray Darling Basin Plan.

The Council of Capital City Lord Mayors originated in 1957 and continues to provide a collective to advocate for the particular issues affecting Australian capital cities.

The Productivity Commission's report on planning, zoning and development assessment systems in Australia details a plethora of other planning related sub committees, working groups, and agency structures associated with the Council of Australian Governments (Productivity Commission 2011 p392).

Commonwealth administration, law and policy

In January 2011, five main Commonwealth government departments had responsibilities relevant to the environment, natural resource management, and matters relevant to urban and regional policy (Table 4.2).

The Department of Sustainability, Environment, Water, Population and Communities (DSEWPC) (www.environment.gov.au) develops and implements national policy and laws relating to environmental protection and heritage, population, and communities (DSEWPC 2010a). It represents Australia in international forums (such as the United Nations Environment Program, and the Commission on Sustainable Development) undertaking international agreements relating to the environment, and administers national legislation on the environment and heritage (discussed further below). It manages the Commonwealth government's environment and heritage portfolios, relating to biodiversity, coasts and marine areas, built and natural heritage, protected areas, water and environmental protection. In late 2010 the department assumed policy responsibility for an emerging population policy, as well as initiatives relating to communities and affordable housing.

The Department of Infrastructure and Transport has responsibility for Commonwealth-funded infrastructure planning and coordination (relating to transport, communications, water and energy facilities) as well as land transport (national highways), civil aviation and airports, and maritime transport (DITR 2010b). Within the Department of Infrastructure and Transport, the Major Cities Unit provides high-level advice to the Australian government on policy, planning and infrastructure matters relating to cities and suburbs (MCU 2010a). It maintains data on key urban indicators relating to the economy, settlement, environmental quality, health, housing, transport, and governance, published in its *State of Australian Cities* report (MCU 2010b).

The Department of Regional Australia, Regional Development and Local Government (DRARDLG) promotes regional development, particularly in non-metropolitan, rural and remote regions, and coordinates national programs for local government (DRARDLG 2010).

The Department of Climate Change and Energy Efficiency develops and implements national research, policy and programs to encourage reduction of greenhouse gas emissions (climate change mitigation) and to assist the community and industry to adapt to unavoidable impacts of climate change that are already underway (DCCEE 2010a). This includes a national framework for greenhouse gas emission reporting by corporations and adaptation to climate change, in particular focusing on adaptation in relation to coasts, water, infrastructure, nationally significant ecological processes, disaster planning and management, and agriculture (Australian Government 2010a).

The Department of Agriculture, Fisheries and Forestry (DAFF) focuses on the management and regulation of these primary industries, but also has a role in managing natural resources.

The Australian Heritage Council is an arm's-length statutory authority that provides advice to the Commonwealth government on matters relating to national heritage. Its functions include advising the Australian government on proposed additions to the National Heritage List (providing protection for places of natural heritage significance) or Commonwealth Heritage List (Commonwealth places of heritage significance). Arrangements for conserving heritage in Australia are discussed further below.

Table 4.2 Australian Commonwealth government departments with responsibilities for the environment, natural resource management, or urban and regional affairs, January 2011

Department name	Functions
Department of Sustainability, Environment, Water, Population and Communities	National policy and laws relating to environmental protection and heritage (natural and built), population (growth and distribution) and communities; international environmental treaties; range of funding programs for environmental initiatives.
Department of Infrastructure and Transport	National urban policy (under development); major cities; funding programs for infrastructure, national transport, communications, energy infrastructure projects; airports and civil aviation.
Department of Regional Australia, Regional Development and Local Government	Regional economic development, local government coordination and assistance, range of funding programs for regional Australia and local government.
Department of Climate Change and Energy Efficiency	Greenhouse gas and energy use reporting and reduction framework; climate change adaptation research, policy development, and funding.
Department of Agriculture, Fisheries and Forestry	Coordination of national level natural resource management, agriculture, fishery and forestry activities and programs.

Source: the Author (January 2011)

While the bureaucratic arrangements and names of these Commonwealth agencies may change over time, the range of functions as summarised in Table 4.2 will more or less remain. However political changes mean that overarching foci and priorities may shift as demonstrated in the ebb and flow of national urban policy in Australia over the past four decades.

International treaties

As noted above, one way in which the Commonwealth government influences environmental matters in Australia is by participating in international forums relating to the environment and entering into international treaties, conventions or agreements on behalf of Australia. International agreements (Table 4.3) are largely administered by the Department of Sustainability, Environment, Water, Population and Communities.

Figure 4.3: Blue Mountains National Park World Heritage Area

The Blue Mountains National Park, which adjoins Sydney's growing western suburbs, is a listed World Heritage Area. This means that it falls within Australia's international treaty obligations under the World Heritage Convention, and is protected under Commonwealth and state legislation. Source: the Author 2004

One of the most influential treaties is the United Nations Convention on Climate Change, arising from the United Nations Conference on Environment and Development (UNCED) held in Rio de Janeiro, Brazil in 1992. The convention committed parties to monitor and reduce their greenhouse gas emissions, and to submit national greenhouse gas inventories of emissions and removals. In 1997, a protocol for establishing legally binding national targets was formed in Kyoto, Japan. Australia formally signed the Kyoto Protocol in late 2007, committing to limit its greenhouse gas emissions between 2008 and 2012 to 108 per cent of 1990 emissions. As an indicator of progress towards meeting these commitments, the Commonwealth Department of Climate Change and Energy Efficiency publishes Australia's National Greenhouse Accounts on an annual basis (DCCEE 2010b).

Table 4.3 Key international treaties or conventions on the environment, January 2011

Title	Description	Date*
International Convention for the Regulation of Whaling	Governs the conduct of whaling throughout the world.	1948
Convention on Wetlands of International Importance 'Ramsar Convention' on Wetlands	Framework for national action and international cooperation on the conservation and use of wetlands. Provides for international listing of 'Ramsar' wetlands.	1971
Convention for the Protection of the World Cultural and Natural Heritage 'World Heritage Convention'	Seeks to protect outstanding natural and cultural heritage. Lists items of world heritage. Australia currently has 16 properties on the World Heritage List, ranging from Uluru Kata Tjuta National Park through to the Great Barrier Reef and the Greater Blue Mountains Area.	1972
Convention on International Trade in Endangered Species of Wild Fauna and Flora	Aims to ensure that international trade in species of plants and animals does not threaten their survival.	1973
Convention on the Conservation of Migratory Species of Wild Animals	Aims to conserve migratory species throughout their range, by conserving or restoring their habitat and addressing barriers to migration.	1979
Convention on the Conservation of Antarctic Marine Living Resources	Seeks to conserve the marine life of the Southern Ocean.	1982
Convention on Biological Diversity	Signed by 150 government representatives at the 1992 Earth Summit in Rio de Janeiro. Intended to result in a range of practical initiatives for the protection of biodiversity.	1992
UN Framework Convention on Climate Change	Framework for intergovernmental actions on climate change. Associated Kyoto Protocol (1997) commits parties to individual targets for reduction of greenhouse gases. The targets are legally binding. Australia signed the Kyoto Protocol in 2007.	1992
UN Convention to Combat Desertification	Aims to combat desertification and mitigate the effects of drought.	2000
Montreal Protocol on Substances that Deplete the Ozone Layer	Establishes a mandatory timetable for phase out of ozone depleting substances, with obligations identified for signatories to the protocol.	1987

Source: Department of Foreign Affairs and Trade 2011. *Date of original agreement/meeting

In addition, Australia has also participated in many other international strategies or agreements arising from international activities. A key example is Agenda 21, the 'action plan' agreed by more than 178 governments, including Australia, also at the 1992 Earth Summit. Agenda 21 has resulted in the promulgation of a range of activities from the global through to the local level and has been particularly influential amongst local government in Australia, as discussed in chapter 9.

There has been criticism that the Commonwealth is able to enter into international treaties which by implication bind the states and territories without their involvement and sometimes, without a strategic legislative framework for implementation (Conacher & Conacher 2000). While there may be some truth in this criticism, in fact many of the conventions listed above have directly influenced national environmental policy and law.

National policies

Participation in many of the international conventions or treaties has directly resulted in the development of national policies to assist in implementing Australia's treaty commitments. Major Australian government policies relevant to the environment and therefore to urban planning are listed in Table 4.4. At the time of writing, a national aviation policy and a national ports strategy were also under development.

Table 4.4: National policies relating to the environment and urban settlement

Policy	Description	Date
National Strategy for Ecologically Sustainable Development	Provides strategic direction for Australian governments to guide policy and decision-making in relation to the national objective of ecologically sustainable development. It addresses many of the priority areas identified by Agenda 21.	1992
National Forest Policy Statement	Jointly developed by Commonwealth, state and territory governments and ultimately signed by all participating governments. Establishes objectives and policies for Australia's public and private forests, for all levels of government. Led to establishment of regional forest agreements (20-year plans) agreed between in each state/territorial government for the long term conservation and management of native forest resources.	1992
National Water Quality Management Strategy	Establishes a framework for managing Australia's water-bodies, including guidelines for water-cycle management plans for each each catchment, aquifer, estuary, coastal water or other waterbodies. Reviewed in 2008.	1992
Commonwealth Coastal Policy	Establishes a framework for Commonwealth and shared government responsibilities for managing the coastal zone, including objectives and principles for management.	1995
Australia's Biodviersity Conservation Strategy 2010–2030	National objectives for the conservation of Australia's biological diversity and a framework for other levels of government to achieve biodiversity conservation. The earlier 1996 version of the strategy resulted in the preparation of biodiversity conservation strategies by the states.	1996; 2010

Policy	Description	Date
Australia's Ocean Policy (1998)	Provides national coordination and consistency for marine planning and management on a regional basis.	1998
National Greenhouse Strategy	Intended to provide a comprehensive, cross-government approach to addressing greenhouse issues. Establishes a set of actions for government.	1998
Australian Natural Heritage Charter	'Best-practice' conservation principles for Australia, based on consensus of a range of heritage experts to assist in establishing and managing natural heritage values in terrestrial, marine and freshwater areas.	1996; updated 2002
National Framework for the Management and Monitoring of Australia's Native Vegetation	Sets national framework for native vegetation monitoring, followed by in 2007 by national strategies for managing introduced species (weeds and pest animals).	1999
Australia's Strategy for the National Reserve System	National guidance for selection, establishment, planning, management, and monitoring of national reserve system, including targets for ecosystem representation, threatened species habitat protection and climate change resilience.	2009
National Waste Policy: Less waste, more resources	National framework for waste management and resource recovery to 2020. Aims to reduce waste generation and improve waste recovery, through national coordination, to reduce greenhouse gas emissions, save energy and water, and improve productivity of land.	2009
Our Cities, Our Future: A national urban policy for a productive, sustainable and liveable future	A framework for policy development and public and private investment in urban areas; organised in relation to three overarching goals: 'productivity, sustainability, and liveability'.	2011
Sustainable Australia, Sustainable Communities - A Sustainable Population Strategy for Australia	A framework for monitoring and responding to population change and distribution, intended to operate in conjunction with the national urban policy and initiatives for regional development.	2011

Traditionally the Commonwealth government has been reluctant to become involved in those environmental and urban land use planning matters regarded to be the domain of the states, territories and local governments. The recent proliferation of policies relating to the environment, shown in Table 4.4 reflects increasing global concern regarding environmental issues since the late 1980s. National intervention in environmental matters is interpreted as, at least partly, actions flowing from international treaty commitments. However, as relationships between urban and regional planning decisions and environmental outcomes solidify, the Commonwealth is becoming increasingly engaged with the development process, through its responsibilities relating to environmental protection and natural resource management, and its new enthusiasm for cities and regions.

As shown in Table 4.4, the national environmental policy spectrum now spans environmentally sustainable development, biodiversity conservation, oceans and coasts, greenhouse gas emissions and waste, with emerging policies focusing on population and urban affairs.

One policy not specifically associated with environmental or urban policy is having increasing influence on Australia's planning systems and law. The National Competition Policy, established in the early 1990s through a series of intergovernmental agreements under the COAG framework, seeks to implement micro-economic reform under the guiding principle that 'competitive markets will generally best serve the interests of consumers and the wider community' (Productivity Commission 2005). An early outcome of the policy was to introduce a requirement for Regulatory Impact Statements to accompany proposed new regulation, and this approach has progressively been applied to new planning laws and policies with a statutory base. As noted in chapter 1, by 2010 the ambit of the policy (renamed Australia's National Reform Agenda) was extended to a review of Australia's planning systems, particularly land use zoning requirements, to assess the extent to which they support the national objective of national competition (Productivity Commission 2010).

Commonwealth legislation

Despite the lack of a direct head of Commonwealth power relating to the environment under section 51 of the Constitution, the Commonwealth government is able to make laws regarding environmental (or planning) issues, even if these matters are also covered by state law (Bates 2006, p51). For instance, if a particular threatened species is protected by both Commonwealth and state law, proposals must comply with both regulations, unless procedures are in place for the Commonwealth to recognise or sanction state assessment as fulfilling Commonwealth requirements. Key Commonwealth laws relating to aspects of the environment are shown in Box 4.2. While in practice the issue of duplication between Commonwealth and state requirements rarely arises in relation to routine land use planning matters, it has emerged in the context of the *Commonwealth Environment Protection and Biodiversity Conservation Act 1999*.

Before turning to a discussion of this act it is important to note that under section 109 of the Constitution, the Commonwealth is immune from state law, unless federal legislation provides for it to be bound. This means that state and local environmental planning laws do not usually apply to the Commonwealth government in relation to its activities on Commonwealth lands, such as airports, Commonwealth reserves and defence lands:

> The effect of this Commonwealth immunity means that the environmental effects of Commonwealth activity cannot be legally controlled by state environmental protection and planning legislation unless the Commonwealth subjects itself to such control (Bates 2006, p53).

This has led to significant concern expressed by state and local governments affected by activities such as airport expansions.

Commonwealth Environment Protection and Biodiversity Conservation Act 1999

As noted above, historically the Commonwealth government has had no formal role in traditional land use planning matters such as the preparation of statutory land use plans, or in the assessment of development proposals (with the exception of plans and developments affecting Commonwealth-managed Crown lands). This changed with the introduction of the *Commonwealth Environment Protection and Biodiversity Conservation Act 1999* (*CEPBCA*), which came into operation in 2000. The act's objectives include the promotion of ecologically sustainable development (Box 4.3).

The *CEPBCA* consolidated responsibilities formerly contained under many other Commonwealth laws and introduced a new role for the Commonwealth government in assessing and approving actions of 'national environmental significance'. The act defines these actions of 'national environmental significance' as actions (projects, developments, undertakings, activities or services of activities) that may affect:

- Australia's world heritage properties
- National heritage places
- Wetlands of international significance, listed under the Ramsar Convention
- Nationally listed threatened species, ecological communities, and listed migratory species protected by international agreements
- Commonwealth marine areas
- The Great Barrier Reef Marine Park
- Nuclear actions (*CEPBCA* 1999, Part 3, Division 1).

In addition to this list, other actions may be specified by regulation following consultation with state government.

The *CEPBCA* also applies to Commonwealth land and actions undertaken by Commonwealth agencies. It implies that apart from activities within Commonwealth areas, the Commonwealth government will intervene only in relation to environmental matters of national environmental significance.

The onus is on the proponent of the proposed development to seek Commonwealth approval for actions that may fall within the jurisdiction of the *CEPBCA* 'controlled actions'. They must then refer the matter to the Commonwealth environment minister. The minister will determine whether or not a matter needs approval under the act. In considering whether to approve an action, the minister must consider social and economic matters, environmental impacts, and the principles of ecologically sustainable development. There are provisions for the public exhibition of matters assessed under this legislation.

To avoid duplication, bilateral agreements have been reached between the Commonwealth government and each state and territory to accredit their environmental assessment processes. However, in most jurisdictions, approval responsibility for *CEPBCA* matters remains with the Commonwealth (Productivity Commission 2011). Further, difficulties in identifying whether and at which stage a project should be referred to the Commonwealth and the lack of defined processes for synchronising applications to state and Commonwealth agencies means that most controlled actions are assessed separately under Commonwealth and state processes (Productivity Commission 2011).

There is provision for strategic 'up-front' assessment during the strategic planning for major proposals (under section 146 of the *CEPBCA*). These strategic assessments can avoid the need for subsequent environmental assessment under the *CEPBCA* as the project proceeds. Strategic assessments can be proposed by state or territorial governments and other project proponents.

Under the *CEPBCA*, 'conservation agreements' may be reached in relation to any matter of national environmental significance or Commonwealth land. These agreements can require the owner of a place to undertake certain activities related to its conservation or remediation (DSEWPC 2010a).

In addition to the *CEPBCA*, the wide spread of Commonwealth legislation relating to the environment as shown in Box 4.2 reflects the diversity of environmental matters now falling within Commonwealth responsibility, despite the lack of a direct constitutional head of power relating to this area. This current framework is largely a product of key legislation enacted during the 1970s under the short-lived Whitlam government (1972–1975) and the subsequent Fraser Liberal government (1975–1983). In 1974 Australia's first real environmental protection legislation was introduced by the now superseded *Commonwealth Environmental Protection (Impact of Proposals) Act 1974*, which was inspired by the enactment of federal environmental protection legislation in the US. The *National Parks and Wildlife Conservation Act 1975* was echoed by similar legislation enacted by the states for their own reserves and the protection of native flora and fauna.

Many of these reserves (and Crown lands not designated as such) are also places of Aboriginal significance and the Commonwealth *Aboriginal Land Rights (Northern Territory) Act 1976* provided a basis for granting certain lands to Aboriginal Land Trusts and for the claiming of unalienated Crown land by Aboriginal groups able to prove traditional ownership. This meant that Aboriginal groups at the so-called resource frontier were able to benefit financially from mining developments through royalty payments, some of which were reinvested in northern towns. It has been necessary to adapt land use planning practice in the Northern Territory to accommodate the unique characteristics of small Indigenous and mining communities in locations where land title has been affected by the granting of land rights (for a history of these events see Lea & Zehner 1986, and Kesteven & Lea 1997). Around 600,000 km^2 has been transferred to collective Indigenous ownership in the Northern Territory – nearly 50 per cent of the total area (Department of Foreign Affairs and Trade 2008).

The *Aboriginal Land Rights (Northern Territory) Act 1976* legislation paved the way for the landmark Mabo decision, which held that Indigenous rights had not been automatically extinguished by colonial settlement of Australia and that in certain circumstances 'native title' may persist and even co-exist with other types of land title (though not freehold title) (*Mabo v. Queensland* [No. 1] 1988 166 CLR 186; *Mabo v. Queensland* [No. 2] 1992 175 CLR 1). The passage of federal native title legislation in the early 1990s established a framework for administering native title claims, as discussed below.

Box 4.2: Commonwealth laws relating to the environment or heritage

Aboriginal and Torres Strait Islander Heritage Protection Act 1984

Antarctic Acts:

  Antarctic Marine Living Resources Conservation Act 1981

  Antarctic Treaty Act 1960

  Antarctic Treaty (Environment Protection) Act 1980

  Australian Antarctic Territory Acceptance Act 1933

  Australian Antarctic Territory Act 1954

Australian Heritage Council Act 2003

Environment Protection and Biodiversity Conservation Act 1999

Environment Protection (Sea Dumping) Act 1981

Fuel Quality Standards Act 2000

Great Barrier Reef Marine Park Act 1975

Hazardous Waste (Regulation of Exports and Imports) Act 1989

Historic Shipwrecks Act 1976

Lake Eyre Basin Intergovernmental Agreement Act 2001

Meteorology Act 1955

National Environment Protection Council Act 1994

National Environment Protection Measures (Implementation) Act 1998

National Parks and Wildlife Conservation Act 1975

National Museum of Australia Act 1980

National Water Commission Act 2004

Natural Heritage Trust of Australia Act 1997

Natural Resources Management (Financial Assistance) Act 1992, section 25(1)

Ozone protection and synthetic greenhouse gas acts:

  Ozone Protection and Synthetic Greenhouse Gas Management Act 1989

  Ozone Protection and Synthetic Greenhouse Gas (Import Levy) Act 1995

  Ozone Protection and Synthetic Greenhouse Gas (Manufacture Levy) Act 1995

Product Stewardship (Oil) Act 2000

State Grants (Water Resources Measurement) Act 1970

Sydney Harbour Federation Trust Act 2001

Water Act 2007

Water Efficiency Labelling and Standards Act 2005

Wet Tropics of Queensland World Heritage Area Conservation Act 1994

Source: DSEWPC 2010a

Box 4.3: Objectives of environmentally sustainable development under the *Commonwealth Environment Protection and Biodiversity Protection Act 1999*

3 Objects of Act

(1) The objects of this Act are:

(a) to provide for the protection of the environment, especially those aspects of the environment that are matters of national environmental significance; and

(b) to promote ecologically sustainable development through the conservation and ecologically sustainable use of natural resources; and

(c) to promote the conservation of biodiversity; and

(ca) to provide for the protection and conservation of heritage; and

(d) to promote a cooperative approach to the protection and management of the environment involving governments, the community, landholders and indigenous peoples; and

(e) to assist in the cooperative implementation of Australia's international environmental responsibilities; and

(f) to recognise the role of indigenous people in the conservation and ecologically sustainable use of Australia's biodiversity; and

(g) to promote the use of indigenous peoples' knowledge of biodiversity with the involvement of, and in cooperation with, the owners of the knowledge.

Commonwealth Environment Protection and Biodiversity Protection Act 1999 (January 2011)

Native Title

The Commonwealth *Native Title Act 1993* provides a legal framework for recognising and enabling the continuation of Indigenous rights and interests in certain lands. It represents the culmination of legislative changes and pressure to incorporate Indigenous rights over land, as discussed above, and directly followed the landmark High Court decision in favour of Eddie Mabo, whose claim to have his native title rights recognised on behalf of the Meriam people was accepted by the Court in 1992. The *Native Title Act 1993* recognises that Indigenous or native rights and interests in their lands were not automatically extinguished by the colonisation of Australia by Europeans.

However since this time many actions that have been undertaken or authorised by the government are inconsistent with the continuation of native title. These actions include the granting of freehold land, such as farms held in freehold title and pastoral or agricultural leases granting exclusive possession, as well as leases for residential, commercial or community purposes and public works. In other circumstances, native title can coexist with other rights relating to the use of vacant and unallocated Crown land, some reserves, some types of pastoral leases, waters and coastal lands that are not privately owned, and some land held by Aboriginal and Torres Strait Islanders (National Native Title Tribunal 2006). In limited areas of Australia, native title rights may be granted as 'exclusive possession', but in other areas 'non-exclusive' rights may include the right to live on the area, access it for traditional purposes, or for hunting or resource gathering activities. While native title does not confer the right to veto development proposals per se it is expected that the rights and interests of native title holders would need to be taken into account during the assessment process (Native Title Tribunal 2006, p3).

Figure 4.4: Aboriginal Tent Embassy, Victoria Park, Sydney

The Aboriginal Tent Embassy established in Sydney's central Victoria Park in 2004 was a symbolic protest calling attention to the forced disconnection between the traditional Aboriginal owners of Sydney and contemporary land settlement, ownership and management. Source: the Author, 2004.

The *Native Title Act 1993* enabled the establishment of the National Native Title Tribunal, providing a process for Indigenous Australians to lodge claims relating to native title. If meeting all requirements associated with a registration test, claimants are then entitled to participate in certain processes relating to the future use of the land, such as negotiation about mining activities. The tribunal also facilitates negotiations and arrangements to enable native title to coexist with other rights pertaining to land using mechanisms such as Indigenous Land Use Agreements (Native Title Tribunal 2010). Some local governments have begun to use the native title framework to establish new cooperative arrangements with Indigenous people over the management and use of lands, waters and resources, and there is potential to use this approach whether or not the land in question is subject to a formal claim.

By September 2010, about 13 per cent of Australia's land mass was covered by native title determinations and a further 15 per cent of Australia's land mass was covered by an Indigenous Land Use Agreement. A total of 139 native title determinations had been made while 449 applications remained pending (National Native Title Tribunal 2010).

While native title recognises rights and interests in land that predate European settlement in Australia and that have continued in an uninterrupted way since this time, 'land rights' relate to an actual grant of land under various state legislation. Land rights laws provide for the granting of land to Indigenous Australians in the Northern Territory, Queensland, New South Wales, South Australia and Victoria. In general, successful land rights claims result in the granting of freehold title or perpetual lease, usually to a community rather than an individual (National Native Title Tribunal 2006).

Building Code of Australia

The Building Code of Australia (BCA) was a joint initiative of all levels of Australian government to achieve national consistency in building and technical standards. In March 1994, the Australian government and state and territory ministers responsible for building regulatory matters signed an intergovernmental agreement to establish the Australian Building Codes Board, which includes representatives from the building industry and is responsible for the BCA. This agreement was reaffirmed in July 2001. The BCA enshrines a comprehensive set of technical provisions relating to structure, fire resistance, access and egress, fire-fighting equipment, mechanical ventilation, lift installations, health and amenity. It is formally implemented through the planning legislation of the states and territories which refer to, and require compliance with, BCA provisions for all approved developments. It is amended on an annual cycle.

Heritage

Provisions for the protection of heritage in Australia are often confusing because there are several different lists and registers identifying items of natural or cultural heritage at national, state and local levels (Table 4.5).

The Australian Heritage Council provides independent expert advice on the nomination, assessment, and management of places on the Commonwealth and national heritage lists. To find out whether a site or building is listed, see the Australian Heritage Places Inventory which contains a searchable database with links to many of the lists outlined in Table 4.5. The inventory is available online (through the link at www.heritage.gov.au).

Each of the states and territories have their own parallel processes for obtaining independent advice on the assessment of heritage matters at state and local levels. It is not uncommon for heritage items to be listed more than once and potentially, subject to an overlaying set of heritage requirements. In general terms, national heritage listing overlays state or local requirements, while Commonwealth-listed areas are subject solely to Commonwealth legislation. We return to the specific arrangements for protecting state and local heritage items in the following chapters.

Table 4.5: Heritage lists in Australia, January 2011

List	Description	Legislation
World Heritage List	Places listed on the United Nations Environmental and Social Cultural Organisation (UNESCO) embody 'universal' values of cultural or natural significance. World Heritage listed properties are protected by domestic laws.	*Commonwealth Environment Protection and Biodiversity Conservation Act 1999*
National Heritage List	Places of 'outstanding' heritage value for Australia. May relate to natural, Indigenous or historical values. Nominations assessed by the Australian Heritage Council who makes a recommendation to the minister for the environment and heritage.	*Commonwealth Environment Protection and Biodiversity Conservation Act 1999*
Commonwealth Heritage List	Natural and cultural heritage places (lands or waters) owned or managed by the Commonwealth government. Nominations assessed by the Australian Heritage Council who makes a recommendation to the minister for the environment and heritage.	*Commonwealth Environment Protection and Biodiversity Conservation Act 1999*
Register of the National Estate	Lists natural, cultural and historic places throughout Australia. New additions to the register closed in February 2007 but it remains a statutory list until February 2012. Replaced by other heritage lists.	*Australian Heritage Council Act 2003*
State and territory heritage lists	Each state and territory manages its own heritage lists subject to protection under state legislation.	State or territorial heritage legislation
Local government lists	Most states and territories also enable local governments to maintain their own lists of heritage items, often attached to local planning schemes.	State or territorial heritage legislation, local planning schemes
National Trust list	A list of National Trust items is maintained within each state and territory. (The National Trust is a community-based, non-government organisation dedicated to heritage appreciation and protection).	
Indigenous site registers	State and territory governments and some local land councils maintain registers of Indigenous places (including religious sites, rock art places, camping sites, and sometimes historical sites). To avoid placing sensitive sites at risk, access to information about these sites may be restricted.	Relevant state legislation relating to the protection of Indigenous heritage

Source: Adapted from (DSEWPC 2010)

Summary and conclusions

This chapter has outlined the intergovernmental arrangements for environmental management and urban land use planning in Australia, focusing particularly on the role of the Commonwealth and the spectrum of national level policies and laws relating to the environment and urban affairs.

There is an increasingly important body of Commonwealth law relating to matters of national environmental significance, (national) heritage conservation provisions and native title, which may need to be considered during plan-making and development assessment. Where this legislation applies to places not directly owned or managed by the Commonwealth, planning processes can become particularly complex because these provisions represent an additional layer to requirements under state and territorial legislation, as discussed in the following chapter.

There has been a distinct groundswell of national level interest in urban affairs and regional development. It has established a national framework to progress important environmental policy agendas relating to environmentally sustainable development, climate change, biodiversity and coasts, and is pursuing new policies for urban affairs and sustainable population. Through this framework, the Commonwealth has articulated a new role in making Australian cities 'globally competitive, productive, sustainable, liveable, socially inclusive and well placed to meet future challenges and growth' (Department of Infrastructure and Transport 2011, p3).

Chapter 5

Frameworks for state and territorial planning legislation and policy in Australia

Australia lacks a national approach to urban and land use planning and the states and territories have evolved their own idiosyncratic planning systems, policies, legislation and approaches. This chapter provides a comparative overview of these systems and highlights key similarities and differences. Understanding the ways in which Australia's different planning systems function assists in transferring knowledge and good practice between jurisdictions. It also provides a basis for broader policy development in establishing a national agenda for urban and environmental planning and in promoting particular priorities, such as ecologically sustainable development or housing affordability.

The chapter begins with an overview of the administrative arrangements governing planning systems in the Australian states and territories, before summarising key legislation and policy relating to urban and environmental planning. Although there is little by way of formal regional governance in Australia, there has been revived interest in recent years in regional and metropolitan planning, largely facilitated by the states, and an overview of these initiatives is provided here. Using the planning system to fund infrastructure for new development has become a contentious policy area in Australia. The third section of the chapter considers local infrastructure contribution systems in each state and territory in the context of these wider debates. Finally, the chapter provides an overview of provisions for dispute resolution through special planning courts and tribunals.

Overview of state and territorial planning jurisdictions

Administrative arrangements for planning systems in the Australian states and territories differ from jurisdiction to jurisdiction. While some jurisdictions have stand-alone planning agencies, in many cases the administration of the planning system is situated within larger government departments. A change of government or ministerial reshuffle often results in a re-organisation of administrative functions. The summary of agencies shown in Table 5.1 is indicative of bureaucratic arrangements for urban and environmental planning and management in Australia at the time of writing.

Related responsibilities for local government, infrastructure, housing, transport, land and property management, are dispersed across other administrative portfolios in most jurisdictions.

Table 5.1: Administrative arrangements for land use and environmental planning in the Australian states and territories June 2011

State/territory	Agencies with environmental policy and land use planning responsibilities
Australian Capital Territory (ACT)	**ACT Planning and Land Authority***
	Department of the Environment, Climate Change, Energy and Water
New South Wales (NSW)	**Department of Planning and Infrastructure**
	Office of the Environment and Heritage
Northern Territory (NT)	**Department of Lands and Planning**
	Department of Natural Resources, Environment, the Arts and Sport
Queensland (Qld)	**Department of Local Government and Planning**
	Department of Environment and Resource Management
South Australia (SA)	Department of Planning and Local Government
	Department of Environment and Natural Resources
Tasmania (Tas.)	**Tasmanian Planning Commission**
	Department of Primary Industries, Parks, Water and Environment
Victoria (Vic.)	**Department of Planning and Community Development**
	Department of Sustainability and Environment
Western Australia (WA)	**Department of Planning**
	Western Australian Planning Commission
	Department of Environment and Conservation

*Bold denotes main responsibility for planning system and processes within jurisdiction.

State and territorial planning legislation frameworks

State and territorial legislation establishes the framework for urban land use planning systems in each jurisdiction. This legislation is summarised in Table 5.2. The table also highlights the key objectives for the planning system identified in each planning act, many of which have been heavily amended since the original acts were passed. These objectives are important because they indicate how the legislation should be interpreted. State level legislative objectives may also set the parameters for the range of objectives and matters that can be addressed within subsidiary planning instruments prepared under the main legislation, and the way in which development proposals are assessed. Decisions contrary to these objectives are generally unlawful.

Most of the state and territorial planning acts now include an objective relating to sustainability, variously referred to as: 'ecologically sustainable development' (NSW); 'sustainable' development or use and protection of land (NT, SA, Tas., Vic., WA); 'ecological sustainability' (Qld); 'ecologically sustainable' (ACT, SA); or the 'maintenance of ecological processes and genetic diversity' (Tas., Vic.). The different emphases are more than just semantic. For instance, an objective of 'ecologically sustainable development' includes broad environmental, social and economic goals, and implies some prioritisation of the environment in evaluating these interests, but remains tied to a model of growth or development. It can be argued that a development focus is appropriate given the context within which urban planning operates – i.e. managing urban change by controlling new development. However, many jurisdictions have chosen to articulate objectives that recognise the innate values of the environment and the ecological processes within which humans are situated and dependent on, rather than implying that development is an end in itself.

Table 5.2: Australian planning legislation

State	Legislation	Key objectives
ACT	*Planning and Development Act 2007*	The objectives of the Act are 'to provide a planning and land system that contributes to the orderly and sustainable development of the ACT' … 'consistent with the social, environmental and economic aspirations of the people of the ACT' … 'in accordance with sound financial principles' (s6).
NSW	*Environmental Planning and Assessment Act 1979*	Objectives include the 'proper management, development and conservation of natural and artificial resources', 'the promotion and coordination of the orderly and economic use and development of land', 'the provision and coordination of community services and facilities', 'ecologically sustainable development', 'the provision and maintenance of affordable housing', and the promotion of public participation (s5). Box 7.1 includes the full objectives of the *EPAA*.
NT	*Planning Act 1999*	'To plan for, and provide a framework of controls for, the orderly use and development of land', with subsidiary goals relating to the sustainable use and protection of the natural environment and resources; protection of amenity; and community consultation (s2A [2]).
Qld	*Sustainable Planning Act (SPA) 2009*	The act aims 'to seek to achieve ecological sustainability' by 'ensuring the process is accountable, effective and efficient and delivers sustainable outcomes', 'managing the effects of development on the environment' and coordinating and integrating planning at local, regional and state levels (s3). Further detail is provided under section 5, states that decision making processes should be 'accountable, coordinated, effective and efficient', 'take account of short and long-term environmental effects of development at local, regional, state and wider levels'. Such considerations relate to climate change, housing diversity and choice, the provision of infrastructure, and community involvement. The full provisions of section 5 are contained in Box 6.1

State	Legislation	Key objectives
SA	Development Act 1993	Objectives are to: 'to provide for proper, orderly and efficient planning and development' by the creation of development plans, 'to enhance the proper conservation, use, development and management of land and buildings', 'sustainable development and the protection of the environment', 'to encourage the management of the natural and constructed environment in an ecologically sustainable manner', 'to advance the social and economic interests and goals of the community', to 'provide for appropriate public participation in the planning process and the assessment of development proposals', to provide for 'cost effective' technical standards for buildings including the adoption of national standards, and increased housing choice and access to affordable housing (s3).
Tas.	Land Use Planning and Approvals (LUPA) Act 1993	Schedule One of the act establishes objectives for Tasmania's resource management and planning system and processes, which include promoting 'sustainable development' and 'the maintenance of ecological processes and genetic diversity', public participation and economic development (Schedule One, Part One). Objectives for the planning process include ensuring that 'the effects on the environment are considered' in plan-making and assessment and providing for 'consideration of social and economic effects when decisions are made' (Schedule One, Part Two).
Vic.	Planning and Environment Act 1987	Objectives for 'planning in Victoria' include providing for 'the fair, orderly, economic and sustainable use, and development of land' and the 'protection of natural and man-made resources and the maintenance of ecological processes and genetic diversity'. Objectives for the 'planning framework' established by the act include ensuring that 'the effects on the environment are considered and provide for explicit consideration of social and economic effects when decisions are made about the use and development of land', 'the achievement of planning objectives through positive actions by responsible authorities and planning authorities', and providing an 'accessible process for just and timely review of decisions without unnecessary formality' (extracts from s4).
WA	Planning and Development Act (PDA) 2005	The purposes of the act include providing 'for an efficient and effective land use planning system in the state', and promoting 'the sustainable use and development of land in the state' (s3).

The inclusion of specific objectives relating broadly to community or social wellbeing recognises that spatial planning decisions affect social outcomes for different individuals and groups in society and that these likely outcomes should be considered during plan-making and when development proposals are assessed.

The objectives for Queensland's planning system bear closer scrutiny, as the *Sustainable Planning Act 2009 (SPA)* is the newest comprehensive planning legislation in Australia. Uniquely amongst the other states and territories, the *SPA* makes reference to climate change as a potentially adverse environmental impact from development, which should be avoided if practical, or otherwise 'lessened'.

More specific provisions in each of these acts relate to local, regional or state level strategic planning processes; matters to consider when developments are assessed; mechanisms for public participation; infrastructure or community services; and systems for dispute resolution and appeal. These are discussed further in the sections below.

State and territorial planning policy frameworks

Terminology surrounding the land use planning system is often confusing. 'Plans' may be drawings or maps, or they may be written documents. They might contain actions and timeframes, thus indicating how an individual agency or group of people 'plan' to achieve a particular series of objectives or strategies. 'Land use' plans contain controls or guidelines governing the use and development of land, and they are usually prepared under some overarching piece of legislation, so they are often referred to as planning 'instruments' to infer or denote their statutory legitimacy. But they might not be called plans! They might be called planning 'schemes', 'ordinances', 'instruments' or some other variation.

'Policy' is another term that is often used in different ways and in some cases, interchangeably with plans or planning instruments. In a general sense, a policy represents a broad approach intended to achieve a particular objective. Usually, the term policy refers to a defined set of objectives and strategies to achieve these objectives, often including decision-making guidelines. One of the powerful ways in which government policies relating to the environment or community or economic wellbeing can be implemented is through planning legislation, and through subsidiary statutory planning instruments prepared under this legislation.

An overarching strategic policy or policy framework for urban planning can engage the community in identifying visions for a particular place and strategies to achieve these. Often such a process is much more accessible for members of the community than the more formal approaches associated with the preparation of a specific statutory planning instrument. As shown in Table 5.3, some Australian states and territories (the ACT, Vic., SA and WA) have implemented a broad or comprehensive approach to articulating state planning policy relating to the environment, urban settlement, industry, housing and infrastructure. These policy frameworks are given statutory weight to guide plan-making and development assessment in each state.

Other states (NSW, Qld, and Tas.), have no overarching policy framework but have provision for specific state policy instruments to address matters of state planning significance.

There are varying procedures to incorporate state planning policies (overarching or specific issue) within local plans. In Victoria and South Australia, for instance, state planning policies are drafted to enable automatic insertion within local planning instruments. In NSW, some State Environmental Planning Policies have been incorporated within the framework for preparing new local environmental plans (discussed further in chapter 7). In Tasmania there is a requirement for state planning policies to indicate how local planning schemes should be adapted to reflect their intent.

Table 5.3: Planning policy framework for the Australian states and territories

State/ territory	Policy instruments	Description
ACT	The Canberra Plan 2008, the Canberra Social Plan and Spatial Plan (2004), Statement of Planning Intent 2010	Policy framework to guide development of the ACT. Includes actions and guidelines relating to social and physical planning.
NSW	State Environmental Planning Policies (SEPPs)	Various issue-based and place-based policies addressing matters of state /regional significance. Statutory instruments prepared under the EPAA. Relate to specific issues (e.g. housing, infrastructure, urban design), particular places (e.g. the Murray Riverine area) and the planning system itself.
NT	Northern Territory Planning Scheme	Land use policy framework for the Northern Territory.
Qld	State Planning Policies (SPPs) prepared under SPA 2009; State Interest Planning Policies (SIPPs)	SPPs address collection of specific issues including development near airports, natural hazards, conservation and housing. SIPPs cover air quality, nature conservation, Queensland waters, and cultural heritage.
SA	South Australian Planning Strategy, prepared under the *Development Act 1993*	Physical and policy framework for range of social, economic and environmental issues. minister must report annually to parliament about its implementation. Integrated with other specialist plans, including the Strategic Infrastructure Plan for South Australia, the Housing Plan for South Australia, Water Proofing Adelaide, and South Australia's Waste Strategy.
Tas.	Planning directives made under LUPA and state policies made under *State Policies and Projects Act 1993*, relate to coasts, protection of agricultural land, and water quality management	Local planning schemes must be amended to incorporate relevant components of state policies. State policies are drafted to provide clear guidance on implementation through local planning schemes. In the event of an inconsistency, the state policy prevails.
Vic.	State Planning Policy Framework (in the Victorian Planning Provisions); prepared under *Planning and Environment Act 1987*	Includes goals, principles and provisions relating to metropolitan development, settlement, environment, housing, economic development and infrastructure.

State/territory	Policy instruments	Description
WA	State planning policies under the *Planning and Development Act 2005* include place and issue specific policies for the environment, coasts, agriculture, urban growth and settlement	Provides a comprehensive policy framework for land use planning in WA. This and other specific Statements of Planning Policy are authorised/prepared under the *Planning and Development Act 2005*.

Strategic metropolitan and regional planning in Australia

Regional planning recognises that some issues – be they environmental, social or economic – cross local government boundaries, and need to be addressed in a consistent and collaborative way. As noted in previous chapters, there is little by way of regional governance in Australia, with the exception of some specific structures designed to address particular regional needs. For instance, the Commonwealth and the Queensland government established the Torres Strait Regional Authority in 1994 to establish regional administrative arrangements for the Torres Strait but this approach has not been widely adopted elsewhere. The Commonwealth has also played a significant role in facilitating and resourcing regional natural resource management initiatives funded under the National Heritage Trust.

In 2009, the Commonwealth government established a new regional framework structured by 'Regional Development Committees' (RDCs). These RDCs include representatives from government, industry and community and are charged with preparing Regional Development Plans (Regional Development Australia 2009).

However the lack of a formal level of regional government in most areas of Australia has meant that the states and territories have played the lead role in regional planning, to the extent that it occurs.

Regional planning processes managed by the Australian states and territories include the development of both statutory, and non-statutory plans or strategies. There are different arrangements for incorporating the provisions of regional plans in local plan-making and development assessment. Usually the plan or instrument itself will indicate the anticipated arrangements for local implementation.

When regional planning processes involve a strategic policy development component, they usually provide opportunities for broad engagement of different stakeholders from different levels of government, industry and community. The long-established regional planning process jointly initiated by local governments in Queensland, and facilitated by the Queensland state government, provides an example of this approach. While these plans have not traditionally had statutory weight, the South-East Queensland Regional Environmental Plan 2009–2031 is now a statutory instrument under the *Statutory Instru-*

ments Act 1992 and has the status of a planning instrument under Queensland's *Sustainable Planning Act 2009.*

Over the past five years there has been a resurgence of more proactive or strategic regional planning, including the identification of specific centres or locations for growth and the organisation of transport and infrastructure investment decisions to reinforce this growth. The South East Queensland regional planning processes is supported by a funded infrastructure investment plan on the basis that significant government investment decisions have a large role in shaping growth outcomes, so such decisions should follow and reinforce strategic growth plans.

Table 5.4: Regional planning arrangements in the Australian states and territories, January 2011

Jurisdiction	Regional planning arrangements
ACT	No specific arrangements. Most planning arrangements relate to the entire ACT.
NSW	Regional strategies (non-statutory). (Some State Environmental Planning Policies [SEPPs] are called Regional Environmental Plans but have now the status of a SEPP).
NT	NT Planning Scheme enables subsidiary planning on area/regional basis.
Qld	Regional plans are joint initiatives between state and local governments. Prepared under *SPA 2009*, regional plans have statutory status.
SA	The overall planning strategy for South Australia includes Greater Adelaide and regional volumes.
Tas.	Regional strategies (under development).
Vic.	Regional metropolitan planning and regional planning arrangements for particular issues or areas (e.g. the Great Ocean Road).
WA	Statutory Regional Structure Plans and Regional Schemes
Cwlth	55 Regional Development Australia Committees to develop non-statutory Regional Development Plans.

As shown in Table 5.4, the Northern Territory, Queensland, South Australia and Western Australia enable some form of statutory regional planning. In Tasmania and Victoria there has been a tradition of sporadic, non-statutory strategic planning between regional clusters of local government areas, but this is becoming more systematised over time. In NSW there has been a retreat from a comprehensive, statutory regional plan, in favour of a non-statutory strategy required to be implemented through local planning instruments. These arrangements are discussed in more detail in the following chapter.

What is metropolitan planning?

Planning for a metropolitan region is one form of regional planning. If broad based regional planning processes fell somewhat out of favour in Australia over the 1980s and 1990s, metropolitan planning largely continued in some form. Metropolitan plans are 'a strategic plan for managing change in urban regions' (Gleeson et al. 2004, p1). As well as their wider strategic scope, metropolitan plans often incorporate or are supported by 'positive planning levers' – programs of land purchase and the development of land by government agencies, generally in relation to large public infrastructure or facilities.

Figure 5.1: New development on Melbourne's fringe

Melbourne's Metropolitan Strategy 'Melbourne 2030' identifies a hierarchy of activity centres and new growth areas, surrounded by an urban boundary. Source: the Author 2003

The process of creating a metropolitan plan is similar to that of other strategic planning processes, proceeding from the identification of 'foundational principles': 'These principles include decisions as to: (i) governmental purpose, (ii) goal(s) for civil society, and (iii) consequences for strategic planning' (Gleeson et al. 2004, p4). Considerations in the development of the plan include the overall focus it will have – whether it will focus primarily on urban growth management or extend to other issues such as transportation, infrastructure or environmental protection; its spatial scope – how the metropolitan region will be defined; and the legal status of the plan – whether or not it will have legal status as a statutory planning instrument in its own right or have the status of a guiding document that must be consulted when relevant decisions are made. The responsibilities for implementing the plan and the arrangements for public involvement are also important considerations in its development (Gleeson et al. 2004).

The status of metropolitan planning in the Australian states and territories is summarised in Table 5.5.

Table 5.5: Metropolitan planning in the Australian states and territories, January 2011

State/territory	Metropolitan plan
ACT	*The Canberra spatial plan* (2004)
NSW	*Metropolitan plan for Sydney 2036* (2010)
NT	No formal arrangements for metropolitan planning
Qld	*South East Queensland regional plan 2009–2031* (2009)
SA	*The 30 year plan for greater Adelaide* (2010)
Tas.	No formal metropolitan planning arrangements
Vic.	*Melbourne 2030: planning for sustainable growth* (2002); updated by *Melbourne @5million* (2008)
WA	*Network city: community planning strategy for Perth and Peel* (2004)

It has been noted that metropolitan strategic planning experienced a resurgence during the 1990s, partly as an attempt to 'enhance city competitiveness under intensified globalisation using public-private partnerships, city marketing and other urban entrepreneurial activities' (Searle 2004, p367). Common policy directions contained in the contemporary generation of Australian metropolitan plans include the promotion of more intense urban and mixed development around transportation hubs like railway and bus interchanges, seeking a greater mix of housing types, such as townhouses and medium-density developments, even in new release areas (traditionally zoned for detached single family homes) and the promotion of affordable housing, encouraging more intense development within existing urban areas, through urban infill policies and the rehabilitation of under-utilised former industrial sites, and attempts to renew and revitalise aging middle and outer ring suburbs characterised by social disadvantage.

There are significant differences between the states and territories vis-à-vis the political will, specific opportunities for, and administrative capacity to support direct government involvement in positive metropolitan plan implementation through large-scale land acquisition, infrastructure investment and the definition of urban boundaries. As noted above, state and territory governments in Australia retain responsibility for approving statutory planning schemes made by local governments regarding the allocation of land uses. In relation to metropolitan expansion, this function is usually coordinated within state government, in theory, to establish strategic policies for the urban growth of the metropolitan region in the context of other state government priorities and decisions. However, in practice, even state government planning agencies have had limited influence over Treasury decisions regarding infrastructure funding, let alone the spatial policy decisions made by other state agencies responsible for transport, roads and other major services.

Therefore for the most part, metropolitan plan objectives are to be implemented by local planning authorities through their detailed statutory plan-making functions and primary role in assessing development applications. In many cases this muddled union of state and local governments makes metropolitan plans difficult to implement in practice. The two exceptions are Brisbane and Canberra (a city state), which are the only Australian metropolitan areas governed by single planning authorities (the Brisbane City Council and the ACT Planning and Land Authority). However, in the case of Brisbane, recent development in the surrounding South-East Queensland region mean that Brisbane may more accurately be understood as a '200-kilometre city', comprising the Brisbane City Council and a number of outer metropolitan councils (Spearitt 2010).

The emerging regional planning model in South-East Queensland includes a strong, funded infrastructure strategy, providing a significant means for overarching plan implementation. Nevertheless, while recognising the strength of the South-East Queensland integrated land use and infrastructure planning model, Brendan Gleeson and Wendy Steele observe:

> The provision of an accompanying regional infrastructure plan was another distinctive feature of the SEQ framework. It also at the same time, however, signalled the rise of infrastructure as a distinct planning modality. The rise and rise of this model, heightened by a national debate about infrastructure deficits, and reinforced by local political concern about growth pressures, may ultimately create an alternative planning force with the capacity to overwhelm and override land use, social and environmental considerations. (Gleeson & Steele 2010 p281)

Such concerns regarding the potential for infrastructure to shape, rather than support, strategic planning decisions, are likely to arise in other jurisdictions too, as Federal and state governments scramble to address major backlogs in infrastructure investment.

Government land development authorities

As part of the implementation of metropolitan plans, there has been a revival of interest in the strategic use of Government land development authorities. Originally established during the Whitlam era in the early 1970s, the land development authorities were intended to facilitate the release of new development areas. Through their land acquisition powers they provided an opportunity to ensure a steady stream of land to market in response to demand (Milligan 2003). As such it was anticipated that the land development authorities would help reduce land speculation and price inflation, maintaining housing supply and affordability. However, during the neoliberal era of the 1980s most land development authorities were recast as government enterprises required to meet commercial operating principles. This undermined their potential strategic influence on land supply and housing affordability, and some States abandoned the model altogether.

Figure 5.2: Welcome to Pentridge Village!

Melbourne's 2030, and subsequent update, Melbourne @ 5 million, emphasises urban renewal through the re-use of former industrial or government sites. As shown above, a former prison is being transformed into a medium-density housing development comprising villas and townhouses. Source: the Author 2003

In the past decade a new generation of government development agencies have emerged (Table 5.6). In many jurisdictions there are specific entities with responsibility for facilitating urban renewal and development, to meet metropolitan planning targets. Some of these, such as Queensland's Urban Land Development Authority, have specific land acquisition and development functions, while others, such as Melbourne's Growth Areas Authority, facilitate the planning and development process for major new release locations.

Local planning in the Australian states and territories

All of the states and territories use different terms to describe their planning instruments. However, while the language differs, in all jurisdictions a single, comprehensive land use plan, prepared under state planning legislation, establishes the development control framework for all or part of a local government area (Table 5.7).

Table 5.6: State/territorial government land development or redevelopment authorities

State/territory	Development/redevelopment authority	Role
ACT	ACT Land and Development Agency	Sells and develops land for ACT government
NSW	Landcom	Government land developer, manages redevelopment of former government sites
	Metropolitan Development Authority (incorporating the Redfern-Waterloo Development Authority)	Facilitates urban renewal in designated areas
NT	Northern Territory Land Development Corporation	Government land developer
Qld	Urban Land Development Authority	Acquires, develops and sells land in designated priority growth areas, coordinates planning framework
SA	South Australian Land Management Corporation	Manages and develops Government land assets
Tas.	n/a	
Vic.	VicUrban	Government land development agency
	Growth Areas Authority	Facilitates implementation of Melbourne 2030 through planning and coordination of designated growth areas
WA	Land Corps	Government land and property developer
	East Perth Redevelopment Authority	Special purpose redevelopment authority

These instruments are usually supplemented by more detailed local plans or policies, as well as higher-level state or regional requirements. When development proposals are assessed, these instruments provide the primary criteria for consideration, as detailed in the following chapter.

Development contributions for local infrastructure

There has been growing interest in Australian urban policy about the ways in which state and territorial planning systems coordinate and fund the infrastructure needed to support new development. In part this interest follows concern that cities and regions have suffered from under-investment in infrastructure over the past three decades, due to continued cutbacks in capital expenditure by governments. These cuts exemplified the shift towards neoliberal economic policies and were exacerbated by the impact of the recession in the 1990s (Nuetze 1995).

Table 5.7: Principal local land use planning instruments in the Australian states and territories

Jurisdiction	Principal local land use planning instruments
ACT	The Territory Plan 2008
NSW	Local environmental plans
NT	NT Planning Scheme enables subsidiary planning on local/area basis
Qld	Local planning schemes
SA	Development plans
Tas.	Local planning schemes
Vic.	Local planning schemes
WA	Local town planning schemes
	Regional schemes
	Development orders
Cwlth	n/a

Aside from direct government funding of infrastructure (through the general revenue stream generated by taxation, through borrowing, or at the local government level through rate revenue), two other basic approaches have been pursued to varying degrees in Australia. The first seeks to shift the costs of infrastructure provision to the end user, but upfront funding is still needed. This upfront funding could be provided by the private sector (which will seek to recoup their investment plus profits), by the public sector (which will need a source of up-front revenue), or through a public-private partnership. The second approach is to seek contributions from developers to pay for the shared or public infrastructure requirements associated with the development itself.

This approach emerged during the post World War Two years, when infrastructure shortages relative to demand beset the reconstruction boom. During this time developers offered to contribute to the costs of the basic services needed to facilitate growth – the provision of roads, drains, sewerage and water (Nuetze 1995, p225). These informal approaches were often formalised by state and territorial planning legislation during the 1980s and 1990s.

Each of the approaches to funding infrastructure (general government revenue, user charges and development contributions) can address different policy objectives (Table 5.8). It is therefore likely that a combination approach, leaning towards general government funding through revenue supported by a user-pays model that should be used sparingly (such as roads, water or energy) is optimal. This approach can then be supported by direct contributions for infrastructure that is closely related to the development and that needs to be provided in the most efficient way (Nuetze 1995). For instance, goals like social equity, public health or clean air would suggest an infrastructure funding model that promotes access to recreational areas and public transport, rather than possibly restricting their use through negative price signals. On the other hand, certain road infrastructure may increase road-based travel and so a user-pays model with strong price signals to recoup negative externalities for the environment and to promote transport alternatives makes policy sense. Clearly however, such a model is not compatible with a fully privatised approach to funding because it is not in the private operator's interest to deter the use of the infrastructure and thus reduce the user-pays funding stream.

Table 5.8: Summary of policy objectives underlying options for urban infrastructure provision in Australia

Approach	Objective
Government funding (general revenue)	Maximise access to and use of public good (e.g. recreation areas, footpaths/cycleways, public transport)
User pays (upfront funding, recouped from user charges)	Discourage use of resource associated with significant externalities (e.g. use of roads by private cars, reliance on non-renewable forms of energy, waste disposal rather than re-use or recycling)
Developer contributions	Provide basic services and infrastructure in efficient way
Development 'impact fees' *	Recoup costs associated with significant negative impacts/ externalities of private development

* Not currently used in Australia in a formal sense.

Finally, requiring developers to contribute to the infrastructure needed to support development – local roads, footpaths, utilities and so on, can promote an efficient development pattern (Nuetze 1995). To maximise this strategic approach, a strong policy framework is needed so developers cannot avoid contributions payments by incrementally 'tacking' onto existing infrastructure, such as linear roads. In this way, the developer contributions framework could ultimately provide a basis for encouraging and rewarding preferred urban forms that save energy, reduce the production of waste, and collect and recycle water, for example. At the same time, development that is associated with a particular negative impact could be required to offset this impact through specific development 'impact' fees, as discussed in chapter 3.

As noted, the international research finds that infrastructure contributions can facilitate urban development by enabling services to be provided upfront, and contribute to increased property values, when the facilities or amenities funded are of a high standard (Mathur et al. 2004). On the other hand, if fees are set too high relative to what the market will bear, or are not effectively utilised for local infrastructure and services, they can have a negative impact on development outcomes (Burge & Ihlanfeldt 2006).

Infrastructure funding and statutory planning in Australia

Opportunities to influence the selection of funding sources for infrastructure provision within the planning system itself in Australia are limited primarily to the developer contributions framework. Arrangements differ significantly throughout the Australian states and territories (Gurran et al. 2009). As shown in Table 5.9, key differences include the circumstances under which funds may be levied, and the purposes to which those funds may be put. Opportunities in SA are particularly narrow, focusing on open space and car parking, while in NSW development contributions can provide for a range of facilities and services, in some cases, including affordable housing. In the NT 'service authorities' such as local councils, may make a contribution plan under which developers are required, as a condition of planning consent, to contribute to car parking and other infrastructure. There are also provisions in the ACT to seek contributions from developers towards the cost of car parking.

Figure 5.3 Infill development and revitalisation in Kingston, Canberra's inner south

Canberra is seeking to revitalise its low density inner suburbs with a combination of medium-density housing and mixed use developments. Source: the Author 2011

Table 5.9 Provisions for infrastructure funding through the development planning process in the Australian states and territories, January 2011

State	Legislation	Description
ACT	*Planning and Development Act 2007*	Non-statutory means to charge for infrastructure or to levy a development infrastructure charge, provisions for change of use charge for variations of a Crown Lease that increase the value of the lease. Infrastructure provision can also be required as a condition of land release, with the cost offset against the amount paid for the lease.
NSW	*Environmental Planning & Assessment Act 1979 (EPAA)*	May require development contributions (cash or in kind) for services and infrastructure, subject to approved contributions plan (S94 EPAA). Must be allocated within LGA itself. May apply flat levy as percentage of proposed cost of development (1–3%). Capped to $20,000–$30,000 per residential lot unless ministerial approval for higher rate.
		Provisions for planning agreements between developers and consent authorities for developer contributions instead of or in addition to S94 contributions (s93F EPAA). Can be applied to a wider range of matters, including affordable housing or environmental conservation, and may be applied across local government areas.
		Additional infrastructure charges for regional infrastructure may be levied in designated 'contributions areas' (s94ED EPAA) declared by minister.
NT	*Planning Act 1999*	Service authorities may make contributions plans for infrastructure or public car parking. Infrastructure is defined as prescribed capital works, or works required as a condition of the development permit to be carried out (s67). ('Service authorities' are a territorial, local government, power or water corporation, or a statutory authority).
Qld	*Strategic Planning Act 2009*	Contributions for 'development infrastructure' may be levied by local councils (a) under a Priority Infrastructure Plan (PIP); (b) through an Infrastructure Agreement (an agreement between council and a developer for infrastructure provision or contributions); (c) conditions on the planning permit requiring the supply of non shared infrastructure (e.g. internal networks and connecting site to shared networks).
		PIP forms part of local planning scheme. Generally includes an Infrastructure Charges Schedule for levies. Low growth councils may use standard or 'Regulated' infrastructure charges. 'Development infrastructure' includes land or works for water, transport, local services (e.g. parks, community halls, libraries).
SA	*Development Act 1993* *Local Government Act 1999*	At time of land subdivision, provisions for dedicating up to 12% for open space (or cash contribution) as well as ceding access roads and contributions for hydraulic connections. Councils can also establish funds for developers to contribute to car parking at a fixed cash rate if this is preferable to on-site parking.
		Under the *LG Act 1999*, 'service rates' and 'service charges' might be used as indirect developer charges.

State	Legislation	Description
Tas.[1]	Land Use Planning and Approvals Act 1993	'Agreements', which may include provision for payment or other contribution for infrastructure, may be made between councils and developers, during development assessment (as a condition of consent); planning scheme provision amendment, or a special planning order. Agreements may be broad in scope, 'services, facilities, works and other uses and developments which provide the basis for meeting economic, social and environmental needs' (s70).
Vic.	Planning and Environment Act 1987	Developer contributions for either 'development infrastructure' or 'community infrastructure' levied through: (a) approved Development Contributions Plan (DCP), enforced through conditions attached to planning and building permits; (b) conditions on planning permits (but unless relating to a DCP these contributions must be works or infrastructure on site); (c) voluntary agreements (registered on title to land). Voluntary agreements may be used when a developer requests an amendment to a planning scheme, or a planning permit.
		Set levies restrict funds able to be collected through DCPs (e.g. $450 per residential dwelling for community infrastructure).
		State agencies may collect additional funds for specific works directly.
WA	Town Planning and Development Act 1928	Developer contributions usually levied through conditions imposed by the Western Australian Planning Commission (WAPC) on subdivision approvals.
		May also be levied through conditions imposed by WAPC or local government on the development of land under a regional or local government scheme.
		Three types of contributions: (a) ceding or dedication of land for roads, primary schools, public open space (10% of development), foreshores, drainage, and other reserves needed for subdivision; (b) construction of infrastructure and transfer to public authorities; (c) contributions to acquire land or undertake works by public authorities). Process predominantly regulated through WAPC operational policies.
		Social infrastructure generally not funded through this process.

Source: adapted from Gurran et al. 2009, Productivity Commission 2009

In establishing the arrangements for local authorities to levy funds from developers towards infrastructure needs and services in Australia, the emphasis to date has been the provision of local facilities. While this emphasis remains in the majority of jurisdictions, new provisions in NSW, Victoria and Queensland, extend this framework to enable the state government considerable powers to seek developer contributions that can be applied to a wide range of purposes (Gurran et al. 2009). This contrast reflects the debates regarding seeking infrastructure contributions through the planning system versus alternative

---

1 Tasmania's *Water and Sewerage Industry Act 2008* will provide an additional framework for infrastructure charging, once operational.

approaches such as user-pays or direct government investment. Clearly, some states have made a deliberate decision to limit the ability of local government to seek development contributions through the planning process, partly due to concern regarding the potential impact of contribution requirements on housing affordability and development activity.

Specialist planning courts and tribunals

Each of the jurisdictions has specialist courts or tribunals to administer and support environmental and planning legislation, shown in Table 5.10.

In general, jurisdictions enable applicants to appeal a refusal to grant development approval, or the conditions of this approval. Opportunities for third party appeals (by parties who are neither the applicant or decision-maker) vary across jurisdictions. As well as disputes, the courts can prosecute breaches of planning laws. These arrangements are discussed further in the following chapter.

Table 5.10 Planning appeal bodies, Australian states and territories, January 2011

Jurisdiction	Planning appeal body
ACT	ACT Administrative Appeals Tribunal
NSW	NSW Land and Environment Court
NT	Lands, Planning and Mining Tribunal
Qld	Planning and Environment Court
SA	Environment, Resources and Development Court
Tas.	Resource Management and Planning Appeals Tribunal
Vic.	Victorian Civil and Administrative Tribunal
WA	State Administrative Tribunal

Summary and conclusions

This chapter has compared the administrative and legal frameworks of Australia's state and territorial planning systems. A key jurisdictional difference to emerge in this review is the extent to which the states and territories have articulated comprehensive state policy frameworks. While Victoria, Western Australia and South Australia have established comprehensive state policy frameworks, the other jurisdictions have provisions for specific issues of state or territorial significance. Another distinction relates to regional planning approaches. While metropolitan planning is undertaken across the majority of state capital cities, non-metropolitan regional planning is most advanced in Queensland, where strong voluntary and collaborative processes for regional strategic planning have been established over the past 15 years. In Queensland, South Australia and Western Australia, statutory regional plans are in operation. NSW has recently undergone a process of developing non-statutory regional strategies that will ultimately inform new local plans.

The chapter also reviewed the different approaches to development contributions across Australia. These arrangements are set to become a more significant component of Australian urban policy. Finally, the different structures for specialist environmental courts and tribunals were outlined. The next three chapters continue the examination of Australian planning systems in greater detail.

Figure 5.4: Community infrastructure, St Kilda Library, Victoria

Source: the Author 2002

Chapter 6

Systems for plan-making, development assessment and planning appeals in the Australian states and territories

There are many similarities in approaches to plan-making, development assessment and dispute resolution across the Australian states and territories. For instance, most jurisdictions use land use zoning as the main form of development control. But there are also distinct differences, particularly in relation to the various layers associated with plan-making and development assessment. Further, the terminology used in each jurisdiction and approaches to development standards and criteria is unique.

This chapter provides a comparative overview of these arrangements, building on the comparison of state planning laws, regional and metropolitan planning arrangements and infrastructure contribution systems discussed in the previous chapter. The summary of systems and processes in each jurisdiction is deliberately brief; the intention is to provide a basis for comparing and understanding the key features of each system rather than to provide a comprehensive operational guide.

Overview of state and territorial planning systems

The legal framework for planning across the states and territories was set out in the previous chapter and legislation summarised in Table 5.2. Each jurisdiction has their own terminology to describe particular elements of the planning system – from land use plans to development application and decision processes.

Planning and development in the Australian Capital Territory

The Australian Capital Territory (ACT) has a unique planning and land management system because of its special status as the nation's capital city and role in accommodating the seat of government. In contrast to the other Australian jurisdictions, land in the ACT is owned by the Commonwealth and subject to a leasehold system. This system was established when the national capital was founded during the early years of Federation. The leasehold system was devised to discourage the rampant land speculation that had already beset cities such as Sydney and Melbourne (House of Representatives 1997). Conditions on leases were intended to better manage and control the development process.

The Commonwealth Government's responsibility for the planning and development of Canberra was exercised via a series of commissions, departments and advisory committees until the ACT achieved self government in 1988. Following self government, the *Australian Capital Territory (Planning and Land Management) Act 1988* established a dual system for planning and land management. All land in the ACT was divided into 'National Land' and 'Territory Land'. Any land not gazetted as National land was transferred to the ACT executive to manage as Territory land, using the leasehold system of land administration.

Figure 6.1 Medium-density development on Canberra's urban fringe

In recent years metropolitan planning strategies have emphasised the need for a diversity of housing types, including attached and medium-density housing, in new release as well as in existing, infill contexts. This complex is situated on the edge of Canberra's northern fringe, and is part of a larger suburban precinct comprising a mix of attached row houses, townhouses, detached dwellings on small allotments, and apartments. Source: the Author 2011

Today the dual planning system consists of two planning organisations, the National Capital Authority and the ACT Planning and Land Authority.

The National Capital Authority has responsibility for the Commonwealth government's ongoing involvement in the planning and development of Canberra. The National Capital Plan sets out the planning principles and policies for Canberra and the Territory, and detailed conditions of planning, design and development for areas that because of their particular importance to the special character of the national capital, are known as

'Designated areas'. Planning and approval of development ('works') within Designated Areas is the responsibility of the National Capital Authority.

The ACT Planning and Land Authority (ACTPLA) has responsibility, through the Territory Plan for setting the land use policies and approving development for all areas of the ACT, with the exception of 'Designated Areas' and 'National Land' – (that is, the land retained by the Commonwealth for its own purposes). Policies of the Territory Plan must be consistent with the broad land use policies set out in the National Capital Plan. Commonwealth and Territory planning and land management responsibilities partially intersect on National Land sites beyond Designated Areas, which are subject to a Development Control Plan. Although the National Capital Authority retains planning and development approval responsibilities for these sites, the Development Control Plan must comply with both the provisions of the National Capital Plan and the Territory Plan.

The *Planning and Development Act 2007* is the Territory's principle planning legislation. It defines three classes of development: development which is 'exempt'; development which is 'assessable'; and development which is 'prohibited'. The Territory Plan includes a zoning system with tables for determining which development fits into these categories according to location. It also contains a series of codes with development standards for particular development types and locations. Most developments require both development and building approval from ACTPLA, although 'exempt' development is generally low impact and does not require specific approval.

Private sector building certifiers are able to approve building applications for dwellings that meet development exemption criteria, for instance, single dwellings meeting the requirements of the relevant precinct code (if any) and the Residential Zones Single Dwelling House Development Code of the Territory Plan.

'Assessable' development is reviewed according to one of three categories. 'Code' assessed development must be approved if it complies with all applicable rules contained in the relevant Assessment Code of the Territory Plan. 'Merit' applications are assessed against the relevant code, and may be approved even if they are non conforming, provided that they meet all relevant Territory Plan criteria, including zone objectives. Merit applications must be publicly notified and public representations are considered during their assessment. The notification requirements depend on the nature of the proposal.

'Impact' applications are assessed against the relevant rules and merit criteria of the Territory Plan, as well as an Environmental Impact Statement (EIS) (unless exempted by the minister for planning). They are required to be publicly notified, and to be referred to relevant public agencies for advice. Public inquiries may be held for impact assessable applications. In determining an impact assessable application, the authority must be satisfied that the proposal satisfies the 'intent, objectives and Statement of Strategic Directions of the Territory Plan' (ACT Planning and Land Authority 2007, p11).

The process for preparing an EIS in the ACT is as follows. Firstly, the proponent requests a scoping document from ACTPLA. In consultation with relevant public authorities, ACTPLA defines the range of matters to be covered in the EIS, which is then prepared by the proponent. The EIS is then publicly exhibited, revised by the proponent in response to any submissions, then considered by ACTPLA, who seeks to resolve any further outstanding issues. Finally, the decision is referred to the minister for approval.

Merit and impact assessable applications must be determined within 30 days if they attract no public representations, and 45 days, if public submissions are received.

While the ACT has shifted in recent years towards the zoning system within the Territory Plan just described, the unique system of leasehold land continues to influence land use and development. This leasehold system of land tenure establishes development rights through lease purpose clauses rather than the range of uses permissible in a particular zone, unlike planning schemes that operate under a freehold system (David Wright, pers. com. June 2011). This system also enables the ACT government to collect contributions for local infrastructure via a change of use charge when lease conditions are amended to permit more intense development. In this way, the ACT's system for development contributions might be described as a system for 'betterment tax' since the charge is linked to value uplift arising from the new use.

Public consultation varies considerably between the two jurisdictions. The *ACT (Planning and Land Management) Act* 1988 sets out the process for preparing, administering and subsequently amending the National Capital Plan. There is no statutory requirement for consultation in respect of works approval. In contrast, the ACT Planning and Land Authority is subject to considerable public consultation obligations. Mandatory public consultation obligations for plan making and development assessments are set out in the *Planning and Development Act 2007*. ACTPLA also engage the Canberra community extensively in preparing plans from the strategic level to more location specific studies such as Master Plans for various commercial centres.

Reviews of planning decisions are heard by the ACT Administrative Appeals Tribunal. Applicants may appeal a refusal or the terms of conditions. There are 'third party' appeal rights (the right to appeal even if not directly a party to the decision as the applicant or the consent authority) for impact and merit track applications undergoing the major notification process (ie. a sign on the property, letters to neighbours, and advertisement in a newspaper).

Managing the interface between Commonwealth and Territorial planning interests has proved challenging. In 2008 a Commonwealth Parliamentary Inquiry on planning in the ACT recommend better integrating the dual planning system and removing the hierarchical relationship between the planning authorities. In particular different opinions arise over 'the strategic metropolitan planning for Canberra … and … 'matters of national significance" (The Parliament of Australia 2008, p156). Such tensions over Commonwealth interference in matters of national planning significance in the ACT echo intergovernmental skirmishes between state and local governments in the other jurisdictions as discussed in the following sections.

Environmental planning and assessment in New South Wales

Environmental planning and development assessment in New South Wales (NSW) is managed under the *Environmental Planning and Assessment Act 1979* and associated Environmental Planning and Assessment Regulation 2000. There is a tiered system of statutory planning instruments, including State Environmental Planning Policies, Local Environmental Plans, and Development Control Plans. Local Environmental Plans assign permissable uses across a local government area, through land use zones, while more detailed design criteria is contained in Development Control Plans. A Standard Instrument set by the state governs the format and content of Local Environmental Plans.

Development is categorised by the need for consent, and the level of assessment required. A broad threefold distinction is set out in the *Environmental Planning and Assessment Act 1979*: development which does not need consent, development which needs consent, and prohibited development. Development which does not need consent includes minor works, known as 'exempt' development, as well as certain types of public works. Development which needs consent includes 'complying development', which must be approved if it meets the relevant requirements; and other development considered on merit against the requirements of the applicable state and local environmental planning instruments and development control plans, as well as public submissions.

Changes to the Act in June 2011 introduced two new categories of development: State Significant Development and State Significant Infrastructure. Criteria for state significance relates to the type of development, its capital value, or its location on a site of significance to the state.

Certain types of development designated in the Environmental Planning and Assessment Regulation 2000 require an Environmental Impact Statement. Like in the ACT, the requirements for the EIS are set by the state planning department. State Significant Developments and Infrastructure also undergo an environmental impact assessment process.

Most applications are determined by local councils, but minor (complying development) applications may be certified by private certifiers. Joint Regional Planning Panels determine more significant matters including development with a capital value over $20 million; certain developments by public authorities and councils, some types of private infrastructure, some coastal and ecotourism developments. The minister for planning is the consent authority for State Significant Development and Infrastructure but consent powers for private development of state significance has been delegated to an independent Planning Assessment Commission. The Planning Assessment Commission also provides advice to the minister on a range of other matters and is able to undertake public inquiries.

Public consultation occurs in relation to most development applications (with the exception of complying development) and, usually, when local plans are made. In all cases there is a mandatory exhibition period during which time written submissions regarding the plan or proposal may be lodged with the relevant authority.

Appeals to the NSW Land and Environment Court may be made by applicants whose development is refused or 'deemed' refused (when a decision is not made within certain timeframes specified by the legislation in relation to types of application). Applicants may also appeal conditions of development approval. Third party appeal rights are limited in NSW predominantly to development that is subject to the environmental impact assessment process. In these cases the appellant needs to have lodged an objection within the specified time.

The NSW planning process has undergone significant reform over the past five years as outlined in the following chapters. A new planning Act is anticipated by the end of 2012.

Development planning and environmental assessment in the Northern Territory

The Northern Territory Department of Lands and Planning is responsible for developing land use policies and strategic plans for local areas. The Northern Territory Planning Scheme is the main instrument for assessing development applications. It consists of zones, policies and development assessment criteria. Interim Development Control Orders may be made for areas subject to the preparation of a planning scheme amendment.

Development consent is required for land subdivision or consolidations and in other situations specified by the Northern Territory Planning Scheme. Building certification is generally required for matters not requiring a planning permit. Applications must be consistent with the requirements set out in the Northern Territory Planning Scheme, unless special ministerial approval is gained. A public environmental report or Environmental Impact Statement may be required under the Northern Territory *Environmental Assessment Act*, to support the application.

Development applications must be made to the Development Consent Authority, or to the minister for planning and lands, depending on the area (Department of Planning and Infrastructure n.d.). The Development Consent Authority is a five-member panel appointed by the minister following the *Northern Territory Planning Act* (s82). The authority contains seven divisions which correspond to the larger population centres of the Northern Territory (Alice Springs, Batchelor, Darwin, Katherine, Litchfield, Palmerston and Tennant Creek), with provisions for local authority representatives to sit on the relevant division.

Planning scheme amendments require public hearings and these are conducted by the Development Consent Authority which makes recommendations to the planning minister. Individuals may request a planning scheme amendment.

Applicants for development permission may appeal within 28 days against a refusal to grant the permit or the conditions of the permit. An applicant may also appeal if the Development Consent Authority has not determined the application within 12 weeks. Third-party appeal rights are available in certain circumstances but generally only for matters within residential zones. Appeals are heard by the Lands, Planning and Mining Tribunal.

Sustainable planning in Queensland

Queensland's planning system, established under the *Sustainable Planning Act 2009*, is referred to as 'Qplan'. The 2009 Act continued Queensland's existing development assessment process, known as the 'Integrated Development Assessment System' (IDAS). The system is described as 'integrated' because it covers approvals for almost all development in Queensland, aside from some mining and petroleum related activities (managed under the *Environment Protection Act 1994*) and certain urban development areas covered by the *Urban Land Development Act 2007* (Department of Infrastructure and Planning 2009). The *Plumbing and Drainage Act 2002* also covers a number of matters relating to local development in Queensland.

Qplan includes plan making arrangements at state and local levels, with standard provisions for local planning schemes. Regional planning is a state government responsibility but undertaken on a cooperative basis between state and local governments, through regional planning committees.

As noted in chapter five, state planning instruments inform plan making and development assessment in Queensland. They prevail over local planning instruments, to the extent of any inconsistency. There are four types of state planning instrument. State Planning Regulatory Provisions can support regional plans, master plans, and infrastructure charging arrangements. Regional Plans are prepared by state government and have statutory weight. State Planning Policies provide a basis for addressing significant policy areas in a consistent way. Standard Planning Scheme Provisions establish the framework for new local planning schemes. They contain both mandatory and non mandatory provisions, definitions, land use zones and overlays.

Local planning schemes are the main instruments against which development applications are considered. They are generally made by local government, but the minister for planning may also make or amend planning schemes. Local planning schemes are intended to have a 20 year planning horizon, but to be updated after a new regional plan is made (Department of Infrastructure and Planning 2009) and must be reviewed every 10 years. As well as incorporating the standard planning scheme provisions, new schemes prepared under the *Sustainable Planning Act 2009*, must identify strategic outcomes and measures to achieve them; and must co-ordinate and integrate 'core matters' relating to land use, development, infrastructure, and valuable features of the local area. Priority Infrastructure Plans are prepared by local government. They are included in local planning schemes to identify infrastructure requirements to support development. Public consultation processes must be followed when local planning schemes are made or amended. Planning scheme policies can support local planning schemes and provide a basis for greater consistency in relation to certain decisions.

Temporary Local Planning Instruments can be prepared to protect an area from 'adverse impacts', provided that the minister is satisfied that there is a risk of serious harm to the environment, and that any delay in making or amending a full scheme would increase this risk.

Other types of plans under the *Strategic Planning Act 2009* include 'master plans' and 'structure plans'. These plans, which contain more detail for specific areas, can be made in a collaborative process involving state, local government, and the private sector. Declared master plan areas are identified in local planning schemes or a regional plan. Structure plans may set out the strategic planning intent for these declared master planned areas and form part of the planning scheme made by local governments. A master plan may contain more detailed information, accommodate significant private involvement in its preparation, and include categories and codes for specific development and a schedule for development completion.

Local governments are generally the authority responsible for deciding proposals, although other referral agencies may have involvement role in assessing proposals. Referral agencies are usually, but not always, state agencies.

The IDAS approach is described as a 'performance based' system because it generally allows almost any proposal to be considered on its merits. The performance-based approach sets standards that describe the desired end result (through the setting of acceptable limits) rather than the prescriptive zoning of land uses in a hierarchy based on land types (Department of Infrastructure and Planning 2008, p1).

There are several categories of development. 'Exempt' development needs no planning approval, and no application is required. 'Self assessable' development must comply with set assessment criteria, but needs no application. The developer has responsibility for checking compliance with these criteria, which operate like conditions of approval. 'Compliance assessable' development requires only a compliance permit to proceed, rather than a full development permit. 'Assessable development' needs a development permit, and may require additional code assessment and or impact assessment processes. Applications for 'prohibited' development may not be made.

Following the application lodgement itself, the development assessment and approval process usually follows four stages These are identified in the IDAS process and include the Application Stage, the Information and Referral Stage, the Notification Stage (for development requiring impact assessment) and the Decision Stage. During the Information Stage, the assessment manager seeks additional information if necessary and refers the application to relevant authorities for their concurrence (agreement that the application may be approved) or advice, if required. If the development is classed as impact assessable, it must be publicly notified. Following consideration of submissions, a decision is made (to approve, to approve with conditions, or to refuse). Once the development permit is issued and the appeal period has expired, the land use may commence, and a process of monitoring compliance with any conditions of approval begins.

If an Environmental Impact Statement is needed under the *Strategic Planning Act 2009*, this is usually requested as an information request at the Application Stage. Environmental impact assessment requirements are prescribed under regulation. In common with other jurisdictions, the terms of reference for a specific project are set on a case by case basis (by the Chief Executive of the planning department) and these terms are publicly notified.

When the terms are finalised, the proponent prepares an Environmental Impact Statement (EIS). This EIS is then publicly exhibited, and may be amended following exhibition to reflect submissions or government agency advice. The proponent then submits the EIS to the department, which may require additional matters to be addressed before issuing its decision.

The planning minister has reserve direction powers to intervene in this process. The state government (the planning minister, the minister for the region in question, or the minister for state development and public works) may call in matters or decide applications under certain circumstances involving a state interest.

Most jurisdictions require development proposals to be publicly notified via a newspaper advertisement, and a sign on the site itself. The sign will contain details about where the development proposal may be inspected, and the closing date for any public submissions.

Figure 6.1: Public notification of a development in Brisbane

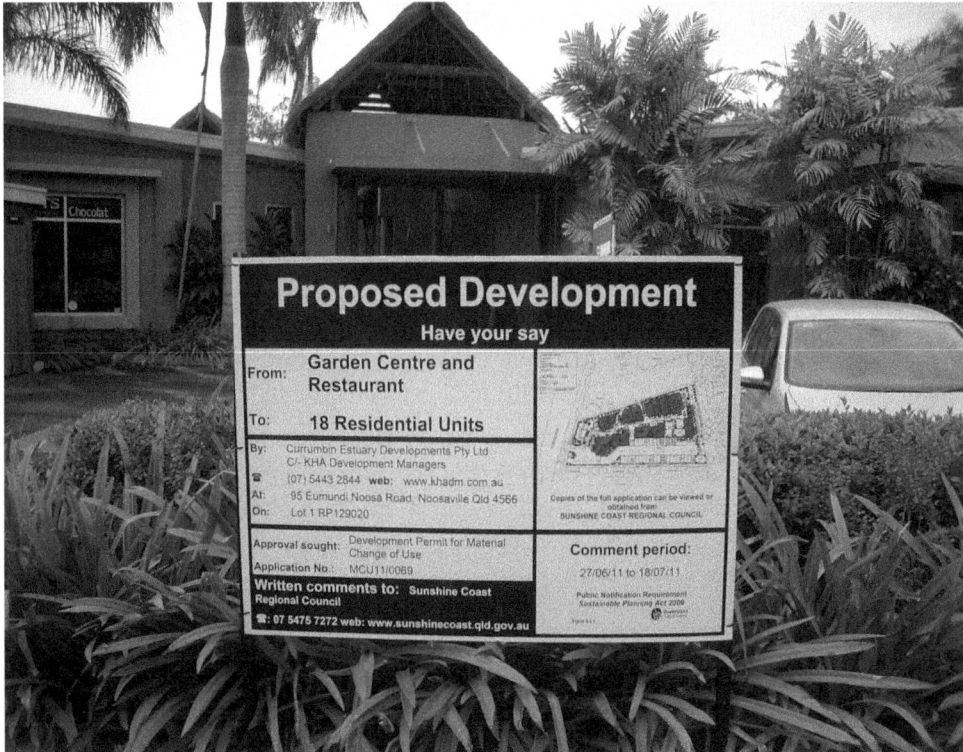

Source: Robin King Cullen 2011

Third party appeal rights are available for development that is publicly exhibited (or notified) and subject to impact assessment (which means the development cannot simply be considered against the standards contained within a code or codes, but must be considered against the whole of the planning scheme). Appeals are made to the Queensland Planning and Environment Court. Third party appeal rights are only available under criteria established by the *Sustainable Planning Act 2009*. A submission must have been properly made during the notification period for third party appeal rights to arise. Third party appeal rights do not apply to conditions or directions issued by a concurrence agency. Some development decisions may be appealed to Building and Development Dispute Resolution Committees.

Development planning in South Australia

The framework for urban planning and development assessment in South Australia is established by the *Development Act 1993* and the Development Regulations 2008. Within this framework, the South Australian Planning Strategy provides state government direction on land use and development. The 2010 Plan for Greater Adelaide is incorporated as a 'volume' of the South Australian Planning Strategy, and is oriented towards a 30 year planning horizon for the greater Adelaide metropolitan region. The minister for planning must report annually to parliament about the implementation of the Planning Strategy, which is supported by the Strategic Infrastructure Plan for South Australia, the Housing Plan for South Australia and the South Australian Greenhouse Strategy.

Development plans set out the land use and development control framework for local areas. Land use zones are used to classify permissible types of development, and 'policies' set out standards and criteria for assessing development proposals. Development plans can be amended through a process initiated by a local council or the minister for planning. The process includes a period for public consultation. Development Plan amendments must be approved by the minister.

The *Development Act 1993* and Regulations 'call up' the South Australian Housing Code (which contains the building rules and standards for dwellings and is read in conjunction with the relevant development plan).

As in many of the other Australian jurisdictions, there has been a trend in South Australia to increase the number of 'complying' developments, which are generally small scale proposals which must be approved if they comply with stated criteria. For instance, the new Residential Development Code was introduced in March 2009 and applies to alterations and additions to existing homes and to small 'backyard structures' (Government of South Australia 2009, p2).

Most development applications are determined by local councils, but a number of matters are assessed by an independent Development Assessment Commission (DAC). These include applications relating to land subdivision; waste management or disposal; certain development in key areas of the state or presenting significant regional impact, applications for development by the state housing authority (Housing SA) and the government's land development authority (the Land Management Corporation); and specified development by councils or involving council land (Development Assessment Commission 2007). Large development applications within the City of Adelaide are now also referred to the DAC, and local councils may also request that the DAC be the assessing authority for a particular application in their area. In addition, the DAC assesses and advises the minister on all crown or public infrastructure development.

Development is categorised as 'complying'; 'non complying' and 'assessed on merit', according to potential impact and consent requirements. Applicants must seek both development plan consent (approval against the provisions set out in the local development plan) and building rules consent (approval against relevant building codes and standards, including the Building Code of Australia). These consents are required before the council can issue final development approval.

Independent Assessment Panels have been established to increase the impartiality and consistency of decision making. The panels are appointed by Council and must include a specialist, independent presiding member, three other specialists and or independent members, and up to three elected councillors or staff. Panels typically consist of seven members, but the Act allows for five or nine member panels in certain circumstances. Elected council councillors must always be in the minority. There is also provision for councils to establish a regional Development Assessment Panel.

There is a special assessment procedure for proposals which are declared by the minister for urban development and planning to be a Major Development, because of economic, social or environmental significance. Once the proposal is declared a Major Development, it is referred to the Development Assessment Commission for it to determine the level of assessment required and to issue Assessment Guidelines. Three levels of assessment are possible: an Environmental Impact Statement for the most complex proposals; a Public Environmental Report, where issues require some investigation but are more clearly defined; and a Development Report for less complex matters.

The assessment documents are released for public comment and submissions. Environmental Impact Statements and Public Environmental Reports must be exhibited for at least six weeks, and a public meeting must be held near the site of the development. Development Reports are exhibited for at least three weeks.

Following this process, the proponent responds to public and state agency comments. The minister then assesses the proposal and prepares an Assessment Report, which is submitted to the state governor for determination. The Development Assessment Commission may determine some major developments on delegation.

There has been a trend for the planning minister to make increased use of these powers to remove development applications regarded to be of state significance, out of local council jurisdiction. New provisions for identifying state significant projects and state significant areas (such as complex redevelopment sites to be planned by state government) are being considered.

Appeals against planning decisions are made to the Environment, Resources and Development Court. Applicants may appeal an unfavourable decision or conditions of consent, while third party appeal rights are available for certain classes of decision providing the application was publicly notified and the third party appellant lodged a formal objection or representation (Steven Hamnett, pers. com. 16 June 2011). Decisions by the governor are not subject to appeal.

Commenting on the South Australian government's increasing tendency to become engaged in metropolitan planning matters, including climate change, an aging population, housing supply and affordability, Stephen Hamnett and Alan Hutchings describe an increasingly interventionist state:

> indicated by its direct involvement in urban redevelopment in transport corridors; its unapologetic use of its *Development Act* and other powers to take control of more broadly defined 'state significant developments'; and a reduction in the discretionary powers which local governments have at present to regulate development within their areas. These changes may mark the end of the trend encouraged by successive state governments since the early 1980s towards a partnership role for local government in planning matters. Certainly, they redefine the terms of that partnership. (Hamnett and Hutchings 2009, p280)

Land use planning and approvals in Tasmania

Land use planning in Tasmania is primarily undertaken under the Resource Management and Planning System (RMPS). The aim of the RMPS is to achieve sustainable outcomes from the use and development of the state's natural and physical resources. The concept of sustainable development provides overall direction for the RMPS and is given expression in a set of objectives common to all Acts within the system. The Tasmanian Planning Commission has the major responsibility for the RMPS which is largely constructed by the *Land Use Planning and Approvals Act 1993*, the *State Policies and Projects Act 1993*, and the *Tasmanian Planning Commission Act 1997*. The Commission sets the strategic and statutory framework for planning, holds inquiries, and assesses major projects and proposals involving the use of public land. The commission also advises the minister for planning and local councils about land use planning matters (Tasmanian Planning Commission 2011).

State policies relevant to land use planning in Tasmania are made under the *State Policies and Projects Act 1993*, and are intended to address matters of state significance in a consistent and coordinated way. There are currently three specific state policies addressing coastal issues, water quality, and agricultural land. The 'national environment protection measures' issued by the Commonwealth Environment Protection and Heritage Council (described in chapter five) are also deemed state policies in Tasmania. The Act also provides for the Governor to declare major development proposals as Projects of State Significance. Such developments are assessed under Part 3 of the *State Policies and Approvals Act 1993*. Criteria for state significance relate to capital investment, economic impact, environmental impact, technical complexity, and infrastructure requirements. Six state significant projects have been declared since commencement of the Act.

The *Land Use Planning and Approvals Act 1993* (LUPAA) establishes the basis for preparing and amending planning schemes and interim planning schemes, assessing development applications, appeals against planning decisions, and agreements for the provision of infrastructure to support a development. Under the Act, planning directives can establish a basis for addressing land use issues, applying across all municipal areas in the state or to only some municipal areas. Currently, there is only Planning Directive No. 1: The Common Key Elements Template. This directive establishes the template as the mandatory format and structure for all new planning schemes.

Local governments in Tasmania prepare planning schemes which articulate the strategic objectives for the area, allocate lands to particular zones, and establish performance criteria for the type of use and development permitted within particular zones and circumstances. In some planning schemes, precincts may be defined which break zones down to allow for more detailed criteria to be adopted in relation to the development controls that are applied. Overlays can also be used to add additional controls or to modify those in place over the top of zones and precincts. Overlays usually relate to areas where special planning considerations or requirements need to apply, such as height controls or noise exposure forecasts for airports, bushfire or flood protection and vegetation protection.

Planning permits are required for most forms of development. Local planning schemes establish whether a permit is needed and the criteria and requirements for development assessment. Planning schemes categorise types of development according to whether they are permitted as a right, may be permitted subject to a discretionary decision of council, or whether the development is prohibited. Developers may simultaneously lodge a development application and a request for a planning scheme amendment. In this case, following the public exhibition of the proposal, council's assessment and any public submissions are forwarded to the Tasmanian Planning Commission, which is responsible for approving new and amended planning schemes.

Applicants may appeal a council decision to refuse an application, or the conditions imposed, within 14 days of receiving the decision. Third party appeal rights apply to a person who has made a written objection to a discretionary development application during the 14 day exhibition period. Again, the appeal must be lodged within 14 days of the decision. Appeals for matters under the *Land Use Planning and Approvals Act 1993* are heard by the Resource Management and Planning Appeals Tribunal (RMPAT).

Recent legislative amendments have created a new planning process under which regionally significant projects can be assessed by Development Assessment Panels. These panels are primarily comprised of experts but also provide for regional representation. The Development Assessment Panel makes the final decision in relation to a Project of Regional Significance, with no right of appeal to RMPAT. Reforms have also established a framework for regional land use and infrastructure plans, which seek to guide settlement patterns and infrastructure investment across the three regions of Tasmania (North, Northwest, and Southern Tasmania). Implementation of these regional-scale plans is intended to be primarily through local government planning schemes.

There are also some areas of development activity that are largely outside the RMPS: forestry operations on land declared as a private timber reserve under the *Forest Practices Act 1985*; mineral exploration in accordance with a mining lease, exploration or retention licence issued under the *Mineral Resources Development Act 1995*; fishing; and marine farming in state waters. However, plans made by the Tasmanian Parks and Wildlife Service under the *National Parks and Reserves Management Act 2002* are subject to the RMPS and are assessed and approved by the Tasmanian Planning Commission.

Planning and environmental assessment in Victoria

The legal framework for planning in Victoria is established by the *Planning and Environment Act 1987* and its associated regulations, the *Planning and Environment Regulations 2005* and the *Planning and Environment (Fees) Interim Regulations 2011*. Statutory planning provisions are established at state and local planning levels. The Victorian Planning Provisions (known as the VPPs) contain the standard provisions for local planning schemes in Victoria. The VPPs establish a structure for local schemes and a set of operational mechanisms for inclusion such as standard zones, overlays for development control and definitions. They also include an overarching state planning policy framework which covers matters including the built and natural environment, landscape and heritage, economic development, housing, transport and infrastructure.

A tailored local planning policy framework allows for more strategic direction for the local area. Planning schemes can formally adopt or include any other document relating to the use or protection of land as well, providing a statutory basis for these documents to be consulted when decisions are made. These are called 'incorporated documents'.

Local planning schemes provide the main instrument for categorising and assessing land use and development in Victoria. Zoning provisions control land according to uses that do not require a permit, those that require a permit, and prohibited uses. Zoning overlays can specify additional information or assessment requirements. Developments which are publicly notified must be exhibited for at least 14 days, and objections to proposals may be lodged during this period. Generally, owners and residents of adjoining land are notified of development applications and have a right to make a representation to the planning authority.

Planning schemes and planning scheme amendments must be approved by the minister for planning, following a public notification and consultation process which usually includes a hearing of the matter before Planning Panels Victoria.

Local councils are the main consent authority, responsible for assessing land use and development applications and issuing planning permits. Many planning permits can be approved by council officers under delegation. Major projects or projects where there are unresolved objections are decided by a council committee or the full council. There is a 60-day period to assess applications before an applicant is able to apply to the Planning and Environment List at the Victorian Civil and Administrative Tribunal (VCAT) on the basis of a 'deemed refusal'.

If there are no objections to a proposal, a planning permit may be issued directly. However, in cases where there are objections to a proposal that the council has decided to approve, it must issue a 'Notice of decision to grant a permit', signalling council's intention to allow the development to proceed, and outlining the conditions of approval. Objectors then have 21 days in which to lodge an application for review of the decision to VCAT.

The minister for planning is able to appoint independent planning panels and advisory committees, and to provide for environmental assessment inquiries. Planning panels are convened to consider planning scheme amendments, and to review planning permit applications associated with scheme amendments or being assessed by the minister. Planning panels consist of independent experts who consider public submissions about proposals and provide advice to the minister through a panel report (reports available at www.dpcd.vic.gov.au/planning/panelsandcommittees/reports).

Advisory committees are appointed to provide advice on particular planning policy areas, review specific development proposals, or matters 'called in' by the minister from the VCAT. They are constituted by a terms of reference, and are able to hold public hearings to elicit public input. The Priority Development Panel has been established to provide expert advice on facilitating strategic planning outcomes and to speed up approval processes.

Development assessment committees are independent statutory bodies to determine projects of metropolitan significance. They relate to specific 'activity areas' of the Melbourne metropolitan region (which are areas defined for their accessibility to transport and concentration, or potential concentration, of commercial and other activities). The development assessment committees include five members with an independent chair, and two members nominated by the minister for planning and the local council.

The *Environmental Effects Act 1978* provides the basis for managing proposals with significant potential environmental impacts. Such projects are referred to the minister for planning to determine whether an environmental effects statement (EES) is needed. If required, a scoping document is issued by the minister, and finalised following a period of public and agency comment. Proponents are then responsible for preparing the EES, and for undertaking public consultation, according to a time schedule agreed with the Department for Planning and Community Development. To provide technical advice to the department and to the proponents responsible for preparing the EES, a Technical Reference Group is usually convened. This group comprises members from state, regional and local agencies. The EES is then exhibited for 20–30 days, during which time public submissions may be made. The minister may convene an environmental assessment inquiry to consider the proposal and any public submissions, before making a final assessment. This assessment is then provided to government decision-makers, who are responsible for making the final determination (Department of Sustainability and Environment 2011).

Planning and development in Western Australia

The Western Australian planning system includes an overarching state strategy, a central-ised statutory regional planning process, and local planning schemes. Planning functions are divided between the minister for planning, the Western Australian Planning Commis-sion (WAPC) and the state government Department of Planning. The WAPC is responsible for policy development and planning decisions, while the department provides professional support. Planning regulation occurs at three levels – the minister for planning, the WAPC, and local government. The minister for planning oversees planning agencies and reviews regional and local planning schemes. The WAPC determines all subdivision applications, administers regional planning schemes, and makes recommendations to the minister. Local government prepares and administers local planning schemes and strategies, and determines some planning decisions under delegation.

Planning controls in WA include a hierarchy of state, regional and local instruments. State planning instruments include the state planning strategy, a comprehensive document providing overarching principles and strategies for action, a Statement of Planning Policy suite and Development Control Policies, used to establish a basis for addressing particular matters in a consistent way, and regional planning schemes which provide a statutory mechanism to coordinate the provision of major infrastructure and set aside areas for regional open space. For instance, the Perth Metropolitan Region Scheme includes a financial dimension (called the Metropolitan Region Improvement Fund) which requires developers to contribute towards public land reservation during the process of land subdivision. Broad land use zones are shown in regional planning schemes designating areas for urban, central city, industrial, rural and deferred urban uses. The WA Residential Planning Codes or R-Codes, as they are called, represent state planning policy for housing density and development standards, such as standards for housing setbacks, privacy and overlooking, and car parking. Other planning policies are developed by WAPC to provide more detail on certain matters, as a basis for more consistent, but flexible, decision-making (Western Australian Planning Commission 2007). If consistently applied, planning policies will be supported by the State Administrative Tribunal, which hears planning appeals.

Local (Town) Planning Schemes usually delineate zones, permissible land uses, and development control provisions. A Local Planning Strategy sets out the overall rationale for the planning approach and direction taken by the authority and forms the first section of the scheme. A 'scheme report' sets out the reasons for adopted policies and provisions. A model scheme text produced by the state provides standard clauses, terms and provisions.

While broad land use zones are usually specified in regional planning schemes, local planning schemes provide more specific detail regarding the intensity of development and locations for specific purposes.

Figure 6.3 The Perth Underground

Planning and urban development in Perth has been supported by strong state government investment in public transport infrastructure, such as the Perth underground system. Source: the Author 2010

Draft schemes are initially considered by the WAPC and the Environment Protection Authority, to consider whether an environmental assessment is required to develop the scheme. Draft schemes are exhibited for at least three months, and local councils consider all submissions received during this period. Submissions relating to environmental matters must be referred to the Environment Protection Authority for their consideration. Consideration of draft planning schemes by the Environment Protection Authority under the *Environment Protection Act 1986* is intended to provide a basis for undertaking necessary environmental assessment upfront, avoiding the need for later environmental impact assessment during the subdivision proposal stage. Following the exhibition period, council then passes a resolution regarding the draft scheme and informs WAPC. The WAPC considers council views and the public submissions, and then reports its advice to the minister, who has the final decision. There are provisions for an Interim Development Order to be made for areas not covered by a regional or local planning scheme.

As well as these local schemes, non-statutory structure plans can provide a framework for coordinating land use, transport, settlement and infrastructure decisions in the context of economic and demographic trends, and environmental protection. Regional structure plans can provide a broad framework for urban boundaries, the location of commercial and other strategic activities, regional open space and environmental protection, and infrastructure. District structure plans are prepared by local governments and contain more detail on land use patterns and transport networks. Local structure plans provide a basis for assessing specific rezoning and subdivision applications, for identifying the location and density of housing, public open space, sites for community and physical infrastructure, roads, cycleways, and footpaths. Local structure plans can be prepared by the landowner or a local council. They must be publicly advertised and approved by the applicable local government and or the WAPC.

Development applications are usually determined by local councils, with the exception of subdivision applications, and projects of regional significance, which are assessed by the WAPC. Consultation requirements for development applications are defined in planning schemes. In July 2011 a new Development Assessment Panel (DAP) approach was established by the state. All planning applications above a threshold capital investment value of $7 million will be assessed by a DAP (comprising a panel of experts and two representatives from local government). Developers with applications of over $3 million in value may also opt to be assessed under this system. In central Perth the threshold investment value is $15 million. Applications for single dwellings or residential development applications of less than 10 dwellings will not be assessed under the DAP system.

The Integrated Project Approvals System manages major state development proposals, generally significant mining and petroleum projects. The system provides a basis for early screening of proposals, scoping of environmental issues, and coordinating local government engagement.

Applications to review planning decisions may be made to the State Administrative Tribunal. In addition to rights regarding the permissibility and decisions of development approval, there are also rights of appeal against 'deemed refusal' of applications. The minister is able to 'call in' some applications before the State Administrative Tribunal for determination.

Summary and conclusions

What can be learned by analysing the different approaches to planning in Australia? Arguably, a comparative analysis of state planning systems and policies could help inform the development of national level initiatives or contribute to a state-level reform in specific policy areas, such as coastal growth or affordable housing. Looking at different approaches to strategic planning and development control may also reveal methods or systems that could be transferred elsewhere. There is a growing interest in such interjurisdictional comparison, as evidenced through the COAG process in relation to capital city planning (COAG Reform Council 2009) and the Productivity Commission's benchmark report on

Australian planning, zoning and development assessment processes (Productivity Commission 2011). These national-level processes may drive reforms for greater consistency and convergence across Australia's planning systems in the future, for better or worse, as discussed at the end of this section of the book.

Clearly much borrowing between the state jurisdictions has occurred over the years. For instance, there are striking similarities between the stated objectives for planning in Tasmania and those for Victoria as outlined in Victoria's *Planning and Environment Act 1987*. It is worth noting however, that there is limited evidence of cross-fertilisation of ideas between local governments in different states and territories, which may be due to the jurisdictional differences at state and territory level, or because of a general paucity of research and information on local planning approaches in Australia. To understand how such practice might be transferred, it is essential to know the contextual differences in legislation and policy that characterise each jurisdiction.

There are also distinct political, economic and community differences which continue to shape the evolution and reform of planning policy and practice. These different socio-political conditions also apply at the local level and are highly subject to change, further influencing opportunities for policy innovation. These themes are reflected in the following two chapters with specific reference to the NSW planning system as it has evolved over the past thirty years under the *NSW Environmental Planning and Assessment Act 1979*.

Chapter 7

Thirty years of environmental planning in New South Wales

The preceding three chapters have provided a comparative overview of Australian urban planning systems across the states and territories. The next two chapters give greater operational detail, using the state of New South Wales (NSW) as an example. Like many of the other Australian jurisdictions, the planning system in NSW has undergone a process of significant change since the original passage of the *Environmental Planning and Assessment Act 1979 (EPAA)*. This chapter and the following, focus particularly on the planning framework as it evolved to what might be described as its nadir in late 2010 and early 2011. By this stage the NSW planning system was viewed by many as a symptom of the deep malaise affecting the state Labor Party government at the inglorious end of a 16-year reign.

A policy narrative reflecting on over 30 years of the *Environmental Planning and Assessment Act 1979* overlays the descriptive explanation of the NSW planning system's contemporary operation in this chapter and the following. This narrative reflects distinctive periods in the progression of NSW planning policy, process and regulation. The first two decades, and particularly the mid 1990s, focused on an environmental agenda, emphasising the containment of suburban sprawl through 'urban consolidation', coastal protection and threatened species conservation. Social impacts of development were also recognised, with important state planning policies to preserve low cost rental housing and to promote housing diversity and choice. The last decade was a tumultuous time of change, in many ways stripping back some of the more progressive environmental policies of the 1990s to facilitate development in the wider context of neoliberalism and national regulatory reform.

The first section of this chapter introduces the NSW planning system as it has evolved since 1979 and outlines the key elements of the ongoing reform process that began in the late 1990s and remained unresolved a decade later. The second section of the chapter outlines the contemporary distribution of administrative responsibilities for the environment, planning and infrastructure in NSW. Key provisions of the *Environmental Planning and Assessment Act 1979*, including planning bodies, state and local planning instruments, and metropolitan and regional planning are then introduced. The *Environmental Planning and Assessment Act 1979* does not operate in isolation and the final section of the chapter summarises other important legislation relevant to environmental and urban planning and management in NSW.

The evolution of the NSW planning system

The first legislation for town and country planning schemes in NSW was introduced in 1945, as an amendment to the *Local Government Act 1919* (the *Local Government (Town and Country Planning) Amendment Act 1945*). This amendment enabled local governments to prepare comprehensive planning schemes for their areas, and required the establishment of an organisation to prepare a plan for the Sydney metropolitan region (Toon and Falk 2003). Consequently, the Cumberland County Council was formed, resulting in the preparation of Sydney's first regional plan (the County of Cumberland Scheme 1951). A Town and Country Advisory Committee advised the Department of Local Government on town planning matters. In 1963 a new State Planning Authority was established, and the functions of the Cumberland County Council transferred to this authority in 1964, ending Sydney's brief experiment with metropolitan regional governance. The State Planning Authority comprised executives of the major state infrastructure agencies as well as local government, and had the capacity to establish regional planning committees, as well as land acquisition and development powers. Describing the State Planning Authority, John Roseth writes:

> Established by a Labor government, the Authority was a true child of the 60s. It saw itself as a planning body in the traditional British sense, a combination of regulator and public developer. The Authority was also the consent authority for major projects, a role for which it had a reputation for long delays. (Roseth 2003, p93)

The Authority was replaced by a five member Planning and Environment Commission in 1974, including one local government and one community representative. The Commission oversaw the preparation of the Environmental Planning Bill 1976, but this was abandoned following a change of State government. The new Labor government established a working group to 'devise a planning system that would provide a clear distinction between State and local responsibilities, involve the public in planning decisions, control coastal development, achieve the conservation of heritage and ensure that the environmental impact of proposals is assessed' (Roseth 2003, p. 106).

Consequently, the late-20th-century NSW planning system was established by a series of five planning Bills relating to environmental planning, the establishment of the Land and Environment Court, and consequential amendments to other acts. The *Environmental Planning and Assessment Act 1979* came into force in September 1980. At the time, the *Environmental Planning and Assessment Act 1979* was regarded as landmark legislation, providing for strong environmental considerations and greater public involvement in plan-making.

The original Act, operational for over 30 years, has changed substantially since its promulgation, and pressure for change began in the late 1990s. In response to criticisms that the planning system was too complex, poorly integrated with the planning arrangements established by other legislation (particularly those relating to natural resource management), and provided insufficient opportunities for genuine public participation, a Green Paper to stimulate public and stakeholder discussion was released in 1999 (DUAP), followed by a White Paper known as 'PlanFirst' (DUAP 1999, 2001). PlanFirst aspired to a whole of government approach to urban, regional, and rural planning through integrated local environmental plans, regional strategies, and comprehensive state level policy direction. Land use zoning, as a form of development control, fell out of favour, with new 'place-based' plans promoted as a novel approach for development control more attuned to local character and aspirations. The northern Sydney local government area of Warringah was the only council to attempt the new model, preparing a comprehensive Local Environment Plan (LEP) based on detailed, precinct level 'locality statements' rather than functional land use zones.

Included within the package of reforms were controversial proposals for a formal tier of regional planning coordinating across natural resource management, environmental conservation and land use planning agencies. The new regional tier was intended to leverage greater community participation in the planning process, and enable more integrated decision-making across government portfolios, particularly at regional and local levels. Following a ministerial level change, the proposals contained in the White Paper were never really adopted. Rather, NSW along with the other Australian jurisdictions, began to focus attention on perceived planning system barriers to business investment and residential development. Dismantling such perceived barriers became the main focus of the planning reform agenda.

Consistent with this pro business agenda, the Environmental Planning and Assessment Act (Infrastructure and Other Planning Reforms) Bill 2005 included a range of sweeping changes to plan-making and development assessment in NSW. In the words of Craig Knowles, then minister for infrastructure, planning and natural resources, the Bill was cast very much in terms of facilitating development and investment in the state:

> The wellbeing of our economy depends on business being able to work with certainty, a minimum of risk, low transaction costs, and appropriate levels of regulation. This bill demonstrates the Government's determination to take decisive action to achieve these objectives. By establishing greater certainty in the assessment of projects of state significance and major infrastructure projects, the bill further assists in the Government's desire to afford opportunities for the private sector to participate in the delivery of our infrastructure programs.
>
> There is no doubt that this bill dramatically improves the climate in which to do business in this state. (Knowles 2005)

Perhaps the most notorious and controversial element of the reform was the introduction of Part 3A to the *Environmental Planning and Assessment Act 1979* which enabled major projects meeting defined criteria to bypass the usual planning requirements and be assessed under a special process. The Bill and subsequent amendments (particularly in 2008) changed the way in which local plans were made, extended the minister's powers in development assessment, and established several new planning bodies. Substantial changes to the infrastructure contribution system have also been made over the past five years.

On 4 April 2011, the new Premier, Barry O'Farrell announced that Part 3A would be repealed and foreshadowed his intention to commence work on a new planning act for NSW in his first eighteen months of office (O'Farrell 2011a).

In this context, the following sections explain the key elements of the NSW planning system as it has evolved up to the state election in March 2011 and in the months following as the new Premier, Barry O'Farrell established his agenda for change.

Environmental governance arrangements in NSW

Planning and environmental responsibilities in NSW have long been divided amongst many different state agencies and statutory authorities, sometimes described as 'silos' (Mant 1998). The administrative division of responsibilities for the environment and planning immediately before and after the March 2011 state election is shown in Tables 7.1 and 7.2.

As shown, a spread of government departments and statutory authorities are responsible for various aspects of urban and environmental planning and decision-making in NSW. The main changes following the 2011 election were the recasting of the former Department of Environment, Climate Change and Water as an 'Office' of Environment and Heritage within the Department of Premier and Cabinet, and the addition of 'infrastructure' responsibilities to the renamed Department of Planning and Infrastructure, also subsumed within the wider premier's portfolio. The dissolution of the former Department of Environment, Climate Change and Water was widely perceived to signify a demotion of environmental and heritage concerns under the new Liberal government regime, but could also be cast as an elevation of these matters to the inner circle of government. By contrast, the marriage of planning and infrastructure signified a clear government commitment to rebuilding urban and regional infrastructure in NSW.

Throughout the progression of the *EPAA* many of the names for key agencies responsible for planning and the environment, as well as senior bureaucrats and the minister for planning, have changed. To avoid confusion, generic titles corresponding with the terms used in the *EPAA* are used in this book to refer to departments, director generals, and the minister for planning and or the environment.

Policy framework for urban and environmental planning in NSW

The state policy framework for urban and environmental planning in NSW is somewhat piecemeal. The *NSW State Plan: investing in a better future* provides the overarching statement of NSW government policy across all portfolios (NSW Government 2010). In its second iteration, its aims include growing 'cities and centres as functional and attractive places to live, work and visit' (p11) and goals are specified for transport, infrastructure, housing and environmental management, although at a high level of generalisation. In addition to the NSW State Plan, there are a handful of specific state level policy documents with implications for urban and regional planning.

Table 7.1: Urban and environmental governance in NSW – key organisations (January 2011)

Agency	Role	Principal legislation (relating to environmental planning)
*Department of Planning (DOP)	Regulated environmental planning and assessment for NSW (spatial land use planning and development assessment). Incorporated NSW Heritage Council, which advised the minister on heritage planning matters.	*Environmental Planning and Assessment Act 1979 (EPAA)* *Environmental Planning and Assessment Regulation 2000 Heritage Act 1977 (HA)*
*Department of the Environment, Climate Change and Water	Broad responsibility for sustainability programs including environmental education and protection, climate change and greenhouse issues, energy, water, catchment management, native vegetation, coastal management and threatened species biodiversity conservation. Incorporated statutory authorities, including the Environment Protection Authority, and the NSW Office of Water. Responsibility for protecting the environment from all forms of pollution, managing waste, and preventing risk to human health. Also incorporated the National Parks Service, responsible for managing protected areas, species, Aboriginal heritage, and archaeological sites. Formal referral/concurrence role for many development applications under the *EPAA*.	*Protection of the Environment Administration Act 1991 and Protection of the Environment Operations Act 1997 (PEOA)* *National Parks and Wildlife Act 1974 (NPWA)* *Catchment Management Authorities Act 2003* *Coastal Protection Act 1979* *Native Vegetation Act 2003* *Threatened Species Conservation Act (TSCA)* *Wilderness Act 1987*
Division of Local Government, Department of Premier and Cabinet	Administration of local government and policy framework for their activities.	*Local Government Act 1993 (LGA)*
Land and Property Management Authority	Management of state Crown lands and state property; incorporating a number of statutory authorities, including the Sydney Harbour Foreshore Authority.	*Crown Lands Act (CLA) 1989* *NSW Aboriginal Land Rights Act 1983* *Sydney Harbour Foreshore Authority Act 1998*
*Roads and Traffic Authority (RTA)	To develop and maintain national and state roads in NSW.	*Roads Act 1993 (RA)*
Natural Resources Commission	To provide the government with independent advice on natural resource management.	*Natural Resources Commission Act 2003*

Agency	Role	Principal legislation (relating to environmental planning)
*Sydney Metropolitan Development Authority (Statutory Authority)	Responsible for urban renewal and development in designated urban renewal precincts of Sydney. Incorporates the Redfern-Waterloo Authority in inner Sydney.	*Growth Centres (Development Corporations Act) 1974* *State Environmental Planning Policy (Urban Renewal) 2010* *Redfern Waterloo Authority Act 2004*
*Transport NSW	To lead and manage public transport policy, planning and implementation in NSW.	A number of acts relating to air, rail and passenger transport.
Landcom	The NSE state-owned development corporation, established to assist the government with its urban development functions. Required to achieve commercial efficiency while meeting social responsibilities.	*Landcom Corporation Act 2001*
Independent Pricing and Regulatory Tribunal (IPART)	Regulate and review pricing policies relating to government monopoly services – e.g. transport, electricity, gas. Review of some local infrastructure contribution plans and advice on appropriate contribution levels.	*Independent Pricing and Regulatory Tribunal ACT 1992*
Independent Commission Against Corruption (ICAC)	Investigates allegations of corruption in the NSW public sector, including state and local government. Actively advocates to prevent corruption through information and educational activities.	*Independent Commission Against Corruption Act 1988*
(Commonwealth) Department for Sustainability, Environment, Water, Population and Communities	Sets Commonwealth policy for the environment, manages the National Reserve Program and assesses developments of 'national environmental significance'.	*Commonwealth Environment Protection and Biodiversity Conservation Act 1999 (CPEBCA)*

* Administrative relocation in March 2011.

NSW Biodiversity Strategy

The *NSW Biodiversity Strategy* (NSW Department of Environment and Conservation 1999), and subsequent *Draft NSW Biodiversity Strategy 2010–2015* (Department of Environment, Climate Change and Water NSW 2010a) established a whole of government policy statement for biodiversity conservation, one of the central objectives of ecologically sustainable development. The document recognises the national strategies for the conservation of Australia's biodiversity and ecologically sustainable development, and acknowledges a 'pressing need to strengthen and improve current activities, policies, legislation, practices and attitudes to achieve the conservation of biodiversity' (p7). The strategy also identifies and maps priority terrestrial and aquatic ecosystems for investment through acquisition or rehabilitation across the state.

Table 7.2: Key administrative changes to urban and environmental planning following the March 2011 state government election

Principle government department	Division name
Premier and Cabinet	Department of Planning and Infrastructure (formerly Department of Planning)
	Office of the Environment and Heritage (contains functions of the former Department of Environment, Climate Change and Water, and the Heritage Office formerly within the Department of Planning)
	Office of the Barangaroo Delivery Authority
	Office of the Sydney Metropolitan Development Authority
	Redfern-Waterloo Development Authority
Department of Transport (formerly Transport NSW)	Roads and Traffic Authority Division
	State Transit Authority Division

Source: Public Sector Employment and Management (Departments) Order 2011

NSW Coastal Policy

Another important policy document emerging from the late 1990s, the NSW Coastal Policy set a framework for coastal planning (Coastal Council of NSW 1997). This includes managing population growth, by identifying appropriate locations for development and recognising limits in particular areas, protecting and managing coastal water quality management, coastal reserves, integration of the different organisations involved in coastal planning, and protection of Indigenous and European cultural heritage. The policy framework was designed to govern local plan-making and development assessment within coastal areas.

The NSW Coastal Policy set the scene for a series of subsequent coastal planning initiatives, particularly in the context of growing concern about climate change. In 2009 the state government released a statement on sea-level rise (Department of Environment, Climate Change and Water NSW 2009b), providing guidance for local governments in planning for and adapting to sea-level rise, and in 2010 a specific coastal planning guideline was issued by the department of planning. The *Environmental Planning and Assessment Act 1979* was also amended to ensure that coastal zone management plans would be considered during development assessment (DOP 2010c).

Integrating land use and transport

A loose policy framework for integrating land use and transport in decision-making was articulated in a series of documents produced in 2001 (Transport NSW and Department of Urban Affairs and Planning 2001). The 'policy package' sought to reduce car travel and improve access to jobs and services through land use planning approaches. Specific guidelines for planning and development of 'urban structures, building forms, land use locations, development designs, subdivision and street layouts', sought to improve access to 'housing, jobs and services, by walking, cycling and public transport', increase 'the choice of available transport', reducing 'dependence on cars', reduce travel demand, support the 'efficient and viable operation of public transport services' and provide for 'the efficient movement of freight' (Transport NSW, RTA and DUAP 2001, p3).

These objectives were to be pursued by ensuring that transport implications are considered at all stages of the development process; by locating businesses and services in the right locations, and encouraging networks of mixed use centres; by using parking decisions as a form of private car demand management; and designing new residential development areas to maximise access to public transport. However while many of these considerations have become standard assessment and design criteria for retail and commercial centres, the policy itself was never formalised. Indeed, by 2010, the integrated land use and transport agenda had become overshadowed by arguments that policies designed to enforce the containment of 'centres' represent barriers to business 'competition' (DOP and Better Regulation Office 2010).

Environmental planning under the NSW *Environmental Planning and Assessment Act 1979* and regulations

Reflecting the environmental consciousness of the late 1970s, the passage of the *Environmental Planning and Assessment Act 1979* introduced the term 'environmental planning' to the lexicon of town and country planners in NSW. Alan Gilpin describes environmental planning as 'the identification by the community of desirable objectives for the physical environment, including social and economic objectives, and the creation of administrative procedures and programmes to achieve those objectives' (1990, p73). This is consistent with the scope of environmental planning envisaged by the primary planning legislation in NSW, the *Environmental Planning and Assessment Act 1979 (EPAA)*.

While the *EPAA* is the main article of planning legislation in NSW, it has operated in conjunction with several other laws relating to environmental protection and management, discussed below.

Generally speaking, the key functions of environmental planning legislation in NSW are to articulate objectives for environmental protection and management (including the protection and management of cultural heritage and the built environment); and establish decision-making responsibilities and processes (including processes for public participation).

A key way in which these functions are fulfilled is in enabling the preparation of subsidiary laws, in the form of land use plans, and by regulating the assessment of land use, development and management activities by individuals and by the government acting on behalf of the community ('the Crown').

By mid 2011, the amended *Environmental Planning and Assessment Act 1979*, as amended, consisted of eight numbered parts and sub-parts as follows:

- objectives and definitions (Part 1)
- administrative provisions, including responsibilities of the minister, department, and director general of planning (Part 2).
- plan-making provisions, for the preparation of environmental planning instruments and development control plans (Part 3).
- development assessment provisions, contained in two parts: Part 4 – for most private development, and Part 5 for certain types of infrastructure, utility, or public works (following amendments passed on 23 June 2011).
- implementation and enforcement provisions (Parts 6, 7 and 8).

Box 7.1: Objectives of the *Environmental Planning and Assessment Act 1979*

The objects of this Act are:

(a) to encourage:

(i) the proper management, development and conservation of natural and artificial resources, including agricultural land, natural areas, forests, minerals, water, cities, towns and villages for the purpose of promoting the social and economic welfare of the community and a better environment,

(ii) the promotion and coordination of the orderly and economic use and development of land,

(iii) the protection, provision and coordination of communication and utility services,

(iv) the provision of land for public purposes,

(v) the provision and coordination of community services and facilities, and

(vi) the protection of the environment, including the protection and conservation of native animals and plants, including threatened species, populations and ecological communities, and their habitats, and

(vii) ecologically sustainable development, and

(viii) the provision and maintenance of affordable housing, and

(b) to promote the sharing of the responsibility for environmental planning between the different levels of government in the state, and

(c) to provide increased opportunity for public involvement and participation in environmental planning and assessment.

Source: Section 5 *Environmental Planning and Assessment Act 1979* (14 January 2011).

The objectives of the *EPAA* are broad, incorporating concepts of ecologically sustainable development and public involvement and participation (as can be seen in Box 7.1). These objectives have been amended and expanded incrementally over time as new issues requiring a land use planning response have emerged.

Ecologically sustainable development is defined with reference to s 6(2) of the *Protection of the Environment Administration Act 1991 (POEAA)* (s6[2]) (see Box 7.2).

Box 7.2: Ecologically sustainable development in NSW legislation

Ecologically sustainable development requires the effective integration of economic and environmental considerations in decision-making processes. Ecologically sustainable development can be achieved through the implementation of the following principles and programs:

(a) the precautionary principle–namely, that if there are threats of serious or irreversible environmental damage, lack of full scientific certainty should not be used as a reason for postponing measures to prevent environmental degradation.

In the application of the precautionary principle, public and private decisions should be guided by:

(i) careful evaluation to avoid, wherever practicable, serious or irreversible damage to the environment, and

(ii) an assessment of the risk-weighted consequences of various options,

(b) intergenerational equity–namely, that the present generation should ensure that the health, diversity and productivity of the environment are maintained or enhanced for the benefit of future generations,

(c) conservation of biological diversity and ecological integrity–namely, that conservation of biological diversity and ecological integrity should be a fundamental consideration,

(d) improved valuation, pricing and incentive mechanisms–namely, that environmental factors should be included in the valuation of assets and services, such as:

(i) polluter pays–that is, those who generate pollution and waste should bear the cost of containment, avoidance or abatement,

(ii) the users of goods and services should pay prices based on the full life cycle of costs of providing goods and services, including the use of natural resources and assets and the ultimate disposal of any waste,

(iii) environmental goals, having been established, should be pursued in the most cost effective way, by establishing incentive structures, including market mechanisms, that enable those best placed to maximise benefits or minimise costs to develop their own solutions and responses to environmental problems

Source: *Protection of the Environment Administration Act 1991*, s6(2) (14 January 2011)

'Environment' under the *EPAA* means 'all aspects of the surroundings of humans, whether affecting any human as an individual or in his or her social groupings' (*EPAA*, s5). This is a highly 'anthropocentric' or human-centred definition of environment (Farrier 2006) but the reference to 'social groupings' implies a recognition of matters that may be beyond the strict physical world itself. This is an important basis for enabling planning decisions to consider social issues beyond the strictly physical impacts of land use change.

Operational matters for environmental assessment and ministerial consideration are set out in the *Environmental Planning and Assessment Regulation 2000*. They include requirements for local environmental plan-making; development contributions and development assessment, and prescribed conditions of development consent fees and charges.

Planning bodies under the *EPAA*

The *EPAA* establishes a number of 'planning bodies'. The minister for planning has over-arching responsibility for most plan-making activities and significant environmental assessment decisions. The director, through the department, administers the planning system, establishes state and regional level policy parameters and requirements, and manages the assessment of state significant projects. Local councils undertake much of the detailed work in preparing local plans and assessing local developments. Rolling reforms to the *EPAA* over the past five years have introduced a number of new bodies including Joint Regional Planning Panels, the Planning Assessment Commission, (local) planning assessment panels, planning administrators, and Independent Hearing and Assessment Panels.

Planning Assessment Commission

The Planning Assessment Commission comprises state government appointees, planning experts, and local government representatives.

Its establishment was intended to de-politicise planning decisions and reduce the number of matters determined by the minister. However, in the year 2008/09 the commission determined only two applications, rising to 17 in 2009/10 (16 of which related to reportable political donations) (DOP 2010a). By comparison, the minister and the department of planning approved over 200 major projects for the same period (and refused an additional two). This situation changed following the March 2011 change of government. In May 2011 the incoming planning minister delegated responsibility for assessing all private development to the PAC, and expanded the PAC's role in identifying and assessing development or infrastructure of potential state significance.

The Commission can also act as a Joint Regional Planning Panel; a planning assessment panel (which can fulfil the role of a local council, if required by the minister); or an Independent Hearing and Assessment Panel (providing independent advice to consent authorities on planning decisions).

Joint Regional Planning Panels

Joint Regional Planning Panels were established across NSW to provide independent expert advice on regional planning decisions. Panel members include representatives of some local councils within the region as well as members selected by the minister for planning. Joint Regional Planning Panels are required to carry out a council's role as a consent authority in relation to certain types of development (discussed further in chapter eight), or act as a planning assessment panel with general consent and plan-making responsibilities of a council.

Planning Assessment Panels

Planning assessment panels have been appointed by the minister to address a range of council functions or in relation to specific responsibilities (DOP 2006a, PS 06-016). Under the EPAA, the minister may appoint assessment panels or Administrators if the council's performance is regarde as unsatisfactory, or if the council agrees to the appointment (s118[3]).

Table 7.3 Summary of local plan-making and development assessment process in NSW under the *EPAA*

Stage	Public involvement	*EPAA*
STRATEGIC PLANNING - PREPARING AN LEP		PART 3
Planning authority prepares a planning proposal		S 55
Planning proposal referred to minister for a 'gateway determination' to determine if a draft plan may proceed to be prepared		S 56
Community consultation on planning proposal, if required by the minister	•*	S57
Variation of planning proposal, and submission to minister		S58
Legal drafting, minister makes local environmental plan, if approved		S59
Development assessment (Under Part 4)		PART 4
Development classified according to consent requirements		76–77
Development application to consent authority (council, private certifier or minister)		78
Public exhibition ('designated development', and or other development that must be notified under an environmental planning instrument or local planning policy)	•	79A
Concurrence and notification to public authorities		79B
Evaluation of environmental, social and economic impacts		79C
Determination and conditions		80
Appeal (by applicant or by objector to designated development)	§	97–99

• Public exhibition/consultation § Meeting/proceedings open to the public *Subject to determination by minister that public consultation is required.

Table 7.4 Planning instruments and plan-making guidance in NSW (January 2011)

Instrument/ guiding document	Public exhibition	Coverage	Authority	Purpose
State Environmental Planning Policies (SEPPs)	×	May be statewide or place specific	Minister for planning	Establish a consistent basis for addressing matters of state or regional significance in plan-making or development assessment
Local Environmental Plans (LEPs)	✓	Locally specific	Minister for planning (approves plan) Local council (prepares and administers plan) OR Minister for planning directs preparation of LEP by Administrator OR minister for planning prepares LEP directly	Regulate location of developments and development assessment
Development Control Plans (DCPs)	✓	Place specific	Local council OR minister for planning	Identify more detailed development control standards
S94 Contributions Plans	✓	May be development or place specific	Local council	Regulate development contributions
S117 Directions, Ministerial Directions, and Planning Circulars	×	May be statewide or place specific	Minister for planning	Regulate/guide the content of local plans
S94E Directions	×	May be statewide or place specific	Minister for planning	Regulate/guide development contribution plans

The NSW planning process

A summary of the main stages of local environmental planning in NSW, from the preparation of local environmental plans (as has occurred under Part 3 of the Act) through to the assessment of development (under Part 4 of the Act) is shown in Table 7.3. As shown, the stages involved in preparing a local plan include a 'gateway decision' on whether the proposal may proceed, followed by community or agency consultation, if required, and finally submission to the minister for the plan to be made as a legal instrument. The development assessment process follows from an application to the planning authority, through an exhibition process, consultation with others if required, to assessment against planning requirements in applicable instruments and the *EPAA*, and finally to the determination.

As shown in Table 7.3, there are two main statutory opportunities for public involvement during the planning process. The first occurs if the minister determines that a planning proposal for a new plan should undergo community consultation. The second occurs if the proposed development is required to be publicly exhibited under an environmental planning instrument or the *Environmental Planning and Assessment Act 1979* and Regulation 2000. At both of these times members of the public may make a written representation to the consent authority regarding the content of the plan or the development application. There has been a clear obligation for the consent authority to consider and seek to address these submissions in making their decision.

Planning instruments and plan-making under the *EPAA*

As noted, the *EPAA* established a tiered system of planning, with state environmental planning policies, and comprehensive local environmental plans having the status of 'environmental planning instrument'. Development Control Plans contain more detail to guide development (Table 7.4).

State environmental planning policies

As highlighted in the comparison of Australian state and territorial planning systems in chapter 5, under the *EPAA* State environmental planning policies (SEPPs) have provided the mechanism for addressing matters regarded to be of state or regional significance in NSW. SEPPs can apply across the whole state or to specific places, sites, types of development, and even particular projects.

They have fulfilled a number of specific purposes for state government, enabling direct state intervention or control over specific matters; allowing the state government to address specific policy issues such as the environment, housing, urban design or transportation; and providing a basis for setting special procedural requirements for the preparation of plans or the assessment of development.

SEPPs are made by the governor. There are no formal requirements for public consultation, but if the SEPP may affect threatened species, the director of planning must consult with the agency responsible for administering the *Threatened Species Conservation Act 1995* (s34A). SEPPs come into operation once they are published on the NSW legislation website (www.legislation.nsw.gov.au).

Status of SEPPs

SEPPs prevail over local environmental plans (LEPs) or subsidiary documents, like DCPs, in the event of an inconsistency.

Once exhibited, the provisions of draft SEPPs are a relevant consideration under the *Environmental Planning and Assessment Act 1979 (EPAA)* in plan making under Part 3 or when developments are assessed under s79C (*EPAA*) (discussed further below), for up to three years.

In recent years, the state government has been in the practice of evaluating new SEPPs, following their first year's operation, and subsequently after five years. The following section summarises some of the key SEPPs that have defined the planning policy landscape in NSW.

Direct state intervention

One of the major functions of SEPPs has been to provide a mechanism for state intervention. Three SEPPs were of particular importance in implementing the state government's rolling reform agenda between 2005 and 2010.

Major projects and development of state significance

The now notorious SEPP (Major Development) 2005 established special development provisions for 'major projects' and 'state significant sites' to be determined by the minister for planning, and for regionally significant development to be assessed by Joint Regional Planning Panels (Box 8.1). It also provided a special process for declaring 'critical infrastructure projects'. Once declared, these so-called major projects and critical infrastructure projects were relieved from the usually planning requirements and development standards set out in environmental planning instruments, and assessed against customised requirements issued by the director general of the department of planning, under Part 3A of the *EPAA* (discussed further in the following chapter). Following the NSW State election in March 2011, the SEPP (Major Development) 2005 was amended to remove residential commercial and retail development and coastal subdivisions from its operation, pending the full repeal of Part 3A of the *EPAA*, to be effected by the Environmental Planning and Assessment Amendment (Part 3A Repeal) Bill, passed in June 2011. The passage of the Bill was accompanied by a commitment to prepare a new SEPP for state-significant development and state-significant infrastructure (Department of Planning and Infrastructure 2011).

Infrastructure

A framework for consistent treatment of more routine public infrastructure was established via the SEPP (Infrastructure) 2007. This SEPP consolidated development controls for many types of infrastructure works, ranging from air transport facilities to gas and telecommunications, bushfire hazard reduction, social and supported housing, rail, road and traffic facilities, and waste or resource management facilities.

The Infrastructure SEPP was regarded by many to be a major innovation in NSW planning law for it overcame inconsistencies in local plans which might otherwise obstruct the efficient delivery of identified infrastructure. This was achieved by identifying and standardising the zones in which these infrastructure or services could be carried out under different assessment provisions of the *EPAA* (as outlined in the following chapter).

Exempt and Complying Development

Reflecting the national trend towards greater codification of standard development types, the SEPP (Exempt and Complying Development Codes) 2008 sought to update and extend existing arrangements for categorising and regulating development of minor environmental impact. It identified classes of development able to be 'exempt' from the need for development approval, and 'complying' development to be approved without merit assessment. Specific codes relating to housing, commercial and industrial development now establish statewide criteria for complying development.

Prior to the introduction of the Codes SEPP, local councils managed the definitions and standards of exempt and complying development within their own local areas. This customised approach was regarded as overly complex and a barrier to standardising basic development types across the state, such as single story dwellings and straightforward home alterations. In 2009–2010, following the introduction of the Code SEPP, 17 per cent of all development approvals in NSW were managed under the complying development process and it is intended that this proportion will continue to increase (DOP 2010a).

State environmental planning policies for the environment, flora and fauna

As noted, the mid 1980s to mid 1990s was a particularly fertile time for environmental policy-making in NSW. The period resulted in a number of SEPPs addressing aspects of environmental protection and management, as summarised in Table 7.5.

Two landmark state environmental planning policies were introduced in the first few years of the new millennium – in part, reflecting new concerns about human induced climatic change. SEPP 71 – Coastal Protection – enhanced the statutory status of elements of the NSW Coastal Policy, covering a range of coastal planning and protection matters including climate change and sea-level rise. The Buildings Sustainability Index (BASIX), progressively introduced since 2004, provides a basis for ensuring minimum energy and water savings are achieved in new residential and commercial development.

Table 7.5 State environmental planning policies relating to the environment, flora and fauna, January 2011

Name of Policy	Year	Description
SEPP No. 14 – Coastal Wetlands	1985	Required that an Environmental Impact Statement be prepared for development proposals that may affect coastal wetlands (including over 1300 wetlands outside the Sydney metropolitan area).
SEPP No. 19 – Bushland in Urban Areas	1986	Required that remnant bushland be protected when new Local Environmental Plans for applicable urban areas are made.
SEPP No. 26 – Littoral Rainforests	1988	Required an Environmental Impact Statement to accompany applicable development applications, and provided for buffer zones to protect littoral rainforests in 18 coastal local government areas of NSW.
SEPP No. 44 – Koala Habitat Protection	1995	Mandated the preparation of a koala habitat plan of management for developments that may threaten core or potential core koala habitat. Plans of management may relate to the area covered by a particular development or be comprehensive and apply to a whole local government area.

Name of Policy	Year	Description
SEPP No. 50 – Canal Estates	1997	Prohibited the establishment of new canal estates to protect coastal and marine environments. (Canal estates are systems of artificial waterbodies interspersed by land that is supplemented by sufficient fill to enable residential or other development. They are associated with significant environmental impacts.)
SEPP No. 71 – Coastal Protection	2002	Protected the NSW coastal zone, by establishing model provisions and objectives for local environmental plans. Sought to ensure a consistent approach to development assessment within the coastal zone, by establishing special criteria and requirements for development assessment.
SEPP (Buildings Sustainability Index BASIX) 2004	2004	Facilitated a statewide approach to the implementation of the Environmental Planning and Assessment Amendment (Building Sustainability Index: BASIX) 2004 which provided for minimum water and energy savings to be achieved on proposed new residential dwellings, alterations or additions. The SEPP over-rode competing provisions in local environmental plans and development control plans. To demonstrate compliance with the SEPP, a BASIX certificate must be obtained, using an online tool, requiring detailed undertakings in relation to solar amenity, energy and water efficiency.

As shown in Table 7.5, while several progressive state policies relating to environmental protection – for instance, protection of wetlands, koala habitat, and minimum water and energy savings – were introduced over the 1980s and 1990s, other key environmental issues – such as climate change adaptation – lacked specific state planning coverage more than a decade later in 2011.

Even when a specific issue is addressed through planning law, it may be several years before the requirement influences outcomes on the ground (Figure 7.1). This is because development consent is generally unaffected by subsequent changes to planning law. In 2010 the *EPAA* was amended to mandate a five-year period of development consent validity, removing the opportunity for local councils to impose a shorter timeframe. A developer only needs to ensure that the development is physically commenced, rather than actually completed, during this time. The extended timeframe for development to proceed was viewed as a way of recognising the difficulties and uncertainties in securing finance for projects to proceed, particularly following the global financial crisis of the late 2000s (DOP 2010a). However the lag exacerbates difficulties associated with adapting planning schemes to reflect important policy changes such as improved environmental standards.

State environmental planning policies for housing, urban development and design

The NSW state government enacted a number of environmental planning policies for housing, urban development and design over an 18-year period between 1992 and 2010. Policies remaining in operation up until early 2011 are summarised in Table 7.6. Several of these policies sought to overcome barriers in local planning laws that would otherwise prevent more diverse housing options, for instance, higher density housing, or housing to meet the needs of seniors or people with a disability. The state government has also used the SEPP mechanism to improve the aesthetic design standards of new medium-density housing.

The NSW government's planning policies relevant to housing are discussed further in chapter 11, within the wider context of national and international approaches to planning for housing choice and affordability.

Figure 7.1 Canal development, Port Macquarie

There is often a time lag between the introduction of new planning policy and legislation and impacts on the ground. This canal estate in Port Macquarie under construction in 2005 was not permitted under state planning policy at the time of its development but was approved before the policy came into effect. Approvals in NSW are generally valid for five years and in general a development only needs to commence within this period of time to prolong the approval further. Source: the Author 2005

State Environmental Planning Policy relating to industry and employment

Industry and employment matters have also been addressed through state environmental planning instruments, with several SEPPs designed to address specific issues relating to particular industries, including SEPP (Mining, Petroleum Production and Extractive Industries) 2007, for assessing and approving development relating to mineral petroleum and extractive materials; and SEPP No. 62 – Sustainable Aquaculture (2000) which categorised aquaculture projects according to their impacts and establishes special consent requirements. SEPP No. 33 – Hazardous and Offensive Development (1992) defined hazardous and offensive industries and storage establishments, and provided a process for assessing and managing this type of development.

Table 7.6 State environmental planning policies relating to housing, urban development and design, January 2011

Name of Policy	Year	Description
SEPP No. 21 – Caravan Parks	1992	Required consent for new caravan parks and camping grounds. Established merit considerations for councils assessing applications for caravan parks, including the need for or availability of low-cost housing.
SEPP No. 36 – Manufactured Home Estates	1993	Applied to Gosford, Wyong, and all local government areas beyond Sydney, and established criteria for the location, design and servicing of manufactured home estates. Recognised the importance of affordability and security of tenure for residents of manufactured home estates and allowed them to be developed on sites where caravan parks are permitted, subject to satisfying merit criteria.
SEPP No. 53* – Metropolitan Residential Development	1997	Required local councils to have an approved residential development strategy in place for achieving urban consolidation, or face controls imposed by the state government. While still operational in 2010, most areas (with the exception of parts of the local government area of Kur-ring-gai) achieved compliance through residential development strategies for higher-density housing completed in the early 2000s.
SEPP No. 70: Affordable Housing (Revised Schemes)	2002	Preserved the provisions to collect development contributions for affordable housing contained in certain local environmental plans (applying to parts of the cities of Sydney and Willoughby).
SEPP No. 65 – Design Quality of Residential Flat Development	2002	Established principles for the design of residential flats, provided for the establishment of local design review panels to advise on proposed new residential flats, and required the engagement of a qualified designer for developments meeting certain criteria (a requirement that is specified in the accompanying regulation).
SEPP (Housing for Seniors and People with a Disability)	2004	Relaxed local planning controls for developments designed for seniors and people with a disability to facilitate the provision of affordable medium-density accommodation (subject to design and locational criteria).
SEPP (Sydney Region Growth Centres)	2006	Provided a statutory implementation mechanism for Sydney's North West and South West Growth Centre land release plans. Established merit considerations for development applications within the growth centres pending the completion of more detailed planning controls, and established standard zoning controls for environmental conservation land, waterways, and areas containing high biodiversity values. Councils within the relevant areas remain the consent authorities for development applications.

Name of Policy	Year	Description
SEPP (Affordable Rental Housing)	2009	Aimed to promote and retain diverse and affordable rental housing across the state, through incentives for affordable housing inclusion (additional floor-space allowance known as a 'density bonus'), provisions to enable accessory dwellings such as 'granny flats' in residential areas, greater flexibility for social-housing providers, and provisions to offset the loss of low-cost rental housing stock, such as boarding houses. Brought together some existing housing policies, dating from the late 1980s.
SEPP (Urban Renewal)	2010	Established a process for identifying and assessing potential urban renewal sites and precincts. It required the director general of planning to undertake a study to support a proposal for potential urban renewal precincts and their appropriate land use and development controls, which should undergo a process of public exhibition and submissions. Proposed development within potential urban renewal precincts is subject to special restrictions.

*Repealed on 3 June 2011

Regional Environmental Plans, deemed state environmental planning policies

Prior to July 2009, 'environmental planning instruments' under the *EPAA* included a regional tier, called Regional Environmental Plans (REPs). To eliminate planning system 'layers', the *EPAA* was amended to remove this formal regional level tier, but existing REPs were deemed to have the status of SEPP. As SEPPs, these former regional plans also operate by influencing local environmental plan-making and or development assessment.

For instance, the Jervis Bay REP 1996, which established a framework for managing conservation and development in the fragile Jervis Bay area on the NSW South Coast, now has the status of a SEPP. It sets out planning provisions for urban development and tourism, while seeking to protect water quality, landscape, cultural and natural heritage.

A complete list of current SEPPs is maintained on the NSW Department of Planning and Infrastructure website: www.planning.nsw.gov.au. This website has links to the latest full-text version of all planning laws, regulations and instruments on the NSW government legislation website (www.legislation.nsw.gov.au).

Determining when SEPPs apply

Each environmental planning instrument contains provisions to explain where and in which circumstances they apply. LEPs usually apply to a whole local government area, or a defined section, such as a town centre. SEPPs may have statewide application such as the SEPP (Infrastructure) 2007, or may apply only to defined areas – such as SEPP No. 44 – Koala Habitat Protection, which operates only in places with potential koala habitat. In some cases, applicability may only be ascertained with reference to a map or schedules accompanying the instrument.

Figure 7.2 Boarding house, Inner Sydney

Boarding houses and certain low-cost rental housing in the greater Sydney metropolitan area are protected under SEPP Affordable Rental Housing 2009, which continued an earlier SEPP to protect low cost rental housing. Source: the Author 2004.

To ensure consistency in new plans and development decisions, the EPAA established a formal obligation to consider the provisions of SEPPs when a plan is made or development application assessed. Determining which SEPPs apply to a particular plan, local government area, or development has been one of the most complex areas of NSW planning law.

By January 2011, more than 55 SEPPs and deemed SEPPs (former REPs) were operational in NSW, representing a significant procedural burden for planners or developers seeking to determine technical consistency with applicable instruments. To address this, new local environmental plans, prepared in line with the state government's template for local plan-making (discussed further below), introduced the potential to signal the SEPPs that apply within a particular local government area.

Local environmental plans

Under the *Environmental Planning and Assessment Act 1979*, local environmental plans (LEPs) are the main statutory instrument for regulating land use and development within a local government area (LGA) in NSW. LEPs set out where particular activities should happen within a local government area and specify the objectives, standards and criteria for development assessment.

Figure 7.3 New residential flats in inner Sydney

New residential flats in former industrial areas, close to transport, such as the Silo Development in Newtown, reflect a combination of state planning policy, from the encouragement of urban consolidation under the former SEPP No. 53 to the improvement of residential flat development (SEPP No. 65). Source: the Author 2006

In 1999, the state government estimated that there were over 300 principal LEPs (comprehensive or single-issue plans) and more than 5300 amending instruments (DUAP 1999). Reduction in the number of local instruments and standardisation of their form has therefore been a particular emphasis of planning reform.

In 2006 changes to the *Environmental Planning and Assessment Act 1979 (EPAA)* introduced a template for standard local environmental plans, precipitating the end of idiosyncratic and heterogeneous local government plan making. To help implement the standard instrument, the minister was given wider plan making powers. However, reflecting the lengthy time periods involved in plan making, by June 2010, nearly four years after the promulgation of the order, only 16 of 152 local government areas had standard local environmental plans in place (DOP 2010a).

Box 7.3 Interpreting SEPPs

As with all environmental planning legislation, it is essential to read SEPPs from cover to cover to ensure that all of the relevant provisions are identified. However, as the instruments appear to have different formats and requirements, they often seem quite difficult to interpret. One way to help interpret SEPPs is to undertake an initial scan of the instrument with some key questions in mind:

- What are the objectives of the instrument?
- Where and under which circumstances does it apply?
- What are the key provisions it contains? In other words, how does it affect plan-making or development assessment?
- Does it establish any particular consent authority or authorities?
- Does it establish any special consultation arrangements?
- Does it establish any other roles or responsibilities, for the minister, council, or another authority?

Following this initial operational 'scan' of the instrument, it is easier to make a more detailed reading taking note of any additional details or provisions that may be relevant to a particular plan or development proposal.

Subsequent reforms have changed the process for plan making, with the objective of simplifying and speeding up the process, and facilitating routine amendments. The new changes, outlined below, essentially sought to reduce the procedural burdens on undertaking straightforward local plan amendments such as rezoning, by customising the research and consultation requirements to the likely impacts of the plan.

Preparing a local environmental plan

Traditionally LEPs have been initiated and prepared by local councils. However under certain circumstances, the minister can initiate an LEP. For LEPs initiated by the minister, a regional planning panel, the director general of planning, or another planning body, may by assigned responsibility for preparing the LEP. The authority responsible for preparing the LEP is known as the 'relevant planning authority'.

Reforms in 2008 established a new process for preparing an LEP. Under these changes, the process begins with a 'planning proposal' explaining and justifying the proposed plan. Proposals are required to set out the objectives and intended outcomes of the plan, the key provisions that the plan will contain, and arrangements for public consultation. A number of specific issues also need to be addressed, including the availability of public infrastructure to support the development, likely social, economic, and environmental effects and approaches to managing these effects. The proposal also needs to address consistency with local strategic directions and other state government planning requirements as outlined in the sections below.

This proposal is then referred to an 'LEP Review Panel' who advises the minister on gateway determinations, including any specific public or agency consultation requirements, requirements for supporting studies, and whether a public hearing is required.

This is known as a 'gateway determination':

> The gateway determination is a checkpoint for planning proposals before significant resources are committed to carrying out technical studies and investigations. It enables planning proposals that are not credible to be stopped early in the process before resources are committed to fruitless studies and investigations, and before State and Commonwealth Public Authorities are asked to commit their own resources to carrying out assessments. (Department of Planning 2009 p6)

Figure 7.4 New housing in Sydney's North West

Source: the Author 2008

In general 'low impact' proposals are exhibited for 14 days and other matters for 28 days.

Following this process, the planning authority must consider any public submissions and the report of any public hearing, before amending the proposal (if required). The final proposal may also need to be reviewed by the relevant joint regional planning panel or the Planning Assessment Commission. If the plan is amended significantly following exhibition, in response to public submissions or other reasons, it must be re-exhibited before it can be finalised (EPAA s68). A legal instrument is then prepared by Parliamentary Counsel before being made by the minister or delegate.

Benchmark timeframes have been specified for the making of local environmental plans. 'Minor spot rezonings' are to be processed within three months, and 'major land release and urban renewal' within six to 12 months (Department of Planning 2009 p15). In practice these benchmarks are rarely achieved.

Content of LEPs

Local environmental plans must be consistent with the objectives of the *EPAA* and may address any combination of matters set out in s26 of the Act. These include:

(a) protecting, improving or utilising, to the best advantage, the environment,

(b) controlling (whether by the imposing of development standards or otherwise) development,

(c) reserving land for use for the purposes of open space, a public place or public reserve within the meaning of the *Local Government Act 1993*, a national park or other land reserved or dedicated under the *National Parks and Wildlife Act 1974*, a public cemetery, a public hospital, a public railway, a public school or any other purpose that is prescribed as a public purpose for the purposes of this section,

(d) providing, maintaining and retaining, and regulating any matter relating to, affordable housing,

(e) protecting or preserving trees or vegetation,

(e1) protecting and conserving native animals and plants, including threatened species, populations and ecological communities, and their habitats,

(f) controlling any act, matter or thing for or with respect to which provision may be made under paragraph (a) or (e),

(g) controlling advertising,

(h) such other matters as are authorised or required to be included in the environmental planning instrument by this or any other Act (*EPAA*, s26).

LEPs must also be consistent with all applicable SEPPs. A series of LEP Practice Notes and Planning Circulars provide information on preparing LEPs, and are available on the Department of Planning website: www.planning.nsw.gov.au.

The LEP 'standard instrument' template

The Standard Instrument (LEPs) Order 2006 (referred to as 'the Order') prescribed the form and content of principal LEPs.

It specified compulsory provisions that must be adopted in new LEPs and optional provisions that may be included if the local council chooses to do so. If adopted, optional provisions must be applied without variation of the standard text.

The Order also provided for the inclusion of additional local provisions if not already covered by any of the mandatory (standard order) provisions or otherwise inconsistent with the standard instrument. These local provisions are intended to address specific issues. A council must justify their inclusion – for instance, by reference to an environmental study or local strategy.

Key provisions of the standard instrument include the following:

- *Aims of the plan:* Specific, locally determined aims for the LEP may be expressed.

- *Application of SEPPs:* A statement that SEPPs prevail over the LEP, and of any particular SEPPs that do not apply to the land covered by the LEP.

- *Land use zones:* The standard instrument identifies more than 30 land use zones that may be applied (Box 7.4). In first moving to the standard instrument, local councils have been able to select the standard zone that most closely approximates their existing zoning or system of land use categorisation. Standard zone objectives are specified in the Order, as well as a list of mandatory permitted and prohibited uses (set out in a 'Land Use Table'). Councils have been permitted to add local objectives to the core zone objectives, and to introduce additional permitted or prohibited land uses.

- *Exempt and complying development:* A definition of exempt and complying development including any specific local categories.

- *Principal development standards:* The standard instrument identifies a range of optional development standards, including a minimum subdivision lot size (to be shown on a lot size map); height restrictions, to be shown as a maximum limit on a height of buildings map; and floor space ratios, to be indicated on a floor space ratio map.

- *Exceptions to development standards:* The Instrument allows the planning authority flexibility to vary a development standard contained in the LEP, within certain parameters.

- *Miscellaneous provisions:* The standard instrument contains a range of compulsory and optional provisions relating to land acquisition by public authorities, the classification of public land (as 'operational' or 'community' land reserved for public purposes), development within the coastal zone (incorporating provisions of the NSW Coastal Policy), heritage conservation, and Crown development and public utilities.

- *Schedules:* Schedules referring to additional permitted uses (on particular land), exempt and complying development, the classification and reclassification of public land, and a list of environmental heritage.

- *Dictionary:* The Standard Instrument contains a dictionary of required definitions for LEPs.

While the capacity to include locally specific provisions and criteria is essential for local plan-making, in practice this has caused difficulties. For instance, although local government areas are required to adopt the same terminology for land use zones, they are not required to adopt all of the possible categories of permitted land uses within a particular zone. Therefore, while land use zones across NSW will share the same names and broad objectives, actual permitted and prohibited uses within these zoning categories may differ. Arguably this has created a more complex and confusing situation than the previous system by which local governments had greater freedom to define land use categorisations in relation to criteria which had evolved over time.

Figure 7.5 Urban Renewal site in Redfern Waterloo

Terrace houses owned by the Aboriginal Housing Company were demolished to make way for a new mixed residential and commercial development, including affordable Aboriginal rental accommodation. The long struggle for planning approval meant that the site remained vacant for several years. Source: the Author 2010

Ministerial directions

In addition to the *EPAA*, the regulations, SEPPs, the Standard Instrument, and planning circulars, the state government has required that certain provisions be retained or included in local environmental plans by making a direction under s117(2) of the *EPAA*. A range of s117(2) directions specify how policy issues are to be addressed in new local environmental plans (such as requirements for business, industrial and rural zones, environment and coastal protection, housing, hazard and risk), or generally to preserve the existing status quo (for instance, controlling major reductions in the availability of open space when new plans are made, or restricting the ability of a local council to reduce existing densities). The mechanism has also been used to facilitate the implementation of regional strategies through local plan-making (under s117(2). Direction 5.1, for regional strategies, and s117(2) Direction 7.1 for Sydney's metropolitan strategy). The Department of Planning and Infrastructure's website (www.planning.nsw.gov.au) contains a list of s117(2) Directions.

Amending LEPs

Amendments to LEPs proceed according to the plan-making process outlined above. However, all mandatory provisions contained in new LEPs are automatically amended when the Standard Instrument itself is amended. The Standard Instrument is reviewed and updated annually, and it is intended that LEPs will be locally reviewed every five years.

Box 7.4 Standard land use zones in NSW

The following land use zones are identified by the NSW standard instrument:

Rural Zones

RU1 Primary Production

RU2 Rural Landscape

RU3 Forestry

RU4 Rural Small Holdings

RU5 Village

RU6 Transition

Residential Zones

R1 General Residential

R2 Low Density Residential

R3 Medium-Density Residential

R4 High Density Residential

R5 Large Lot Residential

Business Zones

B1 Neighbourhood Centre

B2 Local Centre

B3 Commercial Core

B4 Mixed Use

B5 Business Development

B6 Enterprise Corridor

B7 Business Park

Industrial Zones

IN1 General Industrial

IN2 Light Industrial

IN3 Heavy Industrial

IN4 Working Waterfront

Special Purpose Zones

SP1 Special Activities

SP2 Infrastructure

SP3 Tourist

Recreation Zones

RE1 Public Recreation

RE2 Private Recreation

Environment Protection Zones

E1 National Parks and Nature Reserves

E2 Environmental Conservation

E3 Environmental Management

E4 Environmental Living

Waterway Zones

W1 Natural Waterways

W2 Recreational Waterways

W3 Working Waterways

Source: Standard Instrument (Local Environmental Plans) Order 2006; 18 January 2011).

Development control plans

To support the overarching LEPs, development control plans (DCPs) provide more operational standards and criteria for development. They may address the same range of issues as environmental planning instruments, but do not have the same status under the *EPAA*. DCPs are usually made by a resolution of council (following a period of exhibition, during which time members of the public may make submissions). The minister may also order a local council to make, amend, or revoke a DCP, or do so directly (*EPAA* s74F).

DCPs must be consistent with all applicable SEPPs and LEPs. While their provisions are not strictly legally binding, they have been given weight by the NSW Land and Environment Court when consistently applied by the council or other relevant planning authority. DCPs have been used for a wide range of development control purposes – from specifying development standards and requirements in greater detail, to landscape requirements or additional procedures for the assessment of particular types of development.

By 2006, a proliferation of DCPs had emerged in NSW, roughly grouped into three categories:

- comprehensive DCPs addressing detailed development control issues across an entire LGA
- issue-based DCPs addressing a particular issue (which could range from exempt and

complying development to tree preservation or the control of brothels) across an entire local government area. Many LGAs enacted multiple issue-based DCPs

- Site-based DCPs managing development within a particular site or precinct. Sometimes these have been required by an environmental planning instrument before development can be carried out within a particular area. Under the *EPAA* 'master plans' containing detailed development requirements are 'deemed' to have DCP status.

As part of the wider 2006 reforms to reduce the complexity of NSW planning law, the *EPAA* was amended to specify that only one DCP should apply to the same land (s74[c] 2) effectively preventing issue-based DCPs. However, existing DCPs have been able to continue pending the gazettal of a new LEP consistent with theStandard Instrument, or the preparation of a new comprehensive DCP for the local area.

Box 7.5 Interpreting LEPs

How to 'read' LEPs

Like other legislation, LEPs must ultimately be read from cover to cover, to ensure that nothing has been missed. However, the following checklist provides a guide for the purposeful reading of LEPs in relation to specific development proposals.

- Where available, consult the table of contents or list of provisions to gain an overview of the instrument.

- Refer to the objectives, aims or purpose of the LEP to understand and interpret its strategic intent.

- Identify the operational provisions for a particular place or type of development (for instance, the land use zone or locality and permitted activities, development standards, and special provisions). Consult the cadastral zoning map to identify the zoning of the site and surrounding areas.

- Refer to the plan's schedules and definitions, looking for any additional provisions or definitions that may apply to the proposed development or location.

- Lastly, interpret the LEP in conjunction with any other applicable environmental planning instruments or development control plans.

Regional strategies

Like the other Australian jurisdictions, there has been a resurgence in NSW towards a more comprehensive approach to strategic planning at the regional level. In NSW, this regional planning has occurred through non statutory 'regional strategies'. In addition to the established Sydney metropolitan planning process, the state government has initiated strategic regional planning in seven non-metropolitan regions: the Alpine Region, Central Coast, Hunter, Illawarra, South Coast, North Coast, and Western NSW.

Regional strategies address broad themes, relating to settlement and housing, urban character, employment, natural resource management, hazards and transport.

Strategic Regional Land Use Planning

In May 2011 the NSW government announced an additional approach to regional planning, focusing in particular on major industries in non metropolitan regions. The initial concentration will be on managing potential land use conflict between coal, coal seam gas and agricultural industries. Regional Land Use Plans will provide a strategic framework to assess new proposals for coal and coal seam gas industries. Pending the finalisation of the plans, new project proposals for coal, coal seam gas and petroleum extractions will need to submit an Agricultural Impact Assessment as part of their application. Ultimately, Regional Land Use Plans are intended to work together and complement the existing regional strategy framework (NSW Government 2011).

Metropolitan Plan for Sydney 2036

While commitment to non-metropolitan regional planning has been episodic at best, metropolitan level planning for Sydney has continued in some form since the first County of Cumberland Scheme was prepared in 1948 (Toon & Faulk 2003). However, unlike the County of Cumberland Scheme, which was a traditional land use control plan, more recent metropolitan 'plans' have evolved into strategic documents that depend primarily on local councils for implementation through local instruments and decisions. Sydney's latest metropolitan strategy, *Metropolitan Plan for Sydney 2036*, aims to: 'mitigate and adapt to the impacts of climate change'; 'integrate infrastructure, particularly transport, with land use'; 'strengthen governance, monitoring and implementation arrangements'; and 'respond to the challenges of Sydney's faster than previously expected population growth' (NSW Government 2010a). The strategy also aims to address national criteria for capital city planning established by the Council of Australian Governments (COAG) Reform Council. As discussed in the previous chapter, these criteria relate to the integration of land use, infrastructure, transportation, environmental assessment and urban development, and coverage of nationally significant policy issues spanning population growth and change, climate change, social inclusion and community wellbeing, productivity and competitiveness, housing affordability, and matters of national environmental significance (COAG Reform Council 2009).

The Metropolitan Plan responds to a predicted growth in population of 1.7 million between 2006 and 2036, by which time it is expected that Sydney's population will reach 6 million people, rising annually by an average 56,650 persons (NSW Government 2010a). There will be a need for 760,000 new jobs and 770,000 new homes (an increase of 46 per cent). One of the more controversial aspects of metropolitan planning in NSW has been the split of greenfield versus infill development. While the 2010 metropolitan plan aimed to contain 70 per cent of new growth within existing urban areas, the Liberal National Party argued for a more 'balanced' 50/50 split as part of its successful campaign to win the March 2011 election (NSW Government 2010a; Nicholls & Moore 2011).

Figure 7.6 Urban growth areas in Sydney's North West

Sydney's western suburbs have been a traditional focus for housing growth, despite limited transport infrastructure. The new O'Farrell government, which came to power in a landslide victory in March 2011, pledged to redirect 50 per cent of planned growth back to greenfield sites on the urban fringe. Source: the Author 2004

The delivery of the plan is overseen by a committee of local and state government representatives, known as the Metropolitan Plan Delivery Group. A Metropolitan Development Authority (discussed below) will also have a role in implementing the urban development and housing objectives of the plan, in part through the State Environmental Planning Policy (Urban Renewal) 2010, which, as discussed above, establishes a process for identifying and assessing potential urban renewal sites and precincts. As with the regional strategies, a key mechanism for implementing the metropolitan plan is via a ministerial direction (under s117[2] of the *EPAA*), which requires that planning proposals are consistent with metropolitan strategy.

Development authorities

Special purpose development authorities have been created by the state government to oversee the development of specific sites or precincts. The Sydney Metropolitan Development Authority was established in 2010 to facilitate development on strategic urban renewal sites throughout the metropolitan area (Box 7.6).

Another significant authority is the Barangaroo Delivery Authority, established in 2009 under the *Barangaroo Delivery Act 2009* to oversee the development of a controversial 22 hectare waterfront precinct on the Sydney Harbour foreshore.

The prime harbourside site of Barangaroo was declared a state significant site under the former provisions of the SEPP (Major Development) 2005. In 2007 a concept plan for the site was approved under the now discredited Part 3A provisions of the EPAA (meaning that future development proposals consistent with the parameters of the concept plan would not be subject to third-party appeal). However, subsequent changes to the original design of the precinct, which included a Dubai style hotel in Sydney Harbour itself, polarised the community and inspired a colourful campaign of grassroots opposition. The legality of the project was challenged on a number of procedural grounds, including compliance with State Environmental Planning Policy 55 – Remediation of Contaminated Sites due to the management of poisonous substances relating to the site's former usage as a gasworks. Proceedings commenced in the Land and Environment Court in November 2010 and were heard in early February 2011. However, before a judgment had been made, the then planning minister declared that the provisions of SEPP 55 did not apply to projects assessed under Part 3A, issuing an order under s.75R of the *EPAA* only weeks before the state election. This action was widely interpreted as symptomatic of the climate of mendacious behaviour that characterised the government in its dying days. However, the order effectively defeated the legal challenge, a fact noted with some irritation by Justice Biscoe in his decision:

> The applicant would have achieved success in the proceedings but for the Minister's amendment to SEPP 55 made after the trial concluded. If the Minister wished to exclude these two developments … he could have exercised his power to make the amendment at any time after the commencement of the proceedings, if not before. The amendment changed the law on which the case has been fought. (Biscoe J, Australians for Sustainable Development Inc v Minister for Planning[2011] NSWLEC 33 at 306)

Following the change of government, the new Minister for Planning and Infrastructure, Brad Hazzard, announced a review into the Barangaroo development. Reflecting the difficulties associated with securing high value development for NSW while also meeting election commitments to return planning to local communities, the minister used the review announcement as an opportunity to criticise the economic performance of the former Labor government:

> We want all stakeholders to engage in the 'short and sharp' review, which will provide much needed business certainty, and an opportunity for the city to have a say. Barangaroo has the potential to be an economic golden ticket – its projected $6 billion stimulus will create substantial opportunities for the wider NSW community. The NSW Government is hard at work reversing sixteen years of financial mismanagement. Labor's dismal economic record has left us with a multi-billion dollar black hole – which this government is well on its way to repairing. While repairing the economy, we are also making certain the city's voice is heard. (O'Farrell 2011)

Box 7.6: The Sydney Metropolitan Development Authority

The Sydney Metropolitan Development Authority (SMDA) was established as a state development corporation in 2010, under the *Growth Centres (Development Corporations) Act 1974*. The role of the SMDA is to facilitate urban renewal in key sites of the Sydney metropolitan region, by 'working with transport and planning departments to identify precincts for renewal', 'undertake ... planning investigations and feasibility analyses', 'coordinating transport and infrastructure planning', 'borrowing and managing funds and partnering with public agencies and private entities when necessary' (NSW Government 2010a, p1). The SMDA assumed and extended the functions of the former Redfern-Waterloo Authority, which was created in 2004 to develop and renew the Redfern-Waterloo area of inner Sydney. The SMDA is overseen by a board with representatives from the NSW Departments of Planning, Transport, Premier and Cabinet, and Treasury, as well as the federal minister for Infrastructure.

The first location overseen by the SDMA, Redfern-Waterloo, inspired much controversy, centring on the future of The Block, which is the site of the first urban land-rights claim in Australia. Developed by Australia's first housing collective, the Aboriginal Housing Company (AHC), as affordable rental housing, the area became infiltrated by serious drug problems in the 1990s and the AHC began to demolish homes that had become derelict and impossible to manage. The initial Redfern Waterloo Authority plans largely excluded Aboriginal housing from The Block and conflicted with the wishes of the AHC who sought a combination of mixed-tenure Aboriginal housing, commercial, educational and cultural uses. However, in June 2009, the minister approved the AHC's proposed concept plan for the redevelopment of The Block (DOP 2009). At the time of writing, demolition of the original AHC homes was almost complete, but the area retains and is rebuilding its strong Aboriginal community presence.

Other environmental legislation in NSW

In addition to the *EPAA*, several other laws have framed environmental and urban planning in NSW over the past 30 years. These deal with environmental quality and pollution, heritage, natural resource management, threatened species, national parks and native flora and fauna, and local government matters.

Local Government Act 1993 (LGA)

The *Local Government Act 1993* established the administrative framework and operational requirements for local government and councils in NSW. It contained relatively extensive provisions for local government transparency and public participation in decisions made at local government level, including requirements for the availability of minutes of council meetings, and reports of professional planning staff, exhibition of plans and policies prepared by councils, requirements for public meetings or hearings on particular matters, the holding of public polls, and inquiries into the conduct of councils.

The Act requires local government areas to develop a community strategic plan, identifying the 'main priorities and aspirations for the future of the local government area' (s402). The plan should cover a 10-year period and address 'civic leadership, social, environmental and economic issues in an integrated manner', be 'based on social justice principles of equity, access, participation and rights', and reflect an adequate information base in relation to 'social, environmental and economic issues' (s402[3]). The community strategic plan is also required to have 'due regard to the State government's State Plan and other relevant State and regional plans of the State government' (s402[3d]). A community engagement strategy is required to be prepared as a basis for involving the community in the development of the strategic plan. A resourcing strategy must be prepared to demonstrate the allocation of resources to implement strategies in the community plan, through a delivery program.

The *Local Government Act* also provides for management plans to be prepared for public land and reserves under the responsibility of local councils.

The *Protection of the Environment Operations Act 1997 (PEOA)* and the *Protection of the Environment Administration Act 1991 (PEAA)*

Together, the PEOA and the PEAA establish the administrative framework for environmental protection, waste management and reduction, and public education and awareness in NSW. The *Protection of the Environment Operations Act 1997 (POEA)* provides a basis for environmental protection, through measures to prevent pollution and encourage cleaner production, monitoring of environmental quality, and through community education and involvement. Environment protection licences (permission to undertake specific activities) and environment protection notices (orders to carry out specific 'clean-up' or 'preventative' actions) are issued under the *PEOA*. Often such licences are needed before particular developments under the *EPAA* may proceed. The *PEOA* also provides for preparing 'protection of the environment policies' (PEPs) to further the objectives of the Act and for managing cumulative environmental impacts of future activities. These PEPs can include an environmental protection goal, standard, guideline or protocol; and may apply to the whole or a part of the state. They may also be prepared for implementing a National Environment Protection Measure issued by the Commonwealth Environment Protection and Heritage Council (described in chapter 4).

Heritage Act 1977 (HA)

The *Heritage Act* preceded the *EPAA* by two years and has been an important part of the NSW planning system, protecting items of environmental heritage, defined as places, buildings, works, relics, moveable object and precincts. It created a framework for establishing state or local heritage significance, including interim conservation orders to protect a potential heritage item that is at immediate risk. Items of state heritage significance are permanently protected on the State Heritage Register. Items of local heritage significance are listed in local environmental plans. The Act establishes a Heritage Council to advise the minister on heritage matters, including recommendations for the State Heritage Register. The 11 member Council must include the NSW government architect, and the director generals responsible for heritage and planning. The remaining eight members are appointed by the minister but must have expertise in relation to Aboriginal heritage, archaeology, architecture, environmental heritage, history, local government, relevant law, or cultural landscapes and include a nominee from the National Trust of Australia (NSW). The council is resourced by a heritage office situated in the premier's department (following the 2011 state election).

The Heritage Council has established a committee to manage recommendations for listing items on the State Heritage Register and to comment on planning documents affecting significant heritage places. An Approvals Committee provides the Council's consent role, approving or commenting on proposals affecting items listed on the State Heritage Register. Special panels provide advice to the Heritage Council on Aboriginal heritage, archaeology, fire protection, access and services, religious property, history and technical matters associated with heritage conservation. The Heritage Council is guided by the Burra Charter which is recognised as establishing best practice in managing cultural heritage in Australia (Australia ICOMOS 1987).

Figure 7.7 Habitat protection corridor, Hyams Beach

The *TSCA 1995* has been instrumental in shaping development patterns within environmentally sensitive areas, such as this housing development in the popular tourist destination of Hyams Beach, on Jervis Bay. Source: the Author 2003

Native vegetation and catchment management

The *Native Vegetation Act 2003 (NVA)* and the *Catchment Management Authorities Act 2003 (CMAA)* established a new framework for catchment and native vegetation management in NSW. The *CMAA* created 13 Catchment Management Authorities to coordinate natural resource planning on a catchment basis. The Catchment Management Authorities were charged with preparing catchment action plans to address regional natural resource management issues affecting the water catchment. In preparing these plans, Catchment Management Authorities are required to consider the provisions of any applicable environmental planning instrument under the *EPAA*. Catchment Action Plans were required to also comply with and promote statewide natural resource management standards or targets declared by the NSW Natural Resources Commission. In addition to the Catchment Action Plan, the authorities have been required to submit an annual implementation program.

The *NVA* aimed to strike a balance between agricultural management activities and the prevention of salinity, land degradation, and biodiversity loss. It generally sought to prevent broad-scale clearing, protect native vegetation of high conservation value, improve the condition of existing native vegetation, and encourage re-vegetation and rehabilitation of land (s3). A key mechanism was the requirement for landholders to seek consent under Part 4 of the *EPAA* to clear native vegetation (applying only to native vegetation on non-urban lands). Following the preparation and approval of a Property Vegetation Plan, additional consent for clearing, consistent with the plan under the *EPAA*, is not required.

Threatened Species Conservation Act 1995 (TSCA)

The *Threatened Species Conservation Act 1995 (TSCA)* represented a significant environmental turn in NSW policy and law. It sought to conserve biological diversity by protecting both 'endangered' and 'critically endangered' species, populations and ecological communities (which are listed in schedules to the Act). It also recognised species presumed to be extinct; and crucially, the protection of habitat on which they depend.

A scientific committee oversees the listing of species, populations and ecological communities under the *TSCA*. Land that is critical to the survival of an endangered species, population or economical community may be declared by the minister as 'critical habitat'. A species impact statement is required to accompany activities that are proposed to be undertaken on critical habitat.

The *TSCA* provides for recovery plans to be prepared for endangered and critically endangered species, and ecological communities. These plans aim to preserve and restore the habitat of species identified as endangered, vulnerable or presumed extinct and introduce a general obligation on behalf of decision-makers to consider the impacts of proposed developments within the known geographical range of these species, although in practice, these obligations have been difficult to enforce. The real value of these instruments may have been in proposing proactive strategies to raise the awareness of landholders and to encourage the remediation of degraded habitat areas.

Under the *TSCA*, licences are required to undertake activities that may have a significant effect on threatened species. Such licences may be required to be obtained under the integrated development provisions of the *EPAA* (discussed further in the following chapter). There are also specific requirements for assessing affected development under the *EPAA*, including a requirement for the concurrence of the minister responsible for the *National Parks and Wildlife Act 1974*, and the preparation of a species impact statement.

While the *TSCA* relates specifically to threatened species in NSW, and is separate from the threatened species provisions of the Commonwealth *Environmental Conservation and Biodiversity Conservation Act 1999*, it identifies species that are considered to be threatened both in NSW and nationally.

Biodiversity certification, under the *TSCA*

A decade after the introduction of the *TSCA*, a process to to 'switch off' certain requirements of the *TSCA* was introduced. Biodiversity certification has the effect of suspending requirements to consider biodiversity values or threatened species during assessment processes under Parts, 4 and 5 of the EPAA, and means that the provisions of the *Native Vegetation Act 2003* do not apply. A 'biodiversity certification strategy', (a strategy for implementing conservation measures 'to improve or maintain biodiversity values' (s126K[2]) is needed for certification.

Biodiversity banking

The *Threatened Species Amendment (Biodiversity Banking) Act 2006* introduced provisions to enable landholders to acquire 'biodiversity credits' by undertaking enhancements and conservation works on their land. It was intended for these credits to be purchased by developers needing to offset the impacts of their own development (Department of Environment and Conservation NSW 2006). The price of credits is calculated by adding the total cost of managing and reporting on the conservation works over the life of the agreement, plus return to the landholder, (establishment costs, assessment, land value, opportunity cost, and a profit or 'risk margin').

A BioBanking Trust Fund was established to provide payments to landholders for managing the site over time and to ensure that if biobank sites are sold, the new owner is able to continue to manage and conserve the land (Department of Environment and Climate Change 2007). A 'biobanking agreement' sets out the total fund deposit requirement (made when the biodiversity credit is sold) and the schedule of payments to the landholder, which are made annually. A list of 'wanted credits' allows developers or other potential purchasers of biodiversity credits, such as philanthropic organisations, to inform current holders of credits (including local councils and landholders) of the number and type of credits sought. In late 2010, ten developers were seeking nearly a thousand credits for different vegetation and species types.

National Parks and Wildlife Act 1974 (NPWA)

The *National Parks and Wildlife Act 1974* governs the conservation, management and use of natural and cultural heritage in NSW, with an emphasis on Aboriginal places and relics, and the protection of native plants and fauna. It covers the establishment and management of protected areas (including national parks, nature reserves, state conservation areas, regional parks and Aboriginal areas), including the preparation of plans of management. Conservation agreements between the minister and the owner of land may be made to protect areas with scenic, natural scientific or Aboriginal significance, by restricting the use of the area, requiring the owner to undertake certain activities, and providing a basis for financial, technical or other assistance.

Crown Lands Act 1989 (CLA)

The *Crown Lands Act 1989* sets the legal framework for managing Crown land, including conditions for allowing Crown land to be occupied, leased or sold. The Act covers the preparation of plans of management for public reserves. Relevant plans of management must be considered as part of any strategic planning or development assessment process.

Trees (Disputes Between Neighbours) Act 2006

The *Trees (Disputes Between Neighbours) Act 2006* was introduced to allow neighbouring landholders to apply to the Land and Environment Court 'for an order to remedy, restrain or prevent damage to property on the land, or to prevent injury to any person' associated with a tree on adjacent property (s7). The Act only applies to trees within land zoned for residential, village, industrial or business zones, and requires that applicants attempt to resolve the dispute before seeking a court order. A range of matters including biodiversity and heritage considerations must be taken into account before an order can be granted.

Summary and conclusions

This chapter has reviewed the policy and legislative framework for urban and environmental planning in NSW, established over 30 years of the operation of the *EPAA 1979*. Despite, or perhaps because of successive reform initiatives, the NSW urban planning and environmental governance system, remained fragmented and complex by the end of the first decade of the new millennium.

In sum, the *EPAA 1979* established the legal framework for NSW plan-making and development assessment. A hierarchy of environmental planning instruments – state environmental planning policies and local environmental plans set statutorily enforceable objectives, criteria, and standards for land use and development, while development control plans have provided more detailed, and flexible, local level provisions.

Like many other jurisdictions, local plan-making in NSW is in the process of transition to standardised planning instruments. This process is intended to reduce the complexity of local planning controls and so facilitate development assessment processes, but it is ostensibly a modification of form rather than substance. However in moving from the existing mesh of disparate local controls to the new proscribed standards, it is almost inevitable that certain local policies, standards, or regulations will be lost or substantially altered. Time will tell whether matters of substantial policy concern for local communities are upheld or lost in the sieve of translation to the new standard instruments.

Aside from the NSW state plan, which has provided a de-facto policy agenda, NSW lacks a comprehensive policy framework for urban and environmental planning. Instead, key policy issues – relating to the environment and climate change, housing, transport, infrastructure, industry and so on, have been addressed through a kaleidoscope of planning instruments, ministerial directions, departmental circulars and guidance, and 'policy statements'.

Within this mix, there have been some extremely progressive policy interventions. For instance, NSW is the only state in Australia to mandate specific controls to protect low-cost housing stock, and was one of the first states to prohibit canal developments within sensitive coastal areas. State environmental planning policies protecting koala habitat, wetlands and littoral rainforests, represent progressive practice even in international terms, as does the BASIX mechanism for achieving energy and water-use efficiencies through building design. While there are opportunities to enhance the use of these measures, and to extend the scope of environmental and social matters addressed through state policy in NSW more broadly, they provide a sound basis for future progress.

Similarly, the increasing emphasis on strategic metropolitan and regional policy provides a stronger framework for statutory planning and development decisions to take place. However, the ability to suspend and override existing controls under the former Part 3A of the *EPAA*, to facilitate a growing list of major projects – including apartment buildings, suburban shopping centres, and even an international hotel within the waters of Sydney Harbour itself – seriously threatened this strategic policy framework for NSW. The new government wasted no time in announcing the repeal of Part 3A and the return to assessing developments against applicable planning controls set out in state and local environmental planning instruments (Department of Planning and Infrastructure 2011).

According to the new premier:

> The days of giving the planning minister sweeping powers to approve developments at the stroke of a pen with virtually no consultation with local communities are over. (O'Farrell 2011a)

Chapter 8

Development control and environmental assessment in NSW

Throughout this book, a conceptual distinction between strategic or forward planning and development control has been emphasised. In the previous chapter the statutory framework for strategic planning in NSW – the legislation, policies and rules to control particular future actions or developments – was explained. The specific processes and terminology are tied to particular legislation, reflecting the historical evolution of planning law within a particular jurisdiction, as influenced by changing government policy. This has been seen in the progression of the *Environmental Planning and Assessment Act 1979*. As discussed in chapter seven, NSW planning law evolved in the 1980s and 1990s to focus on urban consolidation and environmental conservation; shifting towards regulatory standardisation and codification in the new millennium. This latter shift is particularly pronounced in relation to development and environmental assessment processes, the subject of this chapter.

The chapter first explains the main concepts associated with development control as they have evolved under the *EPAA*, and the categorisation of development according to the level of likely environmental impact and the level of assessment required. It then outlines the different stages in the development application and assessment processes for private developers and for public authorities, including the range of matters that must be considered by consent authorities in making their decision.

One of the important functions of planning systems is to provide a basis for funding the shared infrastructure and services needed to support urban development. The NSW planning system has offered some of the most varied opportunities in Australia for securing contributions by private developers for public infrastructure and services through the planning process, as outlined in the third section of the chapter. Provisions for dispute resolution in the NSW Land and Environment Court and its evolving role in relation to policy development and case law, are discussed in the final section of the chapter.

What is development control in NSW?

It is important to establish what types of activities or developments are controlled within a particular planning jurisdiction. In NSW, the legal concept of development is very broad. The *EPAA 1979* has defined development as follows:

> 'development' means:
>> (a) the use of land, and

(b) the subdivision of land, and

(c) the erection of a building, and

(d) the carrying out of a work, and

(e) the demolition of a building or work

Development is also any 'other act, matter or thing' ... 'that is controlled by an environmental planning instrument'. (*EPAA*, s4[1])

Thus the concept of development has extended to the reservation of land, controlling advertising, maintaining affordable housing and preserving vegetation. The development 'control' framework is the system of legal rules governing development and development processes, including:

- what can and cannot be done on a particular site (generally established through the land use zone or equivalent)
- the parameters or standards governing permissible developments; and,
- the circumstances under which permission for development may be granted – for instance, compliance with particular conditions of consent or other codes.

Control had been defined under the *EPAA* as follows:

'control', in relation to development or any other act, matter or thing, means:

(a) consent to, permit, regulate, restrict or prohibit that development or that other act, matter or thing, either unconditionally or subject to conditions, or

(b) confer or impose on a consent authority functions with respect to consenting to, permitting, regulating, restricting or prohibiting that development or that other act, matter or thing, either unconditionally or subject to conditions. (*EPAA*, s4[1]).

In other words, under the *EPAA* development 'control' has meant the ability to allow, regulate, or prevent particular developments, with or without conditions specifying how the development is to be carried out. This control has been vested in a consent authority – the authority with responsibility for determining a development application, which is generally a local council, but where specified by the *EPAA* or another environmental planning instrument, may also be the minister for planning, a Joint Regional Planning Panel, a local planning assessment panel or administrator, the Planning Assessment Commission, or another public authority.

Classification of development under the *EPAA*

The *EPAA* establishes a threefold classification of development:

- development that does not need consent
- development that needs consent
- prohibited development.

Within each of these categories are further distinctions based on the scale of the development and level of environmental assessment required.

Development that does not need consent

Environmental planning instruments may provide for particular developments to be carried out without the need for obtaining development consent. There are two types of development that fit into this category:

1. *Exempt development* has minimal environmental impact and is specifically defined within local (and some state) environmental planning instruments. A special State Environmental Planning Policy (Exempt and Complying Development Codes) 2008 establishes exempt and complying development codes for state wide application. LEPs prepared under the Standard Instrument define exempt development. All development on land that is critical habitat, or part of a wilderness area (within the meaning of the *NSW Wilderness Act 1987*) needs consent and so is excluded from definitions of exempt development.

2. *Certain kinds of public activities* such as public infrastructure or other works, may be carried out by public agencies without the consent of local planning authorities. These are indicated within the development control tables of local (and in some cases state) environmental planning instruments. This type of development is still subject to an environmental assessment process under the *EPAA,* as discussed below. The new class of State Significant Infrastructure, introduced via the Environmental Planning and Assessment Amendment (Part 3A Repeal) Bill 2011, falls within this category of development.

Development that needs consent

Environmental planning instruments specify development that needs consent. Development that needs consent is usually assessed under Part 4 of the *EPAA*.

1. *Complying development* meets certain predefined development standards established by environmental planning instruments and codes. If these predetermined standards are met, there is no need for additional assessment of the proposal 'on its merits'. Development cannot be complying if it is classed as 'designated' (see below); requires the concurrence of another authority; is to be carried out on land that is a critical habitat, is part of a wilderness area or on land that comprises or contains an item of state or local environmental heritage; or land otherwise identified as an environmentally sensitive area. As noted, the SEPP (Exempt and Complying Development Codes) 2008 establishes exempt and complying development criteria across the state.

   Complying development may be approved by the issuing of a complying development certificate by an accredited certifier or other relevant planning authority, usually the local council. It is covered by Part 4 of the *EPAA*.

2. *Local development* is identified within the planning instrument as requiring consent but which does not meet the set criteria for complying development. The consent authority is usually the local council, which will undertake an assessment of the merits of the proposal against Part 4 of the *EPAA,* and the standards and criteria established by the applicable environmental planning instruments.

3. *Advertised development* is development that must be publicly notified and exhibited, with a specified period for public submissions. Advertised development may be identified in an environmental planning instrument or in the *Government Gazette.*

4. *Regional development* includes development to be determined by a joint regional planning panel under Part 4 of the *EPAA*. Following changes introduced in June 2011, this includes development with a capital value over $20 million; development by local council and development by a public authority requiring consent under Part 4; certain private infrastructure or community facilities with a value over $5 million; eco-tourism facilities with a value over $5 million; and some coastal developments. Development with a capital value of more than $10 million that has been subject to delays, or in areas where a council's performance has been found to be unsatisfactory, due to failure to comply with applicable performance criteria may also be determined by joint regional planning panels (Environmental Planning and Assessment Amendment (Part 3A Repeal) Bill 2011, Schedule 4A(11).) Joint regional planning panels are also consent authorities for particular types of designated development (generally relating to extractive industry, waste management facilities, and marinas).

5. *Designated development* is defined in the Environmental Planning and Assessment Regulation 2000 (EPAR). It is often heavy industry (for instance, intensive agriculture, mining activities, abattoirs) with a high potential for pollution. Place-specific forms of designated development may also be defined within an LEP or SEPP. Proposals for designated development must be accompanied by an Environmental Impact Statement.

6. *Integrated development* is a special class of development defined under section 91 of the *EPAA* because it needs other forms of government approvals such as a state agency permit or licence. The integrated development provisions are intended to provide for upfront agency involvement in the assessment of developments. The agency is able to guarantee that if the development is approved, the relevant permit or licence will be issued to enable the applicant to carry out the activity.

7. *State Significant Development.* The June 2011 amendments to the *EPAA* changed the nomenclature for projects of state significance. The new provisions, and accompanying policy guidance issued by the government establish classes of State Significant Development (SSD) based on the type of development and its capital value (for most classes of development, $30 million is the threshold value). The provisions, which are to be formalised in a State Environmental Planning Policy, also identify particular sites with state significant development, including the Sydney Opera House, the Sydney Olympic Park, Luna Park, Barangaroo, Darling Harbour, and a number of other strategic locations (Department of Planning and Infrastructure 2011). Residential development is no longer considered to be of state significance solely because of its capital value.

Development that is prohibited

If an environmental planning instrument defines a particular development as 'prohibited' within a certain zone or parcel of land, it may not be carried out unless the plan is amended. The Major Development SEPP, in conjunction with Part 3A, provided an avenue for approving major projects and critical infrastructure projects, despite the provisions in an environmental planning instrument. The capacity to approve such non conforming activities has been significantly curtailed under the new State Significant provisions outline above.

Environment and development assessment under the *EPAA*

Development is categorised and assessed under parts 4 and 5 of the *EPAA*. Different terminology is used to describe the party putting forward the application and the authority resposible for the decision under these parts, as summarised in Table 8.1

Table 8.1 Terminology for environmental and development assessment under parts 4 and 5 of the *EPAA*, June 2011

Part	Person/party making application	Project	Assessment terminology	Authority responsible for decision
Part 4	Applicant	Development	Development assessment/environmental impact assessment	Consent authority
Part 5	Proponent	Activity	Review of environmental factors/environmental impact assessment	Determining authority

As shown in the table, the person or organisation making a proposal is called an 'applicant' under Part 4 and a 'proponent' under Part 5; while a 'development' under Part 4 is called a 'project' and an 'activity' under Part 5.

Box 8.1 Major Development assessment under the former Part 3A *EPAA*

Part 3A of the *EPAA* established special procedures for developments declared to be of state or regional significance. The provisions were introduced in 2005 as part of a package of reforms intended to streamline the NSW planning system, facilitate infrastructure development, and encourage business investment in the state.

A special State Environmental Planning Policy (Major Development) 2005 identified the criteria for major development status as well as specific sites regarded to be of state significance. A large number of development types met the criteria for state significance, including, controversially, residential developments of a capital value of more than $100 million. Major infrastructure or other development to be carried out by a public authority (that would otherwise have required an Environmental Impact Statement under Part 5 of the Act) was also covered under the Part 3A provisions. A project could also be declared to be 'critical infrastructure' if the minister regarded it to be 'essential' for the state for economic, environmental or social reasons (under the former Part 75C of the *EPAA*).

The minister for planning was the consent authority for projects under Part 3A, unbound by the environmental assessment requirements of Part 4 and Part 5 of the *EPAA*, including the provisions of environmental planning instruments. If an approval contravened existing planning controls, these controls were subsequently amended. Environmental assessment guidelines were issued on a case by case basis by the director general of planning (as occurs in relation to the environmental impact assessment provisions under Part 4 and Part 5). Proponents prepared and submitted environmental assessments in relation to these requirements, which were then exhibited for at least 30 days. Submissions were then addressed by the proponent in a 'preferred project report' before submission for assessment by the department and determination by the minister. Authority to determine certain matters (relating to reportable political donations or proposals located within the minister's electorate) was delegated to the Planning Assessment Commission in 2008.

Under certain circumstances, Part 3A provided an abridged process of approach for projects prior to detailed consideration. A 'concept plan', outlining the scope of a project and related development options provided a way of obtaining in principle approval prior to detailed project planning and assessment. Subsequent more detailed development applications consistent with the scope of an approved concept plan were guaranteed approval.

Between 2009–2010, 138 applications under Part 3A were made (Department of Planning 2010). Of these, 48 related to residential, commercial, and retail projects, with the remainder spread across infrastructure, industry, and coastal development sectors. Over the same period, 125 approvals were made, 66 of which were determined by the minister, 16 by the Planning Assessment Commission, and the remainder by the Department of Planning.

The Bill to repeal Part 3A established two categories of development: State Significant Development and State Significant Infrastructure, again with separate assessment pathways. While in many ways the new provisions resemble the former Part 3A, accompanying policy documents establish a narrower range of criteria for state significance and delegate Ministerial approval powers to the Planning Assessment Commission or departmental officers, thereby reducing perceptions of political interference in the process. A key difference between the new provisions and the former Part 3A is that applicable environmental planning instruments must be considered during the assessment of State Significant Development. However, exemptions from requirements under other certain legislation, such as the *Coastal Protection Act 1979* the *Fisheries Management Act 1994*, the *Heritage Act 1977*, the *National Parks and Wildlife Act 1974*, remain.

Development applications and assessment (Part 4)

Most development in NSW is subject to the development application and assessment processes set out in Part 4 of the *EPAA*. The process can be summarised as follows:

- intention to develop
- lodging an application
- public consultation
- assessment
- decision (to refuse, approve, or approve with specified conditions)
- possible appeal against decision.

Figure 8.1 Community concern over Part 3A in NSW

This community protest over the expansion of a suburban shopping centre 'Marrickville Metro' in the inner city is indicative of many such attempts by local residents to draw attention to perceived politicisation of the planning process. Local residents expressed particular concern over the decision regarding the shopping centre expansion being taken out of the hands of their local council. Source: the Author 2011.

The application

The owner of the land or a person with the owner's written consent (such as an appointed consultant) may make a development application in NSW. This requirement has prevented speculators securing planning approval for a proposal without advising the landowners. Technically, public authorities are also able to make a development application and need only serve a copy of the application to the owners of the land.

The application itself must contain sufficient information to enable the environmental impact of the proposal to be assessed. Information requirements are usually specified by consent authorities and include the completion of an application form, the submission of a site plan and drawings of the development, and supplementary information outlined in Schedule 1 of the Environmental Planning and Assessment Regulation 2000 (EPAR).

Like most jurisdictions, NSW has set strict requirements for the type of information needed to assess a development application. A development application form will include a description of the development, details of the land (including title), an indication as to whether the land is part of critical habitat or whether the development might significantly affect threatened species, a list of authorities whose concurrence to the development is needed, whether the development is classed as 'integrated' under s91 *EPAA*, and the estimated cost of the development.

For land that is part of a critical habitat, or likely to significantly affect threatened species, populations or ecological communities, or their habitats, a species impact statement is required.

The EPAR requires that site plans indicate:

a. the location, boundary dimensions, site area and north point of the land
b. existing vegetation and trees on the land
c. the location and uses of existing buildings on the land
d. existing levels of the land in relation to buildings and roads
e. the location and uses of buildings on sites adjoining the land (EPAR, Schedule 1, s2[2]).

Sketches or drawings of the proposed development must show:

a. the location of any proposed buildings or works (including extensions or additions to existing buildings or works) in relation to the land's boundaries and adjoining development
b. floor plans of any proposed buildings showing layout, partitioning, room sizes and intended uses of each part of the building
c. elevations and sections showing proposed external finishes and heights of any proposed buildings
d. proposed finished levels of the land in relation to existing and proposed buildings and roads
e. proposed parking arrangements, entry and exit points for vehicles, and provision for movement of vehicles within the site (including dimensions where appropriate)
f. proposed landscaping and treatment of the land (indicating plant types and their height and maturity)
g. proposed methods of draining the land (EPAR, Schedule 1, s2(3).

For applications affected by the SEPP – Building Sustainability Index (BASIX) (discussed in chapter 7), matters relating to the BASIX certificate for the development should be included on the sketch.

In addition to a site plan, and plan or drawings of development, a 'statement of environmental effects' is required (unless the development is 'designated', in which case an Environmental Impact Statement is needed). Applications for non-complying development must be accompanied by a Statement of Environmental Effects, or, if designated, an Environmental Impact Statement.

Statement of Environmental Effects

The Statement of Environmental Effects must indicate:

a. the environmental impacts of the development
b. how the environmental impacts of the development have been identified
c. the steps to be taken to protect the environment or to lessen the expected harm to the environment
d. any matters required to be indicated by any guidelines issued by the director general for the purposes of this clause (EPAR, Schedule 1, s2(4)).

If the development application relates to an application affected by SEPP No. 65 – Design Quality of Residential Flat Development (discussed in chapter 7) special information requirements are stipulated in the regulation.

Development applications for any development subject to BASIX requirements, must also be accompanied by a BASIX certificate or certificates to demonstrate compliance with minimum water and energy savings provisions. These can be obtained online by submitting technical details about the proposal and undertaking certain commitments regarding its design and materials.

Figure 8.2 Exhibition of development application, Marrickville

Source: the Author 2010

Environmental Impact Statements

Schedule 2 of the EPAR specifies the requirements for environmental impact statements for Part 4 applications that are classified as designated (defined in Schedule 3) development (Box 8.2). Specific issues for the Environmental Impact Statement to address are identified in consultation with the director general of planning; and the developer is notified of these requirements.

Evaluating development applications

The *EPAA* sets out a list of matters for consent authorities to consider when assessing development under Part 4 (s79C) (Box 8.3). Relative to the other Australian jurisdications, this list of matters to be assessed is quite comprehensive, and includes the provisions of any environmental planning instrument, and any exhibited draft environmental planning instrument; any development control plan, as well as the likely impacts of the development on the natural and built environment, and social and economic impacts, the suitability of the site, any public submissions, and 'the public interest'.

However, the Act does not state what weight should be given to each of these factors, as long as they are formally considered. Similarly, there is no rule that if consideration of these factors is negative, consent should be denied. Rather, the development application must be considered overall. Nor does the Act provide advice on how to evaluate conflicting factors such as when proposals are likely to have social and economic advantages but may cause environmental problems (Farrier & Stein 2006). Prior to 1997, an even more detailed list of matters to consider when assessing a development under the *EPAA* was specified under the former s90(1) and this list is often used as a guide to assist in the interpretation of issues such as 'social and economic impact'.

Box 8.2 Prescribed format for environmental impact statements NSW

1 Summary

A summary of the Environmental Impact Statement.

2 Statement of objectives

A statement of the objectives of the development or activity.

3 Analysis of alternatives

An analysis of any feasible alternatives to the carrying out of the development or activity, having regard to its objectives, including the consequences of not carrying out the development or activity.

4 Environmental assessment

An analysis of the development or activity, including:

(a) a full description of the development or activity, and

(b) a general description of the environment likely to be affected by the development or activity, together with a detailed description of those aspects of the environment that are likely to be significantly affected, and

(c) the likely impact on the environment of the development or activity, and

(d) a full description of the measures proposed to mitigate any adverse effects of the development or activity on the environment, and

(e) a list of any approvals that must be obtained under any other Act or law before the development or activity may lawfully be carried out.

5 Compilation of measures to mitigate adverse effects

A compilation (in a single section of the Environmental Impact Statement) of the measures referred to in item 4 (d).

6 Justification of development

(1) The reasons justifying the carrying out of the development or activity in the manner proposed, having regard to biophysical, economic and social considerations, including the following principles of ecologically sustainable development:

(a) the 'precautionary principle', namely, that if there are threats of serious or irreversible environmental damage, lack of full scientific certainty should not be used as a reason for postponing measures to prevent environmental degradation. In the application of the precautionary principle, public and private decisions should be guided by:

(i) careful evaluation to avoid, wherever practicable, serious or irreversible damage to the environment, and

(ii) an assessment of the risk-weighted consequences of various options,

(b) 'intergenerational equity', namely, that the present generation should ensure that the health, diversity and productivity of the environment are maintained or enhanced for the benefit of future generations,

(c) 'conservation of biological diversity and ecological integrity', namely, that conservation of biological diversity and ecological integrity should be a fundamental consideration,

(d) 'improved valuation, pricing and incentive mechanisms', namely, that environmental factors should be included in the valuation of assets and services, such as:

(i) polluter pays, that is, those who generate pollution and waste should bear the cost of containment, avoidance or abatement,

(ii) the users of goods and services should pay prices based on the full life cycle of costs of providing goods and services, including the use of natural resources and assets and the ultimate disposal of any waste,

(iii) environmental goals, having been established, should be pursued in the most cost effective way, by establishing incentive structures, including market mechanisms, that enable those best placed to maximise benefits or minimise costs to develop their own solutions and responses to environmental problems.

(Source: EPAR, Schedule 2)

Matters for consideration: provisions of environmental planning instruments

As noted, the provisions of environmental planning instruments, must be considered under section 79C (Box 8.3). Consent authorities should consider not only whether the development is technically permissible within the land use zone, but also undertake an assessment of the merits of the proposal to determine whether it is consistent with the aims and objectives of the zone, and the wider aims and objectives of applicable environmental planning instruments (or exhibited draft instruments). The development standards in these instruments – for instance, controls relating to floor-space, height, or lot size, must be upheld unless the instrument indicates opportunities for discretion. The provisions of development control plans are discretionary but if they are consistently applied, they will generally be supported in case of legal appeal. Even council policies that are not contained in development control plans may be given weight in assessment decisions if they are consistently applied and reflect appropriate consultation and deliberation (Farrier & Stein 2006).

Environmental impact of development

In evaluating the environmental impacts of developments, consent authorities are required under s79C to consider the effect of the proposal on natural resources (such as water, soil, forests); the protection and maintenance of biodiversity; waste disposal and energy use. Consent authorities should also consider whether the proposal relates to critical habitat (under the *Threatened Species Conservation Act 1995*); and whether it may be a matter of national environmental significance under the *Commonwealth Environment Protection and Biodiversity Conservation Act 1999*. There is an implied obligation to consider the principles of ecological sustainability more broadly, consistent with the overall objectives of the *EPAA*.

Impacts on built environment

The definition of environment under the *EPAA* includes both built and 'natural' elements. Factors relevant to assessing the impacts of proposed developments on the built environment include:

- effects on traffic movements
- aesthetic impacts of the development on landscape and scenery, considering things such as size, bulk, appearance and design
- the relationship to other developments on adjoining land or localities (for instance, things such as views, privacy, access, sunlight and ventilation)
- the health and safety of the occupants (Farrier & Stein 2006).

Social and economic impact of development

Principles for assessing social and economic impact of development include:

- respecting the character of an area
- avoiding a reduction in the existing quality of life of residents
- maintaining an adequate spread of services and facilities within a particular area (Farrier & Stein 2006).

These factors might relate to neighbouring amenity – privacy, solar access, views or noise, or to broader considerations such as the impact of a club on a neighbouring residential area. In some cases a relevant consideration may be the impact of development or the redevelopment of buildings on the need for, or availability of, affordable housing.

Decision-makers may also take into account the benefits and costs of proposed development on both existing and potential future businesses in the locality, although the impact of a specific proposal on a particular business is not a relevant consideration. For instance, the potential for a new cinema to revive a local shopping strip and so contribute to wider employment opportunities may be relevant, but the impact of competition from a second cinema on the financial viability of a nearby theatre would not be a basis for consideration.

It is also relevant to consider social and economic impacts of development in relation to establishing a hierarchy of retail and commercial centres, consistent with efficient urban structure and the integration of land use and transportation.

Suitability of the site

There are two primary considerations when considering the suitability of the site:

- does the proposal fit the locality?
- is the site itself suitable for the particular development? (Farrier & Stein 2006)

Relevant issues include basic health and safety (including contamination) as well as exposure to natural hazards (like flooding, bushfires, subsidence, slip, storm events). The future use of land may also be taken into account. For example, will the proposed activity prejudice or rule out future uses which may be regarded as important, like agriculture or mining? Land use conflict between the proposed use and existing or potential uses on adjacent land is a key factor to evaluate – will the development impose constraints on the future development of surrounding land? For instance, will a residential subdivision within a rural area lead to conflicts or opposition to the further development of the area for agricultural or intensive agricultural activities?

The public interest

The concept of public interest takes in a range of issues such as the existence of restrictive covenants on the use of land or design of development; consistency with government policies that might not have legal status, and the circumstances of the case. For example, if in the particular circumstances of the case, an approval may set an undesirable precedent of other inappropriate development within the locality, this is a relevant issue to consider in relation to the 'public interest'. Community reactions to a proposed development may be a relevant matter under this head of consideration. Environmentally sustainable development objectives might also be considered in relation to the public interest given there is no other specific reference to them under s79C (Farrier & Stein 2006).

Submissions

Submissions by members of the public are invited when a development is classified as 'designated' or 'advertised' under an environmental planning instrument. Many local councils have their own notification policy requiring that, at a minimum, neighbours be advised of developments on adjacent land. Submissions regarding development proposals may be by members of the public or by public authorities. Not only must each of these submissions be formally considered by decision-makers, there is also an implication that decision-makers consider how the issues raised can be resolved.

Box 8.3 Matters for consideration when assessing development under Part 4 of the *EPAA*

79C Evaluation

(1) Matters for consideration – general. In determining a development application, a consent authority is to take into consideration such of the following matters as are of relevance to the development the subject of the development application:

(a) the provisions of:

(i) any environmental planning instrument, and

(ii) any draft environmental planning instrument that is or has been placed on public exhibition and details of which have been notified to the consent authority (unless the director general has notified the consent authority that the making of the draft instrument has been deferred indefinitely or has not been approved), and

(iii) any development control plan, and

(iiia) any planning agreement that has been entered into under section 93F, or any draft planning agreement that a developer has offered to enter into under section 93F, and

(iv) the regulations (to the extent that they prescribe matters for the purposes of this paragraph),

that apply to the land to which the development application relates,

(b) the likely impacts of that development, including environmental impacts on both the natural and built environments, and social and economic impacts in the locality,

(c) the suitability of the site for the development,

(d) any submissions made in accordance with this Act or the regulations,

(e) the public interest.

(Source: *EPAA*, s79C[1])

The clock

Strict timeframes have been established by the *EPAA* and EPAR for the processing and assessment of development applications. A consent authority may reject a development application:

- within seven days if it is illegible or unclear, or does not contain the required information
- within 14 days if the proposal is for integrated development and the proponent has not identified all of the relevant approvals required, or include the required additional fees and information needed to assess the development.

An application may be deemed refused if a determination is not made by the consent authority:

- within 40 days (for general development)
- within 60 days (for designated, integrated, or development requiring the concurrence of another authority).

A 'deemed refusal' enables the applicant to appeal to the NSW Land and Environment Court for a decision.

Determination and conditions

The consent authority determines a development application by granting consent to the development, granting consent subject to conditions, or refusing consent to the development. The consent authority must give reasons in writing for refusing consent and for the implementation of conditions. Conditions could relate to the commencement or staging of development, the details of development – for instance, its design, siting and landscaping, or required financial or other contributions. The consent authority may also grant 'deferred commencement consent', which is consent subject to a condition that the development cannot proceed until certain activities have been carried out (*EPAA* s80[3]). A consent authority may also grant a 'partial consent', approving the development with the exception of a specified part or aspect of it, granting full consent at a later time (*EPAA* s80[4–5]).

Post consent

Development consents in NSW generally lapse within five years if the development has not physically commenced within that time.

Following approval, the developer may apply to the consent authority for the consent to be modified if needed (*EPAA* s96). The *EPAA* provides for modification of consents only if the development is 'substantially' the same. If the proposed modification is not of a minor nature, it may be necessary to undergo notification/advertisement procedures again. The state government may also revoke or modify consent if it is no longer compatible with a draft environmental planning instrument (but special notification provisions and financial compensation requirements apply).

Criminal proceedings may be brought if the developer does not comply with the terms of the consent. Councils (and consent authorities generally) are able to give certain orders to comply with a development consent, to complete the development, if it has commenced, to demolish or remove buildings erected without consent and to maintain the public safety (for instance, in the case of demolition or repair of buildings).

State Significant Development (Part 4, Division 4.1)

The 2011 changes to the *EPAA* provided for the new category of State Significant Development to be assessed under the provisions of Part 4 (including s79C) as just described.

The minister has 'call in' powers for projects of state significance that are not identified in a State Environmental Planning Policy, subject to advice from the Planning Assessment Commission. In contrast to previous arrangements under Part 3A, proposals that are wholly prohibited under existing planning controls are not able to be approved, unless the project is 'called in' under these special powers. Proposals that are partly prohibited under existing planning controls may be approved, subject to consideration of an amendment to the planning controls. For probity, authority to make the 'gateway determination' for such an amendment is delegated to the Planning Assessment Commission. Applications for State Significant Development must be publically exhibited for a period of 30 days.

Although the minister is the consent authority for State Significant Development, this role is delegated to the Planning Assessment Commission (for controversial projects) and to senior departmental officers for projects that have attracted fewer than 25 public objections and where the council has not objected.

Environmental assessment under Part 5

Part 5 of the *EPAA* established procedures for regulating development that does not need consent under Part 4 of the Act (but is not exempt development). Usually, Part 5 relates to actions undertaken by 'the Crown'. Rather than the term 'development', Part 5 refers to 'activities', which have a similar meaning, including the use or subdivision of land, the erection of a building, the carrying out of a work, and demolition, as well as any other matter referred to in section 26 of the *EPAA,* unless development consent under Part 4 is required or has been obtained, or the activity itself is prohibited.

In contrast to the term 'consent authority' used for activities regulated under Part 4, Part 5 refers to the 'determining authority', which is the minister or public authority, by or on whose behalf the activity is to be carried out, and any minister or public authority whose approval for the activity is required (*EPAA*, s110). The minister responsible for planning is not necessarily the determining authority for activity under Part 5. If the approval of more than one determining authority is required in relation to an activity, the minister may, by order published in the *Gazette* and in a newspaper circulating throughout the state, identify a 'nominated determining authority'. This is the main authority responsible for assessing the proposed activity.

Part 5 identifies a range of matters that each determining authority must consider when assessing proposals, including the potential environmental impact of activities; the potential impact on wilderness areas and critical habitat, threatened species, populations and ecological communities, and their habitats, and any other protected fauna or protected native plants within the meaning of the *National Parks and Wildlife Act 1974.* The determining authority must also consider potential effects on any conservation agreement entered into under the *National Parks and Wildlife Act 1974*; any plan of management adopted under that Act for the conservation area to which the agreement relates; any joint management agreement entered into under the *Threatened Species Conservation Act 1995*;

and any biobanking agreement entered into under Part 7A of the *Threatened Species Conservation Act 1995 (EPAA, s111)*.

If the determining authority considers that the potential activity may have a significant impact on any of these matters, they must require an Environmental Impact Statement to be prepared in relation to the activity. The 2011 changes to the *EPAA* introduced new terminology to describe these activities as 'State Significant Infrastructure'. State Significant Infrastructure may also be declared under a State Environmental Planning Policy. The minister for planning must approve applications for State Significant Infrastructure'.

An application for State Significant Infrastructure is made to the director general of planning, who issues environmental assessment requirements for the preparation of an Environmental Impact Statement. The Environmental Impact Statement must be exhibited for at least 30 days. Public submissions on the proposal are considered in preparing a final 'preferred infrastructure report', which is then considered by the director general of planning, along with any advice from the Planning Assessment Commission or other public authorities, before making a recommendation to the minister.

State Significant Infrastructure is not subject to the provisions of environmental planning instruments, aside from classification of the proposed activity as permissible without consent. There is also relief from requirements under other certain legislation, including the *Coastal Protection Act 1979*, the *Fisheries Management Act 1994*, the *Heritage Act 1977*, and the *National Parks and Wildlife Act 1974*.

There is provision for staged approval of State Significant Infrastructure, via 'concept proposals' ahead of detailed proposals that can be submitted for subsequent approval.

The minister may also declare 'critical' State Significant Infrastructure, if 'it is of a category that, in the opinion of the minister, is essential for the state for economic, environmental or social reasons' (Environmental Planning and Assessment Amendment [Part 3A Repeal] Bill 2011, 115V). Critical State Significant Infrastructure is granted additional exemption from provisions of state legislation that might otherwise interfere with the carrying out of the activity (115ZG [3]).

Unauthorised building work

On occasion council-approved planning and building regulations are intentionally overlooked by owners, builders or developers in an attempt to evade local controls. The Mayor of Willoughby City in NSW, for example, has found it necessary to write an open letter to the residents explaining a variety of concerns about a growing lack of compliance that extends beyond accidental building work or misinterpretation (Box 8.3).

As emphasised in the letter, 'These actions are usually based on the assumption that if illegal work is discovered by Council, the offender will simply be issued with a fine and be able to lodge an application for approval after the work has been completed' (Reilly 2010). Gaining such a retrospective approval through a section 96 modification application may be seen as cost effective given the reluctance of many councils to order demolition of the unauthorised development. In response to this trend some councils have created Development Enforcement Units to monitor building sites.

It is not only private individuals and developers who undertake activities without observing required planning and assessment requirements. Commenting on the complexity of the NSW planning system, the Environmental Defender's Office has claimed that there have been a number of incidents when state agencies have failed to carry out appropriate environmental assessment requirements under Part 5, or to seek development approval for activities requiring consent under Part 4. One cited example was work authorised by the Department of Education and Training within a nature conservation area earmarked for rehabilitation of an endangered ecological community (Environmental Defender's Office NSW 2010).

Box 8.4 Letter from Mayor of Willoughby City Council regarding unauthorised building works

Council on behalf of the community is concerned when:

- Development applications are lodged that are well outside the standards and have no prospect of Council support.

- Practices where confusing or incomplete drawn plans are lodged with Council with the intention of gaining approval and later using the uncertainty about what has been approved to build something different to what was outlined in the approved application.

- Owners and builders ignore the conditions of an approval they don't like in order to do what they originally wanted to do without getting the changes approved.

- Owners and builders ignore Council altogether and build what they want in the hope that Council will never find out.

Source: Pat Reilly, Willoughby City Mayor, Open letter to the residents of Willoughby City, 20 November 2010.

Development contributions system under the *EPAA*

The *EPAA* has evolved to provide several different avenues for planning authorities to seek contributions from developers for infrastructure or services. These include the levying of contributions under a contributions plan, the use of a fixed fee or levy, negotiated agreements between developers and planning authorities, special infrastructure contributions (typically applying to urban release areas), and contributions for affordable housing.

The NSW contributions planning framework established under section 94 of the *EPAA* evolved partly in response to requests from the development industry for greater rigour and transparency regarding the costs and distribution of funds relating to local urban infrastructure. However, there has been ongoing debate about the operation of this framework, and indeed, approaches to infrastructure contributions nationally (Gurran et al. 2009; Productivity Commission 2011). As outlined in chapter 5 this debate focuses on the costs of contributions, the uncertainty of requirements, and delays between payment and local provision of infrastructure on the ground (Gurran et al. 2009). As explained by Michael Watt, a long-time local government professional, the appropriate use of development contributions depends on the capacity to predict future development scenarios and needs, including land acquisition, the cost of which is invariably higher at the time of acquisition than when the contribution levy was set:

> As a long range planning tool section 94 requires constant and regular review. Adjusting for changes in facilities, services, population needs, land value and capital works costs is a complicated, resource hungry exercise. Alternatives need to be explored which deliver a certainty of outcome and meet the demands arising from development. A valid question for local government to ask is whether it is able to afford urban development and sustain future capital and recurrent costs in the long term (Watt 2003, p114).

Figure 8.3 Council aquatic centre

Local swimming pools are commonly funded through s94 contributions in NSW. Source: the Author 2006

Since 2005 a number of new avenues for local and state planning authorities in NSW to seek developer contributions for urban infrastructure and services have been introduced, as outlined in the sections below. However, responding to concerns about housing afford-ability and a slump in new housing supply, in 2010 the NSW state government announced a 'cap' on local development contributions of $20,000 per new home (subsequently lifted to $30,000 in greenfield areas). While very few local government areas exceeded this amount, the cap represented a particular problem in new release areas dependent on contributions for the basic urban services needed to support new development. By late 2010 a number of local councils were demonstrably unable to provide for new development and a Priority Infrastructure Fund for councils to meet essential works was introduced (DOP 2010).

Contributions for public amenities or services

Under section 94 of the *EPAA,* developers may be required to contribute towards public 'amenities or services' as a condition of development approval. Public amenities and services are not defined by the Act but the *EPAA* states that they do not include water supply or sewerage services (s93C). (Councils are able to require payment for water and sewerage services, or to require developers to construct them, under the *NSW Water Supply Authorities Act 1987).* Contributions may be sought towards the provision or improvement, or to recoup the costs of public amenities and services that have already been provided.

These contributions may be obtained by the consent authority as a condition of development consent, requiring (a) the dedication of land free of cost, (b) the payment of a monetary contribution, or both (EPAA, s94[1]). The consent authority may accept a 'material public benefit' (an in kind contribution other than land) in lieu of a cash or land contribution.

Key principles of reasonableness, nexus, fair apportionment and accountability

Key principles of 'reasonableness' and 'accountability' are intended to underpin the NSW contribution system (DOP 2010d). These principles are important because contribution requirements that contravene such principles may be legally challenged. 'Reasonable' contributions demonstrate a 'nexus' or link between the development and the facilities or services for which the contribution is sought. 'Nexus' requires a causal connection between the development and the contribution. That is, the development should in some way cause or contribute to the need for the amenity or service. There should also be a 'spatial' connection between the location of the development and the provision of the amenities or services. The principle of 'temporal' nexus requires that the amenities or services be provided in a timely way, before or within a reasonable period of time after the development is completed. The notion of 'fair apportionment' – that is, that contributions sought from individual developers represent a fair and consistently applied share of the cost of providing the service – has also been inferred from the concept of 'reasonableness'. However, in practice excessive focus on 'fair apportionment' can lead to complicated contribution formulae and perverse development outcomes, as discussed further below.

In NSW, the principle of 'accountability' is usually demonstrated by the operation of a contributions plan, which sets out the formula for seeking contributions, and a capital works plan showing how contributions will be (and have been) allocated over time.

'Section 94' contributions plans

A contributions plan must be in place before contributions can be collected by a local council under section 94. The provisions for making a contributions plan are set out under section 94EA of the *EPAA* and Part 4, Division 1C of the EPAR. These include ministerial directions to local councils regarding the imposition of local contributions, such as the public amenities or services for which contributions may be applied, the methods for determining required payments, and the maximum amount of payments.

Contributions plans have usually established a formula for needs, using a combination of projected costs associated with meeting all of the projected local infrastructure requirements (such as recreation areas, local roads and paths, community facilities, car parking, stormwater facilities and so on) divided by demand over time, to arrive at an amount per allotment, dwelling, or other development type.

Individual councils, or two or more councils, may prepare and approve a contributions plan. The minister for planning may also 'direct a council, in writing, to approve, amend or repeal a contributions plan' (s94EAA [1]), or undertake this action directly (s94EAA[2]). Contributions plans must be publicly exhibited and any person may make a submission regarding the content of the plan.

Fixed development consent levies (s94A)

Amendments to the *EPAA* in 2005 introduced section 94A enabling the consent authority to impose a levy comprised as a percentage of the proposed cost of the development rather than a contribution calculated by formula. When the consent authority is a local council, this levy must be authorised within the framework of a contributions plan. It must be applied to the provision, extension or augmentation of public amenities or public services (or recouping these costs), although the principle of nexus is not required to be demonstrated. The levy cannot be imposed in addition to any other contributions sought through a contributions plan. While a detailed infrastructure works schedule is still required, the levy provides a simpler approach to calculating development contribution requirements. However, to ensure that the appropriate levy is charged, council must carefully scrutinise development costs nominated by developers.

The EPAR may specify the maximum percentage of a levy. In 2010, this was 0.5 per cent for development valued at $100,000–$200,000, and one per cent for development valued over $200,000. The regulations may also specify different levy amounts for land in specific locations.

The *EPAA* enables the minister or the director general, as the consent authority to directly impose conditions for the levying of developer contributions under section 94 or 94A relating to '(a) land within a growth centre, or, (b) other land within one or more council areas' (s94D[1]). This may be done without the need to prepare a contributions plan.

Ministerial direction under section 94E

As noted, the minister has the power to make directions regarding local contributions (s94E). In late 2010, a direction was made to limit the contribution amount that councils could require as a condition of consent to:

- $30,000 per dwelling or residential lot in greenfield areas
- $20,000 per dwelling or residential lot in other areas.

The direction does not alter existing local contribution plans, but limits the amount that a council can require under these plans as a condition of development consent, in line with the above caps.

To offset some of the funding shortfalls that might arise from the imposition of this cap, the government established a Priority Infrastructure Fund of $50 million providing access to grants for 'essential works' for a two year period. Councils may also seek to overcome infrastructure funding shortfalls by seeking a variation to their local rates. In both cases, existing section 94 contribution plans must be submitted to the Independent Pricing and Regulatory Review Tribunal (IPART) prior to approval. New contribution plans with proposed contributions above the set limits must also be submitted to IPART.

Planning agreements

Also introduced in 2005, planning agreements are an alternative to the fixed contribution requirement just described, and allow more flexibility. They are defined under section 93F as voluntary agreements between a 'planning authority' (or two or more planning authorities) and a person (the 'developer'). The 'developer' is a person:

a. who has sought a change to an environmental planning instrument, or

b. who has made, or proposes to make, a development application (s93F[1]).

Planning agreements are therefore pursued at the time a development application is lodged, or when an application to change an environmental planning instrument is made (for instance, an application for a rezoning). However, the agreements cannot require a development application to be approved or particular changes to an environmental planning instrument to be made. Similarly, the consent authority cannot refuse a development application on the basis that a planning agreement has not been entered into (although the actual enforcement of planning agreements is made through conditions of development consent).

The planning agreement requires the developer 'to dedicate land free of cost, pay a monetary contribution, or provide any other material public benefit, or any combination of them, to be used for or applied towards a public purpose' (s93F[1]). To promote transparency a public notice and exhibition of planning agreements (for a minimum of 28 days) is required (s93G).

The concept of 'public purpose' includes public amenities and services as well as a range of other matters, including:

b. the provision of (or the recoupment of the cost of providing) affordable housing,

c. the provision of (or the recoupment of the cost of providing) transport or other infrastructure relating to land

d. the funding of recurrent expenditure relating to the provision of public amenities or public services, affordable housing or transport or other infrastructure

e. the monitoring of the planning impacts of development

f. the conservation or enhancement of the natural environment (s93F[2]).

Planning agreements are registered to the title of the land, so they are able to be enforced even after a change of owners. Unlike the contributions planning framework under section 94, the principle of nexus does not need to be demonstrated. Contributions sought through a planning agreement may be applied to adjoining local government areas, and councils may join together in securing agreements covering cross-boundary areas.

Planning agreements may be undertaken instead of, or as well as, requirements for contributions under a section 94 contributions plan, however, the complete suspension of any other requirements under section 94 or 94A may only be undertaken if the minister is a consent authority.

Additional approaches to seeking development contributions under the *EPAA*

The *EPAA* provides two other avenues for seeking development contributions through the planning process. These include special infrastructure contributions and dedicated contributions for affordable housing.

Special infrastructure contributions

To facilitate the provision of infrastructure needed to service large urban release areas, the *EPAA* has authorised a further avenue for collecting developer contributions 'for the provision of infrastructure' within 'special contributions areas' under section 94ED.

The minister may make, amend or repeal 'special contributions areas' by order published on the NSW legislation website, after consulting with the 'peak industry organisations that the minister considers to be relevant' (94EG[4]).

A Special Contributions Areas Infrastructure Fund has been established (under section 94EJ), administered by the director general of planning. The fund is to contain any monetary contributions received by a consent authority, proceedings from the sale of land received by a consent authority as an 'in kind' contribution, any money authorised by Parliament, the proceeds of any investments of money in the fund, and any other moneys required to be paid into the Fund under the *EPAA* or other legislation (ss94EK[a-e]).

The fund is to be used to provide payments to 'public authorities for the provision of infrastructure in relation to development' and related administrative expenses (s94EL[1]). 'Infrastructure' in this context is defined as the provision of public amenities or public services, as well as affordable housing, transport, or 'other infrastructure relating to land' (s94ED[1][a]). It may extend to recurrent or maintenance fees associated with these services. Funds may also be directed to the 'conservation or enhancement of the natural environment' (s94ED[1][c]), or used for research or investigation, the preparation of a report, study or instrument. Finally, contributions may be extended broadly to 'any other matter or thing in connection with the exercise of any statutory function' under the *EPAA* (s94ED[1][d][iii]), with the sole exception of water supply or sewerage services.

The principle of spatial nexus does not need to be demonstrated in relation to special infrastructure contributions and the contributions do not need to be spent within the special contributions area. This means that special infrastructure contributions can be levied for regional infrastructure that may not be located within the local government area, but will serve residents across many local government areas within the region (DOP

2006a). However it should be clear that the need for the infrastructure arises as a result of the development, or provides benefits to the development.

The minister is to determine the 'level and nature of development contributions' (94EE[1]) for the provision of infrastructure, and may choose to do so through a levy. When the special contributions area is not a designated growth centre, the minister for planning must either consult with owners of the land and other relevant stakeholders, publicly exhibit the proposed level of collections, or establish an advisory panel prior to determining the amount of contributions that will be sought (or may do any combination of these things).

Part of a development contribution collected in this way may be identified by the minister for provision of infrastructure by a local council. To avoid 'doubling up' on developer contributions, the approval of the minister for planning or a designated development corporation is required before a council can impose a contributions levy within a special contributions area.

Figure 8.4 Affordable housing funded by developer contributions, City West

Source: the Author 2004

Contributions for affordable housing

A special section of the *EPAA* provides specifically for contributions for affordable housing (although as noted above, funds obtained through planning agreements or special infrastructure contributions may also be directed to the provision or maintenance of affordable housing). Under section 94F, a consent authority is enabled to impose a condition of development consent requiring a contribution towards affordable housing, within areas identified by a State Environmental Planning Policy as having a need for affordable housing. In practice, SEPP No. 70: Affordable Housing (Revised Schemes) (SEPP 70) identifies only two local government areas in NSW as having such a need: Willoughby City Council and the City of Sydney (incorporating the Green Square area of the former City of South Sydney and the City West area).

In addition to identification within the SEPP, the consent authority must be formally satisfied that the proposed development 'will or is likely to reduce the availability of affordable housing within the area', 'will create a need for affordable housing within the area', or 'the proposed development is allowed only because of the initial zoning of a site, or the rezoning of a site' (s94F[1]).

The affordable housing contribution may involve:

a. the dedication of part of the land, or other land of the applicant, free of cost to be used for the purpose of providing affordable housing, or

b. the payment of a monetary contribution to be used for the purpose of providing affordable housing, or both (s94F[2]).

The contribution required must be 'reasonable' having regard to 'the extent of the need in the area for affordable housing', 'the scale of the proposed development', and any other contribution made by the applicant under section 94 of the *EPAA* (s94F[3]). Affordable housing requirements under section 94F may not be imposed on development within a 'special contributions area' as defined above.

Arrangements for affordable housing contributions in NSW and Australia are discussed further in the following section of the book.

Dispute resolution, enforcement, and planning appeals under the *EPAA*

Most planning jurisdictions in Australia have established special purpose courts or tribunals for managing disputes in relation to the administration of the planning system. The status, role, and operation, of these bodies differ between jurisdictions as do the range of matters that may be brought before them.

Appeal rights under the *EPAA*

In general, applicants or proponents seeking to carry out a development may appeal to the Land and Environment Court against a refusal or a 'deemed refusal' (so deemed if the application has not been decided within the specified timeframe). They can also appeal against the particular conditions associated with approval. Persons who have lodged a written objection to an application for development that is 'designated' (i.e. requires an environmental impact assessment), may also appeal a decision to approve the development. All of these appeals are also considered again 'on their merits', and parties may even choose to bring forward new evidence or arguments in support of their case.

The NSW Land and Environment Court

The NSW Land and Environment Court was established in 1979 specifically to hear disputes about planning, development, and the environment (under the *NSW Land and Environment Court Act 1979).* The Land and Environment Court has the same status as the NSW Supreme Court.

The composition of the court and its conventions are intended to be less formal than those of other legal courts, and many people who bring matters to the court do not have legal representation. The court is made up of judges and commissioners, who are not lawyers but have specialist expertise (in matters relating to environmental or town planning, architecture, natural resource management, or land valuation).

The court hears eight classes of disputes:

- **Class 1** *Environmental planning and protection appeals*

  These relate to appeals against refusals and deemed refusals to issue development consent, third-party appeals relating to designated development or certain development under Part 3A, and conditions of development approval. Class 1 appeals are 'merits reviews', and the Court's decision replaces that of the original decision and is binding.

- **Class 2** *Local government and miscellaneous appeals and applications, and tree dispute applications*

  These appeals relate to matters under the *Local Government Act 1993,* the *Water Management Act 2000,* the *Trees (Dispute Between Neighbours) Act 2006* and strata/community title legislation.

- **Class 3** *Land tenure, valuation, rating and compensation matters*

  These matters relate to land acquisition and compensation, building encroachment and land access, land valuation, rating and taxation, and Aboriginal land claims.

- **Class 4** *Environmental planning protection and civil enforcement*

  These matters relate to the enforcement of planning or environmental laws – for instance, proceedings to remedy breaches of the *EPAA,* such as unauthorised building work or non-compliance with conditions of development consent. Class 4 matters also provide a basis for judicial review of administrative decisions made under environmental or planning laws.

- **Classes 5, 6, and 7** *Environmental planning and protection – criminal enforcement and appeals in relation to environmental offences*

  Class 5 matters include prosecutions for offences against environmental or planning laws; and Class 6 matters relate to appeals by offenders against convictions for environmental offences in local courts. Class 7 matters are applications for leave to appeal decisions on such matters.

- **Class 8** *Mining jurisdiction*
  These matters are disputes arising under mining and petroleum legislation.

The court publishes practice notes and information about the procedures governing these various classes of dispute. The court also publishes 'practice principles' which are intended to establish consistency in addressing matters not otherwise covered by policy or where policy is ambiguous or unclear. Current planning principles relate to a wide range of matters including the adaptive re-use of buildings, aesthetic considerations, the weight to be given to development control plans, assessment of height, bulk and scale, the role of non-statutory regional planning, privacy, access to sunlight, and views. They are derived from case law and available at the Land and Environment Court website: www.lawlink.nsw. gov.au/lawlink/lec/ll_lec.nsf/pages/LEC_planningprinciples.

Appeals in relation to development assessed under Part 4

As noted above, applicants may appeal to the NSW Land and Environment Court if a decision is not made within a certain timeframe and is thus a 'deemed refusal'.
For development that is not designated, an applicant can:

- appeal the decision of the consent authority or the conditions of consent to the Land and Environment Court (within 12 months), or
- ask the consent authority to review their decision (also within 12 months).
- the applicant may lodge a new application as many times as they choose, if a development application is refused.

There are limited third-party appeal rights (i.e. the right of a person not directly involved in the development as the proponent or consent authority) and these apply principally when an environmental impact assessment is required under Part 4 or Part 5. A third party may also seek judicial review of the decision-making process itself. Such a review would investigate whether all of the required procedures were undertaken and matters considered in making the decision.

Alternative dispute resolution

Once a matter has commenced, alternative dispute resolution processes may be facilitated through the court process. These include voluntary conciliation and mediation proceedings, where an impartial person assists both sides to come to a joint resolution (Smith et al. 2008). A 'neutral evaluation' process is also voluntary, but allows the evaluator to offer an opinion of the likely outcome of the case, if it were decided in court, based on the issues of fact and law.
Appeals against the decisions of commissioners in classes 1, 2, or 3 matters, can be brought to a Judge of the Land and Environment Court, but these appeals must relate only to errors of law rather than the merit of the decision itself. If a decision by a Judge of the Land and Environment Court is appealed, the matter is referred to the NSW Court of Appeal.

The Land and Environment Court does not usually award costs in classes 1, 2, or 3 proceedings unless considered 'fair and reasonable in the circumstances' (Smith et al. 2008 p40).

Independent Hearings Assessment Panels

Many local councils have established Independent Hearings Assessment Panels (IHAPs) to assist in resolving disputes associated with the development assessment process, and to reduce the number of appeals to court. Typically, IHAPs are comprised of an independent panel of experts (such as architects, planners, environmental scientists, solicitors, and heritage specialists) not actively engaged in work within the local area) and community representatives. Developments that have unresolved objections may be referred to the IHAP which will make recommendations to council. Applicants and objectors are usually invited to attend the IHAP meeting and make a representation to the panel. The IHAP meeting provides an independent forum for open discussion amongst members of the panel, applicants, and objectors.

The IHAP process provides an opportunity for all parties to have a say and contribute to decisions, and both applicants and objectors are likely to become more aware about the development assessment process. However, the need to refer a matter to IHAP may be associated with increased assessment times for particular applications.

Summary and conclusions

This chapter has outlined the arrangements for development assessment in NSW as they have evolved under the *EPAA*. Like many of the other Australian states, NSW has attempted to streamline development processes by categorising development according to likely impact and the level of assessment required. Most development is assessed by local councils under Part 4 of the *EPAA*. Relevant matters for consideration in development assessment include environmental planning instruments, and draft environmental planning instruments, development control plans, and the range of other considerations set out under section 79C. Development that may be carried out by public authorities 'without consent' is governed by special provisions set out under Part 5 of the Act. Development that is associated with significant environmental impact is known as 'designated' development and an Environmental Impact Statement must be prepared. 'Major projects' of state significance have been assessed by the minister under Part 3A, not confined to the local or state specific controls that would otherwise apply. At the time of writing, a new regime for identifying and determining State Significant Development and State Significant Infrastructure was being established.

If a development is approved, it is usually subject to a condition requiring the developer to contribute to infrastructure or public services. The provisions for planning for development contributions in NSW have become both extensive and complex. Building on the section 94 contributions planning framework, which provides relatively wide opportunities for consent authorities to require contributions for 'public amenities' and 'public services', new provisions extend to the formal use of planning agreements, fixed levies and special contributions.

Dispute resolution, enforcement of the Act, and appeals against planning decisions, are largely managed by the special purpose Land and Environment Court.

The NSW *EPAA* represented a new approach to urban and regional planning in an era of increased concern for the environment and management of the localised impacts or urban and regional change. It remains the oldest remaining principal planning legislation in Australia, yet it contains and supports a number of significant policy interventions relating to the environment, social equity, housing and public participation in plan-making and local development assessment.

For the first two decades of its operation, the *EPAA* provided the framework for a number of important policy interventions relating to the environment, industry, housing and urban form, and natural hazards. For many years the *EPAA* was one of the few planning laws in Australia to require social impacts of development to be considered, and one of the first to recognise the need to protect threatened species and their habitats. It was the first Australian planning law to recognise affordable housing in its objectives, and to enable local plans to provide for affordable housing inclusion, albeit in a limited way.

However over time, successive amendments to the Act, and the proliferation of subsidiary instruments it has spawned, have left it increasingly complex to interpret. The perceived corrosion of central principles – such as the need for transparent and rigorous environmental assessment of developments against established local and state planning controls has reduced community confidence in the spirit and purpose of the NSW planning system.

Planning system change and convergence

The overview of Australian state and territorial planning systems presented in this section of the book, including the more detailed review of arrangements in NSW outlined in the last two chapters, highlights some converging trends as well as distinct differences in approach.

Firstly, there is a trend towards standardised and codified plan-making through local planning scheme templates, most of which reiterate zoning as the principle means of development control in Australia. As these standard planning instruments are bedded down, state influence in the local planning and assessment process has steadily evolved. In NSW, this is particularly expressed through increasingly direct intervention in local plan-making.

Secondly, there has been a trend towards greater differentiation and separation of development assessment processes according to impact, with minor developments exempt from the need for planning approval through to major proposals requiring an environmental impact assessment process. Queensland, the ACT, and to a lesser extent, NSW, provide examples of this approach. Further, it is clear that procedural approaches to environmental impact assessment are fairly similar across the jurisdictions, aside from the extent of discretion enjoyed by state government in adhering to the statutory development control framework. As discussed in this chapter, the NSW minister for planning has enjoyed almost complete freedom from environmental planning controls when assessing major infrastructure or other projects of high capital value under Part 3A provisions in operation between 2005 and early 2011. While all jurisdictions have equivalent provisions for the minister to 'call in' important projects, these powers are more circumscribed and used more sparingly than has been the case in NSW.

Thirdly, there has been a trend towards more systematised planning for development contributions, which in most cases will result in higher overall charges (Gurran et al. 2009).

If the new systems provide greater stability and predictability in infrastructure obligations and provision, these costs should be offset by adjustments in land value over time, therefore not disadvantaging home buyers or some other developers.

New changes to the statutory planning arrangements of the states and territories may arise as jurisdictions seek to address new national criteria for capital city plans – 'to ensure Australian cities are globally competitive, productive, sustainable, liveable and socially inclusive and are well placed to meet future challenges and growth' (COAG Reform Council 2009). How these aspirations will be pursued through the Australian planning systems given wider pressures to simplify, speed up and standardise planning and development assessment under the National Reform Agenda (COAG Reform Council 2010) remains to be seen.

Box 8.5 Additional reading and resources for section 2

There are a number of useful online resources and, increasingly, government publications, to guide readers on the operation of the Australian planning systems. For independent analysis, there are also several well-researched books on aspects of Australian environmental and planning law and policy.

The following sample is a starting point, rather than a comprehensive guide to the available material.

Australian environmental legislation, policy, planning and management

The key text is Gerry Bates' *Environmental law in Australia*, now in its 7th edition (2010), Butterworths, Australia. This book includes an overview of environment and planning law across state and territorial jurisdictions.

Vortex cities to sustainable cities: Australia's urban challenge, by Phil McManus (2005) is an accessible introduction to the environmental problems affecting Australia's cities, and appropriate policy responses.

To gain an insight into the treatment of heritage, see *Heritage law in Australia* (2005), by Ben Boer and Graeme Wiffin.

The Productivity Commission's (2011) review of Australian planning, zoning and development assessment systems contains a vast compilation of descriptive and comparative material about the operation of planning systems across the states and territories, drawing largely on information supplied by the jurisdictions themselves (Performance Benchmarking of Australian Business Regulation: Planning, Zoning and Development Assessments).

The Commonwealth Government's Major Cities Unit compiles a range of information and indicators on Australia's cities, including the State of Australian cities report (2010), as well as research and discussion papers relating to urban policy and planning (see www.infrastructure.gov.au/infrastructure/mcu/index.aspx).

State planning law and systems

Environmental and planning law in New South Wales (2008) by Rosemary Lyster, Zada Lipman, Nicola Franklin and others remains an important reference.

For a comprehensive reference to planning law in Queensland, see Philippa England's *Sustainable planning in Queensland* (2011).

For more information on planning law in Victoria, see *Statutory Planning in Victoria* (Eccles & Bryant 2006).

For those looking for information on Western Australia, see *Planning perspectives from Western Australia: a reader in theory and practice*, edited by Ian Alexander, Shane Grieve, and David Hedgecock (2010).

The collection of articles in *A climate for growth: planning South-East Queensland*, edited by Brendan Gleeson and Wendy Steele offer fascinating insider accounts of the progression of urban policy and development in that region (2010).

Section 3

Practice: planning for environmental sustainability, climate change, housing choice and affordability

Statutory planning practice demands a particular set of knowledge and skills. Like other policymakers, urban and environmental planners need a deep understanding of the principles or normative goals underpinning their activities. As established in section 1 of this book, these goals relate to both the outcomes of planning intervention – situated within the rubric of environmental sustainability; and the processes supporting planning decisions – which, simply put, should be fair, participatory and efficient. But interpreting high-level environmental, social or economic objectives in relation to a specific place and set of complex stakeholder interests, and translating this spatial strategy into a legally enforceable medium through historically evolved planning regulation, can be extremely difficult in practice. In reality, strategic spatial strategy – expressed in vision documents, community plans or wider policy frameworks – often operates in parallel to, rather than fully integrated within, the statutory planning instruments designed to regulate development in practice. This section of the book examines this interface between important spatial policy and the statutory planning system for development control. It uses environmental sustainability, and housing choice and affordability as primary examples of significant policy themes, and reviews the range of strategic and statutory planning tools that have emerged for environmental conservation, natural resource management, sustainable design and housing diversity, through planning instruments and the process of development assessment in Australia and internationally. The range of tools and mechanisms outlined represent creative approaches that could be modified for incorporation within local planning frameworks irrespective of specific jurisdictional constraints. Chapter 9 focuses on local approaches to environmental sustainability, widely interpreted to include decisions about urban form, energy, water and waste, through to biodiversity conservation and natural resource management. Chapter 10 takes this theme further, examining nascent planning practice in climate change mitigation and in adapting to climate change impacts already underway. Chapter 11 turns to an issue of increasing significance in Australian urban policy – housing diversity and affordability – and the ways in which local governments can use their planning levers to support the wider national housing reform agenda.

Chapter 9

Local planning for environmental sustainability: Australian practice

The planning system offers a very important tool to implement broader government policies, particularly those relating to environmental sustainability, as already noted in this book. In this chapter we examine how Australian local governments have used their own planning powers to promote environmental sustainability in a variety of different ways – from protecting and enhancing biodiversity through to strategies for minimising use of non-renewable resources and encouraging non-motorised forms of transport. The chapter begins by setting out the policy context for local sustainability planning, including a range of key considerations or generic policy objectives to be addressed in land use plans and when assessing developments. It then looks at the broader policy framework processes that may inform, inspire or underpin local planning approaches for sustainability. The final part of the chapter outlines the more innovative planning tools and levers being used by local councils throughout Australia to achieve sustainability objectives.

Policy context: planning for ecologically sustainable communities

The concept of a 'sustainable community' was introduced in chapter 1. As discussed throughout this book, sustainability, particularly ecological sustainability, has become one of the overarching normative goals of urban land use policy and practice – enshrined within policy frameworks from the international through to the national, state, regional and local level in Australia, and given statutory force through national, state and local planning legislation. But what exactly does the concept mean in relation to strategic decisions about the location of future development and the decision-making criteria for assessing that development? In recent years there have been many helpful attempts to articulate the different aspects of sustainability that should be considered in formulating strategic plans and in assessing particular developments against these plans. Adapting the comprehensive planning principles identified for sustainable communities (Beatley & Manning 1997) and within sensitive coastal environments (Beatley et al. 2002, pp198–99; Gurran et al. 2006, p9, pp16–17), the following considerations provide a starting point for promoting environmental sustainability in local plan-making more broadly. They emphasise three linked foci of sustainability planning: the protection and enhancement of biodiversity and ecological processes; urban form – from the design and configuration of buildings through to the strategic location of functions at a metropolitan scale; and resource use and management.

Biodiversity is the 'the variety of life forms, the different plants, animals, and micro-organisms, the genes they contain and the ecosystems they form' (NPWS 1999, p70). Planning processes must protect biodiversity by minimising the impact of urban activities ('urban footprints') on natural systems. For instance, when identifying opportunities for new development or for more intense development, ecologically sensitive areas (such as wildlife habitat or corridors, wetlands and foreshores) must be avoided, and strategies to mitigate any likely impact on ecologically sensitive areas from development on adjacent lands are needed. At the same time it is critical to explicitly prevent further exposure to natural hazards (including hazards that may arise through climate change), or select hazard mitigation strategies that limit environmental disturbance.

Figure 9.1 Water-sensitive urban design, East Perth

Source: the Author 2004

Another way to protect biodiversity is by promoting compact forms of development and encouraging the integration of compatible uses, while maintaining clear separations between urban, rural and natural areas. This can be achieved by urban containment or consolidation strategies which seek to make better use of existing urban areas, including the re-use of sites no longer used for their original purposes. For instance, rather than lying idle or under-utilised, former industrial or brownfield sites may be rehabilitated and re-used, thus making the most efficient use of existing urban infrastructure and land that has already been disturbed by urban development. Often such approaches incorporate additional sustainability elements, such as the ongoing renewal of East Perth, in Western Australia, which has demonstrated leading practice in water-sensitive urban design.

Urban consolidation strategies are often associated with higher-density forms of residential and commercial development, particularly around transportation nodes like railway or bus interchanges. Higher-density and mixed-use housing forms are often appropriate in inner city and suburban contexts, and the influx of new residents may be associated with the revitalisation of areas of poor housing or commercial centres, also an objective of the East Perth redevelopment project (Figure 9.1). In more traditional urban release or greenfield areas, urban containment objectives are often promoted by the introduction of smaller lot sizes and attached dwellings such as villas and townhouses. As well as responding to environmental goals of land conservation, these approaches also reflect changing demographic shifts towards smaller households.

However, neither higher-density development within established areas (sometimes described as 'vertical sprawl'), or a more intense approach to the development of suburban greenfield areas, are inherently sustainable in and of themselves. Many such developments involve high use of 'embodied' energy (all of the energy that is involved in the construction and operation of the building, including the energy needed to produce and transport construction materials). The developments may lead to a dependence on non-renewable resources, for instance, high- and medium-density apartments that depend on airconditioning or prohibit external drying of clothes. In greenfield areas developers often achieve a higher yield of houses on a site on the basis that this is contributing to sustainability goals, but the developments remain car dependent. Alternatively, it is possible to promote urban containment objectives within traditional housing forms (through strata titling) or through the adaptive re-use of existing buildings – an approach which is appropriate for smaller settlements and areas of high historical value – and which also reduces waste. In both cases strong planning regulations are required to achieve development forms that genuinely contribute to sustainability while respecting the prevailing aesthetic or character of an area (Gleeson 2006).

Genuinely sustainable urban forms reduce car dependence and promote the viability of non-motorised forms of transport like walking and cycling, as well as public or 'community' transport (Newman 2006, 2009). This is achieved by providing for compatible mixed uses and compact forms of development, particularly around centres and transport hubs, and providing space for safe pedestrian and cycle routes. These approaches are often described as 'new urbanism'. New urbanism is a design movement that favours traditional street grids, emphasises the neighbourhood unit and the public realm, designing housing and community facilities and services on the basis of pedestrian and cycle accessibility. A variety of other terms are also used to describe forms of development that seek to minimise the amount of land converted for urban development, reduce 'sprawl' and private car dependence, and maximise the use of urban infrastructure. For instance, 'transit oriented development' seeks to increase residential and commercial densities around public transport nodes, often focusing on areas with potential for economic or social revitalisation. 'Smart growth' is a looser term that seeks to limit the shape and impact of urban growth in relation to sustainability principles and viable use of public transportation.

Figure 9.2 Jarlanbah Permaculture Hamlet, Northern NSW

'Eco-communities', such as the 'permaculture hamlet' pictured above, have emerged throughout the world to demonstrate principles of sustainable living through the use of on-site, natural resources in construction and for basic living needs such as food (much of which is grown on-site according to permaculture principles). The Jarlanbah community also aims to be waste neutral. These approaches can be adapted for more urbanised settings. Source: the Author 2004

One of the key objectives of more sustainable forms of building and urban design is to reduce dependence on non-renewable resources and the generation of waste, both in construction and in the ongoing operation of the development. In seeking to minimise the dependence on resources such as energy and water, considerations range from the maximisation of energy efficiency in building design, orientation and configuration, to the use of renewable energy forms from household to the scale of urban region. These approaches also aim to improve urban air quality and reduce the amount of greenhouse gas emissions associated with new development.

Increased contributions to greenhouse gas emissions as a result of human activities are causing the phenomenon known as 'climate change' or 'global warming'. The major gases contributing to this change are carbon dioxide, methane and nitrous oxide. Australia's contribution to climate change is significant: in 1999 it was found that Australia was the worst greenhouse gas emitter per capita and was ranked 134th of 142 countries in a combined assessment of emissions and policy actions (McManus 2005). The leading causes of these emissions are electricity supply (particularly the generation of electricity from coal) and transport (particularly the use of petroleum). Thus initiatives that reduce energy demand and shift energy supply to cleaner sources are imperative. There are opportunities for land use planning to contribute to both demand reduction and energy supply through development controls relating to the design and configuration of buildings, neighbourhoods and urban regions.

In other words, infrastructure provision strategies should support, rather than undermine sustainability goals. For instance, water supply and quality is a crucial component of urban development. Traditional approaches to water provision in Australian cities have resulted in a legacy of environmental damage associated with damming and water diversion, as well as patterns of wasteful water consumption. Such approaches to water supply have also arguably contributed to the very pattern of suburban form in Australia, as observed by Phil McManus: 'The traditional engineering mentality of 'dam, store, purify, pump and pipe' has enabled Australian cities to grow as low-density high-water consumption cities' (McManus 2005, p112). Alternative approaches to water supply, use and management focus on reducing demand (through water saving measures at household and industry scale) and protecting catchments to ensure high water quality and reduce the need for expensive treatment plants. The concept of 'water-sensitive urban design' (WSUD) seeks to better integrate planning and design with the urban water cycle.

There is also a need to consider the minimisation, re-use and recycling of construction, household or industrial waste. Phil McManus documents a discursive shift from concepts of 'waste' to the term 'resource' although he doubts this linguistic transition is more than symbolic: 'The logic of closing the loop to reduce waste is sound, but are we losing, in modifying our language, a motivation for environmental awareness and action?' (McManus 2005, p144). In terms of concrete planning approaches, a key issue is the management of construction and demolition waste and the potential to mandate targets for re-use – especially within urban renewal projects, and strong requirements to assess the entire life cycle of a development, including the viability of adapting the built form as the needs of its occupants change. This may become a particular issue in relation to higher-density residential developments which are likely to be very difficult to reconfigure or adapt in the future.

A broader principle of sustainable resource management is the attempt to source locally produced resource requirements (food, water, and other essential products), and as much as possible, to contain waste within the same area, by retaining spaces for essential production and waste re-use/recycling. If this principle was applied at the metropolitan scale in Australia, remaining areas of agricultural production within and surrounding the urban periphery would be preserved as a high priority. For instance, the city of Santa Monica in California includes as a sustainability indicator the proportion of food served in local restaurants that is produced within the local region and, within this indicator, the proportion of this produce that is grown organically (Gurran et al. 2006).

To facilitate planning within naturally defined limits, the concept of a 'bioregion' – defined by reference to environmental qualities such as a water catchment, or changes in vegetation may be helpful (Dodge 1998). While there have been many formal attempts to define bioregional boundaries for conservation planning or natural resource management in Australia (for instance, the Interim Bioregionalisation for Australia project for determining national conservation priorities), it is not necessary for local planners to define bioregions in a fixed way (EA 2001). Rather, the concept of a bioregion and the permeable relationships between ecological processes (movements of air, water, species etc.) within and between bioregions, provides a basis for aspiring to self-sufficiency. The bioregional concept also provides a reference point in promoting a sense of place through aesthetic designs and controls that recognise and reinforce the natural context, cultural heritage and the contemporary aspirations of the community. This sense of place is reinforced by planning processes that encourage meaningful civic engagement and participation in environmental decision-making. A critical attribute of environmentally sustainable decision-making is the existence of strategies to promote Indigenous input to land use planning and environmental management decisions, respecting needs to fulfil ongoing custodian obligations and protecting traditional resource access rights.

In undertaking their planning activities, local councils work within the policy framework established by national and state governments, as well as their own articulation and interpretation of broader policy goals through strategies or corporate plans. For instance, Local Agenda 21 plans, prepared by many councils in Australia, provide a basis for identifying broad objectives, policies and actions relating to environmental sustainability at the local level. The State of the Environment reporting framework used at the national, state, and local level in Australia, provides a basis for reporting and monitoring achievement towards these goals.

Local policy frameworks, Local Agenda 21 and State of the Environment reporting

Like the Commonwealth and state governments in Australia, most local councils in Australia have their own policy framework within which objectives, strategic directions and activities are articulated. These local policy frameworks may be contained within an overarching corporate or strategic action plan, a series of thematic plans, or a combination of many documents and strategies addressing particular issues. Many local councils in Australia and internationally, now prepare overarching environmental policy frameworks using the Local Agenda 21 model, and many others have developed their own equivalent approaches.

Local Agenda 21

In 1992, the United Nations World Summit on Sustainable Development, held in Rio de Janeiro, resulted in the promulgation of a global framework for implementing sustainability, called Agenda 21. Chapter 28 of this framework focuses on the role of local governments in achieving sustainable development:

> Local authorities construct, operate and maintain economic, social and environmental infrastructure, oversee planning processes, establish local environmental policies and regulations, and assist in implementing national and sub-national environmental policies. As the level of governance closest to the people, they play a vital role in educating, mobilising and responding to the public to promote sustainable development. (Agenda 21, Chapter 28)

Arising from this statement, Local Agenda 21 plans have been prepared by councils throughout the world and in many parts of Australia. In some cases, these plans have provided the basis for significant change to local planning strategies, objectives and mechanisms, although in themselves Local Agenda 21 plans have no statutory weight. Implementation difficulties and a lack of higher-level government support have also been documented as barriers to the effective use of the Local Agenda 21 model in Australia (McManus 2005).

At the Local Government Session at the subsequent 2002 World Summit, held in Johannesburg, South Africa, it was agreed to shift the emphasis in the Local Agenda 21 program to 'action', reflecting a commitment to address barriers to sustainable development, and to promote the adoption of instruments that ensure implementation of sustainability imperatives.

State of the Environment reporting

A key component of sustainability is monitoring, or measuring, progress towards objectives. State of the Environment reporting provides a methodology for monitoring the environmental impacts of interventions and progress towards achieving sustainability goals (for instance, the goals articulated within a Local Agenda 21 plan). State of the Environment reporting began in Australia in response to the National Strategy for Ecologically Sustainable Development (discussed in chapter 4). National State of the Environment reports are prepared every five years by an independent scientific committee and are now mandated under the *Commonwealth Environment Protection and Biodiversity Conservation Act 1999*. Each of the states and territories also prepare regular State of the Environment reports as do many local governments throughout Australia. In NSW, the preparation of regular State of the Environment reports is a requirement under the *Local Government Act 1993*.

The State of the Environment report process can therefore provide a basis for monitoring environmental change and identifying the need for policy intervention or change at the local level. Beyond the mandated requirements for State of the Environment reporting, a range of new models for assessing the environmental performance of cities and urban areas have emerged (see McManus 2005). One of the problems with the State of the Environment framework, particularly at the national level in Australia, is that there are poor links between the reporting process and actual strategies to act on the findings documented in State of the Environment reports (Low et al. 2005).

Planning for environmental sustainability – the basic tools

The planning process itself and the careful application of basic development control mechanisms – land use categorisation, fixing urban boundaries, establishing development standards and criteria for assessment, conditions of consent for development and so on, offer powerful tools to achieve environmental sustainability objectives. One of the most important tools is the power vested in planning authorities to refuse applications for developments that represent an unacceptable environmental impact. When applications are approved, there are opportunities to place conditions on the development to ameliorate, mitigate, or offset environmental impacts. The following sections highlight special considerations associated with planning for environmental sustainability, and ways in which the basic development control tool kit, can be used effectively to achieve environmental goals.

Planning objectives for environmental sustainability

One of the most important components of a land use plan is the statement of overall aims or objectives, because these generally provide a guide to the interpretation of the instrument. Many local councils in Australia have included objectives relating to environmental sustainability in their local planning instruments. These objectives range from broad goals promoting ecologically sustainable development, through to specific aims concerning particular aspects of the local landscape or environment.

It is important to ensure that objectives are clear, and as consistent as possible with legislative and scientific usage of particular terminology (Fallding et al. 2001, p5.1). This helps avoid ambiguity when interpreting the provisions of the plan, and if a decision is disputed in appeal. It is also a principle of good plan-making to clarify the way in which plan objectives relate to the actual provisions of the plan, for example, whether developments must be consistent with the objectives.

The Biodiversity Planning Guide (Fallding et al. 2001) assists local governments in NSW in the preparation of plans that promote and implement biodiversity protection, and provides examples of some key planning goals relating to biodiversity protection:

- Maintaining naturally occurring ecosystems, communities and species
- Protecting and adequately managing areas with high conservation value
- Identifying less sensitive areas which are suitable for development
- Minimising impacts through good planning, design and management
- Restoring lost biodiversity where possible. (Fallding et al. 2001, p5.1).

An example of actual plan objectives for maintaining ecological processes and biodiversity conservation is provided by the planning scheme for the local government area of Cairns in Northern Queensland, which contains two areas of world heritage – the Great Barrier Reef and the Wet Tropics of Far North Queensland. Biodiversity related 'desired environmental outcomes' for the area surrounding and including the small coastal hamlet of Douglas include:

DEO 1 – The unique environmental values of the Shire, which result from its location within the Wet Tropics Bioregion, are maintained and protected for current and future generations.

DEO 2 – Those parts of the Shire located within the Wet Tropics and Great Barrier Reef World Heritage Areas and other adjacent areas of environmental value and ecological significance, are preserved and protected for nature conservation, landscape/scenic quality, biodiversity and habitat values, in particular the protection of the Southern Cassowary and its habitat and to ensure the integrity of natural processes.

DEO 3 – Natural waterways such as the Daintree River, the Mossman River, the Mowbray River and Dicksons Inlet, all wetlands but particularly those on the Directory of Wetlands of Importance in Australia, being the Lower Daintree River, Alexandra Bay and the Hilda Creek Headwater; and all catchments located in coastal areas within the Shire, are managed to protect their ecological processes, enhance water quality, conserve riparian ecological values and landscape/scenic quality, while acknowledging nature-based recreation opportunities.

DEO 4 – The unique environmental character of the Shire comprised of internationally renowned landscapes, ecologically significant rainforest systems, sensitive coastal systems and areas of unsurpassed natural beauty, are maintained in association with sustainable development practices, which seek to minimise the effects of development on the natural environment.

Douglas Planning Scheme August 2006, 2.2.1 (Ecological Processes and Natural Systems)

The City of Victor Harbor in South Australia identifies specific planning objectives to encourage sustainable urban form and to promote forms of non-motorised transport within new residential subdivisions. The objectives also focus on preserving and enhancing sense of place and the unique characteristics of the landscape, consistent with the concept of a sustainable community discussed above:

27 Neighbourhoods and infill development should have a layout which:

(a) integrates movement networks and land-use;

(b) reduces local vehicle trips, travel distances and speeds in residential streets; and

(c) facilitates walking and cycling to daily activities.

28 Neighbourhood identity should be reinforced by:

(a) locating a range of community, retail, recreational and commercial facilities and local employment opportunities at focal points; and

(b) relating development to site features and characteristics, setting, landmarks and views.
(ss27–28, Victor Harbor Development Plan, Consolidated 3 June 2010)

Byron Shire in the far north coast of NSW has identified a comprehensive range of objectives relating to environmental sustainability, including principles to ensure that planning decisions implement these objectives (Box 9.1).

Box 9.1 Aims of Byron Local Environmental Plan 1988

BYRON LOCAL ENVIRONMENTAL PLAN 1988 – REG 2

2 Aim, objectives and guiding principles

(2) Objectives: the objectives of this plan are:

(a) to enhance individual and community (social and economic) well-being by following a path of economic development that safeguards the welfare of future generations,

(b) to provide for equity within and between generations, and

(c) to protect biodiversity, and re-establish and enhance essential ecological processes and life support systems.

(3) Guiding principles: the objectives can be achieved through the implementation of the following guiding principles:

(a) The precautionary principle. The precautionary principle means that where there are threats of serious or irreversible damage to the community's ecological, social or economic systems, a lack of complete scientific evidence should not be used as a reason for postponing measures to prevent environmental degradation. In some circumstances this will mean actions will need to be taken to prevent damage even when it is not certain that damage will occur.

(b) The principle of intergenerational equity. This principle means that the present generation must ensure that the health, integrity, ecological diversity, and productivity of the environment is at least maintained or preferably enhanced for the benefit of future generations.

(c) The principle of conserving biological diversity and ecological integrity. This principle aims to protect, restore and conserve the native biological diversity and enhance or repair ecological processes and systems.

(d) The principle of improving the valuation and pricing of social and ecological resources. This principle means that the users of goods and services should pay prices based on the full life cycle costs (including the use of natural resources at their replacement value, the ultimate disposal of any wastes and the repair of any consequent damage).

(e) The principle of eliminating or reducing to harmless levels any discharge into the air, water or land of substances or other effects arising from human activities that are likely to cause harm to the environment.

(f) The principle of encouraging a strong, growing and diversified economy that promotes local self reliance, and recognises and strengthens the local community and its social capital in ways that safeguard the quality of life of future generations.

(g) The principle of providing credible information in open and accountable processes to encourage and assist the effective participation of local communities in decision-making.

Allocating land uses, development standards and criteria for assessment

Once the objectives of a plan have been defined, a process of allocating or reviewing the activities or land uses that may occur within different areas and specific parcels of land is undertaken. This may be expressed through land use zones or through other approaches to land use categorisation. In most cases objectives for a particular area or zone are specified, a range of activities that may or may not be undertaken are identified, and special provisions applying to the assessment of development within the zone or area are often established.

This process must be informed by the best available data concerning the ecological values of the land, as well as the cultural and economic values of the area and sites within it. In reality, often the available data concerning environmental values – the importance of a parcel of land or patch of vegetation, waterbody, foreshore, dune, or grassland, and so on, for a particular species of plant or animal, or for water catchment integrity, is not adequate to enable a full assessment of the range of potential activities that may with confidence be undertaken on the land, although such an approach would be ideal. Instead it is necessary to undertake a cautious approach in categorising land and in identifying the range of activities that are, or may be, permissible, subject to more specific assessment.

With highly sensitive areas, a common approach may be to permit a range of developments that are likely to be compatible with the overall objectives for the area, subject to the developer undertaking or sponsoring a more detailed level of environmental assessment, which might include flora or fauna impact studies, water quality assessments, and perhaps the creation of special strategies designed to offset or minimise negative impacts identified through these more detailed environmental studies. Environmental protection zones may be identified even within highly urban areas.

In naming zones or other planning controls, the NSW Biodiversity Planning Guide suggests that the name given to the control itself encourage conservation objectives:

> Using terms such as bushland conservation, wetland conservation, national park buffer, sustainable development, scenic protection, residential conservation, or the like may attract purchasers who wish to maintain the values identified by the applicable planning controls. In some areas, property values are higher for environmental and scenic protection than for land identified for less restrictive development. (Fallding et al. 2001, p5.6).

To recognise and protect particularly important areas, a system of 'overlays' may be used. These may apply to land that is generally allocated to a particular range of functions but add an additional set of assessment criteria or requirements. The use of overlays can be an effective way of providing a consistent management approach to environmental issues that cut across several land units. For instance, overlays could be used to recognise and protect areas of natural landscape significance, wildlife corridors, coastal foreshores, buffer zones between protected public areas like national parks and adjoining private lands, or areas important for catchment integrity.

Whatever system of land categorisation or overlay is used, specific provisions to promote sustainability objectives may apply to development within a particular area, or to particular types of development. In general these might include requirements for a particular study or set of studies, actions to mitigate any specific impacts arising from the proposal, special requirements to refer proposals to another state agency for their expert consideration, or particular consultation requirements, such as consultation with traditional owners or a local Indigenous group.

Where the environmental values are such that the planning authority regards the land as requiring permanent protection and management as a nature reserve by a public agency, a planning instrument clause enabling the acquisition of the land is needed. This is because the restrictions effectively foreclose any future economic use of the land by private owners. Before committing an agency to potential acquisition, consultation with the agency in question is usually needed. If the local authority has their own funds for environmental acquisition, there is clearly greater flexibility in adopting this approach.

In addition to ensuring that areas with high biodiversity values are protected, it is important to consider the placement of activities and major facilities through land allocation decisions, as discussed above. In promoting sustainable transportation, for instance, the principle is to ensure that places visited often – schools, shops, recreational areas and so on are not solely car-dependent, and that there are effective connections between pedestrian and cycleways, key destinations, and public transport nodes (Low et al. 2005, McManus 2005, Newman 2006). This can be achieved through careful establishment of permissible land uses, clear criteria for assessing specific proposals, and development standards to ensure individual developments are accessible by many modes of transportation. This means requirements in new and renewing areas, and retrofitting provisions in established areas, if necessary, for footpaths and cycleways that are both separated from roads and connect to main facilities, recreational areas and public transport. Such requirements are not just an additional contribution by private developers, although in some cases this may be necessary or justifiable. They are about ensuring that space is provided for safe, appropriate and appealing pedestrian and cycle routes, and that developments exceeding minimum expectations in this regard are actively encouraged. Requirements might also extend to cycle parking or storage in new developments, or space in office buildings for commuters to shower or change.

Further, in establishing development requirements and standards, it is imperative to promote the most sustainable forms of building design, mindful of the total life cycle of development. This extends from the approach to energy and water use to biodiversity considerations like the planting of endogenous (locally occurring) species in gardens or on rooftops. It involves specifying merit criteria to assess developments, taking into account the total likely impact of particular proposals. For instance, planning instruments could, through merit criteria, provide a basis for positively distinguishing between different forms of infrastructure (provided by the private or public sector) such as those which directly contribute to diminishing contributions to climate change (like wind farms) and those that are associated with a negative impact (like coal-generated electricity stations).

Although water-sensitive urban design principles are not yet widely incorporated in development controls and standards in Australia, there are increasing examples of the approach in relation to specific developments. Further, many councils are beginning to enhance existing controls relating to urban water management to better protect water quality, encourage water recycling, or reduce consumption. For instance, Kogarah Municipal Council in NSW has implemented a water management policy applying to all new developments within the area. The policy requires stormwater management approaches to control, treat, and re-use stormwater onsite (Kogarah Municipal Council 2006).

Setbacks are a traditional development standard or control that can be an effective mechanism to protect water quality, other sensitive ecological features, or to minimise risks associated with natural hazards. Set-backs from riparian areas and river or coastal foreshores are routinely, but not always, included in local planning instruments, or may be required by state legislation or policy. Set-backs could be specified in relation to a particular type of development, with lines varying according to the risk posed by each development type. For instance, more permanent structures like tourist cabins may be associated with higher risk than temporary ones like caravans. In planning for the potential impacts arising from climate change, the simple set- back may become a key line of defence – for instance, by moving development lines away from likely storm surge or flood inundation areas, particularly along the coastline. This may have the added benefit of protecting sensitive biodiversity values and public access.

Many local government areas in Australia have articulated specific development controls for waste minimisation and management. Such controls typically include objectives and requirements regarding the maximisation of re-use and recycling of building and construction materials, encouragement of the selective deconstruction of buildings, rather than demolition, improved building techniques to minimise waste in subdivision and construction, and provisions for ongoing waste management. Provisions may extend to requirements regarding waste storage arrangements within specific developments. For instance, the City of Ryde requires facilities to enable source separation, re-use and recycling within residential, commercial and industrial developments; requirements for on-site composting space (whether or not the occupants choose to use this space) and volume reduction equipment for multi-storey buildings (City of Ryde 2006).

Conditions of consent and planning agreements

These special requirements may be negotiated and formalised through conditions of consent associated with development approval, or through planning agreements running with the title of the land (where these are provided for under state legislation). For instance, planning agreements in NSW may provide for conservation works and studies (discussed further in chapter 10). Voluntary Conservation Agreements are voluntary agreements entered into by landowners who undertake to protect their land for biodiversity conservation. The agreements are usually made between the landholders and the state government agency responsible for environmental conservation, although some local government authorities in Australia also recognise such agreements.

Specific planning approaches and levers

The basic range of development controls described above are essential tools to protect important landscapes, biodiversity and ecological processes, through the use of appropriate land use categorisation or zoning, the application of robust assessment criteria, and appropriate design rules to encourage more sustainable patterns of subdivision and building. Additionally, a number of new and creative approaches to using these basic mechanisms have been adopted by Australian local governments in recent years. These can be categorised as overall approaches designed to achieve urban containment; additional requirements, incentives or offsets designed to minimise the impact of particular developments and encourage best practice in environmental management; and mechanisms designed to facilitate the protection and conservation of the most sensitive areas even when these lands are currently in private ownership or subject to planning controls that permit inappropriate development.

Urban containment

The process of land use categorisation, whether the term 'zone' is used or another combination of approaches, should provide a basis for separating urban and non-urban activities. This is important from a sustainability perspective because dispersed patterns of growth generally consume more land, result in more road-based travel, make the provision of infrastructure uneconomic and inefficient, and degrade landscape qualities. As we have noted earlier, land use zones (and equivalent forms of categorisation based on permissible land uses) are a technique for demarcating the edge of an urban settlement boundary, provided that appropriate constraints to prevent urban development are contained in the non-urban zones. However, these are often undermined by incremental changes or small amendments to the overall plan, permitting specific developments that cumulatively undermine the distinction between urban and non-urban areas. This is a particular concern in popular non-metropolitan coastal regions, where continual pressure for development, particularly on rural lands, erodes established boundaries over time.

Urban growth boundaries

The concept of an urban growth boundary provides a basis for attempting to permanently limit the urban footprint of a community, based on an evaluation of land capacity. Rather than the traditional approach to designating urban land uses within a particular area in relation to forecast development need, urban growth boundaries make the potential 'carrying capacity' of a settlement a fundamental consideration. In the US and in some local government areas of Australia, particularly Victoria, attempts have been made to introduce urban growth boundaries that represent the community's desire for a permanent limit on urban expansion (Gurran et al. 2006). Nonetheless, just like other controls established within statutory planning instruments, urban growth boundaries represent more of a symbolic limit as they can always be revised if the overall plan is amended.

The urban growth boundary approach adopted by the Surf Coast Shire provides a good example of how the concept may be adopted through a local planning scheme. Surf Coast Shire is a rapidly growing community in south-west Victoria, situated about an hour and a half drive from Melbourne, and popular with tourists, retirees and others seeking a permanent lifestyle change. As part of the shire's overall aim to achieve a reputation as 'the most environmentally friendly local government in the world – managing the best preserved coastal environment in the world' (Surf Coast Shire 2000, 21.03-1), the council developed a system of planning controls designed to explicitly contain the majority of new urban development within the existing boundaries of its coastal towns and villages, with the exception of two designated growth nodes (Gurran et al. 2006). Urban growth limits are marked clearly on framework plans contained within the Surf Coast Planning Scheme. This approach does not necessarily mean more medium or high-density development forms that are incompatible with the character of many communities, such as those in rural locations. For instance, the Surf Coast scheme includes a specific design template or 'style guide' to ensure that all new development contributes to the emerging and distinctive Surf Coast style.

Population caps

A related approach is to apply a growth or population cap based on an estimated maximum number of people (or households), that can be accommodated within a specific spatial area, subject to environmental capacity, landscape characteristics and community preferences. In the US and Canada this approach is often converted to a limit on the annual number of applications for particular development types (e.g. residential and commercial) that are able to be approved within a given 12-month period. Another approach is to convert the overall estimation of development capacity (in terms of households and the commercial or other services needed to support them) to residential land that can be released over a defined period of time.

This approach was used by the former Noosa Council in South-East Queensland. Noosa has long been a lifestyle destination known for a spectacular local environment, including several national parks and reserves. Concerns about the capacity of the local area to continue to accommodate high rates of growth while maintaining its environmental qualities and the qualities of life that underpin the area's appeal for visitors and residents, prompted the council to introduce a 'population cap' through its local planning scheme (Gurran et al. 2006).

Rather than determining current land release policies, the population cap represented a calculation of population capacity based on the maximum potential development in the council area permitted under the then Noosa Planning Scheme. Using this method, the 'population cap' stood at between 56,000 and 62,000 residents (Noosa Shire Council 2004), depending on population trends, plus seasonal increases during peak holiday periods. Although eroded by subsequent iterations of the planning scheme, the cap was intended to provide a basis for local businesses and services to begin orienting their focus away from an economy based largely on construction and new housing, towards more sustainable, long-term forms of development.

Special requirements, incentives or offsets

New planning mechanisms promoting greater sustainability tend to combine additional environmental requirements with incentives for better performance, or adopt a flexible approach that allows the developer to demonstrate how they are meeting the additional expectations in relation to their particular development (for instance, through the use of a points system). Typically, planning incentives to encourage the conservation of environmentally significant areas allow additional development potential in less sensitive parts of the same site.

Planning incentives

The Maroochy Plan 2000 is the land use planning scheme for the former Shire of Maroochy on Queensland's Sunshine Coast. The plan's overall objectives, described as Desired Environmental Outcomes, include Environmental Management. One of the main provisions identified under this outcome is the capacity for developers to obtain additional subdivision entitlements on sites of recognised conservation value. To achieve the bonus, the applicant needs to demonstrate that a positive net conservation outcome (i.e. more vegetation will be conserved) can be achieved as a result of the development than would otherwise be the case (Maroochy Shire 2000, 1.6.2 [j]).

Green offsets

Green offsets seek to mitigate any negative environmental impact of a particular development. The objective is to go beyond mere mitigation to achieve a 'net environmental improvement' from development (Brodbeck 2005, p13, Gurran et al. 2006). While offset approaches are calculated in relation to specific developments, it is important to establish a local policy framework for their use, and where possible, to indicate within a statutory land use plan, the parameters under which the offset approach may operate.

It is not necessary for the mitigation strategies to occur within the actual development area. They could include a payment of money to assist in the acquisition of another site of conservation value, or the rehabilitation or revegetation of a degraded area. Offsets have frequently been used in relation to native vegetation removal but in NSW the concept of biobanking radically extends this approach. As discussed in chapter 7, the NSW system of 'biobanking' allows developers to offset the impact of their development by purchasing 'biocredits'.

Points systems to encourage better environmental performance

Points systems are being used in NSW and by some local government areas in Victoria to encourage better environmental outcomes without being overly prescriptive. By articulating a set of 'points' for desired outcomes, and mandating or encouraging proposed developments to combine their preferred approaches, planning authorities can promote greater awareness about sustainable construction and resource use while achieving genuine improvements in building performance. In NSW the state government's mandated BASIX scheme (see Box 9.2) requires a minimum score in relation to water and energy savings.

One of the first local governments worldwide to introduce this approach was the City of Boulder, Colorado in the US. Under the Green Points Program, residential building applicants must achieve a minimum score as specified by the scheme in relation to new construction, additions, and remodelling projects over a threshold of 500 square metres in floor area (City of Boulder 2009, Gurran et al. 2006). As well as improving sustainability performance, the program informs local developers about sustainable building and remodelling, and offers flexibility for developers to select the approaches most compatible with their project. These might include ensuring deconstructed materials are resold, construction debris is recycled, and reclaimed (or sustainably harvested) timber and other recycled building products are used in construction. Other approaches include planting low-water demanding vegetation, insulating homes and applying principles of insulation, passive solar design, natural cooling and using low-toxic interior materials (Gurran et al. 2006). Under the scheme there is capacity to score 'bonus' points for using innovative products or for demonstrating energy or resource conservation standards.

Box 9.2 The NSW Building Sustainability Index BASIX

The NSW Building Sustainability Index BASIX was introduced by the NSW government in 2004, and has been applied progressively to developments and regions since this time. The system now applies to all residential development in NSW, and alterations or additions above a certain threshold. Applicants must achieve a minimum standard in energy and water savings, demonstrated by certification through an online tool. Applicants submit the specifications of their development to the website to obtain certification. The tool also shows developers the different options to achieve targets. Minimum criteria for a BASIX-compliant certificate relate to water, thermal comfort and energy use, and vary according to the location and type of development. The average greenhouse gas reduction for all BASIX-compliant building types across NSW is estimated at 36 per cent (DOP 2007). Features of BASIX-compliant homes include the use of rainwater tanks, efficient appliances, endogenous garden species, good solar orientation, alternative energy systems and grey water systems where feasible.

Clustering

Despite a general shift towards urban containment, there are some instances where large parcels of land with minimum levels of residential development are preferable to more intense uses. Larger lots in certain areas may be desirable for environmental reasons or to maintain the viability of agricultural holdings (preventing inflation due to the conversion of farms for housing), and clustering certain compatible developments (such as rural residential dwellings) within less sensitive areas of a particular site. This approach may be a way of allowing some urban growth while retaining the environmental, scenic, or agricultural values of an area. Clustering is also a way of avoiding land use conflicts between different activities such as residential development and agriculture.

Habitat protection plans

Wildlife habitat protection plans provide a framework for permitting some development while establishing measures intended to protect the overall living environment of particular species. To date, habitat protection plans have focused on particular species of animals under threat, such as the highly iconic koala, as in NSW where state policy requires the preparation of plans to protect core koala habitat before development within areas that contain such habitat can proceed (SEPP No. 44 – Koala Habitat Protection). Port Stephens Council (a coastal tourism destination located about three hours north of Sydney) has prepared a comprehensive koala habitat management plan to signal its expectations regarding developments within affected areas and to provide greater development certainty by articulating these expectations upfront.

Conserving the most environmentally sensitive areas

Rectifying the environmental problems associated with previous planning decisions can be particularly difficult and expensive. Even if there are no legal prohibitions against amendments to planning controls that significantly reduce the development capacity of private land, it is rarely a political possibility. However, incentives can be used to offset the costs to individuals that are associated with conserving a parcel of privately owned land. A system of 'tradable development rights' may also provide a basis for compensating owners for lost development capacity through the private market.

Tradable/transferable development rights

There are costs associated with reducing the development capacity of land (and therefore its value on the property market). The concept of tradable (or transferable) development rights provides an opportunity for owners to preserve significant landscapes or areas of high biodiversity value. The schemes work by allowing landholders to sell theoretical development rights that were nullified by the restrictive designation of their land. Although such schemes are complex to establish, once operational, the approach could provide a market-based form of compensation to landholders.

To avoid any dangers associated with an implication that landholders may be entitled to compensation (market or otherwise) for the existing environmental planning constraints affecting their lands, it might be prudent to limit access to such schemes to situations when additional environmental restrictions or 'down-zoning' of privately owned sites are introduced. While tradable development rights are commonly used in many cities of the US, the approach has not yet been established in Australia. The city of Wollongong on the NSW South Coast, sought to devise a similar mechanism in relation to its majestic Illawarra Escarpment but ultimately was unable to implement it due to legal difficulties (Gurran et al. 2006).

Voluntary conservation schemes

Voluntary conservation schemes provide a formal mechanism for a landholder to voluntarily protect the conservation values of their property. Each of the Australian states have established mechanisms to voluntarily protect private land, often through a conservation covenant or contract that is attached to the title of the land (Bateson 2000). Local councils could assist in this process by bringing landholders and state conservation agencies together. They can also introduce their own voluntary conservation schemes, using a management agreement achieved during a development assessment process, or through a voluntarily imposed environmental zone. Local rate rebates or grants can provide incentives for landholders to enter into such schemes.

An example of this approach is provided by the Cassowary Coast Regional Council in Far North Queensland. Much of the shire is affected by World Heritage Listing, but many other significant lands are in private ownership and not subject to specific protections. To encourage the protection of such lands, the Council introduced a local Voluntary Conservation Covenants program. The conservation covenants, which are actually recognised in the local planning scheme, contain restrictions on the use of the land to ensure it has permanent protection. To encourage take up of the scheme, council has offered incentives such as rates reduction, additional development rights in certain areas, and tax reimbursements (Brodbeck 2005, Gurran et al. 2006).

Summary and conclusions

The strategic policy goals for local sustainability planning involve protecting and enhancing ecological systems and processes, including the configuration and form of urban development, and promoting sustainable transport and resource use. All of these issues have a bearing on one of the most enduring land use planning considerations – that is, planning to avoid exposure to natural hazards, like flooding, erosion, or storm events, but these considerations have taken on a new urgency within the sustainability paradigm because of the potential implications of climate change.

This chapter has showed how these matters are often situated within local policy frameworks such as Local Agenda 21 plans or their equivalent, and how progress towards their achievement may be monitored through the State of the Environment reporting process that is mandatory in many jurisdictions. Basic tools for promoting sustainability through land use planning were outlined, establishing objectives, land uses, development standards, conditions of consent and, of course, refusal of inappropriate developments. These depend on a strategic planning framework that is carefully designed to ensure that all relevant information regarding the environmental impacts of a proposal may be considered by a planning authority and the weight to which such matters should have when deciding on the proposal.

Creative variations of these tools – models for urban containment, habitat protection plans, tradable development rights, and ways to recognise or support voluntary conservation schemes were outlined. This is an exciting and emerging area of planning policy and practice and the range of approaches and examples documented here are by no means exhaustive. For further sources of information and inspiration on designing planning frameworks for environmental sustainability, see the end of this section of the book. The following chapter explores this topic in greater detail by examining emerging principles and practice in planning for climate change.

Chapter 10

Climate change mitigation, adaptation and local planning

Nicole Gurran, Elisabeth Hamin, Barbara Norman

This chapter focuses on one of the most significant environmental challenges facing society today: human-induced climate change. Climate change has been described as an extreme example of market failure and its consequences (Stern 2007; Garnaut 2008):

> Market failure occurs when the market fails to take into account the costs (or benefits) of an action that accrue to firms of people who are not parties to the action. Market failure in relation to the pricing of a resource leads to its overexploitation (or underultilisation). The failure to place a price on greenhouse gas emissions has led to overutilisation of a scarce resource: the atmosphere's capacity to absorb emissions without risks of dangerous climate change … The correction of this market failure is the central task of climate change policy, in Australia and in the world (Garnaut 2008 p299).

As discussed in chapter 1, one of the important rationales for urban planning intervention is to protect the environment from irreparable harm arising from market failure in the land use and development process. Therefore, although economic tools – such as taxes on carbon emissions, or a tradeable carbon 'price' are important measures – on their own, pricing signals do not necessarily provide the level of protection needed to prevent further exposure to the serious risks associated with climate change. Regulation – in the form of environmental protection and planning laws – is an important safeguard against ongoing global 'market failure' to manage greenhouse gas emissions, and to defend communities from unacceptable exposure to future climate change risks.

Planning for climate change requires action on two fronts: spatial policies to reduce or mitigate the causes of greenhouse gas emissions, and strategies to adapt to climate change effects already underway. While there is a growing body of scientific evidence regarding the causes and impacts of climate change, and a proliferation of activities across all levels of Australian government, climate change considerations are yet to be 'mainstreamed' in Australian planning law or practice.

The first part of this chapter introduces the causes and potential implications of climate change. Secondly, the chapter outlines Australian legal, policy and governance frameworks relevant to climate change and planning decisions. Thirdly, drawing on the growing body of research on this subject, the chapter sets out principles for climate change mitigation and adaptation in plan-making and development assessment, referring to examples from Australian and international practice. In conclusion, the chapter reflects on the nascent state of Australian planning responses to climate change and opportunities for local communities to take the lead in mainstreaming climate change considerations across all plan-making and development decisions.

Causes and implications of climate change

The term 'climate change' describes ongoing changes in the earth's atmosphere, some of which occur naturally (Metz et al. 2007). However, over the past two centuries, and particularly the last, these variations have accelerated, due to changing concentrations of the earth's atmospheric gases. These atmospheric shifts are provoked by increased production of gases such as carbon dioxide, described as 'greenhouse gases' because of their overall warming effect on the earth's climatic system. Caused by the burning of fossil fuels, increased production of greenhouse gases has been exacerbated by land use changes resulting in loss of natural systems such as forests and native vegetation, which act as 'sinks' to absorb carbon dioxide (Fisher et al. 2007).

The largest proportion of Australia's total greenhouse gas emissions arise from fuel combustion in the energy sector (53.9 per cent in 2008, Department of Climate Change and Energy Efficiency 2010b). These are mainly attributable to energy generation. The transport sector accounts for 14.6 per cent of total emissions (and rising), with road transport the major contributor (Department of Climate Change and Energy Efficiency 2010b). In other sectors, emissions from agriculture amount to 15.9 per cent of emissions (largely from livestock), and coal, oil and natural gas production contribute 7.3 per cent, most of which is related to coal mining.

Within this context, actions to reduce activities which produce harmful carbon dioxide emissions are a priority (Metz et al. 2007, p101). These include reducing energy requirements in the built environment, shifting to low carbon, renewable energy sources; preserving natural carbon sinks, and enabling new techniques for carbon sequestration or removal. However, even if greenhouse gas emissions were stabilised, major and unpredictable impacts associated with anthropogenic warming and sea-level rise would still be unavoidable (IPCC 2007a, p17).

The impacts of climate change are already being observed in Australia (Henessey et al. 2007). Rising temperatures, more frequent heatwaves, increased rain in the northwest and less in southern and eastern Australia have all been attributed to climate change and consequent water shortages, agricultural impacts and pressure on natural ecosystems. By 2030 temperatures will have already risen by up to 0.9 degrees across coastal areas of Australia (CSIRO 2007), and there is likely to be greater temperature variation and extremes with more very hot days. Some parts of the country will expect more overall precipitation but through more intense rain events, with longer periods between rainy days. Combined with these changes in rainfall and temperature, wind speeds are expected to increase in many parts of the country, with implications for fire seasons and spatial range of bushfire risk (Henessy et al. 2007).

Global sea-level rise threatens coastal ecosystems, settlements and infrastructure, with flooding and extreme waves likely to penetrate further ashore (CSIRO 2007, p11). Australia's natural ecosystems are already under pressure, with many species extinct or threatened, due to loss, isolation, or fragmentation of their habitat. Their capacity to withstand changed rainfall patterns, temperatures, and sea-level rise is significantly compromised. One of the most iconic areas already impacted by climate change is the World Heritage listed Great Barrier Reef (GBR) in Far North Queensland. Due to ocean warming, mass coral bleaching events are predicted to become an annual occurrence by 2030 (Henessy et al. 2007, p527).

Social and economic implications of climate change will vary between geographic areas and across different community groups. In the major cities, hotter temperatures and more frequent storms or flooding cause major disruption due to the density of people and major infrastructure affected. However, in many regional areas, drought, inundation and storm events can ravage the economic base of small settlements, while providing or restoring services and infrastructure to rural and isolated communities can be much more difficult. Table 10.1 illustrates the range of social and economic implications arising from climate change effects, using coastal communities, who face particular threats, as a specific example.

Climate change presents many significant hazards to human health. Health impacts arise in two main categories – the first, associated with sudden cataclysmic events such as cyclones, fires or floods, and the second, to the cumulative impacts of ongoing climate viability. Floods, storms and fires obviously threaten human life and also bring health risks associated with water/vector borne diseases and the spread of infection, and mental health impacts such as trauma, displacement, or loss (Few 2007, p282). As shown in Table 10.1, respiratory, disease, and psychological health conditions are also associated with heatwaves, fires and drought. Many of these hazards can be reduced by careful design or retrofitting of new buildings and public spaces.

Health and safety risks can affect different social groups in different ways, depending on existing health status, level of preparedness, and access to financial resources. Research on health impacts arising from climate change in particular and natural emergencies more widely shows that the very old and the very young, and those with a disability are particularly vulnerable (Cutter & Finch 2007; Few 2007; Rosenkoetter et al. 2007). Lower-income households may experience specific pressures as well – higher energy and fuel costs associated with market-based carbon reduction policies – and be less able to adapt their homes for climate comfort or protection.

Adaptation, vulnerability and resilience

In planning for climate change adaptation, a major goal is to reduce vulnerability by improving capacity to adapt to or accommodate the range of impacts that may arise (Vogel et al. 2007). This is described as 'resilience'. The methodology for scoping and assessing vulnerability to climate change scenarios, can be summarised in a threefold process:

1. compile existing information about potential known risks

2. estimate the capacity of existing systems of processes to adapt to these risks

3. define potential strategies to reduce risk and improve resilience (see Centre for Science in the Earth System 2007; cses.washington.edu/cig/fpt/guidebook.shtml for latest best practice in undertaking a local risk assessment).

Table 10.1 Potential climate change impacts and implications for coastal communities

Potential climate change effects	Impacts for coastal communities
Sea-level rise	Loss of beaches
Coastal erosion	Migration of sand dunes
	Loss of/threat to private property
	Infrastructure threat/damage
	Impact on lifestyle/amenity values
	Biodiversity loss
	Tourism values (especially iconic beaches)
Frequent storm events	Public safety and evacuation capacity
More intense storm events/cyclones	Capacity of emergency services – volunteers, infrastructure (hospitals, shelters, supplies)
Increased rainfall	Damage to infrastructure (energy, water, road, buildings, telecommunications, coastal ports, jetties)
Decreased rainfall	Water shortages (during drought) and contamination (storm events, inundation, flooding, ground water salination/disturbance)
	Agricultural industry impacts – sudden weather events (e.g. cyclone) plus long-term events (e.g. drought)
	Tourism impacts (damage to tourism infrastructure, visitor perception of risk)
	Damage to marine ecosystems from storm/agricultural runoff
Warming sea temperatures, ocean acidification	Damage to coral reefs
	Threats to marine habitat and species, coastal ecosystesm (mangroves, saltmarshes, sea grass)
	Damage to estuaries – biodiversity, tourism and economic values
	Threat to fisheries and recreational fishing
	Threats to port functions
Increased temperatures	Public health, especially frail aged community
Increased humidity	Disease vectors (insects)
	Food spoilage
	Capacity of health services
	Economic impacts of disease
	Peak energy demand increases

Source: Gurran et al. 2008a, p20

'Risk' involves two concepts: the degree of likelihood that a particular event will happen, and the degree of impact that such an event would create (New Zealand Climate Change Office 2004). For instance, there might be a high likelihood of increased coastal erosion in particular locations, but if these locations are isolated, the need to intervene will be lower than if the risk relates to highly settled areas containing significant infrastructure. Similarly, while potential impacts of a major 'one in two hundred year' flood event for a particular community might be catastrophic, the low likelihood of the event occurring means lower level of protection may be acceptable. However under climate change scenarios, old benchmarks will need revision, as the likely frequencies of major flood and other hazards increase. Risk associated with climate change is assessed in the same way, with high probability of a particular event, combined with high potential impact, meaning high risk (Allen Consulting Group 2005; Holper et al. 2006).

Risk assessments already underpin strategic land allocation processes and the definition of design standards, in relation to natural hazards like flooding and bushfire. Many jurisdictions have their own state approaches for assessing and managing these risks, such as the NSW Planning for Bushfire Protection guide produced by the Rural Fire Service (Rural Fire Service 2006).

In considering climate change in strategic land use decisions, much can be learned from established methodologies for planning for natural emergencies. Emergency planning frameworks focus on three stages – pre-emergency, when potential risks should be minimised; direct post-emergency, when immediate health and safety needs – such as secure water, temporary shelter – must be provided, and the longer term phase of rebuilding (Levine et al. 2007). In this phase there are opportunities to enhance long-term settlement resilience and perhaps improve overall planned design. Thinking ahead to this potential eventuality can help prepare communities strive for a better outcome despite other pressures (Handmer & Dovers 2007).

Policy and legal context for climate change and Australian planning

As discussed in chapter 5, the United Nations Convention on Climate Change was agreed at the United Nations Conference on Environment and Development (UNCED) in 1992. This convention established international commitments for monitoring and reducing greenhouse gas emissions, tracked through national greenhouse gas inventories of emissions and removals, though these commitments were not legally binding. A legally binding framework under the Kyoto Protocol followed in 1997 (although Australia did not sign the Kyoto Protocol for another decade, when the Prime Minister Kevin Rudd committed Australia to limiting greenhouse emissions to 108 per cent of 1990 levels, by 2012).

A formal policy framework for climate change planning in Australia was established in 1998 under the National Greenhouse Strategy (Commonwealth of Australia 1998). Following this strategy, each of the states prepared their own greenhouse action plans, as did a number of local councils (Burton 2007). In 2007 the Council of Australian Governments (COAG) articulated a National Climate Change Adaptation Framework 2007–2014, intended to provide a coordinating approach to understanding and managing climate change risks to natural resources, industry, settlements, infrastructure and community health.

In February 2011 the Commonwealth established an independent Climate Commission, with scientist Professor Tim Flannery appointed as the Chief Commissioner. The Commission is intended to help build community understanding and support for climate change responses through public outreach activities. A Climate Change Authority, also independent from the government, was established in July 2011 to advise on reducing carbon pollution, including the setting of targets.

Economic tools

In 2007 the Australian government commissioned economist Professor Ross Garnaut to conduct an independent study on the economic costs of climate change and to evaluate policies for reducing emissions and adapting to risks. The report (Garnaut 2008) emphasised the urgency of action in emissions reduction, but focused on market institutions in approaching mitigation and adaptation responses.

This is consistent with the overall focus of Australian policy on climate change which has emphasised market-based measures to make carbon generation and dependency more expensive. At the time of writing, it was anticipated that a national carbon tax would be implemented in July 2012.

Several of the Australian states and territories (including NSW, Victoria and the ACT) have established 'carbon trading markets' to promote greenhouse gas reduction. A trading scheme, when supported by a regulatory 'cap' on carbon emission entitlements, establishes a 'price' for carbon pollution, so that businesses are encouraged to reduce the impacts of their activities over time (DCCEE 2010a). At the same time, the number of entitlements available in the market place is capped and or reduced each year, increasing the price signal to reduce emissions. The NSW Greenhouse Gas Abatement Scheme, established in 2003, was one of the world's first mandatory carbon trading schemes. The scheme requires electricity retailers to meet mandatory targets by reducing or offsetting (through purchase of abatement measures) greenhouse gas emissions generated by electricity production (Independent Pricing and Regulatory Tribunal 2011).

While much of the emphasis of climate change mitigation policy has focused on using the market in this way, both internationally and in Australia, there is growing awareness of opportunities to reduce greenhouse gas emissions through decisions about land use, settlement planning and infrastructure (Davoudi et al. 2009).

Environmental and planning law

At the national level, the *Commonwealth Environmental Protection and Biodiversity Conservation Act 1999* (*CEPBCA*) contains no specific provisions for climate change. However, the loss of 'terrestrial climatic habitat caused by anthropogenic emissions of greenhouse gases' is listed as a key threatening process (under s183). This means that along with emissions reduction, 'adaptation requirements of species and communities likely to be affected by climate change should be given greater priority' during assessments or decisions made under the Act (Threatened Species Committee 2001).

At the state and territorial level, progress on climate change mitigation and adaption is at different stages of development. Most states have declared emissions reductions targets, with NSW the first to make a policy commitment to a 60 per cent reduction in greenhouse gas emissions (by 2050), expressed in the 2006 State Plan (Durrant 2010). Other states have situated reduction targets in legislation, including South Australia's *Climate Change and Greenhouse Emissions Reduction Act 2007*, which has a target to reduce greenhouse gas emissions to 40 per cent or less than 1990 levels of emissions, and a renewable energy target of 20 per cent of electricity generated and consumed in the state, by December 2014 (ss3-5) (Durrant 2010). South Australia has incorporated adaptation policies within an umbrella climate change plan, and has also established specific planning targets for climate change mitigation (emissions reduction) and adaptation, in the South Australian Planning Strategy. South Australian development plans must promote this strategy, providing a means of bringing explicit emissions reduction targets and policies for adaptation to the sphere of local planning (Durrant 2010).

The Australian Capital Territory's *Climate Change and Greenhouse Gas Reduction Act 2010* aims to reduce emissions reduced by 80 per cent (to 1990 levels) by 2050, and establishes an advisory Climate Change Council.

Victoria's *Climate Change Act 2010* establishes an emissions reduction target of 20 per cent (from 2000 levels) and requires decision-makers to consider climate change when making specified decisions under several pieces of legislation relating to environmental protection, catchment and coastal management, but curiously, not the principle *Planning and Environment Act 1987*. The Act also requires a state climate change adaptation plan to be prepared every four years and provides for climate covenants between the government and community or industry stakeholders.

Queensland is the first jurisdiction to mandate the consideration of climate change during plan-making and development assessment *Sustainable Planning Act* 2009 (s5[1][c]), following on from the Queensland government's stand alone 'Climate Smart Adaptation Plan' (2007–2012).

Several Australian states have planning guidance for managing sea-level rise, and have reviewed flood management requirements to incorporate new climate scenarios, providing a more consistent basis for 'mainstreaming' climate change considerations in plan-making and development assistance.

Coastal risk has been a particular emphasis of evolving planning policy and coastal management law in NSW, with the release of a specific coastal planning policy statement (Department of Environment Climate Change and Water 2009b), and guidelines (DOP 2010c), which promote special development criteria for areas within a 2100 hazard line (the anticipated level of sea-level rise in the year 2100), including provisions that items be relocatable or easily disassembled. However, changes to the *Coastal Protection Act 1979* establish provisions for property owners to undertake emergency coastal protection works without development approval (*Coastal Protection and Other Legislation Amendment Act 2010*). Provisions for addressing risks associated with sea-level rise are also covered by legislation in South Australia, Queensland, and Victoria. By contrast, there has been much less regulatory emphasis on managing exposure to existing, and potential future, bushfire risk (Durrant 2010).

In relation to local planning decisions, most states (including Western Australia, Victoria and NSW) now enforce minimum energy efficiency requirements through statutory planning frameworks or building codes. As discussed in chapter 6, in NSW the

SEPP – Building Sustainability Index (BASIX) promotes climate change mitigation through minimum energy and water efficiency standards for residential development, alterations and additions.

The need to consider potential climate change impacts – both greenhouse gas emissions, and the risks of physical exposure – is also implied by the evolution of environmental law (Durrant 2010). Despite different legislative frameworks, climate lawyer Nicola Durrant argues that environmentally sustainable development goals within environmental protection and planning laws offer sufficient authority for climate change to be legitimately considered in decision-making. In relation to the variety of approaches to environmental assessment in Australian state and territory law, she concludes:

> As a general rule, decision-makers under these legislative schemes would be expected to take into account those matters expressly stated in the statute as well as those implied from their subject matter, scope and purpose. On a proper application of those matters it would be expected that the significant long-term effects on the environment and the community from climate change would be taken into account and balanced against the short-term economic and social interests of the approval of the project. The outcome of this evaluation would be either the refusal of the application, on balance, or approval with the imposition of conditions requiring the mitigation or offset of some or all of the emissions of the project. (Durrant 2010, p225).

But in practice, the extent to which consideration of climate change justify let alone compel a refusal is less clear cut in the absence of legally mandated requirements.

Principals for climate change mitigation and adaption through land use planning

In the context of this wider emergent policy and legal framework for climate change mitigation and adaption, what are the implications for local plan-making and development assessment? Although future impacts of climate change are uncertain, decisions regarding settlement patterns and building design will have lasting impacts – with most buildings and infrastructure designed to a 50–70 year life span (Holper et al. 2006). Thus it is important to ensure that current planning frameworks do not exacerbate contributions to greenhouse gas emissions or increase community exposure to climate threats. Rather, strategic planning decisions should actively facilitate climate change mitigation and adaptation opportunities. In this regard, climate change has presented a new ethical challenge to planning underpinned by a moral imperative to protect quality of life for future generations (Wilson 2009).

Drawing on the growing literature and research on planning and climate change, the following principles should guide planning practice.

Principles

Climate change has been described as 'a dramatic manifestation of the sustainability crisis' (Steele & Gleeson 2010, p109). As such, principles for embedding climate change mitigation and adaptation in planning practice are not inherently different to the wider sustainability agenda outlined in the previous chapter. Indeed the overriding principle is to uphold ecological sustainability in prioritising and designing adaptation and mitigation approaches (IPCC 2007b).

The ecological sustainability framework situates climate change mitigation as long range adaptation activity, prioritising actions to reduce greenhouse gas emissions, and avoiding adaptation approaches that increase carbon pollution or have other negative environmental effects. For instance, while air-conditioning would help households adapt to hotter temperatures in the future, there are negative consequences for energy demand and greenhouse gas emissions. Similarly, hard engineering solutions to sea-level rise and increased coastal erosion can result in disturbed marine and coastal habitat. Where possible, actions that undermine climate mitigation and other sustainability goals should be avoided. Instead, approaches that improve climate resilience by protecting and restoring the capacity for natural systems to adjust to increased climate volatility should be promoted.

A corollary is that it is not sufficient to accept that climate change is unavoidable and thus focus planning responses solely on adaptation:

> As planners and other local decision-makers are becoming more cognisant of the extraordinary dangers that climate change poses – prompting recognition that adaptation measures are urgent – most communities are failing to take sufficient steps to prevent climate destabilisation from presenting even larger dangers in the future. As planners make the 'adaptation turn', then, it is fundamentally important that they also push harder than ever for changes in land use, transportation system, energy systems, water systems and built environment that will dramatically reduce emissions of greenhouse gases. (Howard 2009, p19)

In other words, adaptation planning is a significant and pragmatic response to climate change but must not be viewed in isolation to mitigation.

Given that decisions about the built environment will have lasting impacts for the medium to long term, immediate planning intervention is needed to prevent further risks associated with climate change and support rapid adoption of new approaches if and when required (Gurran et al. 2008a). For instance, the adoption of cyclone-rated building codes in parts of Far North Queensland and the Northern Territory following the devastating Cyclone Tracy that hit Darwin in 1974 has significantly reduced damage to property and lives during subsequent major storm events. By contrast, although 1974 was affected by a series of major floods across the same regions, attempts to establish stronger building codes and development restrictions in flood prone areas have been less successful. Contemporary building materials – such as chipboard kitchens, composite board timber frames, and plasterboard walls – all of which swell if exposed to water – mean that many thousands of new dwellings would be seriously damaged in a significant flood event, as demonstrated in the December 2010/January 2011 floods which resulted in three quarters of Queensland being declared a disaster zone (Molino 2011).

Consistent with the overarching sustainability framework, social equity considerations in climate change planning are critical. Planners must recognise potential for particular groups to be disadvantaged by the costs of mitigation – such as higher energy costs, or costs associated with mandatory new design or technology requirements for construction or appliances. Consistent with the principles of equity, affected communities must also have opportunities to participate in relevant decisions relating to climate mitigation or adaptation that may affect their lives.

Finally, many actions designed to reduce greenhouse gas emissions or improve the capacity to adapt to increased climate volatility are worth doing anyway – and have multiple benefits. Actions with multiple benefits for the environment or community (like enhancing natural ecosystems to improve resilience to climate impacts, or providing more opportunities for non-motorised transport) should be prioritised. Opportunities to mitigate climate change through natural carbon sinks or engineered sequestration techniques represent added value for urban biodiversity and greening projects.

Therefore climate change mitigation and adaptation, alongside broader environmental sustainability criteria, should increasingly become mainstream evaluation criteria when land use plans are being prepared and specific developments assessed.

Planning for climate change mitigation and adaption in practice

The section above outlined five key principles for climate change planning, which can be summarised as: upholding the principles of ecological sustainability; ensuring that adaption and mitigation goals align; promoting social equity; and choosing strategies 'worth doing anyway'. The following section operationalises these principles as a series of techniques or examples for practice. The techniques and processes of planning practice must also respond to new pressures and challenges associated with climate change. Traditional planning practice draws heavily on research and past trends, and seeks to establish a stable framework for controlling predictable future change. However, unpredictability is one of the major challenges associated with climate change. Faced with uncertainty as to the timing, nature and magnitude of risks – many advocate a new approach to planning based on 'adaptive management', where decision and response frameworks are designed to adjust to changing circumstances and information. Such approaches can be designed into statutory planning documents through controls that are triggered when a particular 'threshold' is reached, or when new information comes to light. A second approach is that of 'scenario building', whereby potential 'story lines' about the future are developed as a way of exploring or testing different possible approaches in a more creative way (Wilson 2009).

There are a number of strategies for settlement design and planning with dual goals to improve resilience to climate change impacts, and promote long-term mitigation of greenhouse gas emissions. The UK government national planning policy on climate change establishes a spectrum of such considerations with respect to climate change mitigation and adaptation (Department of Communities and Local Government 2011b). It promotes a regional strategy approach to frame local planning in relation to the location of major infrastructure and to establish new, decentralised energy, water or waste management plants to contribute to community resilience. It emphasises the need to consider the role of infrastructure as travel generators, the distribution of goods and energy opportunities to maximise decentralised, low-renewable energy sources, and the designation of carbon sinks.

Increasingly infrastructure facilities are intended to perform multiple environmental services alongside serving basic settlement needs. For instance, waste water management strategies now tend to emphasise natural or constructed wetland systems, which also contribute to biodiversity, active transportation, leisure and amenity objectives. To promote climate change mitigation, planning schemes should also encourage self-provision of key infrastructure services – like energy, water, waste management, through technologies for micro energy generation, water retention and demand reduction technologies, and waste minimisation, re-use and recycling. If technology is not currently viable, opportunities can be preserved to install carbon neutral and climate resilient forms of infrastructure in the future. Solar access should be protected to ensure future capacity for onsite solar generation. Regulatory burdens to require proposals for renewable energy infrastructure should be minimised, and where possible, the onus shifted to favour renewable energy projects as under planning policy in the UK and New Zealand (Department of Communities and Local Government 2011b; Durrant 2010).

Similarly, there are a number of basic approaches to reducing the carbon impact of transportation systems, and improving resilience to future climate impacts and potential oil scarcity (Newman 2009). New and existing settlements should be designed or reconfigured to reduce trip generation, and to encourage public transport use and active transportation such as walking and cycling. Safe, naturally vegetated walkways and cycleways should connect residential, retail and recreational areas. Travel plans to demonstrate the internal transportation network and connections to major centres, according to the hierarchy of sustainable transport options – walking, cycling, public transport and lastly, the private motor car – should be provided to support proposals for major new residential areas.

Urban design guidelines and building codes for public and private buildings should be designed for future climate scenarios – by maximising cross ventilation and natural building cooling. Basic considerations – such as the capacity to open windows or otherwise cool or illuminate workspaces or homes – are important to reduce energy demand and in case of a power outage during severe weather. Addressing potential urban heat island effects arising from hotter temperatures and heatwaves is an important consideration when preparing urban design guidelines and assessing public and private buildings in built up areas (Corburn 2009). Provisions for urban vegetation, 'green' (planted) roofs, specific colours for building and paving materials may be required to mitigate urban heat. Such strategies are best pursued on a precinct basis, rather than solely in relation to individual buildings. Public space designs must anticipate more severe local climatic conditions, with shading, shelter and appropriate vegetation to cool areas of open space.

In areas likely to be affected by specific climate change risk, a full vulnerability assessment should inform strategic land use planning decisions. Increasingly, such an assessment will need to be undertaken to support major land release or subdivisions or other significant proposals (Gurran et al. 2008a). For instance, the Gold Coast Planning Scheme 2003 has a natural hazards strategy component which includes consideration of future impacts associated with climate change, including sea-level rise and increased risk of storm surge, inundation and fire. In drafting planning instruments and criteria for development assessment, existing information used to support land use planning decisions – including floodplain and bushfire protection thresholds or models – may need updating or reconsideration over time as new data becomes available, particularly in relation to likely increases in the intensity or frequency of these events and projected new geographical range. It may be necessary to reorient natural hazard assessment methodologies from historical events to forecasted impacts associated with climate change scenarios.

In planning for areas where risk is found to be high, decisions fall roughly into three categories: to protect infrastructure through engineered fortification, such as a sea wall, to accommodate threat through planning and design modifications, or to retreat, by relocating infrastructure and activities. Such decisions often need to be made at a local scale, responding and adapting to specific circumstances as they unfold (de Vries & Wolsink 2009).

In planning for new settlements, or for new development within existing areas, it is important to reserve space for emergency access, congregation, shelter and evacuation. In particularly vulnerable areas, locations for intermediate post-emergency recovery, such as temporary housing should be identified. Again, while sites need to be in safe locations, they may be multi-function. Further, preplanning for enhanced settlement reorientation or design following a disaster event can result in greater long-term resilience to climate change impacts. Such long-term planning ensures that intermediate land use decisions do not compromise future opportunities:

> One of the earliest messages to arise from modern disaster recovery research was that public decisions taken in the heat of the emergency period immediately following a disaster often compromise significant opportunities to rebuild a safer community for the future. The pressure exerted by residents and property owners to have their disaster-stricken community rebuilt to its pre-disaster form and condition as quickly as possible remains a powerful factor in local, state, and federal emergency management to this day. There are ways to restrain such pressures and maintain mitigation and other post-disaster goals as high priorities during the process of long-term reconstruction even as the ashes, the rubble, and the water are receding or being cleared away. The secret lies in identifying in advance those decisions that will need to be made after a disaster that are most likely to have long term repercussions for hazard mitigation. (American Planning Association 2005, p48)

In thinking ahead, planning processes must make particular consideration of housing conditions for lower-income or more vulnerable groups. Manufactured home estates and caravan parks represent a significant proportion of lower-cost housing, yet present significant risks during extreme storm or hurricane events. For instance, Polk County, Florida, has developed an explicit disaster recovery planning policy, part of which addresses questions of affordable housing and the needs of low-income social groups.

> One of the challenges in promoting affordable housing is the safety of mobile homes. Although affordable, mobile homes do not promote increased resilience to future disasters in the county's housing stock ... Locations for developments that contain affordable housing should be identified in conjunction with land planners during routine planning processes and discussions. It is also important to ensure that temporary replacement housing locations are carefully regulated so that they do not become unintended permanent replacement housing that may be in conflict with land use regulations or other codes. (Polk County 2009, p59)

Finally it is important to ensure that meeting climate change objectives does not add unnecessarily to the regulatory burden of the planning process. Effective strategic planning means that an explicit, separately undertaken, climate change assessment would not be necessary for most applications. Rather, climate change considerations should be closely integrated with the environmental impact assessment criteria and methodology applying to more significant and complex proposals. These criteria should include explicit consideration of the impact of the proposal on greenhouse gas emissions (production and absorption) and exposure to climate risk – in relation to the specific proposal as well as downstream and cumulative impacts. If the proposal is approved, conditions for limiting, monitoring and offsetting carbon impacts, and for managing and reducing risk should be mandated and enforced.

Conclusion: 'mainstreaming' climate change in local planning practice

Despite growing scientific evidence and policy discourse on the climate 'emergency', Australian planning laws and controls at state and local levels remain largely silent on greenhouse gas emissions and climate risk. Given the imperative for immediate action, it is disappointing that a decade of Australian planning reform has failed to confront major environmental concerns such as climate change, while vigorously pursuing the administrative goals of simplicity, standardisation and speed. Indeed, in many cases the outcomes of planning reform may have been to weaken existing tools and mechanisms for climate mitigation and adaptation. This appears to have been the case in NSW, where the former Part 3A reforms enabled major development proposals to bypass existing controls, further weakening the imperative for decision-makers to adhere to ecologically sustainable development considerations, such as sea-level rise and coastal flooding or the impact of particular industries on greenhouse gas emissions (Durrant 2010).

However it seems that case law and gradual legislative change may together shift climate change considerations towards the mainstream planning agenda. Queensland's new *Sustainable Planning Act 2009* includes reference to climate change, while several of the other states now have legally enforceable provisions for considering certain risks such as sea-level rise when plans are made and developments assessed. Hopefully the introduction of national economic measures for carbon reduction will drive major changes in the built environment and in the re-conceptualisation of urban structure, transport and design.

Even without a strong legal framework, local governments are able to embed climate change considerations across all aspects of strategic planning and development assessment, as well as their wider operational, environmental management and natural hazard activities, as outlined in this chapter. The strategies for low-carbon development, which emphasise local and decentralised approaches to food, energy, water, waste and transportation, and preserving and enhancing biodiversity and natural processes, provide a blueprint for the wider sustainable community agenda, emphasising resilience not only to future climate impacts but also to many of the other economic and social challenges likely to arise during the 21st century.

Chapter 11

Planning for housing supply, choice and affordability

Much of the 'day to day' work of a planner involves regulating the development of housing – considering applications for residential subdivision, the development of new housing estates, apartments or single dwellings, and home extensions. Yet in Australia, many local planning instruments have traditionally failed to include specific policy objectives relating to housing. There is now greater impetus to develop strong local policy frameworks and strategies to address the housing needs of the local community. This is in response to growing concern about the lack of affordable housing within many of Australia's urban and regional areas, and the mismatch between our changing demographic profile and the current housing supply (Milligan et al. 2009). For instance, trends towards smaller households and an ageing population imply that very different types of dwellings will be needed in the future. In this chapter, the Australian policy context for local housing and the relationships between the urban planning process and local housing outcomes are explained. The chapter then outlines the way in which the planning system can encourage greater housing diversity, choice and affordability within the local community. The final part of the chapter looks at the ways in which local government has used such mechanisms in Australia.

Housing policy and assistance in Australia

Traditionally the Commonwealth and state governments in Australia have been responsible for providing housing assistance to people on very low incomes, particularly those with special needs. This has included the provision of 'public' or 'social housing' (housing that is funded by the government and managed by a public or community authority) and direct rental subsidies for people renting in the private market. Increasingly however, resource limitations mean that many of the households formerly able to access social housing must rely on the private housing market. House prices and rents have increased dramatically in Australia over the past decade with the result that moderate income earners are being 'priced out' of the housing market even in suburban areas and regional areas that were once affordable (NHSC 2010).

Australia's housing reform agenda

Much of the government funding for housing assistance was provided through grants from the Commonwealth to the states and territories under the Commonwealth State Housing Agreement (CSHA) originally made in 1945. Since this time, the CSHA has helped finance public rental housing construction provided by state housing commissions and other housing assistance programs delivered by the states and territories. Although the first CSHA was tied to obligations for establishing more robust town and country planning laws and programs for slum clearance in the major cities, these planning activities did not really have a major housing focus (Gleeson & Low 2000). While the Commonwealth continued to fund public housing development, by the late 1970s many homes built with CSHA funds could be purchased by tenants in line with Australia's wider policy emphasis on home ownership (Jones et al. 2007).

This policy, coupled with declining real funds for new public housing construction, meant that by the early 1990s public rental housing was a relatively small sector of a housing system largely dominated by home ownership and private rental. Allocation of public housing became highly targeted towards those in greatest need. Over time, many public housing estates became characterised by entrenched poverty and social disadvantage.

Like many other countries, the design of these public housing estates, often enclosed neighbourhoods or modernist apartment towers, intensified social problems, leading to a stigmatisation of public housing. By the 1980's, new strategies for addressing these chronic problems began to emerge in public housing estates across the UK, parts of Europe and the US. These strategies involved changing the organisational delivery of public housing through greater use of community-based housing providers and tenancy managers, and diversifying the tenure mix of public housing through different approaches to asset management and redevelopment. Australia began to adopt some of these strategies in the mid 1980s, through the Community Housing Initiatives Program (CHIP), which provided funding for local community-based housing schemes, including opportunities for local government involvement through transfer of public housing to non profit community housing providers, and through the renewal of public housing estates, sometimes in partnership with the community and or private sectors. To recognise the new diversity in housing provision, the term 'public' housing expanded to 'social housing' – housing that is funded via public subsidy but managed by either government or non-government providers.

While public housing development declined relative to the overall housing market, the provision of housing by the private sector largely kept pace with household growth, until around the turn of the 21st century. However by this time, a growing gap between the rate of new housing production (roughly between 110,000–130,000 dwellings per annum between 2000–2006) and household growth (around 160,000 new households per year) became apparent (NHSC 2010). This apparent supply deficit has shifted the focus of housing policy concern somewhat from targeted assistance for low-income renters to a wider emphasis on the affordability of home ownership.

Table 11.1 charts Australian household growth rates between 2002 and 2009 against the number of new dwellings produced, and house price movements. As shown in the table, there has been a marked mismatch between household growth and housing rates of supply, and a more than doubling of capital city median house prices over the eight-year period.

The National Housing Supply Council, established in 2008 to monitor housing supply in relation to wider population and economic factors affecting demand for housing, estimates that there was a deficit of 178,400 dwellings in 2009, projected to increase to a shortfall of 640,600 houses by 2029 (NHSC 2010, p73). This supply gap has repercussions across the whole market, with long-term private renters unable to move to home ownership, placing pressure on the price and availability of rental housing (NHSC 2010).

Table 11.1 Household growth, dwelling completions and house prices, Australia, 2002–2009

Year	Household growth	Dwelling completions Australia*	Capital city median house prices $AU
2002	138.1	131,900	193,350
2003	139.7	152,800	242,500
2004	138.3	156,900	282,500
2005	137.1	160,600	310,500
2006	137.4	154,700	350,375
2007	162.1	148,200	390,000
2008	157.4	143,500	421,250
2009	205.9	146,400	444,500

*Gross completions not adjusted for demolitions. Source: ABS 2010; NHSC 2010; based on unweighted sales of established houses.

The CSHA was replaced in 2009 with a new National Affordable Housing Agreement (NAHA) (COAG 2009). The NAHA represents a shift towards a wider policy framework for housing assistance, with more diversified delivery of social housing through the expanded community housing sector. While the NAHA focuses primarily on the social housing sector, in 2008 the Commonwealth initiated an important new program to encourage more affordable housing supply provided by the non-profit and private sector. The National Rental Affordability Scheme (NRAS) offers tax credits against new homes, provided that they are offered to eligible low- and moderate-income households at 20 per cent below market rents. The tax incentives are offered annually for a 10-year period. Modelled on a longstanding program in the US – known as 'low-income housing tax credits' – NRAS has operated in parallel with spatial planning strategies for affordable housing supply, rather than being closely tied to specific planning mandates for affordable housing development requirements for affordable housing inclusion within new communities. However, as demonstrated in the US, such incentive programs improve overall supply of affordable housing, and support the establishment of a strong and influential affordable housing sector (Gilmour & Milligan 2008). In planning for housing development opportunities, ways to support and utilise this emerging sector should be taken into account (Milligan et al. 2009).

The supply of social and affordable housing in Australia received a boost following the global financial crisis of 2009. In responding to the financial crisis, the government's Nation

Building – Economic Stimulus Plan included funding of $5.238 billion for new social housing over three and a half years from 2008–09 to 2011–12, resulting in over 19,000 new homes (Australian Government 2010b). Implementation was supported by state and territorial legislation to fast track projects with stimulus funding, bypassing local planning laws if these represented barriers to rapid project completion.

As well as establishing criteria for capital city strategic plans to promote housing affordability, the Council of Australian Governments (COAG) has also promoted the adoption of targets for affordable housing, national planning system principles to support housing supply, and specific requirements for affordable and diverse housing development through local planning schemes (LGPMC 2010). In April 2010, a new national Housing Supply and Affordability reform agenda was announced by COAG. This agenda focuses on interactions between planning regulation, processes and housing outcomes, including factors which might act as barriers to timely housing supply (COAG 2010a).

Adequate, appropriate and affordable housing

While the National Affordable Housing Agreement signals a wider housing policy framework, Australia does not yet have a comprehensive, system-wide housing policy framework at a national level. In the early 1990s a suite of studies resulted in the preparation of a national housing strategy, which aimed to expand the 'range and supply of adequate, appropriate and affordable housing choices accessible to all Australians', deliver 'more efficient and effective housing provision and land development', and achieve 'urban forms and structures' that contribute to 'safe, quality and sustainable environments' (Commonwealth of Australia 1992). Despite never being formally adopted, many of the ideas canvassed – in particular, an emphasis on moving to a more diverse system of housing assistance through greater involvement of the non-profit sector – have come to pass (Milligan et al. 2009). However, housing and urban policy realms have remained detached. Australian planning law provides limited explicit recognition of affordable housing, with the exception of South Australia (following amendments in 2005), and to a lesser degree, NSW (where affordable housing has been an objective of the *Environmental Planning and Assessment Act 1979* since 2000). The ACT's *Planning and Development Act 2007* alludes to affordable residential housing, and Queensland's new *Sustainable Planning Act 2009* includes reference of housing choice and diversity and aims to promote development which is 'affordable', but stops short of specifically addressing affordable housing per se (Table 11.2).

In the absence of a national – and in many cases, state – framework for government housing policy development, many local governments have identified their own housing policy statements drawing on what has become known as the 'adequate housing model' (Lawson 1995; LGSA 1998; Gurran 2003). These components of adequate housing include affordability relative to household income, appropriateness of housing design in relation to cultural expectations and requirements, household size and life cycle, and the availability of housing in appropriate locations accessible to social networks, services and employment.

In an address to the National Housing Conference held in 2005, Councillor Ann Bennison from the Australian Local Government Association (ALGA) described the ALGA position in relation to housing as follows:

Creating liveable and sustainable communities is the fundamental purpose of local government. That's why planning at the local and regional level is such a critically important part of the housing equation. For its part, local government strives to promote housing development which:

- provides the choice of housing sought by our communities

- offers the best possible quality of life and environment for all residents

- achieves best practice in urban design

- provides appropriate protection and enhancement of heritage character and local and cultural identity

- is ecologically sustainable. (Bennison 2005, p1)

To understand how these goals can be achieved it is useful to consider local government roles in relation to housing in more detail.

Table 11.2: Housing choice and affordability in Australian state and territorial planning legislation

Jurisdiction	Legislation	Reference to housing needs, choice or affordability
ACT	*Planning and Development Act 2007*	Territory plan may make provision for affordable housing (s51)
NSW	*Environmental Planning and Assessment Act 1979*	Affordable housing an objective of the Act (s5)
NT	*Planning Act 1999*	X
Qld	*Sustainable Planning Act (SPA) 2009*	Housing choice and diversity to be considered in decision-making, s5(1)(c). Reference to 'affordable development' as a component of sustainable communities (s11[c][i]).
SA	*Development Act 1993*	An objective of the Act (s3) is to promote or support initiatives to improve housing choice and access to affordable housing.
Tas.	*Land Use Planning and Approvals (LUPA) Act 1993*	X
Vic.	*Planning and Environment Act 1987*	An objective of the Growth Areas Authority is to promote housing diversity and affordability in growth areas (s46AR[d]).
WA	*Planning and Development Act (PDA) 2005*	X
Cwlth	*Commonwealth Environment Protection and Biodiversity Conservation Act 1999*	X

Source: the Author

Box 11.1: What is affordable housing?

Understanding affordable housing and housing affordability

The term 'affordable housing' is used in many different ways by politicians, the media, developers, policymakers, lawyers, academics, and, by people who want to access the housing they aspire to at prices they believe they can afford! In defining affordable housing it is helpful to think about what affordability might mean in terms of housing costs as a proportion of income or expenditure for very low, low or moderate income households (up to 120 per cent of median household income). In a very broad sense, affordable housing for is understood to be accessible for these households on low or moderate incomes to rent or purchase.

In policy discourse, the term 'affordable housing' is often linked to a specific program designed to meet the needs of households whose incomes are not sufficient to allow them to access appropriate housing in the market without assistance (Milligan et al. 2004). This definition could include traditional forms of public or social housing, but many other kinds of affordable housing products may be involved. They include housing for fixed term or secure letting at below market cost, shared home ownership (where an equity partner provides free or subsidised capital to assist a home buyer to access affordable housing) subsidised or discounted home purchase, as well as unsubsidised lower-cost forms of housing delivered through the private market.

In evaluating the need for affordable housing or in deciding who is eligible to access affordable housing that has been subsidised, measuring affordability in relation to household income becomes important. Measurements of affordability are usually calculated with reference to the proportion of household income spent on rent or mortgage repayments (25–30 per cent is generally considered affordable, depending on the base income), or with reference to how the level of 'after housing income' compares to a household budget standard. These calculations do not consider other housing impacts on expenditure such as location, which determines travel costs and employment opportunities, and housing appropriateness (in relation to household size and needs).

Given that planning decisions affect the broad range of housing outcomes – and have a complex relationship to supply and demand factors and to the cyclical and spatial dynamics of housing markets, it is important not to limit any conceptualisation of affordability to a particular model. At the same time, strict legal definitions may be needed in some cases to support the range of planning interventions discussed below. For example in NSW, state planning legislation includes specific definitions of affordable housing tied to programs for leveraging affordable housing contributions through the planning process (see SEPP No. 70 – Affordable Housing – Revised Schemes; SEPP – Affordable Rental Housing [2009]). In South Australia, affordable housing is defined according to location specific price points and rents, derived with reference to the capacity of those on up to a moderate household income to sustain housing payments at or below 30 per cent of their earnings (Milligan et al. 2009).

In summary, affordable housing can be understood as 'housing which is affordable for low and moderate income households across home ownership, private rental as well as public rental tenures' (HLGPM 2005, p1). Many different models of financing and delivering this housing are recognised within this definition, ranging from traditional social housing (owned publicly or privately through housing associations), as well as other forms of sub market and regulated market housing for purchase or rent.

Housing functions of local government

In broad terms, local government responsibilities for housing include identifying current and projected community needs for housing of a particular type and tenure, regulating the supply of residential land and housing stock in response to projected needs, coordinating the provision of infrastructure and services to support existing and future housing development, and in some cases, directly providing housing to people with special needs (for instance, seniors, people with a disability, or those on low incomes). To use a traditional conceptualisation, local governments are concerned with both 'production' and 'consumption' aspects of housing (Beyer 1965) (Table 11.3).

As shown in Table 11.3, local government responsibilities for housing extend from identifying appropriate locations for new residential land through to the provision of 'hard' and 'soft' infrastructure, like transport, utilities, recreation, schools, hospitals, community services, and information and advocacy activities.

Many local governments, in Australia and internationally, develop a local housing strategy or equivalent to provide a strategic framework for their housing activities. Local housing strategies are intended to provide a comprehensive framework for responding to local housing issues, relating to population change, housing market trends, coordination of housing or community services, protection of urban amenity, environmental sustainability and efficient land use, and economic and community development.

Local housing strategies usually combine three key elements:

- *the housing 'study' component* – an identification of housing needs (demographic trends as well as other relevant socio-economic data) and housing conditions (housing type, tenure, costs, and market trends)
- *the housing 'policy' component* – containing an aim/s and more detailed set of objectives
- *the housing 'strategy' component* – concrete measures to implement these objectives.

  Typically these measures cover the range of activity areas identified above, including, but not limited to, land use planning. (Goss & Blackaby 1999; Gurran 2003a)

These elements of the strategy may be contained within a stand-alone document or be embedded within other strategies or plans prepared by council.

The process of developing a local housing strategy can provide a basis for:

- identifying potential sites for new residential development and redevelopment in response to projected housing need
- reviewing existing planning controls to ensure that they meet local housing objectives
- initiating or facilitating local housing projects in response to specific local needs, in partnership with the development industry, community housing providers and other levels of government

- improving council systems for monitoring and responding to local housing needs
- coordinating housing responsibilities in a strategic way, across all relevant sectors of council.

Table 11.3 Housing roles of local government

Production aspects	Consumption aspects
Identifying residential land	Identifying and monitoring housing needs
Setting residential development controls (including subdivision design)	Collaborating with other housing providers (private, public, community sector) to assist groups in housing need
Environmental/social assessment of proposed residential development	Coordinating or delivering appropriate support services (e.g. services for the aged, homeless or crisis resource centres)
Facilitating land parcels and residential subdivision	Undertaking information/advocacy activities at the local level and to higher levels of government
Collaborating with other housing providers (private, public, community sector) to facilitate appropriate housing supply	Financial assistance (e.g. rate relief) for low-cost housing providers
Donating land for residential development	Managing local housing stock
Producing housing units	

Source: Gurran 2003, p396

Sometimes a council will decide to prepare a housing strategy in response to a specific issue that has emerged within the community – such as a need for affordable housing, or for housing to accommodate special needs groups such as the aged.

How does urban planning affect housing outcomes?

In order to understand the ways in which planning mechanisms can be used strategically for housing, it is important to examine in greater detail the way in which planning decisions influence housing outcomes. Many of the urban planning responsibilities of local government discussed throughout this book have important impacts on housing outcomes within the community. Planning decisions can affect the availability of residential land, the timing and costs associated with development, the design and configuration of new housing, and the preservation of existing sources of low-cost housing stock. For instance, the allocation of land to particular uses, through land use zoning or other forms of categorisation, determines the amount of potential land for housing, and the location of new residential development in relation to transport, services, employment and educational opportunities. Development controls influence the way that new housing is designed and configured, and can affect the appropriateness, affordability and the likely cost and tenure of new developments. New developments lead to a loss of existing sources of affordable housing. On the other hand, these impacts might be managed through conditions of development approval, for instance, through the use of developer contributions to fund community infrastructure, or, potentially, affordable housing.

Figure 11.1 Affordable housing in Baltimore, US

In Baltimore, US, the local government has initiated urban renewal schemes to encourage affordable home ownership in the inner city. Developers are able to access a range of planning concessions and other financial and tax incentives, in return for producing affordable housing that is available for low- to moderate-income earners to purchase. Source: the Author 2003

Many of the matters addressed through a local housing strategy relate to the planning, functions of local government.

Thus housing considerations must be taken into account at every stage of the planning process – from the identification of residential land through to setting development controls, and assessing particular developments against these controls. Whether a local housing strategy is in place or not, there are a number of ways in which the planning system can be used to encourage greater housing diversity, choice and affordability.

Figure 11.2 Redevelopment in The Entrance, NSW

Processes of urban renewal and gentrification are often associated with a loss of lower-cost housing, as shown in relation to this development site in the rapidly growing Central Coast of NSW. Source: the Author 2005

Planning for housing supply and choice

As noted, basic planning mechanisms like the allocation of land for residential or other purposes (typically through zoning) and the enactment of building controls, shape the location, configuration, design and availability of housing within a particular area (Gurran et al. 2008b). In planning for current and future housing need, a fundamental consideration is whether there is sufficient residential land for projected housing demand, supported by appropriate local and regional infrastructure. A mismatch between the demand and availability of particular housing types can lead to inflation of house prices or rents. An undersupply of housing or residential land has negative consequences for the environment (over-consumption of a scarce resource) and unless carefully managed, will result in dispersed, poorly serviced, development. Conversely, an oversupply of residential land may reduce land prices to the extent that landowners choose not to sell, again leading to a supply blockage that may have particular impacts for the rental market.

Box 11.2. Policy arguments supporting the retention and provision of affordable housing

There are a number of policy arguments to support the use of planning approaches for the retention and provision of affordable housing. These include:

- the need to remedy regulatory and systemic barriers to the production of affordable housing within the land use planning system

- the need to minimise and offset the impact of urban planning and residential development processes on the availability of low-cost housing

- the need for planning systems to provide for and facilitate greater housing diversity to achieve social mix and to support economic prosperity

- the potential to leverage more subsidised housing stock for low-income people, in better locations; and

- in some cases, the opportunity to recapture some of the gain associated with planning decisions, or to create additional financial gain through incentives and to apply this profit to achieving public objectives. (Gurran et al. 2008b)

In other words, it is important to address any inadvertent impacts for housing affordability that result from systemic or other deficiencies in the planning system overall. Secondly, ensuring equitable access to affordable housing opportunities contributes to the central planning goals of promoting social equity and supporting economic interests in urban development. Thirdly, the planning process provides opportunities to secure locations for affordable housing that might not otherwise be accessible, in the same way that the process of land allocation recognises the need to assign land for recreation, infrastructure and other community goals. Finally, the increased value assigned to certain lands through the planning process presents an opportunity to share in some of this private gain for broader public benefit.

Depending on the forecast housing need of a particular community, it may be necessary to reclassify appropriately located land to allow it to be used for residential purposes or for higher-density residential development. When reviewing a planning framework or introducing new controls for an undeveloped area, it is important to consider whether planning controls regarding residential subdivision and the design of housing support local housing goals or policies, considering the following:

- Do overall planning objectives support local housing goals? As discussed in chapter 5 and 6, most local planning instruments in Australia contain overall objectives. As these objectives provide important guidance about how the plan should be interpreted, there is an opportunity to include objectives relating to a local housing policy for housing diversity, choice and or affordability.

- Do existing controls on the size of residential allotments support housing affordability and environmental sustainability? Large minimum allotment sizes are often associated with higher house prices and may also result in dispersed urban forms which cause biodiversity loss, inefficient infrastructure provision and reliance on the private car. On the other hand in some environmentally sensitive areas large minimum allotment sizes may be necessary to preserve important habitats or landscape features. If such controls result in affordable housing shortages they can be offset by other planning mechanisms designed to promote affordable housing across a local area or region (discussed further below).

- Do existing residential zones provide for sufficient housing diversity (such as an appropriate mix of smaller and larger dwellings, adaptable housing, and housing for the aged), consistent with forecast housing needs? In some locations, environmental or cultural heritage considerations, or community preferences, may mean there is very strong aversion from existing homeowners to new housing forms perceived to be inconsistent with the prevailing streetscape. In such cases, creative approaches are needed – for instance, planning controls that permit the adaptation of existing buildings for seniors accommodation or for boarding houses, or for additional accessory dwellings on large lots (subject to design criteria and building standards). Frequently planning instruments permit 'diversity', but the designs submitted by private developers do not reflect this. Thus it may be necessary to mandate particular housing mixes or configurations, as discussed below.

- Do residential design codes support housing affordability and diversity goals? Excessive development control requirements can increase the costs of producing housing. As noted in chapter 3, even a small increase in required building setbacks within an area may have a significant impact on house prices. Other controls associated with increased housing prices include prohibitions on certain housing types, including medium-density housing, group homes for people with a disability, manufactured housing and accessory dwellings, requirements for wide streets and excessive parking space requirements (APA 1991, 1997, 2001; HUD 2005; Pendall 2000).

- Is existing local and regional infrastructure adequate? What infrastructure co-ordination and funding mechanisms are needed to ensure that new housing is accessible to transport, jobs, services and recreational opportunities?

Planning for affordable housing

Approaches to promote affordable housing through planning can be conceptualised along a spectrum that begins with protecting existing sources of affordable housing supply, and moves through promoting new affordable housing opportunities via the private market, to directly producing dedicated affordable housing stock (Gurran et al. 2008b).

The following information is drawn substantially from Australian Housing and Research Institute (AHURI) study on international practice in planning for affordable housing (Gurran et al. 2008b). While the mechanisms referred to are largely informed by international practice (particularly in the UK and the US), there are significant differences in the legal frameworks, funding, subsidy and housing delivery arrangements to support affordable housing in those nations. Therefore the approaches described here are tailored to the Australian context, where statutory constraints limit the extent to which the planning system can be used to leverage contributions for affordable housing. Given these constraints and underpinned by adequate capital resources to support affordable housing development, the planning system can be used to:

- limit and mitigate the loss of low-cost housing
- promote more lower-cost housing options in the private market and make it easier for non-profit housing developers to build new affordable housing supply
- where opportunities to assist the production of new affordable housing are created as the result of a planning decision, implement processes for the set aside of land or housing or for financial contributions to a local housing program.

Figure 11.3 Affordable housing in Pyrmont Ultimo

Medium-density housing developed by the City West Housing Company in Pyrmont Ultimo is provided as subsidised rental housing for people on low to moderate incomes. Source: the Author 2004

In addition, there are a number of more proactive forms of hybrid intervention, particularly through government land organizations or special development authorities. These authorities can use their land development and planning powers to secure affordable housing outcomes, while leveraging other government resources in creative ways.

Protecting existing sources of affordable housing

Existing sources of low-cost accommodation, such as low-cost rental flats, boarding houses, private hotel rooms, shop-top apartments, caravan parks or manufactured home estates, and older housing stock, are often under pressure from processes of urban consolidation and or gentrification. Urban renewal strategies can improve the quality and amenity of decaying residential areas. However lower-cost housing opportunities are often lost and lower-income households may be displaced.

As these processes of change are regulated by the planning system, there are opportunities to address potential impacts on low-income residents. Techniques can seek to directly protect existing supplies of affordable housing, for instance by controlling the demolition or change of use of particular housing types like boarding houses or caravan parks. A social impact assessment requirement for development applications relating to such proposals can help mitigate their impacts, for instance by requiring developers to contribute to the costs of re-housing tenants, or by donating money to a local affordable housing fund.

Promoting new sources of affordable housing

Good planning can help reduce the cost of producing housing and encourage lower-priced housing opportunities through the private market. In part, this may mean addressing any existing problems within the planning system that are associated with a restriction in housing supply or which otherwise lead to unnecessary housing production costs like inefficiency and delays in assessing developments, or high administrative fees.

Unnecessary barriers to lower-cost housing can be addressed by eliminating excessive development controls, and ensuring that a genuine diversity of housing types are encouraged across as many residential/mixed use areas as possible. For example, the NSW Housing Code promotes this agenda by establishing minimum criteria for housing across the state, providing fast and certain approval for of proposed dwellings complying with the code. To maximise opportunities for diverse and flexible housing, the code allows many standard housing developments and modifications as 'of right', such as 'granny flats' (small, self-contained units on a single title, able to provide accommodation for extended family, or lodgers) and 'attic conversions'. Approval is available within 10 days, subject to lot size, orientation, and specified design criteria.

Specific incentives for residential development that is likely to contribute to more affordable housing opportunities within the local area, such as shop-top or student housing (enabled through an increased development entitlement under controlled circumstances) can also be introduced. Similarly, a local housing strategy or planning instrument could establish specific criteria for affordable housing and offer certain exemptions from planning requirements for housing developments that meet these criteria (like reduced landscaping or car parking, and in some cases, additional floor-space capacity).

Producing new affordable housing

There are opportunities through the planning process to seek contributions towards the direct production or subsidised delivery of dedicated affordable housing for low- to moderate-income households. These opportunities may be articulated through a variety of voluntary or mandatory mechanisms (and often using a combination of approaches). These approaches can be classified as follows (Gurran et al. 2008b):

• *Voluntary planning incentives*

These incentives can be offered through a planning scheme to generate new dedicated affordable housing stock or funds to produce it. Incentives can offset the costs of residential development or provide opportunity for additional profit, with a proportion of this profit applied to an affordable housing program. Incentives could include permission for additional development capacity, or reduced landscaping, parking or open space requirements. Often developers are able to select from available planning incentives or concessions to offset the costs of complying with mandatory affordable housing requirements. The NSW SEPP – Affordable Rental Housing (2009) includes a floorspace bonus for developments including affordable housing, as discussed further below.

Figure 11.4 Protections on rooming houses in St Kilda, Victoria

The Port Phillip Planning Scheme, applying to the inner Melbourne suburb of St Kilda, includes objectives to promote the retention of low-cost single occupancy rental accommodation, known as 'rooming houses' in Victoria. Source: the Author 2003

- *Mandatory requirements (inclusionary zoning and compulsory developer contributions or impact fees)*

  Perhaps the most commonly known mandatory mechanism for generating dedicated affordable housing stock through the planning process is known as 'inclusionary zoning', where legally enforceable planning controls require a set proportion of speci- fied new development within a defined area (or zone) to be dedicated for affordable housing. There are many operational variations of this basic model, such as the amount of affordable housing contribution to be required, whether the contribution must be provided on-site as dedicated for affordable housing (in perpetuity or for a specified time frame), or whether a financial payment in lieu is acceptable. Mandated require- ments can be offset by other incentives or subsidies that are not necessarily provided within the planning system itself, such as favourable tax benefits or concessions. These incentives or subsidies can make mandatory requirements much more effective and reduce developer opposition to their introduction. Similarly, mandatory planning requirements optimise the take-up of subsidy or incentive programs intended to encourage affordable housing development by the private sector. There are provisions for mandatory affordable housing inclusion in specific areas of South Australia, NSW, and Queensland, discussed further below.

- *Mandatory requirements (negotiated agreements)*

  A similar approach to inclusionary zoning involves a legally enforceable planning requirement for developers to contribute to affordable housing, but the actual level of contribution is determined on a negotiated, site-by-site basis. In NSW, the cities of Canada Bay and Randwick have developed policies to signal that affordable housing contributions will be sought through negotiated planning agreements applying to certain types of development.

- *Site/master planning (negotiated planning agreement)*
  In many jurisdictions there is not necessarily an overarching requirement within the local plan for affordable housing, but planning authorities are still able to seek a contri- bution from developers towards affordable housing on a site-by-site, negotiated basis (Gurran et al. 2008b). This is a common practice in relation to major redevelopment areas, and negotiated provision of affordable housing (through on-site inclusion or the payment of a financial contribution) has been secured in relation to key urban renewal areas over the past decade, including the Melbourne Docklands in Victoria, the Carlton United Brewery site in central Sydney, and the Glenside Hospital site in Adelaide (Gurran et al. 2008b).

Current state of practice in planning for affordable housing inclusion

There is often community resistance to the development of new affordable housing at the local level and some local government representatives have actively opposed local affordable housing initiatives in the past. However, in many other cases much of the most innovative work in this policy area has occurred at the local community level, sponsored by local councils. The main ways in which local governments in Australia have used their available planning powers to promote affordable housing are:

- increasing the supply of land zoned for housing purposes, particularly for higher-density residential development, in inner urban and in outer metropolitan areas, to provide greater housing supply relative to demand, to provide opportunities for lower entry points to the housing market, and to provide a greater supply of housing stock that is likely to become available through the rental market.

- amending the objectives of planning instruments to reflect local affordable housing goals, often reinforced by decision-making criteria that require a consent authority to consider affordable housing issues when assessing a development.

- making sure that lower-cost forms of housing are permissible where appropriate, such as shop-top housing, boarding houses and manufactured homes.

- making sure that the planning instrument encourages or permits residential conversions that include additional low-cost housing forms, such as 'granny flats', 'garden flats' or 'accessory dwellings' (Gurran et al. 2005; Squires & Gurran 2005).

Figure 11.5 Boarding houses operated by the Brisbane Housing Company

Some councils have acted directly to prevent the loss of low-cost housing in their areas. Brisbane City Council purchased these two boarding houses to prevent displacement of low-income residents. The properties were transferred to the non profit Brisbane Housing Company for management as affordable rental housing. Source: the Author 2003

Figure 11.6 Affordable housing in the UK

Reading, in England's high-growth South East, has experienced major housing affordability pressures. The land use planning framework provides a basis for ensuring that a significant proportion of new development is affordable to households on very low, low, and moderate incomes. A sophisticated delivery system, including dedicated affordable housing developers (such as the above Lifebuilding Company) is able to access capital funding for affordable housing development under the UK Social Housing Grant and this maximises the leverage planning authorities can use to secure as contributions for affordable housing through the planning system. Source: the Author 2003

Due to the lack of a strong legal framework for addressing affordable housing in state planning law, local government initiatives in protecting, promoting and securing affordable housing during development processes remain patchy (Gurran et al. 2008b).

The City of Port Phillip, in inner Melbourne, was one of the first local governments to pursue affordable housing. Using its own non-profit Housing Association, established by the council in 1985, Port Phillip has secured over 500 dwellings for affordable rental housing, using a combination of negotiated planning outcomes, council resources and land. Another pioneering local authority is the inner eastern Sydney council of Waverley, which in the late 1990s established a density bonus model for developers contingent upon a contribution for affordable housing (usually provided as a cash contribution) (Gurran et al. 2008b). Both councils remain active in pursuing affordable housing through their planning frameworks.

As detailed in chapter 8, the NSW *Environmental Planning and Assessment Act 1979* offers some limited opportunities for securing affordable housing through negotiated planning agreements, in the context of an application for rezoning or development application. By mid 2008, two inner Sydney councils – the City of Canada Bay and Randwick City Council – had developed supporting policy frameworks to promote such agreements (Gurran et al. 2008b).

The Brisbane City Council in Queensland has undertaken a number of initiatives designed to promote affordable housing retention and development, including the establishment of the non-profit Brisbane Housing Company, in partnership with state government. In building the company's portfolio, which numbers over 700 properties, the council has been able to provide some planning concessions to development standards such as car parking and landscaping requirements. In addition to these activities at local government level, there are several ways in which higher levels of government can, and have, contributed to affordable housing inclusion through the planning process.

NSW has provided some avenues for protecting and promoting more diverse and low-cost housing forms, through a series of state policy instruments dating from the late 1980s. These addressed the loss of low-cost rental accommodation in metropolitan Sydney and overcame local planning system barriers to the development of housing for people with special needs. Their provisions are now largely contained within the SEPP - Affordable Rental Housing (2009), which also relaxes some planning requirements applying to residential flats for affordable housing, and encourages more flexibility in the existing housing stock by permitting accessory dwellings (popularly called granny flats) and boarding houses (single-room occupancy dwellings) in residential zones across the state. The policy also introduces a standard density bonus formula for certain types of projects incorporating affordable rental housing.

In Queensland, the planning system supports some site-specific affordable housing initiatives managed by the special purpose Urban Land Development Authority (ULDA). Under its affordability charter, the authority has a minimum target for 15 per cent of dwellings within its redevelopment areas to be affordable to low- and moderate-income households (Urban Land Development Authority 2009). As well as surplus funds secured through the redevelopment process, these targets are pursued through mandatory affordable housing requirements (meaning that a percentage of dwellings provided must meet affordable housing criteria); and the optional take up of density bonus providing an additional affordable housing development contribution. In 2009, ULDA anticipated exceeding its benchmark in three of its major development areas in inner Brisbane, with around 19 per cent of the total 14,800 dwellings earmarked for affordable rental and home purchase (Urban Land Development Authority 2009, p13).

South Australia has established a comprehensive framework for enabling local councils to promote affordable housing during plan-making and development assessment. Amendments to South Australia's *Development Act 1993* in 2006 operationalised the state affordable housing target of 15 per cent affordable housing in to be secured in new development areas (established in the State Housing Plan). These provisions are able to be included in local development plans, through the plan amendment process for a rezoning. Although initially applied to the redevelopment of government sites, local development plans have adopted the targets when major new residential areas are released or rezoned for higher-density housing. Unlike in NSW, where the emphasis has been on securing dwellings to be managed as affordable rental housing by a social housing authority, the South Australian model enables homes to be offered for sale to eligible moderate-income earners. Developers must show how they will meet the affordable housing targets, including release of a set proportion of dwellings for sale to eligible households within a defined affordability range. A government mortgage scheme supports the scheme by ensuring eligible households can access home finance. In 2008, around 400 new dwellings for affordable home purchase were achieved under this mechanism (FAC 2009).

Summary and conclusions

As shown in this chapter in relation to housing, the planning process provides many important opportunities to pursue strategic policy goals. In sum, these relate to allocating land, establishing development controls or incentives, considering particular development proposals, and setting conditions of development approval. Internationally, consensus has emerged that local governments are well placed to promote the goals of appropriate, affordable and available housing, and there are sound policy arguments to pursue these goals through the planning system. These arguments relate to the need to address any inadvertent impacts for housing affordability that result from deficiencies in the planning system, to promote social equity and support economic interests (such as the provision of labour force housing) to secure locations for affordable housing that might not otherwise be accessible, and, in some cases, to leverage additional resources to subsidise the provision of dedicated affordable housing supply. Several local governments in Australia have been innovative in planning to protect existing sources of affordable housing, to promote the development of new lower-cost housing in the private market, and in some cases, to secure resources through the planning system to help provide additional subsidised housing for groups in need. Some state jurisdictions are beginning to support and extend these activities through amendments to their planning legislation.

This section of the book has examined the potential to use local planning powers creatively to promote sustainability, with reference to the range of strategic planning tools for promoting environmental sustainability, climate change and housing diversity, choice and affordability that have emerged in Australia. While nascent national urban and housing reform agendas appear fixated on procedural simplicity, standardisation and speed – shedding planning regulations under the banner of ignominious red tape – the role of local planners in reinforcing the principles underpinning ecologically sustainable development – environmental protection and enhancement within a context of global climate change, economic prosperity and social equity – is more important than ever.

Box 11.2: Additional readings and resources for section 3

There are many practical resources for those seeking additional guidance on incorporating sustainability, climate change, or housing considerations in local planning. Many information sources are available online, and include links to emerging local practice. The following references are a starting point.

Local sustainability planning and sustainable urban form

The Biodiversity Toolbox for local government contains many useful resources for biodiversity planning, particularly in Australia

(www.environment.gov.au/biodiversity/toolbox/).

More applied advice on statutory land use planning for biodiversity conservation is contained in the Biodiversity guide for NSW local government (Fallding et al. 2001). While written for a strategic planning framework that has since been superseded, the principles in this comprehensive manual are transferable to other statutory arrangements.

The 'ICLEI' - Local Governments for Sustainability is an international association of local governments and representative organisations interested in sustainable development. Their website: www.iclei.org contains links to the Australasian chapter and projects relating to climate change, water, and waste management.

Also see the environment network for Australian local governments at www.environs.org.au.

Try www.newurbanism.org for information about new urbanist and transit oriented development approaches and projects.

Timothy Beatley and Peter Newman's book Green urbanism down under: learning from sustainable communities in Australia (2009), is a source of positive examples of local sustainability initiatives across Australia.

Planning and climate change

There are a growing number of useful publications and guides relevant to planning for climate change mitigation and adaptation.

The edited collection of articles on climate change Planning for climate change; strategies for mitigation and adaptation for spatial planners (Davoudi et al. 2009), is an excellent introduction to debates and practice in climate change and planning.

Nicola Durrant's Legal responses to climate change (2010) is an important Australian reference for statutory planners.

The ICLEI website contains a wealth of information for local governments wishing to develop climate mitigation strategies, and is increasingly providing information and resources for adaptation planning. The 'Local government climate change adaptation toolkit', 'Cities for climate protection Australia adaptation toolkit', published by ICLEI and the Australian government Department of Climate Change, Melbourne, Australia, is an important resource.

The National Climate Change Adaptation Research Facility (NCCARF) website www. nccarf.edu.au/ contains comprehensive information on research and practice in relation to climate change adaptation, including specific resources for local government.

Housing policy, practice and research

For Australian readers, classic texts are *Housing Australia* by Chris Paris (1993) and *Home truths: home ownership and housing wealth in Australia* by Blair Badcock and Andrew Beer (2000).

The Australian Housing and Urban Research Institute website (www.ahuri.edu.au) contains an online library of housing and urban research funded by the institute, and links to the key data sets relating to housing.

The National Housing Supply Council monitors housing supply, market trends and affordability in Australia – through State of Supply reports published by the Australian government (National Housing Supply Council 2010).

National Shelter (www.shelter.org.au) is the national peak body aiming to improve housing access, affordability, appropriateness, safety and security for low-income people or those who may face disadvantage in the housing system. The site contains links to state and territorial branches, including Shelter NSW (www.shelternsw.infoxchange.net.au), which maintains information, case examples, and policy relevant to planning for affordable housing.

The NSW Department of Housing maintains the online 'NSW local government housing kit' with resources and case studies relevant to preparing local housing strategies and planning for housing diversity and affordability at the local level, including an interactive database for producing key housing indicators at local government level: www.housing. nsw.gov.au/Centre+For+Affordable+Housing/NSW+Local+Government+Housing+Kit/

The 'Affordable housing national leading practice guide and tool kit' provides national level guidance on strategies to plan for affordable housing at the local level, across different geographical and market contexts: www.housing.nsw.gov.au/ Centre+For+Affordable+Housing/Affordable+Housing+Resources/Affordable+Housing+ National+Leading+Practice+Guide+and+Tool+Kit/ ..

Conclusion

Urban land use planning in Australia: strengths, weaknesses, and priorities for reform

This book began by asking why urban planning was important. It put forward a series of reasons for public intervention in the development process – to correct market deficiencies that could threaten valued environments, to encourage fairer outcomes in urban development, to enable public input in decisions about urban growth and change affecting the whole community, and to coordinate the potentially competing goals and interests vested in the urban development process. These functions fit with concepts of planning as urban governance (Gleeson & Low 2000), proactively regulating and supporting spatial change in cities and regions according to democratically defined strategic policies consistent with the overall goal of ecological sustainability.

In ideal terms, planning as urban governance should mediate across the public and private sectors and civil society in pursuing greater social equity, through spatial planning policies that promote equitable access to quality employment, education, housing, recreation, and transport opportunities, as well as the benefits of attractive, high quality built and natural environments. This includes the creation and preservation of healthy living environments, building on the origins of urban planning through the public health reforms of the late 19th century. While in advanced industrialised societies, basic sanitation and safety of the built environment can now be taken for granted, new public health issues such as obesity (linked to a sedentary lifestyle and lack of proximity to outlets for fresh food), or childhood asthma (linked to urban air pollution), require attention.

Urban planning aims to secure ecological integrity through processes of urban change, by preserving important areas of biodiversity, water catchments and landforms by containing urban expansion (though not necessarily through 'vertical sprawl'), using more flexible, lower-impact forms of infrastructure, as well as minimising the use of non-renewable forms of energy and dependence on motorised forms of transport. Another objective is the promotion of economic vitality, through local and regional planning strategies that make and preserve places for business and creativity, recognise and reinforce organic clusters and networks of emerging industries, and focus on local or endogenous strengths and assets.

The quality of the planning process may be just as important as its physical or spatial outcomes. The primary objective is to achieve broad community engagement in urban policy setting and plan-making. Information sources and decision-making processes must be as transparent and deliberative as possible, actively seeking input from diverse community representatives and individuals. High-quality processes of public involvement in community and environmental decision-making build and reinforce the important social networks and civic discursive spaces that make strong communities of place.

So expectations are high. Setting out in broad terms the generic features and processes of planning systems and the more applied mechanisms of development control, we turned to the reality of urban and environmental policy and planning in Australia. It would not be difficult to cast this review as a sustained critique of the urban planning systems and procedures at state and local levels in Australia. In recent years there have been many such justifiable critiques of the urban planning system from academics, community advocates and industry bodies in Australia. A central contention of the first edition of this book related to a distinct lack of urban and regional policy leadership at a national level, and, in NSW the glaring lack of overarching policy at the state level to lead and inspire urban and environmental governance and land use planning at smaller spatial scales. This final chapter considers these issues in the context of national urban reform, as well as the practical opportunities for local governments and planners to build on existing mechanisms through innovative local plan-making.

Planning reform in Australia

Impetus for planning reform across the Australian states and territories has grown steadily over the past decade, as outlined in section 2 of this book. At the national level, pressure for urban policy and planning system change is now being driven by the COAG Reform Council (COAG 2010a), although the planning system is under scrutiny at a number of different levels of government and in relation to several, potentially competing goals, ranging from economic competitiveness, to housing affordability, and climate change resilience.

There are many arguments in favour of planning reform – several of which have been canvassed in different sections of this book. In relation to economic competitiveness, there are concerns that interjurisdictional differences may create inefficiencies in the decision-making processes, and support 'anti-competitive' behaviour by favouring incumbent businesses and the status quo. While some of these concerns reflect a misconception of the nature of a planning system, inconsistent requirements and complex approval processes may undermine efficient development processes, contributing to lower-investment within particular locations. For these reasons, the Productivity Commission's review of Australian planning systems represents an important basis for identifying where change may need to occur (Productivity Commission 2011).

In relation to environmental sustainability and climate change mitigation and resilience, clear changes are needed to ensure that strategic planning processes consider the potential impact of particular urban configurations and development types on greenhouse gas emissions, and reduce risks associated with future climate change effects. While there are signs that jurisdictions are beginning to establish provisions for considering increased sea-level rise and inundation in the plan-making and development assessment process, wider climate change considerations are far less developed.

Growing concerns about an undersupply of housing relative to existing and projected population growth and increasing evidence of housing stress amongst low- and moderate-income groups has also turned the spotlight onto planning systems and perceived blockages to new supply (NHSC 2010). With some exceptions – notably South Australia which now enshrines affordable residential development in new release and urban renewal areas, for the most part – state governments have responded to housing affordability problems by reviewing the quantity and speed of new residential land release, development assessment times, and by tinkering with the development contribution system (Milligan et al. 2009).

The COAG Reform Council agenda – relating to housing, capital city planning systems, and regulation (COAG Reform Council 2009) – followed a decade of extensive and ongoing planning system change which has been underway across many of the States and territories since the late 1990s.

Table C.1 Planning reform in Australia, 2005–2009

Jurisdiction	Key reform documents	Date
ACT	Introduction to *Planning System Reform*	2008
	Planning and Development Act	2007
NSW	Environmental Planning and Assessment Amendment Bill 2008	2008
	Improving the NSW planning system	2007
NT	Planning Act	2007
Qld	*Sustainable Planning Act 2009*	2009
	Planning for a Prosperous Queensland	2007
SA	Better Planning, Better Future	2008
Tas.	Review of the Planning System of Tasmania Final Steering Committee Report	2009
Vic	*Planning & Environment Act 1987* Review Discussion Paper	2009
	Making local policy stronger	2007
	Cutting red tape in planning	2006
WA	Building a better planning system	2009
	Planning and Development Act	2005

Source: Adapted from Gurran et al. 2009

In the past decade, each of the Australian states and territories has embarked on or completed major reforms to address perceived complexity, unnecessary bureaucracy, and time delays in planning processes (Gurran et al. 2009). As noted in earlier chapters of this book, the state of Queensland has had two new planning acts since 1997 (the *Integrated Planning Act 1997*, replaced by the *Sustainable Planning Act* in 2009). In NSW the planning system has undergone comprehensive change. In 2000 the government foreshadowed the abandonment of land use zoning but, as detailed in chapter 7, introduced a system of state-mandated zones in 2006. This standardisation process has required local authorities to entirely rewrite their own planning schemes, in many cases freezing other plan amendment processes in the interim. Western Australia completed a total overhaul of its planning system with the passage of a new planning act in 2005; a new and comprehensive review of the planning system in that state was announced again in 2008.

This decade of planning reform across most of the Australian states and territories appears to have coincided with mounting concern about the economic competitiveness of cities, serious reservations about the sustainability and resilience of Australia's major growth regions, and a deepening of Australia's housing affordability problems and socio-spatial polarisation and disadvantage. In other words, central drivers for planning reform – such as sluggish rates of housing production and escalating house prices – appear to have been largely impervious to recent planning system change. This may reflect the fact that some of the central, and intertwined issues affecting urban Australia today – economic growth, housing affordability, and social inclusion – are not so sensitive to manipulation through statutory planning, explaining why reform to statutory planning systems appears to have been largely ineffectual in addressing these major concerns, in the short term at least. Reform itself may exacerbate some of the problems that gave rise to it as changes to land use regulations cause market uncertainty, while the implementation process can suspend decisions as new instruments and processes are rolled out. A drive for speed in planning decisions may have unanticipated consequences – as shorter timeframes for planning decisions may simply mean reduced flexibility and faster refusals.

If an underlying focus of planning reforms is to make planning 'cheaper, faster, simpler' in the words of the South Australian government (2009) – it is important to consider what may be lost in this agenda, particularly given the other central concerns of Australian urban policy, such as environmental sustainability and climate resilience. As emphasised throughout this book, strong, place-specific planning objectives, standards and criteria are needed to ensure that new development is situated in locations where it can be properly serviced by public transport and other important physical and social infrastructure; that remaining productive lands are preserved to ensure food security in the future; that opportunities for existing and prospective forms of low-carbon energy production and waste management are maintained; that important ecosystems, biodiversity and landscapes are protected; and that new and existing communities are able to withstand and adapt to future climate risks. Strategic and integrated spatial planning, infrastructure and transportation investment – supported by strong regulatory implementation – is crucial to achieving these wider community goals.

Opportunities for proactive urban policy and governance in Australia

It is useful to consider several scales of operation in analysing approaches to reform in urban governance and planning processes in Australia:

- systemic reforms targeting impediments to the implementation of strategic policy within state, territorial, or local government legislation and practice; including information and feedback mechanisms to review and amend elements of the system where needed
- procedural reforms to the operation of local/regional/state/national decision processes, and particularly statutory plan-making and development assessment processes

- planning policy content reform (especially at state or local levels) to ensure that planning instruments reflect strategic national, state, regional or local policy goals
- planning assessment reform (particularly at local and state levels), to ensure that assessment practice supports these strategic policy objectives.

A reform process could focus at a single level or scale, or address all levels simultaneously.

As noted, several emerging structures provide a basis for supporting greater strategic leadership in urban policy at the national level in Australia. These include the forum for national policy development and enhancement provided by the Council of Australian Governments (COAG), and specific sectoral ministerial and intergovernmental committees, as well as the collaborative framework of the Intergovernmental Agreement on the Environment. The establishment of the Major Cities Unit and a government portfolio on 'sustainable population' provide an opportunity to establish an integrated framework for Australian urban and regional policy, including population, social and economic wellbeing, environment and natural resources, and infrastructure.

Federal leadership within a national approach is necessary because the states on their own can rarely pursue strategies extending beyond their jurisdictional boundaries. Further, a national policy framework is crucial because spatial planning itself (the domain of the states and territories) clearly cannot deliver all of the solutions. Rather, spatial land use planning is an implementation tool within the broader framework of urban governance.

National policy development and standards

At a more applied level, federal cooperation has already achieved consistency in building standards, minimising duplication of effort. The articulation of national standards, such as the Building Code of Australia, means specific jurisdictions no longer need to establish and maintain such basic controls themselves. This approach can be used more broadly where specific policy relevant standards and models for obtaining and evaluating information to support assessment against these standards, are established at the national level, or, by states. The BASIX policy established by the NSW government provides an example of this model in relation to energy efficiency and water savings. With the cooperation of the states and territories a federal Australian adaptation of the BASIX model integrated through the legislation of each planning jurisdiction, could apply to a broader scope of environmental considerations, in construction and in ongoing resource use and management.

Natural hazard protection and management (particularly including climate change) is another area well suited to the establishment of national uniform standards and requirements. A nationally consistent approach to identifying areas subject to natural hazards and potentially exposed to increased risks associated with climate change (including sea-level rise) would provide a sound basis for local planning response. The approach would need to be supported by a consistent methodological source of information for identifying risk and assessing the potential impact of actions that might exacerbate this risk, as well as for evaluating approaches to offset or mitigate these impacts.

A national approach to identifying housing needs and articulating housing objectives and strategies to achieve these through complementary actions both within and beyond the spatial planning system itself is also critical. A more comprehensive approach to housing policy in Australia is proceeding under the umbrella of the National Affordable Housing Agreement, and through the work of the National Housing Supply Council, but significant cleavage between different sectors of the housing market remains (COAG 2009; NHSC 2010). This has resulted in an ongoing disconnect between the policy goals for housing assistance and affordability, and the policy levers for supporting them through the spatial planning process.

The Commonwealth government has demonstrated strong capacity in supporting community engagement models, particularly in rural and regional areas, such as the national Landcare program and the variety of local participatory programs funded under the Natural Heritage Trust. The Regional Development Committees established by the Commonwealth government also seem promising, with their potential links to the allocation of regional infrastructure funds (Regional Development Australia 2009). These models, while not linked to statutory planning processes per se, might well be replicated within urban areas. Under a federal urban policy framework such groups and networks might also become more involved in formal strategic planning processes managed by state and local governments.

National urban policy research priorities

In developing the national or federal urban policy agenda, it is important to acknowl-edge research needed to support such policy development. Borrowing from the effective research and policy development role demonstrated by the US Department of Housing and Urban Development, many of Australia's critical urban and environmental planning research needs can be grouped under the umbrella of 'barrier identification'. For instance, what barriers currently impede more sustainable strategic planning or development assess-ment? What are the land use planning obstacles to the implementation of more sustainable technologies, forms of transport, better urban design, more efficient infrastructure, water and energy use, within our cities and towns? Similarly, which regulations make the cost of housing production greater or impede the development of more affordable housing forms? It is also critical to evaluate the impact of shifts in planning policy towards more concentrated urban development and the relationship between these forms and continu-ing socio-spatial polarisation (Randolph 2004; Randolph & Holloway 2004). In answering these questions a necessary starting point is an understanding of the existing state of local planning frameworks, and the ways in which local plans in Australia currently promote sustainability in general and address more specific components (such as sustainable trans-port, biodiversity protection, renewable energy, or affordable housing) – in particular. The interactions between these urban policy and planning frameworks, and the delivery infra-structure – including the private development sector – needs far greater attention.

Opportunities to enhance state and territorial planning systems

The comparative review of state and territorial planning systems in Australia reveals opportunities to enhance planning systems in different ways. For instance, Victoria and South Australia show how comprehensive state policy frameworks can effectively inform local statutory plan-making, while Queensland shows how regional planning can provide a focus for regional collaboration across government, business and community-based groups. The performance-based planning frameworks implemented within Queensland and Tasmania provide a model for flexible development assessment while incorporating a baseline element of certainty for landowners and developers. Initiatives to streamline and standardise development assessment processes for simpler developments have been implemented across most of the states and are being introduced in the ACT, addressing concerns that uncertainties, complexities, or delays within the planning system can deter investment within a particular area or make housing more expensive.

When considering the capacity for state planning systems to promote environmentally and socially sustainable outcomes, a key issue is what the legislation requires (or enables) the decision-maker to take into account when assessing developments. All states now include references to sustainability goals within the objectives of their principal planning legislation and some refer specifically to social and economic objectives, but it has proved difficult in the past to ensure that the integrated range of factors associated with sustainability are considered or given weight when developments are assessed. Planning systems remain focused on the physical aspects of development and managing measurable impacts, so if the capacity to consider less clearly defined social or environmental goals in assessing developments is to be taken seriously by decision-makers and the courts, planning legislation and instruments need to make such goals and decision criteria explicit.

There are opportunities in all states to use local planning objectives to more strategically pursue goals (relating to issues like valued environments, energy use or transport, water saving and protection, housing diversity and affordability, and so on), and to use standard mechanisms (for instance, zoning provisions, overlays, incentives, conditions of consent, or planning agreements), to develop more proactive approaches to environmental sustainability or community wellbeing. Several states have demonstrated that such planning can be supported by strong policy frameworks that establish important goals of state significance.

Processes for monitoring the quality, content and outcomes of planning processes are not well developed in any of the Australian state or territorial planning jurisdictions. While there is an increasing trend towards 'performance monitoring' of local government planning services, for instance, the time to process a development application or rezone a parcel of land, there is very little attempt to measure the quality of Australian plans on a more holistic basis – such as the extent to which higher-level policies are reflected in planning instruments and the implementation of plans themselves. It is likely that if indicators were developed in relation to plan objectives, more weight would be given to these matters in development assessment because the approach would facilitate a more concrete form of evaluation.

Can planning change?

There have always been limitations associated with the capacity for land use planning to achieve change on the ground (Taylor 1998). To date, plans made under state and territorial planning legislation in Australia have largely been limited to matters able to be enforced through statutory means. For this reason, they are often described as 'reactive': while they contain objectives for the future development of a place, their provisions are only triggered when an activity requiring consent is initiated. Recently, however, there are many examples of how 'proactive' strategies can be encouraged or directly promoted through statutory land use plans.

At the same time it is important to remember that land use planning is by no means a complete solution or answer to goals such as ecological sustainability, greater social equity or economic wellbeing. Nor is the planning system the sole cause of unsustainable forms of urban growth, expensive housing, falling rates of home ownership, or depressed economies, as the various critics of planning like to claim. A poorly functioning planning system can exacerbate these problems in the ways outlined in this book. On the other hand, an optimum spatial land use planning system within the context of strong urban and environmental governance, can make a substantial contribution to enhancing and protecting the natural and built environments we value, renewing urban or regional areas in decline, and a fairer distribution of housing, educational, employment and recreational opportunities across our cities and towns.

Australia's planning systems need to change – and to support and provoke change – as do planning systems everywhere. Planning systems must undergo a process of continual adjustment in response to community aspirations and new scientific knowledge and to the ongoing changes amongst society and the places we inhabit. At the same time, a statutory planning system – from the broad goals and procedural requirements articulated in principal planning legislation to the particular objectives, considerations and controls regulating development in a specific place, provides a key safeguard against negative forms of change. Thus a degree of stability, a commitment to goals, standards and requirements that have been collaboratively determined by communities of place (Healey 1997) or by democratically elected representatives, is crucial for planning systems and processes. The safeguards in this established decision-making framework – for environmental integrity, for social fairness, and for investment certainty, is the raison d'être of planning.

Debates such as those described at the beginning of this book – questioning the value of land use planning, its potentially negative impacts on the very economic, environmental or social values that inspire it – provide welcome scrutiny of the mechanics of a system that is often overlooked in academic discourse and research. Such debates are also inevitable when the stakes of planning decisions are so high, and the outcomes so contestable. This is what makes planning such a stimulating and vital process to become engaged in, as a professional, as a community member, or as a scholar. But debates need to be informed by an understanding of the actual objectives, controls and processes that underpin urban planning in practice. This book seeks to further this understanding. Hopefully it shows how, rather than tolling the death knell of the 'Australian dream', our urban planning systems have the potential to recognise and address the multiplicity of urban dreams and critical environmental realities that now define contemporary Australia.

Glossary

Affordable housing – housing that is accessible for households on low or moderate incomes to rent or purchase. Generally, 25–30% of income spent on rent or mortgage is considered 'affordable', depending on income.

Biodiversity – 'The variety of life forms, the different plants, animals, and micro-organisms, the genes they contain and the ecosystems they form' (NPWS 1999, p70).

Brownfield development – the remediation and re-use of previously developed land (brownfield land), for example land that has been used for industrial or commercial purposes.

Community consultation – formal opportunity for members of the public to comment on proposed policies or interventions.

Conditions of consent – conditions attached to development approval, imposed by the planning authority.

Consent authority – the principal body responsible for assessing a particular development proposal. A consent authority may be a local, state, or Commonwealth authority, depending on the nature of the proposal.

Council – in Australia, 'council' refers to the elected representative body of a local government area. The term is often used interchangeably with 'local government area'.

Developer contributions – contributions from private developers to a planning authority or local council for the provision of infrastructure or other services.

Ecologically sustainable development – 'Using, conserving and enhancing the community's resources so that ecological processes, on which life depends, are maintained, and the total quality of life, now and in the future, can be increased' (NPWS 1999, p70).

Environmental impact assessment – formal analysis of the likely impacts of a proposed development, including environmental, cultural, historical, social, economic, or health impacts and impacts on other qualities of life (Bell 2000; Gilpin 1990).

Environmental planning instrument – *The NSW Environmental Planning and Assessment Act 1979* identifies three types of 'environmental planning instrument' – state environmental planning policies, regional environmental plans and local environmental plans.

Development assessment – formal process of assessing the impacts of development proposals, undertaken by a planning/consent authority in relation to statutory requirements.

Greenfield development – development on land that has not previously been used for urban development (e.g. 'rural land').

Local government area (LGA) – spatial boundary of local government jurisdictions.

Merit criteria – matters that must be formally considered by a planning authority when assessing a development (usually specified in the relevant statutory planning instrument).

Planning authority – the body responsible for establishing statutory development controls within a particular area and/or for assessing development proposals. Depending on the nature of the development and the planning jurisdiction, planning authorities may be local, or state/territorial bodies.

Social impact assessment – a formal assessment of 'the impact on people and society of major development projects; social impacts are defined as those changes in social relations between members of a community, society, or institution resulting from external change' (Gilpin 1990, p184).

Sustainable development – 'Development that meets the needs of the present without compromising the ability of the future generations to meet their own needs' (Bell 1995; WCED 1987).

Urban containment – managing or limiting the physical expansion of urban areas.

Urban renewal – redevelopment of decaying urban areas by the private or public sector (Gilpin 1990).

Zoning – a mechanism, generally enforced by a statutory planning instrument, for the spatial separation of land uses.

References

AHURI – see Australian Housing and Research Institute

APA – see American Planning Association

COAG – see Council of Australian Governments

CSIRO – see Commonwealth Scientific and Industrial Research Organisation

DAFF – see Department of Agriculture, Fisheries and Forestry (Cwlth)

DCCEE – see Department of Climate Change and Energy Efficiency (Cwlth)

DOP – see Department of Planning (NSW)

DIPNR – see Department of Infrastructure, Planning and Natural Resources (NSW)

DITR – see Department of Infrastructure and Transport (Cwlth)

DOPBRO – see Department of Planning and Better Regulation Office (NSW)

DRARDLG – see Department of Regional Australia, Regional Development and Local Government

DSEWPC – see Department of Sustainability, Environment, Water, Population and Communities (Cwlth)

DUAP – see Department of Urban Affairs and Planning (NSW)

EPHC – see Environmental Protection and Heritage Council

HIA – see Housing Industry Association

HUD – see Department of Housing and Urban Development (US)

IIED – see International Institute for Environment and Development

ISOCARP – see International Society of City and Regional Planners

MCU – see Major Cities Unit

NPWS – see NSW National Parks and Wildlife Service

TCPA – see Town and Country Planning Act 1990 (UK)

UNCHS – see United Nations Centre for Human Settlements

UNEP – see United Nations Environment Program

WCED – see World Commission on Environment and Development

Abel N, Farrier D, Tatnell B & Mooney C (1999). A rangeland enmeshed: the legal representative and administrative framework of the western division of New South Wales. Unpublished report for the NSW Department of Land and Water Conservation.

ACT Planning and Land Authority (2007). New planning system: introduction to planning system reform: development assessment. Canberra: ACT Planning and Land Authority. [Online]. Available: www.actpla.act.gov.au/topics/significant_projects/change/planning_system_reform_project [Accessed 21 April 2011].

Alexander I, Greive S & Hedgcock D (2010). *Planning perspectives from Western Australia: a reader in theory and practice.* Bentley: Fremantle Press.

Allen Consulting Group (2005). *Climate change risk and vulnerability: promoting an efficient adaptation response in Australia.* Final Report to the Australian Greenhouse Office. Canberra: Department of the Environment and Heritage.

Alonso W (1964). *Location and land use: towards a general theory of land rent.* Cambridge: Harvard University Press.

American Planning Association (APA) (2001). APA policy guide on factory built housing. Adopted by a Chapter Delegate Assembly, 11 March 2001. New Orleans.

American Planning Association (APA) (1997). APA policy guide on community residences. Adopted by Special Delegate Assembly, 21 September 21 1997. New Orleans.

American Planning Association (APA) (1991). The supply of public and subsidized housing. Adopted by the Chapter Delegate Assembly New Orleans, Louisiana, 24 March 1991. [Online]. Available: www. planning.org/affordablereader/policygudes/subsidizedhousing.htm [Accessed 21 November 2006].

Anthony J (2006). State growth management and housing prices. *Social Science Quarterly*, 87(1): 122–41.

Anthony J (2003). The effects of Florida's growth management act on housing affordability. *Journal of the American Planning Association*, 69(3): 282–95.

Aplin G (1998). *Australians and their environment: an introduction to environmental studies.* Melbourne: Oxford University Press.

Australia ICOMOS (1987). *The Australia ICOMOS charter for the conservation of places of cultural significance (the Burra Charter).* Burwood, Australia: ICOMOS Incorporated. [Online]. Available: www. icomos.org/burra_charter.html [Accessed 20 April 2011].

Australian Bureau of Statistics (2010). Catalogue 6416, House price indexes, eight capital cities. September 2010. Canberra: ABS.

Australian Council of Local Government (ACLG) (2010). Australian Council of Local Government, assorted webpage material. [Online]. Available: www.aclg.gov.au [Accessed 6 January 2011].

Australian Government (2010a). *Adapting to climate change in Australia: an Australian Government position paper.* Canberra: Australian Government. [Online]. Available: www.climatechange.gov.au/en/ government/adapt/adapting-to-climate-change-paper.aspx [Accessed 20 April 2011].

Australian Government (2010b). Nation building economic stimulus and jobs plan: social housing.

[Online]. Available: www.economicstimulusplan.gov.au/housing/pages/default.aspx [Accessed 7 February 2011].

Australian Greenhouse Office (1998). *National greenhouse strategy*. Canberra: Australian Government. [Online]. Available: www.australianpolitics.com/foreign/environment/ngs.pdf [Accessed 7 February 2011].

Badcock B & Beer A (2000). *Home truths: property ownership and housing wealth in Australia*. Melbourne: Melbourne University Press.

Baker R, Davies J & Young E (2001). Managing country: an overview of the prime issues. In R Baker, J Davies & E Young (Eds). *Working on country: contemporary Indigenous management of Australia's lands and coastal regions* (pp1–23). Melbourne: Oxford University Press.

Barker K (2006). *Barker review of land use planning: final report, recommendations*. London: HM Treasury.

Barker K (2004). *Review of housing supply. Delivering stability: securing our future housing needs*. London: Final Report, Office of the Deputy Prime Minister. [Online]. Available: www.barkerreview.org.uk/ [Accessed 20 April 2011].

Barrett CD (2001). *Everyday ethics for practicing planners*. Washington: AICP.

Bates B (2010). *Environmental law in Australia*. 7th edn. Chatswood: LexisNexis Butterworths.

Bates B (2006). *Environmental law in Australia*. 6th edn. Chatswood: LexisNexis Butterworths.

Bateson P (2000). *Incentives for sustainable land management: community cost sharing to conserve biodiversity on private lands; a guide for local government*. Canberra: Environs Australia and Environment Australia.

Beatley T (1995). Planning and sustainability: the elements of a new (improved?) paradigm. *Journal of Planning Literature*, 9(4): 383–95.

Beatley T, Brower DJ & Schwab AK (2002). *An introduction to coastal zone management*. 2nd edn. Washington: Island Press.

Beatley T & Manning K (1997). *The ecology of place: planning for environment, economy and community*. Washington: Island Press.

Beatley T & Newman P (2009). *Green urbanism down under: learning from sustainable communities*. Washington, DC: Island Press.

Beder S (1993). *The nature of sustainable development*. Newham, Victoria: Scribe Publications.

Been V (2005). Impact fees and housing affordability. *Cityscape: A Journal of Policy Development and Research*, 8(1): 139–85.

Bell F (2000). *ESD from A to Z: a basic information source on ecologically sustainable development and environmental issues in Australia*. Sydney: Earth Foundation Australia Ltd.

Bennison A (2005). Address to the National Housing Conference on 28 October 2005. Perth: Australian Local Government Association.

Berke P, Ericksen N, Crawford J & Dixon J (2002). Planning and Indigenous people: human rights and environmental protection in New Zealand. *Journal of Planning Education and Research*, 22(2): 115–34.

Berkes F & Folke C (Eds) (1998). *Linking social and ecological systems: management practices and social mechanisms for building resilience*. New York: Cambridge University Press.

Beyer GH (1965). *Housing and society*. New York: Macmillan.

Blake R & Collins P (2004). Planning and land acquisition. In A Golland & R Blake (Eds). *Housing development: theory, process and practice* (pp123–63). London: Routledge.

Blomley N (2004). *Unsettling the city: urban land and the politics of property*. New York: Routledge.

Boer B & Wiffin G (2005). *Heritage law in Australia*. Sydney: Oxford University Press.

Bramley G, Bartlett W & Lambert C (1995). *Planning: the market and private housebuilding*. London: University College London Press.

Bramley G & Leishman C (2005). Planning and housing supply in two-speed Britain: modelling local market outcomes. *Urban Studies*, 42(12): 2213–44.

Brodbeck S (2005). Green offsets. *New Planner*, 13–15.

Burge G & Ihlanfeldt KR (2006). Impact fees and housing affordability. *Journal of Urban Economics*, 60: 284–306.

Burke, T. (2011). Gillard Government delivers first sustainable population strategy, Media release 13 May 2011. Canberra, The Hon Tony Burke MP, Minister for Sustainability, Environment, Water, Population and Communities.

Burton D (2007). *Evaluating climate change mitigation strategies in South East Queensland*. Urban Research Program Research Paper 11, March 2007. Brisbane, QLD: Urban Research Program (Griffith University).

Byrne J, Gleeson B, Howes M & Steele W (2009). Climate change and Australian urban resilience: the limits of ecological modernisation as an adaptive strategy. In S Davoudi, J Crawford & A Mehmood (Eds). *Planning for climate change: strategies for mitigation and adaptation for spatial planners* (pp136–50). London: Earthscan.

Carley M & Smith H (2001). Civil society and new social movements. In M Carley, P Jenkins & H Smith (Eds). *Urban development and civil society: the role of communities in sustainable cities* (pp192–200). London: Earthscan.

Centre for Science in the Earth System (The Climate Impacts Group). Joint Institute for the Study of the Atmosphere and Ocean University of Washington and King County, Washington (2007). Preparing for Climate Change: a guidebook for local, regional and state governments. Washington. [Online]. Available: www.cses.washington.edu/cig/fpt/guidebook.shtml [Accessed 10 June 2011].

City of Boulder (2009). Green building and green points guideline booklet. City of Boulder Colorado. [Online]. Available: www.bouldercolorado.gov/files/PDS/green_points/902.pdf [Accessed 7 January 2011].

City of Ryde (2006). City of Ryde Development Control Plan 2006 Final. [Online]. Available: www. docstoc.com/docs/34876642/City-of-Ryde---Development-Control-Plan-2006 [Accessed 19 April 2011].

COAG Reform Council (2010). National partnership agreement to deliver a seamless national economy: part 1–27 deregulation priorities. Canberra: COAG

Coastal Council of NSW (1997). *NSW coastal policy*. Sydney: NSW Government. [Online]. Available: www.planning.nsw.gov.au/plansforaction/pdf/CPPARTA.PDF [Accessed 31 May 2011].

Commonwealth of Australia (1998). *National greenhouse strategy*. Canberra: Australian Government Publishing Service.

Commonwealth of Australia (1992). *National strategy for environmentally sustainable development*. Canberra: Australian Government Printing Service.

Conacher A & Conacher J (2000). *Environmental planning and management in Australia*. South Melbourne: Oxford University Press.

Connell J & Lea JP (2002). *Urbanisation in the island Pacific: towards sustainable development*. London: Routledge.

Corburn J (2009). Cities, climate change and urban heat island mitigation: localising global environmental science. *Urban Studies*, 46(2): 413–27.

Council of Australian Governments (2010a). Housing reform agenda and timeline. Canberra: Council of Australian Governments. [Online]. Available: http://agencysearch.australia.gov.au/search/search.cgi? query=Housing+reform+agenda+and+timeline&collection=agencies&form=simple&profile=pmc_coag [Accessed 20 April 2011].

Council of Australian Governments (2010b). About COAG. [Online]. Available: www.coag.gov.au/ about_coag/index.cfm [Accessed 9 June 2011].

Council of Australian Governments (2009). National affordable housing agreement. Canberra: Council of Australian Governments. [Online]. Available: www.fahcsia.gov.au/sa/housing/progserv/affordability/ affordablehousing/Pages/default.aspx [Accessed 20 April 2011].

Council of Australian Governments (1997). Heads of agreement on Commonwealth and State roles and responsibilities for the environment. Canberra: Council of Australian Governments. [Online]. Available: www.environment.gov.au/epbc/publications/coag-agreement/index.html [Accessed 20 April 2011].

Council of Australian Governments Reform Council (2009). COAG Communiqué 7 December 2009. Canberra: Council of Australian Governments. [Online]. Available: www.coag.gov.au/coag_meeting_ outcomes/2009-12-07/docs/20091207_communique.pdf [Accessed 21 May 2011].

Cronon W (1996). The trouble with wilderness: or, getting back to the wrong nature. In W Cronon (Ed). *Uncommon ground: rethinking the human place in nature* (pp69–90). New York: WW Norton and Company.

Crook A & Whitehead C (2004). Social housing & planning gain: a post-Barker Review. Paper presented at the ENHR Conference 2 July–6 July 2004. UK: University of Cambridge.

Crook T, Currie J, Jackson A, Monk S, Rowley S, Smith K & Whitehead C (2002). *Planning gain and affordable housing: making it count*. York: Joseph Rowntree Foundation.

CSIRO (2007). *Climate Change in Australia - technical report 2007*. Canberra: CSIRO.

Cullingworth B & Caves R (2009). *Planning in the USA: policies, issues and processes*. 3rd edn. New York: Routledge.

Cullingworth B & Caves R (2003). *Planning in the USA*. 2nd edn. New York: Routledge.

Daly M & Pritchard B (2000). Sydney: Australia's financial and corporate capital. In J Connell (Ed). *Sydney: the emergence of a world city* (pp167–88). Melbourne: Oxford University Press.

Davoudi S, Crawford J & Mehmood A (Eds) (2009). *Planning for climate change: strategies for mitigation and adaptation for spatial planners*. London: Earthscan.

Department of Climate Change (Cwlth) (2009). *Climate change risks to Australia's coast, a first pass national assessment*. Canberra: Australian Government, Department of Climate Change.

Department of Climate Change and Energy Efficiency (Cwlth) (2010a). Assorted web material. [Online]. Available: www.climatechange.gov.au [Accessed 5 January 2011].

Department of Climate Change and Energy Efficiency (Cwlth) (2010b). *Australian national greenhouse accounts*. Canberra: Australian Government.

Department of Communities and Local Government (UK) (2011a). What is a sustainable community? [Online]. Available: www.idea.gov.uk/idk/core/page.do?pageId=9574571 [Accessed 19 April 2011].

Department of Communities and Local Government (UK) (2011b). The plan-led system. [Online]. Available: www.planningportal.gov.uk/planningsystem/planledsystem [Accessed 19 January 2011].

Department of Environment and Climate Change (NSW) (2007). *BioBanking, biodiversity banking and offsets scheme: scheme overview*. Sydney: NSW Government.

Department of Environment and Conservation (NSW) (2006). BioBanking, a biodiversity banking and offsets scheme; guide to the Threatened Species Conservation Act Amendment (Biodiversity Banking) Bill 2006. Sydney: NSW Government.

Department of Environment, Climate Change and Water (NSW) (2010a). *Draft NSW biodiversity strategy 2010–2015*. Sydney: Department of Environment, Climate Change and Water. [Online]. Available: www.environment.nsw.gov.au/biodiversity/nswbiostrategy.htm [Accessed 31 May 2011].

Department of Environment, Climate Change and Water (NSW) (2010b). *NSW coastal panel*. [Online]. Available: www.environment.nsw.gov.au/coasts/coastalpanel.htm [Accessed 19 January 2011].

Department of Environment, Climate Change and Water (NSW) (2009a). *Overview of the biodiversity credit market*. Sydney: NSW Government. [Online]. Available: nativevegetation.nsw.gov.au/resources/biobanking/099335creditmo.pdf [Accessed 20 April 2011].

Department of Environment, Climate Change and Water (NSW) (2009b). *Sea level rise policy statement*. Sydney: NSW Government. [Online]. Available: www.planning.nsw.gov.au/LinkClick.aspx?fileticket=uk mXcVJesYA%3D&tabid=177 [Accessed 31 May 2011].

Department of Foreign Affairs and Trade (Cwlth) (2011). Australian treaties database. [Online]. Available: www.dfat.gov.au/treaties/index.html [Accessed 5 January 2011].

Department of Foreign Affairs and Trade (Cwlth) (2008). Indigenous land rights and native title. [Online]. Available: www.dfat.gov.au/facts/indigenous_land_rights.html [Accessed 7 February 2011].

Department of Housing and Urban Development (US) (2005). Why not in our community? Removing barriers to affordable housing, an update to the Report of the Advisory Commission on Regulatory Barriers to Affordable Housing, February. US Department of Housing and Urban Development, Office of Policy Development and Research. [Online]. Available: www.huduser.org/Publications/pdf/wnioc.pdf [Accessed 20 April 2011].

Department of Infrastructure and Planning (Qld) (2009). Your guide to the *Sustainable Planning Act 2009*. Qplan: My street. Our State. Brisbane: Queensland Government. [Online]. Available: www.dip.qld. gov.au/resources/publication/25821-dip-sust-pocket-guide.pdf [Accessed 20 April 2011].

Department of Infrastructure and Planning (Qld) (2008). Regional planning information sheet: a history of regional planning in Queensland. Brisbane: Queensland Government.

Department of Infrastructure and Transport (Cwlth) (2011). *Our cities, our future: a national urban policy for a productive, sustainable and liveable future.* Canberra: Australian Government.

Department of Infrastructure and Transport (Cwlth) (2010a). Department of Infrastructure and Transport, assorted website material. [Online]. Available: www.infrastructure.gov.au [Accessed 5 January 2011].

Department of Infrastructure and Transport (Cwlth) (2010b). Our cities: building a productive, sustainable and liveable future. Canberra: Department of Infrastructure and Transport.

Department of Planning (NSW) (2010a). *2009–2010 Department of Planning annual report.* Sydney: NSW Government. [Online]. Available: planning.nsw.gov.au/LinkClick. aspx?fileticket=3is8uRn36Sc%3D [Accessed 20 April 2011].

Department of Planning (NSW) (2010b). Local development contributions practice note for the assessment of local contributions plans by IPART November 2010. Sydney: Department of Planning, Independent Pricing and Regulatory Tribunal. [Online]. Available: www.planning.nsw.gov.au/ SearchResults/tabid/39/language/en-AU/Default.aspx?Search=fact+sheet+local+contributions [Accessed 21 April 2011].

Department of Planning (NSW) (2010c). *NSW coastal planning guideline: adapting to sea level rise.* Sydney, NSW: Department of Planning.

Department of Planning (NSW) (2010d). Reforms to local development contributions, planning circular PS 10-022, 16 September 2010. Sydney: NSW Government. [Online]. Available: www.planning.nsw.gov. au/SearchResults/tabid/39/language/en-AU/Default.aspx?Search=PS+10-022 [Accessed 21 April 2011].

Department of Planning (NSW) (2010). A guide to preparing local plans. Sydney: NSW Government.

Department of Planning (NSW) (2009). Major development monitor 2009–10. Sydney: NSW Government.

Department of Planning (NSW) (2007). BASIX Fact Sheet. [Online]. Available: www.basix.nsw.gov.au/ docs/BASIX_fact_sheet.pdf [Accessed 19 April 2011].

Department of Planning (NSW) (2006a). Commencement and implementation of the *EP&A Amendment Act 2006*, Planning circular PS06-016 issued 5 July 2006. [Online]. Available: www.planning.nsw.gov.au/PlanningSystem/Circularsandguidelines/PlanningSystemCirculars/tabid/81/language/en-AU/Default.aspx [Accessed 19 April 2011].

Department of Planning (NSW) (2006b). Performance monitoring of the planning system. Planning circular PS06–017. [Online]. Available: www.planning.nsw.gov.au/PlanningSystem/Circularsandguidelines/PlanningSystemCirculars/tabid/81/language/en-AU/Default.aspx [Accessed 19 April 2011].

Department of Planning (NSW) (2006c) Standard instrument (Local Environmental Plans) Order 2006, Planning circular PS 06–008. Issued 3 April 2006. [Online]. Available: www.planning.nsw.gov.au/PlanningSystem/Circularsandguidelines/PlanningSystemCirculars/tabid/81/language/en-AU/Default.aspx [Accessed 19 April 2011].

Department of Planning and Better Regulation Office (NSW) (2010). *Promoting economic growth and competition through the planning system: review report*. Sydney: NSW Department of Premier and Cabinet. [Online]. Available: www.betterregulation.nsw.gov.au/targeted_reviews/promoting_economic_growth_and_competition_through_the_planning_system [Accessed 21 April 2011].

Department of Planning and Infrastructure (2011). Proposed state significant development and infrastructure classes: policy statement, June 2011. Sydney: NSW Government.

Department of Planning and Infrastructure (NT) (n.d.). Northern Territory planning scheme: user guide. Darwin, Nothern Territory Department of Planning and Infrastructure. [Online]. Available: www.nt.gov.au/lands/planning/scheme/ [Accessed 20 April 2011].

Department of Planning and Local Government (SA) (2006). Summary: Development (Panels) Amendment Bill 2006. Adelaide: Government of South Australia.

Department of Regional Australia, Regional Development and Local Government (Cwlth) (2010). Assorted website material. [Online]. Available: www.regional.gov.au [Accessed 5 January 2011].

Department of Sustainability and Environment (Vic.) (2011). How does the EES process work? Melbourne: Victorian Government. [Online]. Available: www.dpcd.vic.gov.au/planning/environment-assessment/environment-assessment-process-in-victoria2 [Accessed 20 April 2011].

Department of Sustainability, Environment, Water, Population and Communities (Cwlth) (2011). Sustainable Australia, sustainable communities: a sustainable population strategy for Australia. Canberra: Australian Government.

Department of Sustainability, Environment, Water, Population and Communities (Cwlth) (2010a). Assorted website material. Canberra: Department of Sustainability, Environment, Water, Population and Communities, DSEWPC [Online]. Available: www.environment.gov.au [Accessed 5 January 2011].

Department of Sustainability, Environment, Water, Population and Communities (Cwlth) (2010b). A sustainable population strategy for Australia: issues paper. Canberra: Department of Sustainability, Environment, Water, Population and Communities, DSEWPC. [Online]. Available: www.environment.gov.au/sustainability/population/publications/issues-paper.html [Accessed 20 April 2011].

Department of Urban Affairs and Planning (NSW) (2001). Plan first: review of plan making in NSW White Paper. Sydney: NSW Government. [Online]. Available: www3.ekf.tuke.sk/re/Strategia%20a%20 analyzy/white_paper_final.pdf [Accessed 20 April 2011].

Department of Urban Affairs and Planning (NSW) (1999). *Plan making in NSW, opportunities for the future: discussion paper*. Sydney: NSW Government.

Development Assessment Commission (SA) (2007). Role of the DAC. Adelaide: Government of South Australia. [Online]. Available: www.dac.sa.gov.au/index.cfm?objectid=E9352240-F203-0D46-A098A75AE6209C2B [Accessed 20 April 2011].

Development Assessment Forum (DAF) (2001). Good strategic planning guide: strategic land use planning underpinning local government planning and development systems and processes. Canberra: Commonwealth Department of Transport and Regional Services. [Online]. Available: www.daf.gov.au/ reports_documents/index.aspx [Accessed 19 April 2011].

de Vries J & Wolsink M (2009). Making space for water: spatial planning and water management in the Netherlands. In S Davoudi, J Crawford & A Mehmood (Eds). *Planning for climate change: strategies for mitigation and adaptation for spatial planners* (pp191–204). London: Earthscan.

Dixon J & Fallon L (1989). The concept of sustainability: origins, extensions and usefulness for policy. *Society & Natural Resources: An International Journal*, 2(1): 73–84.

Dodge J (1998). Living by life: some bioregional theory and practice. In J Dryzek & D Scholsberg (Eds). *Debating the earth: the environmental politics reader* (pp365–73). Oxford: Oxford University Press.

Douglass M (2002). From global intercity competition to cooperation for livable cities and economic resilience in Pacific Asia. *Environment and Urbanization*, 14(1): 53–68.

Dunn KM (2005). Repetitive and troubling discourses of nationalism in the local politics of mosque development in Sydney, Australia. *Environment and Planning D-Society & Space*, 23(1): 29–50.

Durrant N (2010). *Legal responses to climate change*. Sydney: The Federation Press.

Eccles D & Bryant T (2006). *Statutory planning in Victoria*. 3rd edn. Annandale: The Federation Press.

England P (2011). *Sustainable planning in Queensland*. Annandale: The Federation Press.

England P (2004). *Integrated planning in Queensland*. 2nd edn. Annandale: The Federation Press.

Environment Australia (EA) (2001). Description of IBRA regions. [Online]. Available: www. environment.nsw.gov.au/bioregions/BioregionsExplained.htm [Accessed 19 April 2011].

Environmental Defender's Office NSW (2010). The state of planning in NSW, with reference to social and environmental impacts and public participation. Sydney: Environmental Defender's Office, NSW Nature Conservation Council, Total Environment Centre. [Online]. Available: www.edo.org.au/edonsw/ site/publications.php [Accessed 20 April 2011].

Environmental Protection and Heritage Council (EPHC) (2010). National environment protection measures explained. [Online]. Available: www.ephc.gov.au/nepms [Accessed 11 January 2011].

Evans-Cowley JS & Lawhon LL (2003). The effects of impact fees on the price of housing and land: a literature review. *Journal of Planning Literature*, 17(3): 351–59.

FAC (2009). *Department for Families and Communities Annual Report 2008–09*. Adelaide: Government of South Australia.

Fallding M, Kelly A, Bateson P & Donovan I (2001). *Biodiversity guide for NSW local government*. Hurstville: NSW National Parks and Wildlife Service (NPWS).

Farrelly E (2006). Beauty, exclusionism, stuff: the basis of community? In R Freestone, B Randolph & C Butler-Bowden (Eds). *Talking about Sydney; population, community and culture in contemporary Sydney* (pp135–45). Sydney: UNSW Press.

Farrier D & Stein P (2006). *The environmental law handbook: planning and land use in NSW*. 4th edn. Sydney: Redfern Legal Centre Publishing.

Fensham P & Gleeson B (2003). Capturing value for urban management: a new agenda for betterment. *Urban Policy and Research*, 21(1): 93–112.

Fingland S (2009). WSROC Submission to the Inquiry into NSW Planning Framework. WSROC Ltd Penrith: WSROC.

Fisher B S, Nakicenovic N, Alfsen K, Corfee Morlot J, de la Chesnaye F, Hourcade, J C, Jiang K, Kainuma M, La Rovere E, Matysek A, Rana A, Riahi K, Richels R, Rose S, van Vuuren D & Warren R (2007). Issues related to mitigation in the long-term context. In B Metz, OR Davidson, PR Bosch, R Dave & LA Meyer (Eds). *Climate change 2007: mitigation. Contribution of Working Group III to the Fourth Assessment Report of the Intergovernmental Panel on Climate Change* (pp169–250). Cambridge, UK and New York, US: Cambridge University Press.

Florida R (2003). *The rise of the creative class: and how it's transforming work, leisure, community and everyday life*. North Melbourne: Pluto Press.

Forrester J (1995). Planning in the face of power. In JM Stein (Ed). *Classic readings in urban planning* (pp437–55). New York: McGraw-Hill Inc.

Forster C (2004). *Australian cities, continuity and change*. 3rd edn. South Melbourne: Oxford University Press.

Freehills (2007). An overview of recent Australian climate change litigation. [Online]. Available: www.freehills.com.au/2016.aspx [Accessed August 2008.

Freestone R (2010). *Urban nation: Australia's planning heritage*. Victoria: CSIRO Publishing.

Freestone R (Ed) (2000). *Urban planning in a changing world: the twentieth century experience*. London: E & FN Spoon.

Freestone R & Hamnett S (2000). *The Australian metropolis*. Crows Nest, Australia: Allen & Unwin.

Friedmann J (1986). The world city hypothesis. *Development and Change*, 17(1): 69–83.

Frost L & Dingle T (1995). Sustaining suburbia: an historical perspective on Australia's growth. In P Troy (Ed). *Australian cities, issues, strategies and policies for urban Australia in the 1990s* (pp20–38). Cambridge: Cambridge University Press.

Garden FL & BB Jalaludin (2009). Impact of urban sprawl on overweight, obesity, and physical activity in Sydney, Australia. *Journal of Urban Health-Bulletin of the New York Academy of Medicine*, 86(1): 19–30.

Garnaut C (2000). Towards metropolitan organisation: town planning and the garden city idea. In S Hamnett & R Freestone (Eds).*The Australian metropolis, a planning history* (pp46–64). Sydney: Allen & Unwin.

Garnaut R (2008). *The Garnaut Climate Change Review final report*. Melbourne: Cambridge University Press.

George RV & MC Campbell (2000). Balancing different interests in aesthetic controls. *Journal of Planning Education and Research,* 20(2): 163–75.

Gilmour T & Milligan V (2008). Stimulating institutional investment in affordable housing in Australia: insights from the US. 3rd Australasian Housing Researchers' Conference, Melbourne, 18–20 June 2008. [Online]. Available: mams.rmit.edu.au/09qxapy6qg4y.pdf [Accessed 20 April 2011].

Gilpin A (1990). *A dictionary of environment and planning*. South Melbourne: Oxford University Press.

Gleeson B (2006). *Australian heartlands: making space for hope in the suburbs*. Crows Nest: Allen & Unwin.

Gleeson B & Low N (Eds) (2000). *Australian urban planning: new challenges, new agendas*. Crows Nest: Allen & Unwin.

Gleeson B, Darbas T, Johnson L & Lawson S (2004). *What is metropolitan planning?* Urban Policy Program, Research Monograph 1, July 2004, Brisbane: Griffith University.

Gleeson B & Steele W (Eds) (2010). *A climate for growth: planning South-East Queensland*. Brisbane: University of Queensland Press.

Golland A & Gillen M (2004). Housing need, housing demand and housing supply. In A Golland & R Blake (Eds). *Housing development: theory, process and practice* (pp45–70). London: Routledge.

Goss S & Blackaby B (1998). *Designing local housing strategies: a good practice guide*. London, UK: Chartered Institute of Housing.

Government of South Australia (2009). Simpler, faster, cheaper. The new residential development code: frequently asked questions. Adelaide: Government of South Australia.

Greed C (2000). *Introducing planning*. London: The Athelone Press.

Gunn JH & Noble B (2009). A conceptual basis and methodological framework for regional strategic environmental assessment (R-SEA). *Impact Assessment and Project Appraisal,* 27(4): 258–70.

Gupta S, Tirpak D A, Burger N, Gupta J, Höhne N, Boncheva A I, Kanoan G M, Kolstad C, Kruger J A, Michaelowa A, Murase S, Pershing J, Saijo T & Sari A (2007). Policies, instruments and cooperative arrangements. In B Metz, OR Davidson, PR Bosch, R Dave & LA Meyer (Eds). *Climate change 2007: mitigation. Contribution of Working Group III to the Fourth Assessment Report of the Intergovernmental Panel on Climate Change* (pp745–808). Cambridge, UK and New York, US: Cambridge University Press.

Gurran N (2003a). Housing policy and sustainable urban development: evaluating the use of local housing strategies in Queensland, New South Wales and Victoria. Australian Housing and Urban Research Institute Final Report. Canberra: Australian Housing and Urban Research Institute.

Gurran N (2003b). Positioning Australian local government housing for a new century. *Urban Policy and Research,* 21(4): 393–412.

Gurran N (2001). Sustainable territories? Communities and national parks in New South Wales. Unpublished PhD Thesis, Faculty of Architecture, University of Sydney.

Gurran N, Hamin E & Norman B (2008a). *Planning for climate change: leading practice principles and models for sea change communities in coastal Australia*. Sydney: National Sea Change Taskforce and the University of Sydney Planning Research Centre.

Gurran N, Milligan V, Baker D, Bugg LB & Christensen S (2008b). *New directions in planning for affordable housing: Australian and international evidence and implications*. AHURI Final Report Series (12). Sydney: Australian Housing and Urban Research Institute, Sydney Research Centre.

Gurran N, Milligan V, Baker D & Bugg LB (2007). International practice in planning for affordable housing: lessons for Australia. Australian Housing and Urban Research Institute (AHURI) Positioning Paper. [Online]. Available: www.ahuri.edu.au/publications/p60322/ [Accessed 19 April 2011].

Gurran N & Phibbs P (2003). Reconciling Indigenous and non-Indigenous land management concepts in planning curricula (pp76–88). Proceedings of the Australian and New Zealand Association of Planning Schools (ANZAPS) Conference, Auckland, 2003.

Gurran N & Phibbs P (2004). Indigenous interests and planning education: models from Australia, New Zealand and North America (pp68–82). Proceedings of the Australian and New Zealand Association of Planning Schools (ANZAPS) Conference, Perth, 2004.

Gurran N, Ruming K & Randolph B (2009). *Counting the costs: planning requirements, infrastructure costs and residential development in Australia*. Australian Housing and Urban Research Institute Final Report Series, AHURI, Melbourne. [Online]. Available: www.ahuri.edu.au/publications/download/70393_fr [Accessed 21 April 2011].

Gurran N, Squires C & Blakely E (2005). Meeting the sea change challenge: sea change communities in coastal Australia. Report for the National Sea Change Task Force, Planning Research Centre, University of Sydney.

Hall P (2003). The end of the city? The report of my death was an exaggeration. *City: analysis of urban trends, culture, theory, policy, action*, 7(2): 141–52.

Hall P (1996). *Cities of tomorrow: an intellectual history of urban planning and design in the twentieth century*. Oxford: Blackwell.

Hamnett S & Freestone R (Eds) (2000). *The Australian metropolis, a planning history*. Sydney: Allen & Unwin.

Hamnett S & Hutchings A (2009). Urban development and planning. In J Spoehr (Ed). *State of South Australia: from crisis to prosperity?* (pp265–85). Adelaide: Wakefield Press.

Handmer J & Dovers S (Eds) (2007). *Handbook of disasters & emergency policies & institutions*. London, UK: Earthscan.

Harding R (Ed) (1998). *Environmental decision-making: the roles of scientists, engineers and the public*. Leichhardt, NSW: The Federation Press.

Healey P (1997). *Collaborative planning: shaping places in fragmented societies*. London: Macmillan.

Hendler S (Ed) (1995). *Planning ethics: planning theory, practice and education*. New Jersey: Rutgers Center for Urban Policy Research.

Henessy KB, Fitzharris BC, Bates N, Harvey S, Howden M, Hughes L, Salinger J & Warrick R (2007). *Australia and New Zealand, Climate Change 2007: impacts, adaptation and vulnerability*. Contribution of Working Group II to the Fourth Assessment Report of the Intergovernmental Panel on Climate Change. Cambridge, UK: Cambridge University Press.

Hirt S (2007). The devil is in the definitions – contrasting American and German approaches to zoning. *Journal of the American Planning Association*, 73(4): 436–50.

HM Government (2005). *Securing the future: delivering UK sustainable development strategy*. The UK Government Sustainable Development Strategy. Presented to Parliament by the Secretary of State for Environment, Food and Rural Affairs by Command of Her Majesty, March 2005. [Online]. Available: www.defra.gov.uk/publications/files/pb10589-securing-the-future-050307.pdf [Accessed 28 April 2011].

Hoch J, Dalton C & So F (2000). *The practice of local government planning* (2000) (3rd edn). Ann Arbor, Michigan: American Planning Association for the ICMA University by the International City/County Management Association.

Holper P, Lucy S, Nolan M, Senese C & Hennessy K (2006). *Infrastructure and climate change risk assessment for Victoria: a report to the Victorian Government*. Victoria: CSIRO.

House of Representatives (2009). House of Representatives Standing Committee on Climate Change, Water, Environment and the Arts House of Representatives Committee Report. Managing our coastal zone in a changing climate: the time to act is now. Canberra: Australian Government. [Online]. Available: www.aph.gov.au/house/committee/ccwea/coastalzone/report.htm [Accessed 21 April 2011].

House of Representatives (1997). Bills Digest No. 135 1997–98 Australian Capital Territory (Planning and Land Management) Amendment Bill 1997. Canberra: Commonwealth of Australia.

Housing Industry Association (HIA) (2003). *Restoring housing affordability: the housing industry's perspective*. Australia: Housing Industry Association Ltd.

Housing, Local Government and Planning Ministers (HLGPM) (2005). Framework for national action on affordable housing. 4 August 2005, [np] Australia.

Howard J (2009). Climate change mitigation and adaptation in developed nations: a critical perspective on the adaptation turn in urban climate planning. In S Davoudi, J Crawford & A Mehmood (Eds). *Planning for climate change* (pp19–32). London: Earthscan.

Howe R (2000). A new paradigm: planning and reconstruction in the 1940s. In S Hamnett & R Freestone (Eds). *The Australian metropolis: a planning history* (pp80-97). Sydney: Allen & Unwin.

Howe R (1995). Local government and the urban growth debate. In P Troy (Ed). *Australian cities, issues, strategies and policies for urban Australia in the 1990s* (pp179–95). Cambridge: Cambridge University Press.

Huxley M (1994). Panoptica: utilitarianism and land-use control. In K Gibson & S Watson (Eds). *Metropolis now: planning and the urban in contemporary Australia* (pp66–88). Leichhardt, NSW: Pluto Press.

Hyden G (1998). Governance for sustainable livelihoods: operational issues. Paper commissioned by the United Nations Development Program (UNDP).

Independent Pricing and Regulatory Tribunal (2011). Greenhous Gas Abatement Scheme overview. [Online]. Available: www.greenhousegas.nsw.gov.au/overview/scheme_overview/overview.asp [Accessed 10 February 2011].

Intergovernmental Agreement on the Environment (1992). [Online]. Available: www.environment.gov. au/about/esd/publications/igae/index.html [Accessed 8 June 2011].

Intergovernmental Panel on Climate Change (IPCC) (2007a). Climate Change 2007: Climate change impacts, adaptation and vulnerability. Summary for Policy Makers, 6 April 2007.

Intergovernmental Panel on Climate Change (IPCC) (2007b). *Climate Change 2007: mitigation. Contribution of Working Group III to the Fourth Assessment Report of the Intergovernmental Panel on Climate Change.* B Metz, O R Davidso, P R Bosch, R Dave & L A Meyer (Eds). Cambridge, United Kingdom and New York, NY, USA: Cambridge University Press.

Intergovernmental Panel on Climate Change (IPCC) (2007c). Glossary of Terms used in the IPCC Fourth Assessment Report. [Online]. Available: www.ipcc.ch/publications_and_data/publications_and_data_glossary.shtml [Accessed 10 June 2011].

International Institute for Environment and Development (IIED) (2001). Good governance for good urban environments. Briefing Paper 8. Briefing Paper Series on Urban Environmental Improvement and Poverty Reduction, Human Settlements Programme, IIED, London.

International Society of City and Regional Planners (ISOCARP) (2001). *International manual of planning practice.* 4th edn. The Netherlands: ISOCARP, UNESCO, Ministry of Housing, Spatial Planning and the Environment (VROM-RPD).

Jackson S (1997). A disturbing story; the fiction of rationality in land use planning in Aboriginal Australia. *Australian Planner*, 34(4): 221–26.

Jackson S (1996). Urban development and Aboriginal land and sea rights in Australia. In R Howitt, J Connell & P Hirsch (Eds). *Resources, nations and Indigenous peoples: case studies from Australasia, Melanesia, and South East Asia* (pp90–103). Melbourne: Oxford University Press.

Jojola T (1998). Indigenous planning: clans, intertribal confederations and the history of the All Indian Pueblo Council. In L Sandercock (Ed). *Making the invisible visible: a multicultural planning history* (pp100–19). Berkeley: University of California Press.

Jones A, Phillips R & Milligan V (2007). *Integration and social housing in Australia: challenges and options.* AHURI Positioning Paper Series (102). Brisbane: Australian Housing and Urban Research Institute, Queensland Research Centre.

Keeble L (1959). *Principles and practice of town and country planning.* 2nd edn. London: Estates Gazette.

Kesteven S & Lea JP (1997). *Jabiru and the Aborigines of the Kakadu Region.* Darwin: Australian National University North Australia Research Unit.

Knowles C (2005). Craig Knowles, Minister for Infrastructure and Planning, and Minister for Natural Resources, Second Reading Speech, Extract from NSW Legislative Assembly Hansard and Papers Friday 27 May 2005.

Kogarah Municipal Council (2006). Water management policy & web-calculator, NSW Sustainable Water Challenge Awards 2006. [Online]. Available: www.wsud.org/case-studies/planning-and-policy-projects/ [Accessed 19 April 2011].

Lafferty W (1998). The politics of sustainable development: global norms for national implementation. In J Dryzek & D Scholsberg (Eds). *Debating the earth, the environmental politics reader* (pp266–84). New York: Oxford University Press.

Lawson J (1994). *Australian local government housing survey.* Canberra: Australian Housing and Urban Research Institute.

Lea JP & Zehner RB (1986). *Yellowcake and crocodiles: town planning, government and society in Northern Australia.* Sydney: Routledge.

Lennon M (2000). The revival of metropolitan planning. In S Hamnett & R Freestone (Eds). *The Australian metropolis: a planning history* (pp149–67). St Leonards, NSW: Allen & Unwin.

Levine J, Esnard AM & Sapat A (2007). Population displacement and housing dilemmas due to catastrophic disasters. *Journal of Planning Literature*, 22(1): 4–15.

Liberty RL (2003). Abolishing exclusionary zoning: a natural policy alliance for environmentalists and affordable housing advocates. *Boston College Environmental Affairs Law Review*, 30(3): 581.

Local Government and Planning Ministers Council (LGPMC) (2010). Joint meeting of Local Government and Planning Ministers Council and Housing Minister's Conference, 12 February 2010, Communique. Canberra: Local Government and Planning Ministers Council.

Local Government and Shires Association (LGSA) (1998). Planning tools to improve local housing outcomes. Seminar Notes. New South Wales: LGSA.

Low N, Gleeson B, Green R & Radovic D (2005). *The green city: sustainable homes, sustainable suburbs.* Sydney: UNSW Press.

Lyster R, Lipman Z, Franklin N, Wiffen G & Pearson L (2007). *Environmental and planning law in New South Wales.* Sydney: The Federation Press.

Major Cities Unit (MCU) (2010a). Assorted website material. [Online]. Available: www.infrastructure. gov.au/infrastructure/mcu/index.aspx [Accessed 5 January 2011].

Major Cities Unit (MCU) (2010b). State of Australian cities. Canberra: Major Cities Unit, Infrastructure Australia. [Online]. Available: www.infrastructure.gov.au/infrastructure/mcu/soac.aspx [Accessed 21 April 2011].

Mant J (1998). Place based LEPs. University of Technology, Sydney, Lecture Series, 1998.

Maroochy Shire (2000). Maroochy Plan 2000. Maroochy: Maroochy Shire Council.

Marshall N (2003). Public involvement techniques: an annotated description. Unpublished guide. N Marshall, University of NSW.

Marshall N & Roberts R (1997). That thing called public involvement. *Plan Canada, The Journal of the Canadian Institute of Planners*, 37(3): 8–11.

Mathur S, Waddel P & Blanco H (2004). The effect of impact fees on the price of new single family housing. *Urban Studies,* 41(7): 1303–12.

McManus P (2005). *Vortex cities to sustainable cities: Australia's urban challenge.* Sydney: UNSW Press.

Metz B, Davidson OR, Bosch PR, Dave R & Meyer LA (Eds) (2007). *Climate Change 2007: mitigation. Contribution of Working Group III to the Fourth Assessment Report of the Intergovernmental Panel on Climate Change.* Cambridge, United Kingdom and New York, NY, USA: Cambridge University Press.

Milligan V (2003). How different? Comparing housing policies and housing affordability consequences for low income households in Australia and the Netherlands. *Netherlands Geographical Studies,* 318.

Milligan V, Gurran N, Lawson J, Phibbs P & Phillips R (2009). *Innovation in affordable housing in Australia: bringing policy and practice for not-for profit housing organisations together.* AHURI Final Report Series (134). Sydney: UNSW-UWS Research Centre, Sydney Research Centre and Queensland Research Centre. [Online]. Available: www.ahuri.edu.au/publications/download/60504_fr [Accessed 21 April 2011].

Milligan V, Phibbs P, Fagan K & Gurran N (2004). A practical framework for expanding affordable housing services in Australia: learning from experience. Final Report. Melbourne: Australian Housing and Research Institute (AHURI).

Minnery J & Bajracharya B (1999). Visions, planning processes and outcomes: master planned communities in South East Queensland. *Australian Planner,* 16(1): 33–41.

Molino S (2011). Buildings resist bushfires, earthquakes and cyclones: but not floods. *Sydney Morning Herald,* 10 February 2011.

Monk S & Whitehead C (1999). Evaluating the economic impact of planning controls in the United Kingdom: some implications for housing. *Land Economics,* 75(1): 74–93.

Moran A (2006). *The tragedy of planning: losing the great Australian dream.* Victoria: Institute of Public Affairs.

Morison I (2000). The corridor city: planning for growth in the 1960s. In S Hamnett & R Freestone (Eds). *The Australian metropolis: a planning history* (pp113–30). Sydney: Allen & Unwin.

Mumford L (1961). *The city in history.* London: Martin Secker & Warburg.

Municipal Association of Victoria (MAV) (1999). *Housing: your basic infrastructure.* Victoria: Institute for Social Research, Swinburne Institute of Technology.

Naess A (1989). *Ecology, community and lifestyle: outline of an ecosophy.* Translated and revised by D Rothenberg. Cambridge, New York: Cambridge University Press.

Naess A (1983). The shallow and the deep, long range ecology movement: a summary. *Inquiry,* 16: 95–100.

National Competition Council (2011). National Competition Policy, assorted web material. [Online]. Available: ncp.ncc.gov.au/pages/home [Accessed 25 February 2011].

National Housing Supply Council (NHSC) (2010). *Second state of supply report.* Canberra: Department of Families, Community Services and Indigenous Affairs.

National Native Title Tribunal (2010). Three approaches to negotiating native title. [Online]. Available: www.nntt.gov.au/What-Is-Native-Title/Pages/Approaches-to-Native-Title.aspx [Accessed 6 January 2011].

National Native Title Tribunal (2006). National Native Title Tribunal. [Online]. Available: www.nntt.gov.au/Pages/default.aspx [Accessed 21 April 2011].

Nelson A, Pendall R, Dawkins C & Knaap G (2002). The link between growth management and housing affordability: the academic evidence. A Discussion Paper Prepared for the Brookings Institution Center on Urban and Metropolitan Policy, Washington.

New Zealand Climate Change Office (2004). *Coastal hazards and climate change: a guidance manual for local government in New Zealand*. Wellington, New Zealand: New Zealand Climate Change Office.

Newman P (2009). Transitioning away from oil: a transport planning case study with emphasis on US and Australian cities. In S Davoudi, J Crawford & A Mehmood (Eds). *Planning for climate change: strategies for mitigation and adaptation for spatial planners* (pp70–82). London: Earthscan.

Newman P (2006). Sustainable transport for sustainable cities. *Issues*, 76: 6–10.

Nicholls S & Moore M (2011). Green light for urban sprawl. *Sydney Morning Herald*, 8 February 2011.

Noosa Shire Council (2004). Population carrying capacity in Noosa Shire. Noosa: Noosa Shire Council.

Norman B (2010). *A low carbon and resilient future: a discussion paper on an integrated approach to planning for climate change*. Canberra: Department of Climate Change and Energy Efficiency. [Online]. Available: www.climatechange.gov.au/search.aspx?query=A%20low%20carbon%20and%20resilient%20future%3a%20a%20discussion%20paper%20on%20an%20integrated%20approach%20to%20planning%20for%20climate%20change&collection=agencies&profile=climatechange [Accessed 21 April 2011].

NSW Government (2011). Strategic regional land use: a new approach to planning for resources and our region, fact sheet May 2011. Sydney: Department of Planning and Infrastructure.

NSW Government (2010a). *Metropolitan plan for Sydney 2036*. Sydney: NSW Government, NSW Department of Planning. [Online]. Available: www.metroplansydney.nsw.gov.au/Home/MetropolitanPlanForSydney2036.aspx [Accessed 21 April 2011].

NSW Government (2010b). *NSW state plan: investing in a better future*. Sydney: NSW Government. [Online]. Available: www.stateplan.nsw.gov.au/sites/default/files/State-plan-2010-web.pdf [Accessed 21 April 2011].

NSW Department of Environment and Conservation (1999). *NSW biodiversity strategy*. Sydney: NSW Government. [Online]. Available: www.environment.nsw.gov.au/biodiversity/Strategy1999-2003.htm [Accessed 31 May 2011].

Nuetze M (1995). Financing urban services. In P Troy (Ed). *Australian cities: issues, strategies and policies for urban Australia in the 1990s* (pp220–45). Melbourne: Cambridge University Press.

O'Faircheallaigh C (2010). Public participation and environmental impact assessment: purposes, implications, and lessons for public policy making. *Environmental Impact Assessment Review*, 30 (2010): 19–27.

O'Farrell B (2011). Barangaroo review open to public media release, 31 May 2011. Sydney: Barry O'Farrell MP, Minister for Western Sydney.

Oxley M (2006). The gain from the planning-gain supplement: a consideration of the proposal for a new tax to boost housing supply in the UK. *European Journal of Housing Policy*, 6(1): 101–13.

Oxley M & Dunmore K (2004). Social housing, affordable development and the role of government. In A Golland & R Blake (Eds). *Housing development: theory, process and practice* (pp95–120). London: Routledge.

Paris C (1993). *Housing Australia*. South Melbourne: Macmillan Education.

Pendall R (2000). Local land use regulation and the chain of exclusion. *Journal of the American Planning Association*, 66(2): 125–42.

Polk County (2009). Polk County Post Disaster Recovery Plan. Polk County, Florida. [Online]. Available: www.polk-county.net/WebsiteSearchResults.aspx?menu_id=394&id=0&ItemID [Accessed 21 April 2011].

Productivity Commission (2011). Performance benchmarking of Australian business regulation: planning, zoning and development assessments. Productivity Commission Draft Research Report. Canberra: Australian Government. [Online]. Available: www.pc.gov.au/projects/study/regulationbenchmarking/planning/draft [Accessed 21 April 2011].

Productivity Commission (2010). Performance benchmarking of Australian business regulation: planning, zoning and development assessments. Productivity Commission Issues Paper. Canberra: Australian Government. [Online]. Available: www.pc.gov.au/projects/study/regulationbenchmarking/planning/issues [Accessed 21 April 2011].

Productivity Commission (2005). *Review of National Competition Policy reforms: Productivity Commission Inquiry Report No. 33*. Canberra: Productivity Commission. [Online]. Available: www.pc.gov.au/__data/assets/pdf_file/0016/46033/ncp.pdf [Accessed 21 April 2011].

Productivity Commission (2004). *First home ownership, Report No. 28*. Melbourne: Productivity Commission. [Online]. Available: www.pc.gov.au/__data/assets/pdf_file/0016/56302/housing.pdf [Accessed 21 April 2011]

Quigley J & Rosenthal L (2005). The effects of land use regulation on the price of housing: what do we know? What can we learn? *Cityscape: A Journal of Policy Development and Research*, 8(1): 69–110.

Randolph B (2004). The changing Australian city: new patterns, new policies and new research needs. *Urban Policy and Research*, 22(4): 481–93.

Randolph B & Holloway D (2004). The suburbanisation of disadvantage in Sydney: new problems, new policies. *Opolis*, 1(1): 1.

Read P (2000). *Belonging: Australians, place and Aboriginal ownership*. Oakleigh, Victoria: Cambridge University Press.

Regional Development Australia (2009). Regional development Australia: what is it? Roles and responsibilities. Canberra: Regional Development Australia. [Online]. Available: www.rda.gov.au/about/files/RDA_National_Roles_Responsibilities.pdf [Accessed 21 April 2011].

Reilly P (2010). Open letter to the residents of Willoughby City. 20 November 2010. Chatswood, NSW: Willoughby City Council.

Rittel H & Webber M (1973). Dilemmas in a general theory of planning. *Policy Sciences*, 4: 155–69.

Rognor HH, Zhou D, Bradley R, Crabbé P, Edenhofer O, Hare B, Kuijpers L & Yamaguchi M (2007). Introduction. In B Metz, OR Davidson, PR Bosch, R Dave & LA Meyer (Eds). *Climate change 2007: mitigation. Contribution of Working Group III to the Fourth Assessment Report of the Intergovernmental Panel on Climate Change* (pp95–116). Cambridge, UK and New York, US: Cambridge University Press.

Rosenkoetter MM, Covan EK, Cobb BK, Bunting S & Weinrich M (2007). Perceptions of older adults regarding evacuation in the event of a natural disaster. *Public Health Nursing*, 24(2): 160–68.

Roseth J (2003). The 1970s: the end of post-war optimism. In J Toon & J Falk (Eds). *Sydney planning or politics: town planning for Sydney region since 1945* (pp91–110). Sydney: Planning Research Centre, University of Sydney.

Rural Fire Service (2006). Planning for bushfire protection. Sydney: NSW Fire Service. [Online]. Available: www.rfs.nsw.gov.au/dsp_content.cfm?CAT_ID=900 [Accessed 21 April 2011].

Russell R (2003). Equity in Eden: can environmental protection and affordable housing comfortably cohabit in suburbia? *Boston College Environmental Affairs Law Review*, 30(3): 437.

Sandercock L (2004). Towards a planning imagination for the 21st century. *Journal of the American Planning Association*, 70(2): 133–41.

Sandercock L (1998). *Towards cosmopolis: planning for multicultural cities*. Chichester, England: John Wiley.

Sandercock L (1990). *Property, politics, and urban planning: a history of Australian city planning, 1890–1990*. New Brunswick: Transaction Publishers.

Searle G (2004). Planning discourses and Sydney's recent metropolitan strategies. *Urban Policy and Research*, 22(4): 367–91.

Self P (1995). Alternative urban policies: the case for regional development. In P Troy (Ed). *Australian cities: issues, strategies and policies for urban Australia in the 1990s* (pp246–64). Melbourne: Cambridge University Press.

Sherry N (2010). Performance benchmarking of Australian business regulation: planning, zoning and development assessments, Terms of reference. Canberra: Productivity Commission. [Online]. Available: www.pc.gov.au/projects/study/regulationbenchmarking/planning/termsofreference [Accessed 21 April 2011].

Smith J, Glassborow K & Camenzuli L (2008). *A practitioner's guide to the Land and Environment Court of NSW*. Sydney: NSW Young Lawyers. [Online]. Available: www.lawsociety.com.au/SearchResults/index.htm?ssSiteBasic=true&ssUserText=%22A+practitioner%E2%80%99s+guide+to+the+Land+and+Environment+Court+of+NSW%22 [Accessed 21 April 2011].

Spearitt P (2010). The 200-kilometre city. In B Gleeson & W Steele (Eds). *A climate for growth: planning South-East Queensland* (pp39–58). Brisbane: University of Queensland Press.

Squires C & Gurran N (2005). Planning for affordable housing in coastal sea change communities. Paper presented to the National Housing Conference 2005, Perth, 26–28 October 2005.

Steele W (2009). Australian urban planners: hybrid roles and professional dilemmas? *Urban Policy and Research*, 27(2): 189–203.

Steele W & Gleeson B (2010). Planning in climate change. In B Gleeson & W Steele (Eds). *A climate for growth: planning South-East Queensland* (pp24–46). Brisbane: University of Queensland Press.

Stern N (2007). *The economics of climate change: the Stern Review*. Cambridge: Cambridge University Press.

Sulman J (1921). *An introduction to the study of town planning in Australia*. Sydney: Government Printer of New South Wales.

Surf Coast Shire (2000). Surf Coast style. Surf Coast Planning Scheme, Surf Coast Shire Council, Victoria.

Swan W (2011). Budget speech 2011–12. Canberra: Wayne Swan MP.

Tasmanian Planning Commission (2011). Tasmanian Planning Commission. [Online]. Available: www.planning.tas.gov.au/home [Accessed 11 January 2011].

Taylor N (1998). *Urban planning theory since 1945*. London: Sage.

The Parliament of Australia (2008). *The way forward; inquiry into the role of the National Capital Authority*. Canberra: Parliament of Australia.

Thomas I & Elliott M (2005). *Environmental impact in Australia assessment: theory and practice*. Sydney: The Federation Press.

Thompson S (2007). *Planning Australia: an overview of urban and regional planning*. Melbourne: Cambridge University Press.

Thompson S (2000). Diversity, difference, and the multi-layered city. In R Freestone (Ed). *Urban planning in a changing world: the twentieth century experience* (pp230–48). London: E & FN Spoon.

Threatened Species Committee (2001). Loss of terrestrial climatic habitat caused by anthropogenic emissions of greenhouse gases. Listing Advice and Information Sheet. Canberra: Australian Government. [Online]. Available: www.environment.gov.au/biodiversity/threatened/ktp/greenhouse.html [Accessed 21 April 2011].

Toon J & Faulkner J (Eds) (2003). *Sydney planning or politics: town planning for Sydney region since 1945*. Sydney: Planning Research Centre, University of Sydney.

Transport NSW and Department of Urban Affairs and Planning (2001). Integrating land use and transport: overview. Sydney: NSW Department of Urban Affairs and Planning.

Transport NSW, Roads and Traffic Authority and Department of Urban Affairs and Planning (2001). Integrating land use and transport; improving transport choice: guidelines for planning and development. [Online]. Available: www.planning.nsw.gov.au/programservices/pdf/prg_transport.pdf [Accessed 19 April 2011].

Troy P (Ed) (1995). *Australian cities, issues, strategies and policies for urban Australia in the 1990s*. Cambridge: Cambridge University Press.

United Nations Centre for Human Settlements (UNCHS) (2000). Good urban governance: a normative framework. Preparatory Committee for the Special Session of the General Assembly for an Overall Review and Appraisal of the Implementation of the Habitat Agenda, Nairobi. United Nations Centre for Human Settlements. [Online]. Available: www.bestpractices.org/learning/frameurbangov.pdf [Accessed 28 April 2011].

United Nations Environment Program (UNEP) (2003). The Melbourne Principles for Sustainable Cities, United Nations Environment Program, Division of Technology, Industry and Economics, Integrative Management Series No. 1. [Online]. Available: www.unep.or.jp/ietc/focus/MelbournePrinciples/English.pdf [Accessed 28 April 2011].

UN-Habitat (2002). *The role of cities in national and international development.* Nairobi: World Urban Forum.

Urban Land Development Authority (2009). Affordable housing strategy. Brisbane: Urban Land Development Authority. [Online]. Available: www.ulda.qld.gov.au/01_cms/details.asp?ID=145 [Accessed 21 April 2011].

Vogel C, Moser SC, Kasperson RE & Dabelko GD (2007). Linking vulnerability, adaptation, and resilience science to practice: pathways, players, and partnerships. *Global Environmental Change* 17(3–4): 349–64.

Watson S & McGillivray A (1995). Planning in a multicultural environment: a challenge for the nineties. In P Troy (Ed). *Australian cities, issues, strategies and policies for urban Australia in the 1990s* (pp164–78). Cambridge: Cambridge University Press.

Watt M (2003). Developer contributions. In J Toon & J Falk (Eds). *Sydney planning or politics: town planning for Sydney region since 1945* (p114). Sydney: Planning Research Centre, University of Sydney.

Weaver A, Pope J, Morrison-Saunders A & Lochner P (2008). Contributing to sustainability as an environmental impact assessment practitioner. *Impact Assessment and Project Appraisal,* 26(2): 91–98.

Wells NM, Evans GW & Yang Y (2010). Environments and health: planning decisions as public-health decisions. *Journal of Architectural and Planning Research*, 27(2): 124–43.

Western Australian Planning Commission (2007). An introduction to the Western Australian planning system. Perth: Department for Planning and Infrastructure. [Online]. Available: www.planning.wa.gov.au/Publications/1468.aspx [Accessed 21 April 2011].

Wilson E (2009). Use of scenarios for climate change adaptation in spatial planning. In S Davoudi, J Crawford & A Mehmood (Eds). *Planning for climate change; strategies for mitigation and adaptation for spatial planners* (pp223–35). London: Earthscan.

Witten J (2003). The cost of developing affordable housing: at what price? *Boston College Environmental Affairs Law Review*, 30(3): 509–53.

World Commission on Environment and Development (WCED) (1987). Our common future, report of the World Commission on Environment and Development. UN Documents. [Online] Available: www.un-documents.net/wced-ocf.htm [Accessed 9 June 2011].

Zehner R & Marshall N (2007). Community participation: to be involved or not involved: is that the question? In S Thompson (Ed). *Planning Australia* (pp247–62). Sydney: Cambridge University Press.

Index

www.ingramcontent.com/pod-product-compliance
Lightning Source LLC
Chambersburg PA
CBHW041119280326
41928CB00061B/3460